JACK KEMP

JACK ★ KEMP

The Bleeding-Heart Conservative

Who Changed America

Morton Kondracke

and Fred Barnes

Sentinel

SENTINEL

An imprint of Penguin Random House LLC
375 Hudson Street
New York, New York 10014
penguin.com

Courtesy of the Jack Kemp Foundation: Insert pages 1 (top, bottom), 2 (middle), 3 (top, bottom), 6 (top), 7 (top, bottom), 8 (bottom)

AP Photo/NFL Photos: page 2 (top)

AP Photo/WJZ: page 2 (bottom)

Heinz Kluetmeier/Getty Images: page 4 (top)

AP Photo/John Duricka: page 4 (bottom)

Diana Walker/Getty Images: page 5 (top)

Polyconomics Institute: page 5 (bottom)

AP Photo/Stephan Savoia: page 8 (top)

ISBN 978-1-59184-743-4

Printed in the United States of America
1   3   5   7   9   10   8   6   4   2

Set in Dante MT Std
Designed by Alissa Rose Theodor

For Marguerite and Barbara

CONTENTS

———

Introduction 1

One
QUARTERBACK 13

Two
SUPPLY-SIDER 29

Three
TURNING POINT 55

Four
REAGAN REVOLUTIONARY 78

Five
FRONT LINE 103

Six
COURAGE 128

Seven

TAX REFORMER *150*

Eight

FREEDOM FIGHTER *171*

Nine

ALSO RAN *195*

Ten

POVERTY WARRIOR *217*

Eleven

VEEP *252*

Twelve

FOURTH QUARTER *288*

Thirteen

LEGACY *319*

Acknowledgments *329*

Notes *331*

Index *373*

JACK KEMP

INTRODUCTION

———

J ack Kemp was the most important politician of the twentieth century who was not president, certainly the most influential Republican.[1] No one has yet written the story of his impact on America and the world. His life and legacy need to be recognized—and that's starting to happen. In this era of political bleakness, both Republicans and Democrats are citing him as a model of what politicians ought to be. That is one of the four reasons why we have written this book.

Above all, Jack Kemp merits a prominent place in American political history because he was Congress's foremost advocate for supply-side economics and the man who steered Ronald Reagan toward adopting it. Hence, he deserves partial credit for not only pulling America out of the deep malaise of the 1970s but also for helping to win the cold war and convert much of the world to democratic capitalism.

The '70s were a dismal decade. It was the era of stagflation—simultaneous high unemployment and soaring inflation. And also of geopolitical reverses: it was the post–Vietnam era, when the Soviet Union invaded Afghanistan; its Cuban allies advanced in Africa and Central America; and revolutionary Iran held Americans hostage for 444 days. And it was an era of bottomed-out national morale—its nadir when President Carter blamed the acquisitiveness of the American people for the country's seemingly incurable ills.

In the 1980s it all turned around. The "misery index" (unemployment plus inflation) fell from 23 in 1980 to 7.7 in 1986.[2] The Soviet empire retreated, tried to reform itself, and then collapsed. Among American citizens, satisfaction with the condition of the country rose from a low of 12 percent in July 1979 to 69 percent in June of 1986.³ And around the world—especially in Eastern Europe, but also in Latin America and Asia—democratic capitalism was deemed to be "the end of history."

Jack Kemp was at the center of the great turnaround. He did not invent supply-side economics: the combination of lower tax rates, particularly on individual income, and a stable dollar. That was the work of two young economists, Robert Mundell, later a Nobel Prize winner, and Arthur Laffer. But once converted by journalist-agitator Jude Wanniski of the *Wall Street Journal*, Kemp became the leading political evangelist of the supply-side movement. Lowering tax rates, he argued, would create incentives for work, savings, and investment—and produce booming growth in a way that Keynesian public spending programs had not. His tax bill—Kemp-Roth, a three-year, 30 percent across-the-board cut borrowed from John F. Kennedy's 1963 proposal—became the vehicle for the supply-side revolution.

Kemp's enthusiasm for supply-side economics was contagious, and he spearheaded a national movement that amounted to both a political and intellectual revolution in economics. In Congress, senior Republicans resented the presumptuous backbencher, still in his forties, who was treading on tax turf. They also doubted his economics. But junior Republicans unhappy with their party's lack of vitality joined Kemp's campaign—among them the future Speaker Newt Gingrich, the future Senate majority leader Trent Lott, future senators Connie Mack and Dan Coats, and longtime party leader Vin Weber. Kemp forged links with policy thinkers in Washington and New York, including Irving Kristol and Mundell, and Robert Bartley, editorial page editor of the *Wall Street Journal*. Kemp's office and living room became scenes resembling graduate seminars where the Washington–New York nexus came together for debate, but with major policy change as its aim. That aim was achieved; Kemp-Roth became official party policy in 1978. Even GOP graybeards who had previously scorned him signed on.

Then he recruited Ronald Reagan, who made Kemp's proposal a centerpiece of his 1980 presidential campaign and, once elected, the basis of Reaganomics. The Reagan tax cuts of 1981 and 1986—reducing the top rate from 70 percent to 50 percent, then 28 percent—set off an economic boom that lasted into the 2000s.

The achievements of the 1980s were mainly Reagan's, but their economic underpinning was Kemp's. No Republican politician of the twentieth century who was not president transformed the country the way he did—not Henry Cabot Lodge, Robert Taft, or Nelson Rockefeller. Earl Warren did, but as chief justice, not as governor of California. Nor did any Democrats except possibly Hubert Humphrey, the leading early advocate for civil rights, and Edward Kennedy, author or bipartisan coauthor of dozens of health, education, and civil rights laws.

––––––

Our second reason for writing about Kemp is that he embodied a spirit sorely missing in today's politics—in both parties. Kemp was positive, optimistic, idealistic, energetic, growth- and opportunity-oriented. He was incapable of personal attack and negative campaigning, even when it cost him. "The purpose of politics," he said, "is not to defeat your opponent as much as it is to provide superior leadership and better ideas than the opposition."[4] He criticized liberals and Democrats, but also "green-eyeshade," austerity-minded, "Herbert Hoover" Republicans. His criticisms were always based on their ideas and policy proposals, never their motives or personal flaws. He believed—as he said again and again—that "ideas change history." He wanted to change history for the better.

He wanted his own party to once again be "the party of Lincoln." Even before very conservative audiences, he argued that the GOP should again become the "natural home of African-Americans," as it had been from Lincoln's time to Franklin Roosevelt's. He insisted it could happen if Republican policies brought growth and prosperity to inner cities. It was unrealistic, probably romantic. But it was sincere. It was famously said of him that as a pro-football star, he'd "showered with more African-Americans than most Republicans had ever met." He lamented that his party had been largely absent from the civil rights movement and regarded the "Southern strategy" to win white votes at the expense of blacks a "disgrace."[5]

Kemp believed in what he called the American Idea—that the Declaration of Independence was a universal document, that everyone everywhere deserved the right to advance as far as his or her talent and effort would lead. The American idea was Kemp's version of Lincoln's bedrock principle that the "right to rise" was the central idea of the United States and applied to black slaves as well as white workers.[6] And like Lincoln, he believed it was the job of government to enable people to achieve their aims and remove obstacles—especially, in Kemp's view, high taxes.

We hope this book will inspire—or embarrass—present-day politicians to see there is a better way to conduct their business. To fight, yes, but over ideas for making America better. And to search for common ground to solve America's problems and secure a future for every citizen.

———

Our third reason for writing this book is simply that Jack Kemp led a fascinating, inspiring life. His father, Paul, was his model of entrepreneurial capitalism. His well-educated mother, Frances, was his cultural and intellectual spur. They both were Christian Scientists, which produced in Kemp a lifelong optimism, a faith that thinking positively can change the future, that failure is never final, that "when one door closes, another opens."

Kemp grew up a sports fanatic, deciding at age five that he wanted to be a professional quarterback. By will and determination, he overcame repeated obstacles and became one, a star quarterback, first for the San Diego Chargers, then the Buffalo Bills. He remained a quarterback in mentality all his life. He was a natural leader, the captain of nearly every team he ever joined and president of the American Football League Players Association. In the turbulent 1960s, he fostered racial integration of AFL teams and cities. He never stopped applying lessons from football to life and politics—quarterbacking as capitalism, the huddle as cooperative endeavor, booing as no big deal, the next play as the chance to win.

He was a physical education major and a mediocre student at California's Occidental College, but he became a self-taught intellectual—

deeply read in economics, an expert in defense and foreign policy, and an avid consumer of history books, especially biographies of his heroes Lincoln and Winston Churchill. After Reagan won the presidency, Kemp became the number three leader of House Republicans. He was a Reagan loyalist but had the courage to oppose his president—and took heat for it—when he thought Reagan was being led astray on economic and foreign policy.

In 1988, he was deemed by many to be Reagan's natural political heir. He ran for president urging voters to join him in "the progressive, conservative, radical, revolutionary Lincoln Emancipation wing of the Republican Party."[7] He finished a distant third behind conventional Republicans George H. W. Bush and Bob Dole. As Bush's housing secretary, he fought a losing battle to make the plight of the urban poor a national priority. He also could not resist meddling in foreign and economic matters not in his portfolio. His fellow cabinet members were not amused.

After Bush lost to Bill Clinton in 1992, Kemp started out as the clear favorite of the party faithful for 1996. But he lost support by opposing California's anti-immigrant Proposition 187 in 1994 and otherwise flouting conservative Republican orthodoxy. He passed on running. Then he was plucked from near obscurity by Dole, his long-standing foe, to run for vice president. But he couldn't do what number twos are expected to do—attack the opposition. Bill Clinton's ethics, personal and political, were a ripe target, but in debate with Vice President Al Gore, he whiffed.

The Dole-Kemp candidacy was doomed in any event because the president was popular and peace and prosperity reigned. But Kemp made a statement late in the race in Grand Rapids, Michigan, that summarized his experience and mentality:

"Wow, almost forty years ago, I started my professional career with the Detroit Lions as their third-string quarterback. And they said I would never make it. I came from the wrong schools. I was too short. I threw too hard. I was too optimistic. I didn't have it. I tell you what. I never gave up. I got traded, sold, hurt, cut, booed, knocked out, but I never gave up. Bob Dole in his career never gave up. . . . Bob Dole and Jack Kemp are fighters. We believe in the American dream."[8]

———

Personally, writing this book has given us the opportunity to revisit our experience as journalists. Barnes, who became a conservative in the 1970s and was a close friend of Kemp's foremost journalistic booster, columnist Bob Novak, got to know Kemp in 1981. Curious about what supply-side economics was all about, he traveled with Kemp to Buffalo for a weekend and scarcely got to ask a question. Kemp talked nonstop, determined (as always) to make a convert. Thereafter, Barnes interviewed Kemp numerous times, got close to his staff, and wrote dozens of articles about him, his favorite issues, and his political prospects, first in the *Baltimore Sun*, then in the *New Republic*. He and his family became friends of the Kemps as well. His wife, Barbara, still attends Joanne Kemp's weekly Bible study meetings, and his daughter, Karen, was active in Kemp's presidential campaign in Virginia in 1988. She was slated to attend the Republican National Convention, but didn't after Kemp lost the state's primary.

Kondracke, once a liberal (though not very), was pitted every week against Bob Novak on TV's *McLaughlin Group* and was a longtime supply-side skeptic who thought Reagan's admitted economic successes were the result of Keynesian deficit spending, not tax cuts. Kondracke knew Kemp, admired his "bleeding heart" predilections and obvious sincerity, and wrote about him intermittently for the Capitol Hill newspaper *Roll Call*. Then, in 2011, he was retained by the Jack Kemp Foundation to conduct more than a hundred recorded interviews for its Oral History Project. He then spent two academic years holding the Jack Kemp Chair in Political Economy at the John W. Kluge Center for Scholars at the Library of Congress researching Kemp's career. He's read Kemp's words and seen him through the eyes of fellow football players, staff members, congressional and cabinet colleagues, other journalists, and the Kemp family.[9] All of which has deepened his respect, especially for

Kemp's courage in bucking his party and even his president, his inclusiveness, and his refusal to see politics (in Newt Gingrich's phrase) as "war without bloodshed." Kondracke asked numerous interviewees how it was that this competitive star, playing one of America's most violent sports, wouldn't "hit" a political opponent. The repeated answer was: "Because he was a quarterback!"

———

Finally, and most important, we have written this book because we believe that America is in trouble, perhaps more deeply in trouble than in the 1970s. And we think that Jack Kemp's spirit—and his policy ideas—could again help the country turn around.

The American Dream is dimming. Workers have the *right* to rise, but they are not rising. The median income of American households in 2013 was 8.7 percent below what it was in 1999 after climbing by 20 percent during the '80s and '90s.[10] At the same time, workers' contributions toward health-care premiums have risen almost four times faster than their wages.[11] People born in the lowest fifth in income distribution have just a 9 percent chance of reaching the top fifth, showing no improvement over the past thirty years. And there has been no progress in fifty years in closing the wealth gap between whites and minorities.[12] As the economy recovers from the Great Recession, 95 percent of the nation's income gains have been reaped by the top 1 percent of earners.[13] Meantime, while the official unemployment rate has dropped, the underemployment rate has recovered much less.[14] And millions have dropped out of the labor force.

The slowing of economic opportunity has deleterious psychological, social, and political effects. In 1992, 41 percent of Americans were confident that their children's lives would be better than theirs; in mid-2014, only 21 percent were optimistic. A CNN/ORC (Opinion Research Corporation) poll showed 59 percent believed "the American dream has become impossible for most people to achieve."[15] Whether it's a cause or an effect, America's social capital is also flagging. The out-of-wedlock birthrate, heavily correlated with a life of poverty, has doubled since 1980.[16]

In a speech to the 1979 International Longshoremen's Association convention, Kemp said that "in a stagnant or contracting economy, politics becomes the art of pitting class against class, rich against poor, white against black, capital against labor, Sunbelt against Snowbelt, old against young."[17] The increasingly savage polarization of American politics today is at least partly the result of citizens' fear and anger that "others"—"the 1 percent" or "the 47 percent"—are profiteering at their expense.

This polarization makes it impossible for Democrats and Republicans to solve other deep problems: an immigration system that everyone agrees is "broken"; an education system that costs double per pupil what it did in 1981[18] yet produces high school graduates only a quarter of whom are ready for college;[19] infrastructure ranking nineteenth in the world;[20] a health-care system that costs more per capita than any country in the world except Switzerland's;[21] and a gross federal debt already 103 percent of GDP, nearly as high as at the end of World War II,[22] and destined to climb as the baby boom generation ages.[23]

We do not doubt that poor leadership is heavily to blame for the country's condition. Good leadership turned a bad situation to good in the 1980s. But it's not obvious who can provide it today. We hope today's would-be leaders will try to follow Kemp's example.

Conditions are different from those in the Kemp era. Kemp could be careless about the size of the national debt and he opposed nearly every effort to reform entitlements or reduce benefits. For much of his career, he thought the supply-side formula—reducing marginal tax rates and returning the dollar to the gold standard—would guarantee growth, prosperity, and hope. Until he was HUD secretary, he believed in John Kennedy's dictum, "A rising tide lifts all boats." Then he became convinced that "some boats are stuck on the bottom" and can't rise without government help.

We suspect we know some of what Kemp would favor now—for certain, "family friendly" tax reform; lowering rates for individuals, capital gains, and corporations; eliminating special interest loopholes but providing generous credits for families with children and expanding the earned income tax credit for the working poor. At times he called for making workers' payroll taxes deductible from their income taxes. He was and would be for education vouchers to give families maximum choice in selecting their children's schools. He did and would favor comprehensive immigration reform that offered a path to citizenship to illegal immigrants with clean records. He always backed expanded free trade. He would continue advocating a new gold standard.[24] He would have persisted in favoring enterprise zones and vouchers to enable the poor to find housing in the private market. He would certainly urge his party to promote growth, not austerity, and be concerned with the advancement of all Americans, not just the GOP base. He was a "big tent" Republican, ever urging expansion of the party's appeal.

He would surely oppose the big government, Keynesian drift of the increasingly liberal Democratic Party, which deems high-tax, rich-benefit, and highly regulated European social democracies as model societies in spite of their chronically high unemployment rates.[25] Kemp said that the goal of Lincoln's Republican Party was not "the construction of a safety net under which people should not be allowed to fall, but . . . of a ladder upon which people can climb." He said, "Yes, we need a safety net, but it should be a trampoline, not a trap. And, right now, it's a trap." The measure of compassion of the party of Lincoln, he said, "should not be how many people need help, but how many people do not need to be on government assistance because they're now on that ladder of upward mobility that Lincoln called the desire to improve one's lot in life."[26]

Kemp opposed the impulse of liberals to redistribute wealth rather than create it and to disparage those who get rich rather than see them as entrepreneurs and job creators. But he was equally dismayed at the tendency of some in his own party to *exclude* blacks, Hispanics, union members, the poor—and the tendency to award subsidies and tax breaks to wealthy interests while imposing austerity on the less favored. When Reagan's deficit-obsessed budget director, David Stockman, sought to raise taxes on beer and gasoline, Kemp demanded, "Dave, if we truly face a 'budgetary Dunkirk,' why are food stamps, AFDC, Medicaid and

Head Start touchable, but not Exxon, Boeing and Gulf Oil?"[27] Had he been alive, he would have asked the same in 2014 when House Republicans attempted to reduce food stamp spending but maintained crop subsidies for rich farmers.

———

Kemp had his flaws. He was undisciplined and impatient. He could not force himself—or be forced by aides—to make a short speech, and it hurt him politically. He mystified audiences with references to obscure historical figures and lost them with lectures on the gold standard. He over-promised when asked to help GOP candidates, driving his schedulers crazy. He was chronically late and sometimes reckless behind the wheel trying to make it to events or airports. He barked at aides and blamed them when something went wrong, then made up (usually without apologizing). He played one staff member off against another—evidently to maintain control. His loyal congressional staff worked around it.

He was mistaken on some key issues, especially policy toward the Soviet Union. Reagan, much wiser than nearly every international affairs "expert," understood that the Soviet Union was fundamentally weak and could be defeated if pushed hard enough. He also wanted to bargain with adversaries, though only from strength. Reagan proved more of an optimist than Kemp, and also more of a pragmatist. And he won the cold war.

But Kemp's virtues far outweighed his faults. He was passionate about ideas—relentless, in fact, to the point that members of Congress sometimes hid to avoid his lectures and importuning. He held no grudges and had no enemies, thinking there was no one he couldn't convince if he worked on them long enough. On the football field, he looked at opponents—"the people who tried to knock my head off on Sunday"—as friends. His political adversaries were "opponents, not enemies." A close friend, ex-education secretary and drug czar Bill Bennett, once told him, "Jack, if you believed in original sin, you'd be president." Kemp did not believe anyone was a hopeless sinner.

Above all—and this is the main reason we have written this book—he was positive, optimistic, and in the best sense of the words he used to describe himself, "progressive," "populist," "radical," "conservative," and "liberal minded." He thought large: about changing the whole basis of U.S. economic policy, fiscal and monetary; about government as "the Good Shepherd" leaving no lamb to be lost; about spreading freedom and prosperity around the world. His was a spirit that barely survives in the mean politics of the present day. We hope this book will help change that.

One

QUARTERBACK

I n the San Diego Chargers' second game of the 1962 season, Jack Kemp, the team's quarterback, threw an eighty-yard touchdown pass. As he released the ball, he crashed his hand onto the helmet of a blitzing defender, severely dislocating the middle finger of his right hand. Kemp kept playing and put the finger back in place between plays, but the injury turned out to be serious, requiring doctors to fuse the finger's main joint. When the doctor asked how he wanted it, Kemp told him to bend it in the shape of a football so that he could keep on passing. He had a "football finger" for the rest of his life.[1]

Kemp's finger wasn't the only part of him that was permanently devoted to the quarterback position. His whole personality and leadership style, whether on the field or in the Capitol, would forever reflect his time in team leadership. Years after his football career was over, his GOP adversary Bob Dole referred to Kemp as "the Quarterback." Dole didn't mean it as a compliment. He was implying that Kemp was a dumb jock, out of his league making tax policy, Dole's specialty. In fact, Kemp was anything but stupid or uneducated. In a deep sense, though, Dole was right. A quarterback is who Kemp was and always wanted to be—from his childhood through his career, and all the way to the end of his life.

The quarterback uses his brain as much as his body. The quarterback is the leader. He has a vision of how victory will be won. The quarterback calls the plays—or at least did so in Kemp's day, the 1950s and 60s—and then executes with the help of ten teammates. A team's success or failure depends more on the quarterback than any other player. "He never denigrated other positions," said Kemp's son Jeff, also a pro quarterback. "He knew you needed everyone. . . . But he also said that someone has to take the risk, someone has to step up, someone has to cast the vision, someone has to have confidence when others are faltering or worried or fearful."[2] Whether on the field or in the Capitol, Kemp aspired to be that person.

———

The seeds of that destiny were planted in Kemp's childhood. He was born in 1935 in Los Angeles to Paul and Frances Kemp and grew up in the Melrose neighborhood, next door to Hollywood, along with three brothers—Paul Jr. (seven years older), Tom (five years older), and Dick (four years younger).

Paul Kemp was a quiet man. He quit high school to join the navy during World War I, but his entrepreneurial flair and belief in hard work made up for his lack of formal education. After the war, along with his brothers Jack and Willard, he started a company that sold Henderson motorcycles in the western states. When the Depression hit, the company failed, partly due to Willard's mismanagement, but the brothers refused to declare bankruptcy. Despite nearly being evicted from their home, they paid off all their debts. Financial integrity became a point of pride in the Kemp family.[3]

Brothers Paul and Jack proved resourceful in starting over, and their example planted the seeds of Jack's respect for free markets and entrepreneurs. They used their leftover inventory of motorcycles to open a messenger and delivery service. By the late 1930s they had developed a successful, six-truck delivery service that could support their families. The brothers had breakfast every morning during their working careers and, after retiring, talked by phone every day. Their affection deeply impressed Jack and his brothers.

Frances had an even greater impact in shaping the lives of the Kemp brothers, especially Jack's. "We were a matriarchal family," said Dick Kemp, who described her as having "an assertive intellect."⁴ Frances was an unusually well-educated woman for her time. She graduated from the University of Montana and earned a master's degree from the University of California at Berkeley, then worked as an administrator and social worker for the Los Angeles school system, a job that often had her practicing her fluent Spanish when she hauled truants from the barrio back to school. She was no less assertive in teaching and correcting her sons.

She encouraged her boys to debate at the dinner table and took them to concerts at the Hollywood Bowl. "She was . . . very much in tune with the world's affairs, and pushed us intellectually all the time," Paul Jr. said. "We'd sit there at the dinner table and what started out as a discussion would end up as a big battle . . . between us. Mother would foster that. . . . She would ask questions and we'd tease each other about pronouncing words. Dad would get up and throw his napkin down in disgust and walk away. He couldn't take the dissension."⁵

Jack thrived on the back-and-forth. He was aggressive and argumentative. Paul Kemp thinks he inherited his competitive instinct from his mother. She "encouraged a winning attitude, saying, 'You will win. You can win. Don't worry about it. You'll win.'"⁶ She distrusted the influence of other boys and told them not to run with the crowd. "She liked the fact that [her sons] would think for themselves and be independent thinkers," Paul said. Jack absorbed her advice totally. When her sons left the house each day, she'd tell them, "Be a leader!" Kemp did the same to his children.

Jack's mother and father were Republicans. The family joke was that in 1932, Jack's father was still driving voters to the polls hours after Franklin Roosevelt had been elected. Jack inherited the Republican gene. He also inherited a faith gene. It was Jack's grandmother, Elva Kemp, who led the family to Christian Science. According to family legend, when Elva was a young woman in pre-statehood South Dakota, a horse fell into a hole and couldn't be rescued. The owner was about to euthanize it when someone suggested calling a Christian Science practitioner to pray. He came, and the horse was rescued. Elva converted on the spot.[7] When her husband died, Elva rented a railcar and moved her eleven children to California. In her later years, she lived with Jack's family. She was known as Grandma Sunshine.

Elva's religion influenced both of Jack's parents, and their faith intensified when their first son, Paul, was sick with asthma. According to Christian Science, all reality is spiritual; thus sickness, evil, and failure are illusions. As a result, will and effort can overcome any obstacle. From this belief, Jack got his extraordinary drive to turn his hopes into reality. Later in life, when one of Jack's daughters said she was ill and couldn't go to school, Jack admonished her: "You can! You can do anything if you think you can do it."[8]

Under the influence of his wife, Joanne, a strong evangelical Presbyterian, Kemp formally left Christian Science and regularly attended her church. But privately he drifted in and out of Christian Science in later years. And its teachings were the underpinnings of his view of life. If he was losing a game, his son Jeff said, his father's attitude was "this is a temporary distraction to the ultimate goal. We will win next week. We will turn it around in the 4th quarter. We'll win next season."[9]

———

Winning was one of Kemp's obsessions from an early age. He described his childhood as "all sports, all the time." When he wasn't playing games with his brothers—football, baseball, basketball, or made-up sports—he'd play by himself.

Fitting in as the third of four boys was both a challenge and motivator for Jack. He especially wanted to match Tom, a great athlete and his lifelong hero. Paul said Kemp was always a fierce competitor, "pushing, pushing to win, pushing to achieve,"[10] and he accepted no less from his brothers. Dick once lost a game and said, "So what if I lose?" Jack was appalled. He teased Dick about it for years afterward.[11]

Kemp decided at age five that he wanted to be a professional quarterback. As a sixth grader, he was assigned to compose an essay on a great invention. He wrote about the origin of the forward pass.[12] At LA's Fairfax High, he became quarterback and captain of the football team, and he dreamed of going further. "You have to understand my brother," his brother Tom said. "When Jack was a kid he would fantasize about what he wanted to do with his life. He had a mental picture of himself playing football, and he wasn't going to rest until he got there. He believed it was his destiny."[13]

Jack was a successful football player in high school and was named second team All City, but he was not recruited by a single major football school. Tom had played quarterback and baseball at USC. But USC—and UCLA—ignored Jack, deeming him too small (five feet ten, 175 pounds). He settled on attending Occidental College, also in LA, to train under freshman coach Payton Jordan,[14] whom he greatly admired.

Kemp's chief interest at Oxy, as it is called, was football. He majored in physical education and was a mediocre student at best. But he showed talents outside the classroom. His roommate, Jim Mora, a tight end on the football team and later coach of the New Orleans Saints, says, "There was always something special about Jack. Maybe it was his leadership qualities, but he was always somebody that you knew was going to be maybe beyond the ordinary."[15]

Despite his drive, Kemp did not start for the freshman team. But one day Coach Jordan summoned him for a "confidential" talk. He told Kemp that if he was willing to work hard, he had the talent to make the National Football League. Kemp was thrilled. He took Jordan at his word and began working harder at practice and workouts. In those days, quarterbacks were not supposed to lift weights on the theory they'd develop the wrong muscles. But Kemp lifted anyway, to bulk up and build the strength that would make him a professional. With Kemp the conversation had the desired effect. And the weight training paid off. Before long he was able to throw a football eighty yards, and throw it hard.[16] On his very first play with the Occidental varsity, Kemp completed a sixty-yard touchdown pass. He was a sixty-minute man, playing safety on defense. He also punted. By his junior year he was the varsity starting quarterback. As a senior, he became team captain and was the third-leading passer among small colleges and was named honorable-mention Little College All-American.

Kemp was fortunate that Oxy's football team used a pro-style offense that allowed the quarterback to pass a lot. Other schools in Southern California used a single-wing formation that relied on a running attack, and the quarterback was essentially a blocker who ran occasionally but rarely passed. That wasn't Kemp's style. His childhood hero was Los Angeles Rams Hall of Famer Bob Waterfield, a pure passer. That's what Kemp wanted to be.

Kemp's passing was his ticket to professional football. By his senior year, Kemp, six feet tall and weighing two hundred pounds, had finally grown to NFL quarterback size, though making it in the NFL was still a long shot. But his arm caught the attention of professional teams, and he was chosen in the seventeenth round of the NFL draft by the Detroit Lions, the 203d player picked.

Kemp's professional career did not get off to an easy start. He was not an instant hit at the Lions' training camp. Bobby Layne, the team's hard-drinking Hall of Fame quarterback, dismissed Kemp as a ninny when he ordered a soft drink at a quarterback's meeting. Layne informed Kemp he wouldn't make it in pro football until he started drinking alcohol, which Christian Scientists avoid.

Further complicating Kemp's early career, Lions head coach Buddy Parker quit the team in the middle of training camp and moved to the Pittsburgh Steelers. He took Kemp with him, but not because he was convinced of Kemp's talent. Parker's home town was Kemp, Texas, and he'd latched onto Kemp as a kind of good luck charm. He didn't keep Kemp for long.

———

At Occidental, Kemp's most important moment was meeting, in his junior year, an attractive sophomore named Joanne Main. Jack and

Joanne dated casually for a year and a half, sometimes going to Malibu in Jack's red MG and eating in restaurants by the Pacific Ocean. "He was interesting to talk to and be around, and he was a strong personality," Joanne said. When Kemp graduated and went off to play professional football, Joanne completed her senior year, dating others. "But about once a week or every other week he'd call, usually on Sunday nights . . . after a game. And we would write letters, too, probably once every other week."[17]

When Jack came home in December after his first season in the NFL, he proposed. He arranged for his friends to leave him and Joanne alone for a few minutes at a New Year's Eve party. And Jack brought an engagement ring. "I was absolutely stunned," Joanne said, because they'd never discussed marriage. Nor had they talked about his plans for a career in professional football, and now he wanted to get married in July before he had to show up at the Pittsburgh Steelers training camp. "I had lots of other guys that I had gone out with who really did like me," Joanne said. "But I didn't have anybody else that I felt like I did about him. I don't know why that was. I think it was just a conglomeration of who he was." She said yes.

After proposing, Kemp did six months of army service. And following their wedding on July 19, 1958, at Joanne's home church in tiny Fillmore, California, they flew to Pittsburgh. Though Jack was cut by the Steelers and moved from team to team, Joanne was happy. "I loved that football life," she said.[18]

––––––

Kemp got to play in four games for the Steelers in the 1957 season and looked forward to more playing time in 1958. It was not to be. Kemp was an excellent punter, but in an exhibition game against the Rams in LA, Parker told him to kick the ball away from Jon Arnett, the premier kick returner in the league. Kick it out of bounds if you have to, Parker said. But Kemp wanted to impress his family and Joanne, who were in the stands, by punting over Arnett's head. Kemp boomed the kick, but

Arnett caught it and returned it for a touchdown. As Kemp walked off the field, Parker promptly fired him. "Kemp, you may make it in the NFL, but not with the Pittsburgh Steelers," he barked.[19]

Kemp was not discouraged. The New York Giants quickly signed him to their taxi squad, whose players practiced with the team but didn't suit up for games. He was on the sidelines for the 1958 NFL championship game, which the Giants lost to the Baltimore Colts in overtime in the so-called Greatest Game Ever Played. But he got a full share of the loser's bonus—$1,230—thanks to star running back Frank Gifford's intervention on behalf of the taxi squad. The bonus allowed the Kemps to buy their first house, in Orange County, California.[20]

The next season, the Giants found themselves with too many quarterbacks, so they dispatched Kemp to the Calgary Stampeders of the Canadian Football League. However, the CFL required teams to carry a quota of Canadian citizens, so he was ruled ineligible. The San Francisco 49ers signed him as their third-string quarterback behind Y. A. Tittle and John Brodie. But Kemp was again ruled ineligible because he'd played in Canada that year. It was his fifth cut in two seasons.

For once, Kemp was crestfallen. His parents drove to Calgary to bring him home. His mother refused to let her son be discouraged. "She expected him to grow in the experience," Dick Kemp said. "Mom said that when one door closes, another door of opportunity would open," a precept familiar to Christian Scientists and a byword for Kemp and his family.[21]

The door that opened was the American Football League, the junior rival to the NFL created in 1960. For Kemp, the AFL was a godsend. Kemp came close to signing with the Buffalo Bills in 1960, but the team balked at his demand for a no-cut contract, and the deal fell through. Having been cut so many times, Kemp wanted job security. Fortunately, General Manager Frank Leahy and Coach Sid Gillman of the Los Angeles Chargers gave it to him, and he moved back to California.

Kemp was thrilled to play in Coach Gillman's pass-oriented offense, and the two became close friends. "Sid Gillman was like a surrogate father to Jack," Paul Kemp said. Gillman said numerous times publicly that if he'd had a son, he'd want it to be Jack Kemp. "It caused quite a stir in the press."[22]

Kemp caused a stir on the field too. As starting quarterback for the Chargers in 1960, Kemp led the team to a 10–4 record and a Western Division championship. He set his career highs for pass attempts, completions, pass yardage, and touchdowns. His career was finally taking off—and seeds for something more were also being planted.

The league championship game against the Houston Oilers was a revelation to Kemp. He was shocked to discover that the families of black players had to sit in end zone seats while white players' families were in sideline seats. And though Chargers' owner Barron Hilton owned a hotel in Houston, the black players roomed separately in a dormitory at the University of Houston. As an NFL player, Kemp had seen very little racial segregation because the league had no teams in the South. The experience in Houston stunned him.

Next time a racial problem arose, Kemp wasn't quiet. In 1961, the Chargers—now the San Diego Chargers—played a game in Dallas, where Hilton also owned a hotel. The white players were supposed to stay there, while the black players were to be housed in a hotel miles away in Grand Prairie. "Jack went to Sid Gillman and said, 'This is not acceptable,'" said punter Paul Maguire.[23] "'Either we stay as a team or we don't play.' And Kemp was the guy that actually did it. We all ended up in the crappiest hotel in Grand Prairie, Texas. [But] it was absolutely the right thing to do."

———

After two full seasons with the Chargers, Kemp became the Bills' quarterback through a miscue by Gillman. In the second game of the 1962 season, against the New York Titans (later the New York Jets), Kemp suffered his famous injury, resulting in his permanent "football finger." To activate another player while Kemp recovered, Gillman tried to hide him on the "injured reserve" list, hoping other teams wouldn't notice.

But three did notice and claimed Kemp. AFL commissioner Joe Foss ruled that the Bills were first, and the team obtained Kemp's contract for $100 in what football historian Ed Gruver called "the greatest steal in AFL history."[24] Kemp joked, "I didn't mind them getting me for 100 bucks, but when they asked for change, that really bothered me."[25] Gillman was devastated, and Kemp wasn't pleased. He didn't like going to Buffalo, but under AFL rules, he didn't have a choice.

Though accidental, Kemp's arrival in Buffalo was enormously beneficial to Kemp and to the city. In his first home game, in late 1962, he led the Bills to a 23–14 win over the Dallas Texans (now the Kansas City Chiefs). Completing twenty-one passes for 248 yards and two touchdowns in the game, he was carried off the field by victory-starved Buffalo fans.[26] His victories continued. Kemp led the Bills to AFL championships in 1964 and 1965, earning a reputation as a winner and stirring the economically depressed city's spirits.

Kemp was a risk-taking leader. "The rule for quarterbacks is that their best friends are the sideline and the turf," said Ed Rutkowski, who sometimes played that position as well as wide receiver and defensive back. Kemp ignored the rule. Rather than slip out of bounds or slide to the ground before being hit, he ran head-on into linebackers. As a result he suffered eleven concussions in his career, among many other injuries. Kemp joked about a *Buffalo News* headline reading "Kemp Suffers Concussion," with a subhead reading, "X-Rays of Head Reveal Nothing."[27]

Bills fans, notoriously tough on players when they didn't perform well, had a love-hate relationship with Kemp. Rutkowski joked years later that football players had become soft since the years when he was a quarterback. "When we played, if I threw an interception or we had a bad play, people would throw garbage at us and beer cans and rotten tomatoes. And that was when we were coming out of our house!"[28]

Rutkowski recalled one game in which the Bills were performing especially badly, fumbling and getting intercepted, and the boos were deafening. In the huddle, Kemp said to his team, "Let's shut 'em up." With the Bills on their own twenty-yard line, he called a long pass play with all-star Elbert ("Duby") Dubenion the intended receiver. Kemp lofted the ball to a racing Dubenion, who caught it for a sixty-nine-yard touchdown. The Bills walked off the field to a standing ovation.[29]

Coach Lou Saban created a quarterback controversy when the Bills drafted star Notre Dame quarterback Daryle Lamonica in 1963. Would Kemp start, or Lamonica? Lamonica, later dubbed "the Mad Bomber," could throw even farther than Kemp. And as an Italian American and a Catholic, he acquired an army of devoted fans in Buffalo. When Kemp was faltering, the fans demanded Lamonica, and vice versa. The rivalry bothered Kemp, though he and Lamonica got along well personally. Finally, approaching a game the Bills needed to win in order to clinch the division championship in 1964, Coach Saban wouldn't say who would start. Fed up, Kemp told Saban, according to broadcaster Rick Azar, "Coach, I know you want to win. Let me tell you—I can win for you. I can win for this team."[30] Saban let Kemp start and he led the team to a 24–14 win and, weeks later, to the AFL championship.

Besides being an on-field star, Kemp was elected president of the AFL Players Association in 1963 and held the position until the league's merger with the NFL in 1969. He was also an effective mediator in Buffalo. Kemp didn't like it that white players were always assigned white roommates, and blacks roomed with blacks, so he got it changed. He also supported a black players' boycott of the AFL All-Star game to protest racial discrimination in New Orleans. In 1964, Kemp's intervention kept the Bills' star running back, Cookie Gilchrist, on the team after he refused to play in one game because he wasn't getting the ball often enough. Kemp persuaded Gilchrist to apologize and Saban kept him on the team. He helped win the AFL championship, though Saban cut him the following year. When the AFL and NFL merged in 1970, AFL players, recognizing his leadership skills, wanted him to be president of the new combined union. Instead, he negotiated a compromise under which tight end John Mackey of the Baltimore Colts became president. They became friends for life.

Over seven seasons Kemp led the Bills to two AFL championships and four division championships. He was an AFL Pro Bowler in seven seasons and AFL Player of the Year and Most Valuable Player in 1965. He was AFL championship game MVP in both 1964 and 1965. He holds the AFL record for the most yards gained passing in a career, 21,130. In 1961 and 1964, he led the league in longest pass completions, 91 and 94 yards, respectively, and in those years as well as 1967, in yards per pass attempt and completion. He was number one in total offense in 1960 and 1963.[31]

He also became one of the best-paid players in the AFL—but fell well short of Joe Namath's record-setting starting salary of $427,000 at the New York Jets in 1965. Kemp's last contract with the Bills, which he negotiated for himself, was $50,000.[32] In Kemp's day, a good veteran player could earn $25,000 or $26,000. A promising rookie might get $7,500, plus a signing bonus of $300.

For all of Kemp's achievements, he is virtually certain never to make it into the Pro Football Hall of Fame. His 46.7 percent career pass-completion record—and his throwing more interceptions (183) than touchdown passes (114)—doesn't qualify him, according to the late *Buffalo News* sportswriter Larry Felser, a Hall of Fame judge.[33] Teammates have lobbied for his admission as a historic figure and for his Players Association role, but Felser said it's unlikely to happen.

Kemp missed the entire 1968 season after defensive end Ron McDole fell on his right knee in training camp. He played in 1969, but the season was a 4–10 disaster despite the arrival of Heisman Trophy winner O. J. Simpson. Recognizing that his best years were behind him, Kemp decided to retire. Roone Arledge, the president of ABC Sports, offered him a job as a TV color commentator. But Kemp wasn't interested. He had other plans: politics.

———

Kemp had been an indifferent student in college, but as a football player, he became an avid reader of newspapers, news magazines, and books on economics, history, and politics. He used big words with his team-mates, who laughed and called him "the Senator."[34]

When he joined the Chargers in 1960, he met Herb Klein, editor of the *San Diego Union*, and became fascinated with politics. Klein became Kemp's mentor and, along with *Union* sports editor Jack Murphy, encouraged Kemp to give speeches, first to promote the Chargers and later to address more political themes. Klein also persuaded Kemp to write columns for the *Union*. They spent hours talking about sports, which Klein loved, and politics.

In Buffalo, Ed Rutkowski said, "I would always be talking about the game plan and Jack would start talking about politics."[35] On buses and planes to away games, his teammates read *Playboy* and *Sports Illustrated*, while Kemp devoured *U.S. News*, *National Review*, the *Wall Street Journal*, and books. In 1965, he attended two seminars at the Foundation for Economic Education (FEE), a small think tank at Irvington, New York, dedicated to free markets. FEE expanded Kemp's reading list to include such dense classics as Friedrich Hayek's *The Constitution of Liberty* and *The Road to Serfdom*, Ludwig von Mises's *Human Action*, and Milton Friedman's *Capitalism and Freedom*. Kemp lugged boxes of these and other books to the Bills' training camp at Niagara University.

Kemp became an evangelist to teammates for conservatism and the Republican Party. He converted Rutkowski, who later became his top Buffalo-based congressional aide and then Erie County supervisor.[36] Kemp drew players and the traveling press into political discussions. "Jack used to come down to my seat, looking for a debating partner," said Felser. "He was fun to debate with," but he didn't always win: "I was an FDR Democrat, still am."[37] Not everyone liked his politics; when Kemp campaigned for Barry Goldwater in 1964, it stirred newspaper criticism in heavily Democratic Buffalo. But Kemp didn't back down.

In 1967, Klein helped Kemp get a job during the off-season as an intern in California governor Ronald Reagan's communications office. The internship was a first step into active politics, but it had a downside. The job led to a rumor of homosexuality that took decades—and investigative reporting by columnist Robert Novak—to be knocked down definitively. In 1967, columnist Drew Pearson broke the story of Reagan's firing a "homosexual ring" on his staff. Pearson reported the ring involved "an athlete" whom he didn't name. Rumors spread immediately that the athlete was Kemp, who had copurchased a property near Lake Tahoe with one of the ring's participants. Kemp said it was merely an investment and that he had never stayed there.

Novak began investigating the scandal in 1978. He tracked down one of the gay principals, who was "adamant that Kemp was not part of the homosexual group" and reported his denial in a column.[38] But the rumor continued to circulate in the political community. Novak wrote he was told that it kept Reagan from considering Kemp as his vice presidential running mate in 1980, and it cropped up again when Kemp ran for president in 1988. It didn't die until Novak recounted all the evidence disproving the rumor in his 2007 autobiography, *The Prince of Darkness*.[39]

By the time his football career ended, Kemp had developed political savvy and had become an excellent speaker. His speeches, once vaguely about leadership, were now full of concrete economic and political content. Observing him, Al Bellanca, the chairman of the Erie County (Buffalo) Republican Party, told Kemp he'd make a good candidate for Congress, and Kemp agreed. "If you could take the boos of 47,000 people in War Memorial Stadium, you could take the heat in politics," he said.[40] It soon became his favorite line at campaign events.

Kemp still had three years to go on his no-cut contract when he announced for Congress in March 1970. The seat he sought, New York's Thirty-ninth District, included part of the city of Buffalo but mostly encompassed working-class suburbs of Erie County. Kemp jokingly threatened that if he was not elected, he'd return to play for the Bills.

Winning the Thirty-ninth District was a challenge. The district had been represented by both Republicans and Democrats, but since 1964 the seat had been occupied by Democrat Max McCarthy. It was now open because McCarthy had decided to run for the U.S. Senate, and there was every reason to believe his constituents would continue to vote Democratic. Tom Flaherty, the Democrat nominated to replace McCarthy, was a Buffalo attorney and former city official who had an ethnic advantage in the heavily Catholic district. Kemp countered by bringing in ex–Notre Dame coach Frank Leahy to speak for him, along with O. J. Simpson, Lou Saban, and Daryle Lamonica, and he asked Ed Rutkowski, then a Democrat, to help run his campaign. Rutkowski says he offered to change his registration to Republican, but Kemp urged him not to, pointing out that his Democratic affiliation would look good in Buffalo.

At age thirty-five, Kemp was full of youthful energy, but some said his youth was a liability. His football stardom, largely an asset, also risked making him seem unserious. As Rutkowski later recounted, "People were saying, 'We recognize the name Jack Kemp, but what the hell's a football player think he's doing running for Congress?'" The creative director of an advertising agency retained by the campaign told Kemp he looked "too boyish," so he had his team draw wrinkles on Kemp's face to make him seem older in campaign ads. They also encouraged him to develop a deeper voice.[41] That didn't work: Kemp retained a high-pitched, raspy voice for life.

Kemp initially was reluctant to directly ask people for their support. But he learned to greet workers arriving at Bethlehem Steel's factory gates, where his charisma could win them over. Joanne organized coffee klatches for voters, and that won them over too. In a debate, Flaherty brought up Kemp's support for Goldwater in 1964, whereupon Kemp got Flaherty to admit that he'd supported Lyndon Johnson, then still deeply unpopular. Anyway, he said, the 1970 election was not about 1964, but about the future.

Kemp's friendliness with organized labor was a point in his favor. After six years as president of the AFL players' union, he regarded collective bargaining as "a sacred right."[42] Most Republicans favored right-to-work laws that ban compulsory unionization, but Kemp never endorsed them. He later said he belonged to "the Lane Kirkland wing of the Republican party," referring to the then-president of the AFL-CIO.[43]

Kemp's hard work and celebrity paid off. He won the election with 51.6 percent of the vote. Elated, he and Joanne prepared to move to Washington with their three children—Jeff, then eleven years old, Jennifer, eight, and Judith, five. Their fourth child, Jimmy, was born in 1971 during Kemp's first year in Congress.

Along with his quarterback's approach to leadership, Kemp kept an important memento of his years on the field. In his congressional office, he hung a giant picture of himself about to be demolished by 6-foot-9, 315-pound Chargers defensive tackle Ernie Ladd—a reminder to himself and visitors that, whatever the challenges of politics, he'd been through worse. "Pro football gave me a good sense of perspective to enter politics. I'd already been booed, cheered, cut, sold, traded and hung in effigy," he would later say.[44]

Five-year-old Jack Kemp certainly never considered preparation for politics a side advantage to playing football, but his thick skin would stand the young congressman in good stead as he set out for D.C. He didn't know it yet, but he was soon to be the champion of a new economic model. Washington's elites would not appreciate the young congressman's big ideas.

Two

SUPPLY-SIDER

When Kemp arrived in Congress in 1971, he was basically a novice in economics. He'd read the free market classics—Hayek, von Mises, Friedman—but was scarcely policy savvy. Within seven years, though, he became the most important tax writer of his era, one of the most important of the twentieth century, and the political leader of an intellectual revolution in economics—all without ever once having an official role in tax policy. Along the way he experienced defeat after defeat. But then he won.

Kemp got into tax policy to relieve the economic suffering of his constituents. When he arrived in Washington, Buffalo and blue-collar suburbs like Cheektowaga, Tonawanda, and Lackawanna were hurting. Plants were closing, and unemployment was rising, reaching 11.2 percent in 1972, nearly double the national average.[1] As if living in the Rust Belt wasn't hard enough, Buffalo was also beginning to exhibit symptoms of the economic disease that sapped the entire nation in the 1970s—stagflation.[2]

Stagflation—the phenomenon of simultaneous high inflation and high unemployment—was an impossibility according to conventional economic thinking. Rising unemployment was supposed to lower prices because demand for goods and labor would fall. And good times would lead to inflation. Yet by the time the 1970s ended, prices were rising at

13.5 percent a year, while unemployment rose to 7.1 percent of the work-force in 1980. (Buffalo's unemployment rate in 1976 was 16 percent.) The malady cut America's postwar growth rate nearly in half—from 3.6 percent per year, the average from 1950 to 1973, down to 1.6 percent for the next decade.

The presidents of the era—Republicans Richard Nixon and Gerald Ford and Democrat Jimmy Carter—had no idea how to break the dismal cycle. Neither did most economists, liberal or conservative. Nixon's wage and price controls had no effect. Nor did Ford's "Whip Inflation Now" campaign or Carter's advice to turn thermostats down.

In his early years in Congress, Kemp didn't know what to do either. Eager to help his district, he did what a liberal Democrat might do—help local officials beg industries not to leave and lobby for public works projects to replace lost jobs. As a conservative he also called for limits on federal spending and opposed President Nixon's wage and price controls.

As the economy worsened during the stagflation years, the stock market lost 70 percent of its value as people with money invested in gold, oil, land, even oriental rugs. Retirees on fixed incomes were plunged into poverty as inflation ate up their pension checks. Workers demanded ever-larger wage increases to keep up with the cost of living, which kept the cycle going. And their wage hikes evaporated because higher incomes pushed them into higher tax brackets (top rate: 70 percent), feeding the government rather than their families.

Concerned about his suffering constituents, Kemp realized he'd have to better understand economics, so he began studying. When he met Irving Kristol, the neoconservative intellectual, Kemp asked for a reading list. Six or eight weeks later, he asked for another list. "I gave you one," Kristol said. "I read all those," Kemp replied. "I want a new list." Kristol was amazed. Kemp aides weren't. "He always had five books going at the same time," said Kemp speech writer John Mueller.[3]

Kemp's studies led him to the idea that cutting taxes would help employers and workers. His first step was to find a new chief of staff who understood both public works policy and taxes. He found Randal Teague, an official in Nixon's Office of Economic Opportunity, and hired him in 1973. The two men immediately set to work drafting a bill.

Their first effort wasn't promising. Copying the business-friendly essentials of a bill by GOP senator Paul Fannin of Arizona, Kemp and Teague named Kemp's first tax bill the Savings and Investment Act of 1974. But Teague referred candidly to it as "a Chamber of Commerce wish list."⁴ Arthur Laffer called it an "old line, right-wing" capital forma-tion act.⁵ It consisted entirely of corporate tax breaks: credits and swifter write-offs for investment in equipment, lower corporate taxes, and more exemptions from capital gains taxes. It did nothing to cut sky-high indi-vidual tax rates, later Kemp's successful supply-side formula.

Though it directly benefited business, Kemp viewed his bill more as a job creator. He represented a blue-collar district, after all. And unlike most Republicans, he was not only worker friendly, but also union friendly. One inspiration for the bill was an advertisement he saw in a Buffalo newspaper. In large letters, it read LATHE OPERATORS WANTED*. In small letters beside the asterisk, it added "Bring Your Own Lathe."⁶ Kemp believed that if tax laws made it cheaper to buy lathes, there'd be more lathes and more jobs for lathe operators and everyone connected to their industry.

Kemp used the lathe story to convince working-class constituents that though he was a conservative Republican, he had their interests at heart. He argued in a 1975 House speech that there were two paths to a growing society. "The workers can work harder and longer," he said, or "we can have more and better tools." The history of industrial prog-ress belonged to inventors who create "better tools" for workers and find investors to fund them.⁷

Kemp's proposal went nowhere. When Gerald Ford succeeded the Watergate-ruined Nixon—Kemp took a noncommittal "Let the evidence be our guide" stance on Watergate—the new administration opposed Kemp's bill. Its reasoning: tax revenue would be lost, and the federal defi-cit (then $53 billion, nearly a postwar high) and inflation (then 9.1 percent) would increase. The *Wall Street Journal* editorial page, not yet in Kemp's camp, opposed the bill on the same grounds.

In Congress, few Republicans supported Kemp's bill either. Many agreed with Ford's cautious economics. Others were furious that a non-member of Ways and Means was treading into tax territory, and they let him know it. Some senior officials considered Kemp a "dumb jock" over his head (as well as out of his lane) on policy matters—and they envied his celebrity. One ally, ex-representative Bob Livingston of Louisiana,[8] said that even later in Kemp's career "there was a lot of grumbling because Jack had the ability to appeal to the press in a Reaganesque fashion. A lot of guys . . . resented it. They didn't have that capacity and also they frankly took the old view that you count the beans and don't worry about growth—and Jack was about growth."

Some of Kemp's harshest criticism came from members of the Chowder and Marching Club. As a famous former football player and as president of his freshman class in Congress, Kemp had been admitted to the elite club of GOP representatives, where leaders gathered for policy chats and socializing at 5 p.m. on Wednesdays. After Kemp's bill was introduced, the C&M, stodgy and committed to House tradition, became a whipping post for Kemp as senior Republicans expressed disapproval with his upstart plans. A fellow C&M member, then-senator Bill Brock of Tennessee, said, "Jack was viewed as a maverick and a bit of a trouble-maker for getting off the track the Ford administration was on. . . . There were very tense conversations. . . . There were several of those meetings, by the way, not just one."

Kemp returned from one C&M meeting more shaken than Randy Teague had ever seen him. "People said he was barking up the wrong tree . . . not doing them any good," Teague said. "He just felt like he was hitting a wall."[9] But he recovered and worked to overcome opposition in his party—though success took awhile.

On the football field, Kemp was used to being the play caller and he brought his quarterback mentality to Washington. "He was a real take-charge guy," said Al Bemiller, Kemp's center for eight pro seasons. "You didn't talk in his huddle. You listened."[10]

But Kemp learned that football and politics had different rules. "I'd call a play and expect everyone to carry out his assignment," Kemp told an interviewer. "I quickly realized it isn't that way in government. Leadership here means finding out where people want to go and figuring out a way to take them there. That's what democracy is all about. A football huddle is not a democracy."[11] If Kemp was to make changes in tax policy, he would have to persuade.

Irrepressible as always, Kemp became relentless in trying to win others over—fellow members, political audiences, the press, economic professionals, even liberals—to support his views. Full of zeal to attract colleagues to his team, he worked the House floor relentlessly and would return to his office with names of potential allies. He'd tell Teague to get in touch with the legislative assistants of the members he'd talked to and firm up a relationship.[12] Kemp sought converts at committee meetings and while riding the underground train connecting congressional offices and the Capitol. "He'd work on them when he spoke for them at a fundraiser," Teague said. It never stopped.

His energy and enthusiasm were often greater than his tact and sensitivity. Members ducked into offices or headed for another hallway to escape an impromptu Kemp lecture. If he sensed someone in an audience was unconvinced on a point, he would keep talking to win over the skeptic. It made for long speeches and weary listeners. And it prompted a joke: Kemp is in the clutches of a Gestapo agent who snarls, "Vee have vays of making you stop talking."[13]

So intense was Kemp's proselytizing—especially after he discovered supply-side economics—that many of his colleagues describe his enthusiasm in religious language. Representative Dan Lungren of California says he was "John the Baptist," paving the way for Ronald Reagan. Others call him their "spiritual leader." The result of his initial evangelism was an embryonic Kemp team. It was smaller and less committed to

Kemp personally than the later crew that included Newt Gingrich, but it gathered around him on at least this one issue.

———

When Kemp was in his capital-formation phase, seeking to create jobs by incentivizing business investment, the supply-side movement was still developing. Supply side's intellectual fathers were Robert Mundell, then a hippie-looking Canadian academic, and Arthur Laffer, a precocious, fast-talking University of Chicago professor. Their formula to fight stagflation was to lower individual tax rates to foster growth and control the supply of money in the economy to dampen inflation. Their theories challenged all prevailing economic wisdom and were initially scorned.

Mundell, long-haired and soft-spoken, earned his PhD in economics at the Massachusetts Institute of Technology.[14] In 1958, at age twenty-six, he concluded that the path to prosperity for slow-growth America lay in the Federal Reserve's tightening of the money supply and raising interest rates (to control inflation and attract foreign investment) while Congress and the president (then Dwight Eisenhower) lowered taxes to stimulate domestic investment and foster economic growth.

The theory was at odds with accepted economic and political dogma. Democrats worshipped John Maynard Keynes, the famed British economist who declared that the Great Depression resulted from a collapse of private demand for goods and services, and prescribed government spending to replace and stimulate it. Keynes's followers believed—and believe to this day—that government spending is the remedy for slow growth. They acknowledged that rising budget deficits would result in higher inflation. Their solution was to loosen monetary policy and raise taxes—that is, print dollars to dilute the federal debt while hiking taxes to bring budgets into balance. Mundell said Keynes was wrong and that excessive increases in the money supply were the main cause of inflation.

Even though Richard Nixon declared that "we are all Keynesians now," mainstream Republicans weren't. The party advocated tight monetary policy, decreased government spending—and increased taxes, when necessary, to balance budgets. Deficits, most Republicans believed, were what caused inflation. Mundell insisted that they, too, were wrong and that high taxes hobbled the economy.

Mundell's introduction of a third model—tight money and low taxes—aroused immediate opposition among economists when he proposed it in academic papers in the late 1950s and early 1960s. Then, by a circuitous process unrelated to him, John F. Kennedy proposed policies aligned with Mundell's ideas in 1962 and 1963, and Congress enacted them in 1964 after his assassination. The Kennedy cuts trimmed corporate tax rates from 52 percent to 48 percent and reduced the top individual rate from 91 percent to 70 percent. Meanwhile, the Federal Reserve restricted the money supply. The results, as Mundell had forecast, were higher interest rates and a surge in foreign investment. The changes produced the economic boom of the mid-1960s. The unemployment rate fell from 5.7 percent in 1963 to 3.6 percent in 1968 and the deficit dropped from $7.1 billion in 1962 to $1.4 billion in 1965. Mundell's academic work gained him, at age twenty-eight, a tenured professorship in the University of Chicago economics department, the most prestigious in the country.

In spite of the success of his ideas, Mundell then had little impact on economic thinking or longer-term national policy. Keynesians were impervious to challenge, bending the evidence to fit their theory. The leading economists of the era—Walter Heller, Kennedy's chief economic adviser, and Paul Samuelson, author of the most widely read college economics textbook—argued that Kennedy's tax cuts accelerated growth not by stimulating work, investment, and supply, but by putting more spending money into peoples' hands and increasing demand.

Unfortunately for the economy, immediately after Lyndon Johnson passed JFK's tax cuts, he embarked on two massive spending campaigns, the Great Society and the Vietnam War. To pay the bills, Johnson and Congress raised taxes. But tax revenues failed to keep up with spending, and deficits mounted. Johnson badgered and bullied the Fed to print money to monetize the debt, ignoring an important half of the supply-side formula. In hindsight, it's clear Johnson's late-1960s policies set loose a new problem with a new name—*stagflation*—and a decade of economic decline in the 1970s.

Arthur Laffer, meanwhile, gained a tenured appointment in Chicago at age thirty-one, before he'd even finished his PhD. He took leave from his position there to become chief economist in Nixon's Office of Management and Budget (OMB). In 1971, Laffer relied on Mundell's ideas to predict that the nation's gross national product that year would be $1.065 trillion, $20 billion higher than the consensus forecast of national economists. For this he was denounced—most cruelly, by Nobel Prize winner Paul Samuelson, who delivered a lecture at the University of Chicago titled "Why They Are Laughing at Laffer." He attacked the basis of Laffer's calculations and ridiculed him personally for not having finished his PhD thesis. But Laffer was ultimately vindicated when his GNP prediction proved accurate.[15]

Laffer finished his dissertation and received his doctorate from Stanford, but Samuelson's ridicule made him an outcast at Chicago. Mundell, his friend and ally, had left to teach in Canada. So before leaving Chicago for the University of Southern California in 1976, Laffer spent much of his time with fellow conservatives in New York and Washington where he met the third supply-side "original."

Jude Wanniski was a colorful intellectual seeker, strategist, polemicist, and journalist. He had been a leftist at UCLA[16] before becoming a devoted Democrat and eventually transforming into a champion of free markets. He had a wild reputation and dressed in black shirts, white ties, and gaudy jackets, carryovers from his early years as a journalist in Las Vegas, where he had also become an accomplished gambler. Style aside, Wanniski was a spellbinding purveyor of schemes and ideas—and, for years, one of Kemp's closest advisers.

Wanniski encountered Laffer while working for the *National Observer*, a now-defunct sister paper of the *Wall Street Journal*. He became an editorial writer for the *Journal* in 1972, moving to New York but traveling often to Washington. He first met Mundell in May 1974 at a conference on inflation hosted by the conservative American Enterprise Institute think tank in Washington. The two instantly connected, and when they returned to New York after the conference, Wanniski slept on Mundell's couch for several days instead of going home to New Jersey. Laffer described Wanniski as "my closest friend after my father,"[17] though their relationship later soured over business rivalries. Delighted to have encountered a kindred spirit, the two men, along with Mundell, joined an economic and political discussion group at a New York financial district restaurant, Michael 1, where they brainstormed ways to spread their economic ideas.

December 1974 was a decisive month for the Mundell-Laffer-Wanniski movement that still did not have a name. That month Laffer drew his famous "Laffer curve" on a napkin for President Ford's deputy White House chief of staff, Richard Cheney. Laffer's curve, a bell curve turned on its side, showed that at 0 percent and 100 percent tax rates, the government gets no revenue—at 100, because no one works and pays taxes—while somewhere in between (Laffer didn't say exactly where) workers, business owners, and investors have an incentive to produce to their maximum, the economy flourishes, and government collects optimum revenues. High taxes in an unspecified "prohibitive range" discourage enterprise and cost the government revenue.

Also in 1974, Wanniski wrote his first economics column for the *Journal,* "It's Time to Cut Taxes," a summary of Mundell's views.[18] In his column Wanniski summarized the argument Mundell had been making since 1961: inflation could be curbed by tightening the money supply, and stagnation could be cured by cutting tax rates. "The national economy is being choked by taxes—asphyxiated," Wanniski quoted Mundell as saying. "It is simply absurd to argue that increasing unemployment will stop inflation. To stop inflation, you need more goods, not less."

Wanniski expanded on his *Journal* article in the Spring 1975 issue of the *Public Interest,* edited by Irving Kristol. His article was titled "The Mundell-Laffer Hypothesis: A New View of the World Economy" and fundamentally was a long discourse on Mundell's monetary views. His and Laffer's tax views got less treatment, with just a footnote describing the thinking behind the Laffer curve.

With Wanniski's columns, Mundell's arguments, and Laffer's famous curve, the three men were refining and tightening their economic theories. Now they needed a politician to pay attention.

———

Curiously, for someone well wired in Washington, Wanniski did not meet Kemp until January 1976. The meeting, when it happened, was transformative for both men. Wanniski came to Kemp's congressional office in the morning without an appointment and sent his card in to Kemp, who immediately burst out of his room, exclaiming "Wanniski! I've just been thinking about how I was going to meet you." He said he'd been reading Wanniski for a long time and wanted to discuss his ideas in person.

They started talking about economics at 10 a.m. They talked all day. Wanniski canceled other appointments and followed Kemp around Capitol Hill. In the evening, Kemp took Wanniski to his home in suburban Bethesda, Maryland, where Joanne prepared dinner, and they continued talking until midnight. "It was exhausting," Wanniski recounted. "He was draining me of everything I know. He was squeezing my head."[19] By the time the day was over, Kemp was convinced of the merits of Mundell's and Laffer's ideas.[20]

Wanniski also was impressed. "I had spent hours with other senators, representatives, and even the Treasury Secretary and nobody understood what I was talking about," he said. "Kemp grasped the notion of monetary reform immediately. That day I came back and told my staff, 'I've just fallen in love.'"[21]

Together, Kemp and Wanniski would become a formidable team, Wanniski with the *Journal* platform and Kemp with political energy. Laffer said, "Jack and Jude together were deadly."[22] The relationship was not always smooth—Laffer said they sometimes fought "like schoolgirls"—

but for years their arguments were temporary, as the substance of their agreements kept them together. Kemp and Wanniski talked at least once a day, sometimes more often, according to Kemp's economic aide, Bruce Bartlett.[23] They were "so close . . . talking to one was like talking to the other."

Kemp's advancement became Wanniski's major project. In 1979, he said, "I think Jack will be the next President. . . ." And of Kemp's ability to spread the economic "theology" they shared, Wanniski said, "Every now and then something happens like this. The last time was Christ."[24]

It was Wanniski who coined the term "supply-side economics," converting it from a derisive label into a revolutionary banner. At a 1976 symposium on inflation at the Homestead resort in Virginia, American Enterprise Institute economist Herb Stein, once Richard Nixon's chief economist, observed that a new theory was gaining notice, propounded by "supply-side fiscalists." Among professional economists, he jibed (unfairly)[25] that its adherents numbered "maybe two." Stein's remarks were conveyed to Wanniski, who was seeking a better label for his idea set than "the Mundell-Laffer Hypothesis." He decided to run with "supply side"[26] because it provided a good counter to Keynesian "demand-side" economics. Kemp's wife often urged them to call it "incentive-oriented economics,"[27] but "supply side" stuck.

Under Wanniski's influence, Kemp became a tax cutter first and a budget balancer hardly at all. In 1975, before meeting Jude, he had sponsored a bill, the Fiscal Integrity Act, that mandated balanced budgets and capped government revenues as a percentage of GDP. In December 1975, he had argued that tax cuts—even those he sponsored—had to be matched with spending reductions.[28]

Wanniski was convinced supply-side cuts would stimulate the economy enough to keep it healthy and abhorred Republican calls for spending cuts or budget balancing. In an article in his old paper, the *National Observer*, he wrote that Democrats prospered politically by playing the role of "the Spending Santa Claus." Instead of allowing only Democrats to be seen as gift givers, Republicans "should be the Santa

Claus of Tax Reduction." At the time, Republicans were so "hypnotized" by the need for balanced budgets that they persistently argued for tax hikes to dampen inflation when the economy was booming. And they demanded spending cuts to balance the budget when the economy is in recession. "Either way, of course, they embrace the role of Scrooge," Wanniski complained.[29]

After his conversion to supply-side economics, Kemp continued advocating spending restraint in principle, but in a 1978 profile in *Fortune*, he was quoted as saying, "I don't worship at the shrine of the balanced budget."[30]

Thoroughly convinced of supply side's virtues, in March 1976, Kemp announced that a revised version of his Savings and Investment Act, renamed the Jobs Creation Act, had 106 sponsors. Besides the original corporate tax breaks, the bill now included a 10 percent across-the-board cut in individual taxes. Consultant Norman Ture, an advocate for capital-formation tax policy, concluded that the bill would add $150 billion to U.S. GDP; create five million new jobs over a decade; and add little, if anything, to the federal deficit. The Ford administration, unconvinced that lowering rates would increase revenues, opposed the measure.[31]

Wanniski used all of his influence to support Kemp and push the bill. In a September 1976 *Wall Street Journal* column, he countered the Treasury Department's opposition, pointing to the success of the Kennedy cuts. In Kennedy's case, he wrote, instead of costing the Treasury $89 billion from 1962–64, as government economists estimated, tax cuts led to economic growth that increased revenues by $54 billion.

In the same column, Wanniski lamented that both President Ford and his Republican challenger, Ronald Reagan, believed that tax rate cuts had no revenue-increasing effects. If the supply-siders were able to win over a presidential candidate who agreed with them, their movement would be strengthened. But gaining that powerful an ally in the 1976 election didn't seem likely.

Though Kemp had worked as an intern for Reagan and had been rebuffed by Ford, Kemp stayed neutral in their battle for the 1976 Republican presidential nomination. Yet the party's Kansas City convention was an important moment for Kemp—and would have launched him onto the national stage had all gone as planned. Invited to introduce House Republican leader John Rhodes, he prepared to address a nationally televised political event for the first time. Wanniski played a double role: as Kemp's speechwriter and as a journalist covering Kemp. On the day of the speech, Wanniski published a *Journal* column[32] touting Kemp as the speaker House Republicans most wanted to address the convention and hoping Kemp's speech would communicate the urgency of electing a Republican Congress that could carry out his economic plans.

In the speech, Kemp barely mentioned Rhodes. Instead, he delivered a rousing cry for Republicans to go on the offense and "move the American people with our ideas." He called for the GOP to adopt a platform of reduced spending, lower taxes, private-sector jobs, and a stable currency. He contrasted this agenda with that of Democrats, whose forty years of dominating Congress "carried the seeds of its own destruction—double-digit inflation resulting in nearly double-digit unemployment." There is "only one way to reform Washington," he said, "and that is to reform Congress" by ousting Democrats and installing Republican leaders."[33]

The speech was forcefully delivered, but TV cameras covering the convention cut away for commercials during Kemp's introduction and it was never seen or heard by the public. So much for Wanniski's attempt to spring Kemp and supply-side economics to the national stage.

Undaunted, Kemp, or at least Wanniski, tried another gambit. With the nomination not yet secured by Ford, Wanniski approached Reagan aide Martin Anderson with a proposal: if Reagan would make across-the-board rate cuts part of his platform, Kemp would deliver New York delegates to Reagan. Those delegates would have brought Reagan close to matching Ford's count, but it was unlikely Kemp could actually deliver the New York delegation. Reagan was interested but noncommittal, which wasn't good enough for Wanniski. "Jude wanted a formal acceptance," Laffer said. "'Oh, we love it,' was not precise enough for Jude."[34]

The ploy—hardly the last Wanniski would invent to advance Kemp and his ideas—went nowhere.

Reagan failed to wrest the GOP nomination from Ford, and Ford went on to lose the presidential election to Democrat Jimmy Carter. Democrats gained just one seat each in the House and Senate, but combined with their post–Watergate victories in 1994, they held two thirds of the seats in the House and sixty-one in the Senate. Kemp was reelected with 78.2 percent of the vote. He was secure in his district, and Wanniski's influence had raised his profile. But he hadn't yet acquired the platform he would need to bring supply-side economics mainstream.

––––

Despite the supply-siders' apparent cohesion, Kemp's advisers were actually often at odds. Arguments over policy nuances and historical credit for developing supply-side economics led to personal enmity. One spat between Kemp economic staffer Paul Craig Roberts and Wanniski came close to fisticuffs in a stairwell.[35] Kemp aide John Mueller described meetings in which Laffer, Mundell, Wanniski, and former drugstore magnate Lew Lehrman engaged in shouting matches as the strong-minded economists struggled over differences in policy and tactics.[36]

One major disagreement was over the impact supply-side tax rate cuts would have on tax revenues. Conventional thinkers of both parties calculated that lower rates had to shrink revenue. Supply-siders argued that cuts would stimulate growth and swell government revenues. But would the resulting revenues exceed the nominal cost of the cuts? Laffer and Wanniski were persistently bullish, contending that tax cuts would pay for themselves. Roberts, who went from Kemp's staff to the House Budget Committee and later Reagan's Treasury Department, argued that rate cuts wouldn't pay for themselves, but the growth they fostered would replace *part* of the forgone revenue. He was appalled at Laffer's and Wanniski's position, charging that the two "covered the supply-side movement with hyperbole" used by its enemies to discredit it.[37]

Kemp was unequivocal on this point. He argued that tax rate cuts *did* pay for themselves, basing his conclusion on Kennedy economic adviser Walter Heller's testimony that the 1960s cuts "paid for themselves inside one year." Kemp argued that after the Kennedy cuts, revenues increased for five straight years and cited a Library of Congress study showing that though the Treasury had estimated $89 billion in losses from 1963 to 1968, revenues actually went up by $54 billion.[38]

Roberts moved from Kemp's staff to become chief GOP economist at the Budget Committee in August 1976—the better, he later wrote, to advance supply-side policy. He was replaced in December by Bruce Bartlett, four years out of college and a former staffer for libertarian representative Ron Paul of Texas. Kemp hired him after a hasty interview he conducted dressed in his tuxedo on his way to one of Ford's last White House dinners. Bartlett remembers Kemp asking whether he was "a supply-side fiscalist." Bartlett said, "I swear to God I'd never heard that term in my life. But I didn't have anything to lose, so I said, 'Well, sure. Who isn't?'"[39] To this day, he's not sure why he was chosen ahead of dozens of others considered for the job. But he was to play a central role in the development of Kemp's policy.

———

Bartlett's first task in 1977 was to canvass House Republican offices and re-sign cosponsors for the Jobs Creation Act, which had never passed. Meantime, Kemp sent out a confidential memo to all GOP members of Congress on February 22, 1977, urging support for a House budget amendment to be offered the following day. The amendment contained a 22 percent across-the-board reduction for all taxpayers, offering what Kemp called "constructive alternatives to programs of the national Democratic Party."

Floor debate was intense and provided a perfect showcase for Kemp's arguments. The amendment, sponsored by Roberts's new boss, Representative John Rousselot of California, was attacked by Democrats, notably by Representative Paul Simon of Illinois, who called it "the old trickle-down theory." House majority leader Jim Wright of Texas joined in, calling it "regressive," principally benefiting the rich, and asserting that cutting taxes would swell the budget deficit.

Kemp seized the opportunity to refute both Democrats, teaching supply-side economics with Wanniski's Kennedy punch. To Simon, a kindly liberal and later a senator and presidential candidate, he was deferential and respectful. He said benefits would not trickle but "would literally cascade down—or, in President Kennedy's words, 'a rising tide lifts all ships.'"

Answering Wright, a mean-spirited partisan, Kemp was tougher. He argued that Kennedy had proposed similar cuts without ever having Democrats accuse him of favoring the rich. When Kemp raised the Laffer argument that the government gains no revenue at a 100 percent tax rate, Wright stalked off the floor with a parting shot: "For the record, I would like to agree with the gentleman that 100 percent taxation is not a very good idea. I suppose everyone would agree with that. I am not aware that anyone has made any such suggestion." Kemp retorted, "Mr. Chairman, I appreciate hearing from the other side of the aisle that they do not plan to raise the tax rates any higher. That is progress, I guess." As Wright walked out, Kemp called after him, "Mr. Wright, I am speaking to you!"[40]

Despite Kemp's passionate arguments, the GOP substitute was voted down, 258–148, with ten Republicans voting with Democrats (though twenty-five Democrats supported it). But it was a victory for Republicans in that it established tax cuts as Republican policy. Roberts called it "a historic date [that] marked the origin of the Kemp-Roth bill and the resurrection of the Republican party."[41] He was right. Republicans began introducing tax cuts in later bills, and gained political favor by painting the Democrats as the party of high taxes.[42] Though only a minority of Republicans in the Senate supported permanent rate cuts, the Republican House members showed near unanimity in voting for the cuts in 1977.[43] The tide had begun to turn.

————

Four months after the House debate—on July 14, 1977—Kemp and Senator William Roth introduced a new bill: Kemp-Roth. Their press conference to unveil the proposal was attended by only one reporter, from Roth's home state of Delaware, so the measure attracted no immediate public attention. Within a year, however, it became official Republican policy.

Bartlett recalls the birth of Kemp-Roth this way:

> *I was sitting in my cubicle—this was . . . March or April of 1977—and Jack poked his head in and said something to the effect of "We keep talking all the time about the Kennedy tax cut. Why don't we just replicate it? Let's get rid of all this baggage and just do a clean, straight duplication of the Kennedy tax cut." I said, "Fine," of course. . . . But, it wasn't that obvious what that meant because obviously the tax code was different. . . . So I talked to a lot of people to ask them, "If you were going to redo the Kennedy tax cut today, how would you do it?"* [44]

Bartlett's search led him to economist Norman Ture. Ture had been a staffer for Wilbur Mills, the Arkansas Democrat who chaired the Ways and Means Committee from 1958 to 1974. Ture had helped Mills originate what became the Kennedy tax cuts. At Bartlett's request, he agreed to help shape the new cuts. Bartlett also talked to Laffer and others in the Kemp orbit, and the brain trust agreed that the plan should reduce the top rate from 70 percent to 50 percent and the bottom from 14 percent to 8 percent, making an overall 30 percent cut that approximated Kennedy's.

Kemp needed a cosponsor for his bill. William Roth, a member of the tax-writing Senate Finance Committee and a moderate Republican, came to Bartlett's attention when he sent Kemp a handwritten note of praise. Kemp and his team lunched in the Senate Dining Room with

Roth and his aides, and they found themselves broadly in agreement on Kemp's plan to reduce income tax rates for individuals. Kennedy's bill also had cut corporate tax rates, so Kemp and Roth decided to propose cutting that rate from 48 to 45 percent. Roth just had one concern: worried that Kemp's bill would cost too much revenue, he asked for a smaller reduction to the bottom income tax rate and suggested phasing in the cuts over three years. Kemp agreed.[45]

––––––

As Kemp and Roth prepared their bill, a pivotal player arrived out of the blue. Bill Brock, after losing his bid for reelection to the Senate in Tennessee in 1976, was elected Republican National Chairman in 1977. The RNC boss held a challenging job, given the balance of power in Washington. Republicans had lost the White House and after the devastating 1974 post–Watergate elections, the GOP was reduced to 37 Senate seats and 143 House seats. Democrats now had enough votes to block any GOP filibuster in the Senate and the two-thirds margin required to overturn vetoes in the House. Brock's party was laid low—"clobbered," he said.[46] He was eager to attach the GOP to something new and positive, and swiftly became one of Kemp-Roth's major boosters.

"We were, at least in perception, anti-women, anti-minority, anti-union, anti-poor," Brock said. "Every negative you could put on the Republican Party had been done because of Vietnam, civil rights, Nixon, Watergate. I was trying to create a different kind of party and it was a deliberate objective of getting women elected, minorities elected, young people, blue collar, union. And we needed a catalytic agent. . . . Kemp, with his big-tent approach and his new ideas, could be that catalyst."

Brock was a conventional conservative, no supply-sider. But he also had been politically astute enough, as a House member, to urge giving the vote to eighteen-year-olds. He also supported Wisconsin representative Bill Steiger's bill to cut taxes on capital gains. So when Kemp suggested his tax cuts as a party position, Brock loved the idea. Kemp "talked about the income tax as something that affected every individual. . . . So that became really, really attractive to me," Brock said.[47] In late September 1977, Brock got the full Republican National Committee to adopt Kemp-Roth as official party policy.

Brock's intention was to use the issue to win congressional seats in 1978 and prepare a platform for the presidential candidate of 1980 to run on. A month after the RNC vote, Ronald Reagan made a radio address similar to a *Washington Post* column he'd written just before the 1976 election.[48]

> *Twice in this century, in the 1920s and the early 1960s, we cut taxes and the stimulant to the economy was substantial and immediate. . . . Jack Kemp, a young Congressman from New York who used to quarterback the Buffalo Bills, has introduced a job creation bill five times in this session and each time he gets more support, the last time, 195 votes across party lines. Jack Kemp's bill would reduce the deficit, which causes inflation because the tax base would be broadened by the increased prosperity. We should help him."*

It was an indication that future President Reagan leaned toward the supply side, but Kemp had yet to fully convert him.

———

The year 1978 proved to be a bonanza for tax cutting and supply-side economics. In January 1978, Kemp and Roth reintroduced their bill, which had made political but not legislative progress in 1977. Disdained by Democrats who controlled House committees and procedure, the bill came to the House floor on March 15, 1978, as a Republican amendment to the Full Employment and Balanced Growth Act. An arch-Keynesian effort by Democrats to stimulate employment and fight inflation, the bill originally had been introduced in 1974. Cosponsored by Senator Hubert Humphrey (D-MN) and Representative Augustus "Gus" Hawkins (D-CA), it was popularly known as Humphrey-Hawkins, though

Humphrey had died of bladder cancer two months before. The bill declared it the responsibility of the federal government to promote full employment, economic growth, and price stability, and its provisions were far-reaching. It required the president every year to set short- and medium-term economic goals and required Congress to set specific targets for reducing unemployment and inflation. It also authorized federal aid to states and cities, as well as the creation of temporary government jobs if the goals were not met. The bill aimed to reduce unemployment, then at 7.1 percent, to 4 percent by 1983. It sought to reduce inflation, then at 6.4 percent, to 4 percent by 1983 and 0 percent by 1988. And it significantly expanded the Federal Reserve's responsibilities, creating new mandates to manage monetary policy to spur long-run growth in addition to maintaining price stability.

During debate on the House floor, Kemp delivered a powerful speech, cleverly associating Kemp-Roth with Humphrey-Hawkins. "What I am proposing fits perfectly with the goals of the Humphrey-Hawkins bill," he declared. "I am merely providing a tested means for achieving the goal of full employment": a 10 percent per year cut in individual income tax rates over three years and a 1 percent per year cut in corporate rates. He told the House that "the Keynesian answer to inflation is unemployment and the Keynesian answer to unemployment is inflation and neither strategy works or is acceptable any longer."

He dwelt at length on the effect of "bracket creep" on average workers—a 100 percent increase in wages had led to a 150 percent increase in taxes and prices since 1965. And he challenged the House: "If one does not vote to lower the rates across the board, then by definition one is voting to raise the tax rates now and in the future. The result will be more taxes, few jobs and less output."

Majority Leader Wright objected. He charged that Kemp wanted to replace the bill's goal of full employment and substitute "a complicated formula of specific and permanent tax reductions every year." He called the bill "an alluring promise to hold out to the American people" that could be "a cruelly illusory one." He also cited a Congressional Research

Service estimate that Kemp-Roth would cost the Treasury $150 billion by 1983, and joined his ally, Paul Simon, in claiming the amendment would increase the deficit.

Kemp insisted Kemp-Roth complemented Hubert-Hawkins and reminded the House that the Kennedy cuts had paid for themselves. His counterargument did not prevail. The House voted down Kemp-Roth by 216–194.[49] The next day, the House passed Humphrey-Hawkins by a vote of 257–152.

Though defeated, Kemp-Roth was far from dead. In April 1978, Representative Marjorie Holt (R-MD) returned it to the House floor as an amendment to the House budget resolution, with caps on spending added. To everyone's surprise, it passed on a voice vote. Embarrassed Democrats demanded a roll call and defeated the amendment just barely, 203-197. Kemp's ideas were not winning yet, but they were gaining traction.

Democrats in Congress might have been wedded to Keynesianism, but Kemp-Roth highlighted a political reality: calls for tax cuts were sweeping the country.[50] Wanniski published his supply-side manifesto, *The Way the World Works,* and it became a best seller, making Arthur Laffer a household name. A month after the House defeated Kemp-Roth, thirteen Democrats on the Ways and Means Committee joined all twelve Republicans to approve Steiger's bill reducing the tax rate on capital gains from 40 percent to 28 percent. To everyone's shock, on June 6, supply-sider Jeffrey Bell defeated four-term liberal Republican incumbent Clifford Case in the New Jersey Senate primary, a victory for Kemp, who had campaigned for him. (Kemp tried to persuade Reagan to support Bell too, but he declined.) The same day, California voters passed Proposition 13 by a two-to-one margin, sharply limiting property taxes.

With tax cut fever sweeping the nation, Brock, Kemp, and GOP congressional leaders saw to it that every House Republican candidate running in the 1978 midterm elections backed Kemp-Roth. Brock loaded prominent politicians aboard chartered airplanes for "fly arounds" to multiple cities, campaigning for the cuts. Kemp campaigned with missionary zeal for his bill and for Republican candidates that year. One memorable speech[51] amounted to a stinging critique of his own party and called for a "Republican Renaissance."

> *Sooner or later, you have to accept the fact that Democrats have been running the show because they've been beating Republicans . . . for the same reason that the Yankees beat the Dodgers. . . . They're better at what they do. . . . What you hear from some Republicans is that Democrats [win] because the poor, ignorant voters just don't know what's good for them. . . .*

Kemp insisted that Republicans needed to stop complaining about the cost of welfare, stop whining about balancing the budget, and think hard about how to stimulate growth. Kemp went on to propound his "two wagons" theory of politics. The Republicans loaded the wagon (with goods and services), while the Democrats unloaded it (to the public)—both necessary jobs if the load was to benefit society. Calling Republicans the party of growth and the Democrats the party of distribution, he warned that Republicans had stopped doing their necessary job and were trying to do the Democrats' work. "Surely it's obvious that you can't unload the wagon faster than you load it. Sooner or later, it's empty and you are living hand to mouth," a good description of the nation's sorry condition of mid-1970s stagflation.

Kemp finished the speech by touting Republican policies—notably Kemp-Roth—that would produce more wealth and prosperity. "The party must not become more Democratic, but more democratic," he said, urging that Republicans be concerned with the welfare of all, not "elitist" or "patronizing." He insisted that the party of "economic growth (real, not inflated) can't lose and the Democrats know it. The idea is too powerful."

Meantime, to promote Kemp-Roth in Congress, the sponsors' offices collaborated in publishing a newspaper, *Tax Cut News*. The publication kept colleagues informed about developments in the policy battle and reprinted supportive editorials and articles. Kemp's staff exploited multiple ways to sell each Kemp action, turning floor statements or committee testimony into op-eds, stump speeches, and Dear Colleague letters. Kemp's staff called him a "scrambling quarterback" as he boosted his tax cuts, campaigned for Republicans, and tended to his work on the Appropriations Committee.

————

In July, Kemp-Roth gained new life when Democrat Sam Nunn of Georgia introduced a variation of it, similar to Representative Holt's, in the Senate. On July 14, a Senate Finance subcommittee held a daylong hearing on the bill before a packed room of witnesses and spectators—evidence of the political force that tax cutting had gained.[52] Kemp testified in favor of the bill, along with Republican economists Herbert Stein and Alan Greenspan, former chairmen of the White House Council of Economic Advisers. So did economic consultants Norman Ture and Michael Evans, and a representative of the U.S. Chamber of Commerce. Opposed were Emil Sunley, a Treasury Department deputy assistant secretary, speaking for the Carter administration, and a lobbyist for the AFL-CIO.

The pro-Kemp-Roth witnesses said that inflation had pushed taxpayers into higher and higher brackets, forcing them to pay ever-higher marginal tax rates—the rate on the next dollar they earned. In 1965, they pointed out, only 18.8 percent of taxpayers were paying marginal rates of 20 percent or more. By 1975, it was 53.3 percent, leading to a serious erosion of incentives to work and invest. And without Kemp-Roth, taxes would continue to rise.[53]

The idea—and importance—of marginal tax rates was something Kemp had to explain again and again. He may have done it most clearly in a *Fortune*[54] interview: "Let's say your income is taxed 10 percent on Monday, 20 percent on Tuesday, 30 percent on Wednesday, 40 percent on Thursday, 50 percent on Friday and so on. For most people, sometime around Friday, you'd decide not to work anymore." Inflation and "bracket creep" were systematically and inexorably pushing middle-income workers toward Friday levels of tax.

Some Democrats accused Republicans of offering the proposal not as serious policy, but to take political advantage of the nation's tax-cutting mood. Republicans were cleverly capitalizing on the mood, but Kemp's allies were completely serious, even if many conventional Republicans harbored reservations. Democrats showed unmistakable signs of political desperation. In August, Carter let Congress know that he would sign Steiger's amendment cutting capital gains rates, but not Kemp-Roth or the Nunn amendment. Bartlett said,[55] "Democrats knew they had to pull out all the stops to defeat it. And they did." Speaker Tip O'Neill tried to force the Rules Committee to prohibit any vote on Kemp-Roth, then allowed it to be voted on, but only as part of a motion to recommit Democrats' tax bill to committee, not as an amendment to the bill itself.

On August 10, Kemp-Roth was once again voted down in the House, 240–177. But this time it had the support of all but three Republicans: Millicent Fenwick of New Jersey, Paul Findley of Illinois, and Charles Whalen of Ohio. And this time, thirty-seven Democrats defected from their party position to support the bill.[56]

Kemp-Roth was also defeated in the Senate Finance Committee in September. Roth offered three versions, all of which went down by narrow margins. But Kemp-Roth still was not dead. In October, the Senate passed the Nunn amendment—dubbed "Son of Kemp-Roth"—by a two-to-one margin. On October 12, the House voted 268–135 to instruct its conferees working out differences with the Senate to accept the Nunn amendment.

The following day, Carter announced he would veto the entire Revenue Act of 1978 if it contained Nunn's amendment. Astounded, Evans and Novak wrote in their column, "It is unthinkable that the president would commit the ultimate folly of vetoing an election year tax cut. But the unthinkable is commonplace in Carter tax policy." Carter canceled a planned weekend trip to Camp David to stay in the White

House and monitor his aides' efforts on Capitol Hill to kill the measure in the House-Senate conference.[57]

It was duly killed.

On November 6, the day before the midterm elections, Carter signed the Revenue Act of 1978. It did contain individual tax cuts in the form of a widening of tax brackets and reducing the number of tax rates, increasing personal exemptions from $750 to $1,000 and increasing the standard deduction from $3,200 to $3,400. This was all small stuff, insufficient to impede the tax cut wave. The measure also reduced the corporate rate from 48 percent to 46 percent. It did contain Steiger's cut in capital gains rates to 28 percent, but no other supply-side reduction.

————

Despite Carter's sinking approval rating and widespread public support for supply-side ideas, the midterm elections fell short of Republican expectations. Democrats kept their substantial post–Watergate majorities in both the House and Senate. Republicans gained three Senate seats and fifteen House seats. Kemp was reelected with a stunning 94.8 percent of the vote with only a Liberal Party candidate running against him—the biggest margin of his House career.

Looking toward the 1980 presidential campaign, some after-action analyses actually blamed Kemp-Roth for the failure to gain more seats. David Gergen, Ford's communications director, later a backer of George H. W. Bush against Reagan in 1980 and a Reagan White House aide, wrote in the *Washington Post*[58] that the Republican platform of cutting taxes without increasing spending cuts was a political misstep. Gergen acknowledged that Kemp-Roth had its virtues and that "Jack Kemp himself took off like a flaming meteor across the sky, as Republican audiences throughout the country, tiring of the same old rhetoric from the same old crowd, warmly welcomed a dynamic new star." But reflecting the conventional wisdom of senior Republicans, Gergen believed that supply-side thought was wrong. He argued that while Newt Gingrich of Georgia and Bill Armstrong of Colorado won on the Kemp-Roth platform, most

GOP challengers "were thrown in the defensive by born-again conserva-tive Democrats arguing that Republicans were fiscally irresponsible."

This argument was fallacious. The *Wall Street Journal* scoffed, taking direct aim at Gergen's analysis in an editorial titled "Some Blunder."[59] It noted that Republicans had won 57 percent of the year's Senate races, six new governorships, and three hundred seats in state legislatures—"all by running on the wrong issue!" Kemp himself said that the '78 election showed that Republicans had seized the political initiative with their new ideas.[60] "I'm not suggesting that it is ended or completed, but I think clearly that liberals did not dominate the 1978 elections. You don't hear people call themselves fiscal liberals anymore." The GOP had proved that it had a message appealing to working people, he said.

Indeed, a dramatic beginning had been made. Kemp had gone from being a newcomer to a driving force in the campaign for supply-side economics. He was building a national reputation. He hadn't achieved his goals, but he was advancing a revolutionary bill. The question now was whether he or another candidate would carry his radical ideas for-ward into the highest office in the country.

Three

TURNING POINT

"J ack should run for president. The future of Western Civilization depends on it!"[1] Jude Wanniski, ever volatile and Kemp's biggest supporter, voiced this opinion at a gathering of Kemp supporters as the 1980 primaries approached. He was hyperbolic, but not alone in his conviction. In 1978, Irving Kristol told journalist Martin Tolchin that Republicans didn't want another Ford-Reagan race and were ready to move on to a new generation, with Kemp "the best able to communicate with the American people."[2] Former CBS president Frank Shakespeare, ex-Reagan policy adviser Jeff Bell, and former ambassador Larry Silberman began commissioning polls and plotting strategy. Ronald Reagan was considered the top contender for the Republican nomination, but the supply-siders weren't convinced he could be trusted. He certainly wouldn't be more faithful to the cause than Jack Kemp.

Kemp was the Republican star of 1978, and he spent 1979 tirelessly evangelizing for his tax cut plan. But he gave his presidential boosters no serious encouragement. He planned to run for the U.S. Senate if ailing incumbent Jacob Javits retired. And he wanted to support Reagan for president. The only question was whether Kemp-Roth rate cuts would be the centerpiece of Reagan's campaign. If Reagan committed, Kemp would be on board. In the meantime, he kept his options open, worrying Reagan's people that he might run for the nomination and at least cut into Reagan's support.

———

The idea of a Kemp presidential bid in 1980 was not completely far-fetched. Bell was actively courting Republican leaders in New York on behalf of a Kemp candidacy.[3] Wanniski touted Kemp to everyone he spoke to. And Kemp was one of columnist Robert Novak's "projects." The Evans and Novak column, which appeared three times a week in the *Washington Post,* constantly promoted Kemp and tax cuts.

A Kemp profile by Martin Tolchin, a well-regarded political reporter for the *New York Times,* spurred the Kemp buzz. Published in *Esquire* in October 1978, it described Kemp as "suddenly the hottest young prop-erty in the Grand Old Party."[4] It quoted Wanniski: "I think Jack will be the next president. I've asked him to tell me when he's not running." GOP National Chairman Bill Brock gave Kemp credit for identifying "our most important issue"—sharp reductions in individual tax rates. Kemp "turns people on," Tolchin wrote. "You see it when he enters a room. He exudes confidence . . . working a crowd like an old-time reviv-alist, he casts a special spell among hard-driving, self-made entrepre-neurs on the make in Middle America." He also noted that Kemp had African American supporters and regarded trade union collective bar-gaining "as a human right," increasing his voter appeal.

The article wasn't a total puff piece. It quoted Ford's former chief economic adviser, Herbert Stein, an unflagging critic of supply-side eco-nomics, saying Kemp-Roth would cost the Treasury $100 billion over three years. Other (unnamed) conservative economists, Tolchin wrote, "liken Kemp to a medicine man with one quick cure for all ills." And Tolchin quoted an anonymous "senior Member of the House" calling Kemp "hard to live with," a "monomaniac," and a "one-issue wonder."

For Kristol, Wanniski, and others, the piece was a cause for hope. So was the long article in *Fortune*[5] that said Kemp had "begun to alter the face that the Republican Party presents to the world" and "in the process, he has become a national leader of the party." The article concluded, "Some of Kemp's admirers see him on the national ticket two years hence, possibly even as a presidential candidate. This suggestion was reported to him somewhat jocularly two weeks ago. 'You're not supposed to laugh at that,' said Kemp, laughing."

For John Sears, Reagan's campaign manager, such articles and others were a cause for apprehension. A New York lawyer turned political strategist, he'd helped Richard Nixon win the 1968 Republican presidential nomination and served on Nixon's White House staff. In 1976, he managed Reagan's unsuccessful presidential bid, then signed up to run his 1980 campaign. Sears and other Reagan backers feared that Reagan, sixty-eight years old in 1979, was seen as too old to run for president. Kemp, then forty-four, might be a potent rival. Even if Kemp could not win the nomination, he might draw off enough conservative support to undercut Reagan and allow another contender—George H. W. Bush, Bob Dole, or Howard Baker—to take the prize.

Sears sought to bring Kemp into the Reagan orbit, if only to discourage him from running. He encouraged Reagan to support supply-side ideas and attract potential Kemp voters, especially northeasterners and workers. Years later, Sears flatly denied ever fearing that Kemp would run,[6] insisting he aimed to make Kemp Reagan's campaign cochairman because his views on race would moderate Reagan's image. "How would you ever think a Congressman from suburban Buffalo was any threat to a man who had a national constituency that numbered in the 30 percentiles—just solidly behind him?" Sears said.

But Reagan aide Martin Anderson, Jeff Bell, and other Kemp allies believe otherwise. Novak wrote that Sears was disturbed by conservative James J. Kilpatrick's column of May 6, 1978, saying that Reagan "was getting a little long in the tooth" and suggesting Kemp should run. Sears, Novak wrote, took a possible Kemp campaign so seriously that he "walked Reagan into the supply-side movement to nullify Kemp and prevent him from cutting into Reagan's conservative base."[7] Kemp's chief of staff, David Smick,[8] also interpreted Sears's attention to Kemp as designed to forestall his candidacy. In 1978 and 1979, he said, Sears told Kemp to bide his time on the presidency and run for another office instead—especially governor of New York in 1982.

It didn't work. Kemp did intend to run for the Senate in 1980 if Javits retired, but the governorship didn't interest him. It involved administering bureaucracies and would give Kemp less impact on national policy than he had as a House member with a national platform. Bell, who had known Sears since 1968, thought Reagan's manager was "deathly afraid" Kemp would run. "That was his biggest fear about Reagan's path to the nomination."[9]

Following Kilpatrick's column, Kemp arranged a lunch with Reagan aide Peter Hannaford to allay his fears. He reiterated his support for Reagan and insisted he would not run. "You have my word in blood," he told Hannaford.[10]

But the pledge did not stick. Hannaford mentioned the meeting to Novak, who called Wanniski for comment. Horrified at what he saw as a rash promise, Wanniski did his best to undermine the pledge and persuade Kemp to run. He informed Hannaford that Kemp's support was predicated on Reagan's acceptance of supply-side doctrine. He claimed Reagan's refusal to campaign for supply-sider Jeffrey Bell of New Jersey against liberal Republican Clifford Case amounted to a break in the compact. Wanniski said the pledge also was invalid because Hannaford had leaked word of it to Novak.[11] He argued that there was an irresistible tide building behind Kemp. "It was a tortured argument that I doubted Kemp really bought into," Novak wrote. "But Wanniski exerted tremendous influence on Kemp, and the Congressman found an excuse for reneging on his pledge."

Besides Kemp's on-again, off-again endorsement, other factors led the Reagan forces to fear Kemp might run. In July 1978, when the Republican National Committee endorsed Kemp-Roth as party policy, Novak found committee members eager for a new face to lead the party and speculated that Kemp would win a secret ballot as 1980 favorite. Another Reagan aide, Lyn Nofziger, attended that Detroit RNC meeting and heard the Kemp buzz. He assured Novak that Kemp was on board with Reagan. When Novak cited Nofziger's remark, Kemp announced publicly—via a Novak column—that he was not bound by the pledge and "may announce his own candidacy" in November.[12]

In early 1979 Kemp published a book, *An American Renaissance: A Strategy for the 1980s* (Kemp acknowledged that the book was "organized" by Wanniski.) It read like a campaign manifesto: *"There is a tidal wave coming equivalent to the one that hit in 1932 when an era of Republican dominance gave way to the New Deal."*[13] It contained enough policy recommendations to be a campaign platform, and included a stirring call:

> There are no natural bounds to the human spirit and its accomplishments, except insofar as we are cramped by human timidity and fear or by human institutions. In the 1980s, the first decade of the American renaissance, these are the bounds that we must pit ourselves against, so it can be said of our nation in our time, "To her, and to her especially, belongs the future."[14]

Few could read those words and be sure Kemp wouldn't run for President. But the Buffalo Congressman kept everone guessing.

———

Besides promoting his book, Kemp spent much of 1979 touring the country to advance the newest version of Kemp-Roth, dubbed "Kemp-Roth II." He authored op-ed columns and delivered speeches on the House floor, reprints of which his office circulated widely. Kemp was acting like a presidential candidate.

The new bill was sweeping. It again called for 10 percent across-the-board individual tax rate cuts annually for three years and the indexing of incomes against inflation. It added domestic spending reductions of one percent of GDP per year for four years to bring federal spending to 18 percent of the national economy.[15] It was not an austerity measure, since Kemp expected the economy to grow so robustly that 18 percent would allow for adequate government funding. Unfortunately for Kemp, consideration of the bill was blocked by the failure of House members to agree on details and by new congressional budget rules requiring revenue losses to be offset by specific spending cuts.

Faced with such hurdles, Kemp decided against pushing the bill on Capitol Hill. Instead he hit the road to bring his case directly to voters. In July 1979, Kemp delivered a highly praised (and widely distributed) speech to the International Longshoremen's Association convention in Miami. He told the trade unionists that Republicans had long been wedded to "Herbert Hoover, root-canal economics."[16] But he insisted they were switching to growth economics. He accused "pessimistic" Democrats of favoring low growth and high unemployment. President Carter "promised in 1976 not to use recession to control inflation [but] he is doing exactly that."[17]

Kemp's criticism was bipartisan. It included a dig at a 1976 national Republican candidate who'd advanced—in Buffalo—the "asinine" theory that achieving a balanced budget took priority over fighting unemployment. The reference was to Bob Dole, Gerald Ford's 1976 running mate and Kemp's fierce critic.[18]

In the speech, Kemp made the concept of bracket creep vivid. A teacher who got a $60 pay raise would pay $66.48 in taxes when pushed into a higher tax bracket, *lowering* her income by 13 percent. "When Longshoremen bargained for a pay increase of 30 percent over three years, they ended up with a net pay loss of 14 percent," he said.

A lack of economic growth would destroy national unity, he said, and force citizens to "compete for pieces of a smaller and smaller pie." He warned that U.S. policy was actively shrinking the pie. Indeed, in 1979, unemployment averaged 7 percent and inflation 11 percent, driving the "misery index" to 18 percent.[19] Federal deficits jumped from $40 billion in 1977 to $60 billion in 1979 and $74 billion in 1980. The deficit was the largest since World War II, despite "bracket creep," which swelled federal tax revenues by 16.6 percent.

Adding to his presidential appeal, Kemp could relate to working-class audiences, unlike most Republicans. Though opposed by the AFL-CIO, he was often endorsed by local union affiliates, including building trades and maritime unions. Politically astute, he reminded the Longshoremen that Jack Kennedy had called for tax cuts, inviting them to support Kemp-Roth II as part of JFK's legacy. But he took a dig at Kennedy's successors in the White House, both Democrats and Republicans: "Ever since Kennedy we have been afflicted with leaders who think life is a zero-sum game where one group wins only if someone else loses." These words suggested he thought he'd do a better job in the Oval Office.

———

Kemp made Reagan a special target of his supply-side outreach. Reagan had supply-side instincts and liked tax cuts. But he regularly advocated traditional Republican austerity economics as well. A centerpiece of his 1976 campaign was the "welfare queen," an African American woman in Chicago he asserted was fraudulently collecting $150,000 a year. He contrasted her with "hard working people" who paid their bills and taxes.[20] Kemp supported welfare reform, but he championed upward mobility for the urban poor and shunned use of racially tinged language. Cutting welfare was not a growth strategy, he argued.

Reagan had been an economics major at Eureka College in the pre-Keynesian era, as he recalled in his autobiography.[21] But "my experience with our tax laws in Hollywood probably taught me more about economic theory than I ever learned in a classroom or from an economist, and my views on tax reform did not spring from what people called supply-side economics."

In Hollywood, he was a victim of high marginal tax rates. The top rate was 94 per cent. Reagan paid lower tax rates for the first dollars he earned in a year, but the more he made, the higher his rate. "After a certain point, I received only six cents of each dollar I earned and the government got the rest." He began asking himself, he wrote, whether it was worth taking on more work. A central purpose of supply-side economics was to lower marginal rates—the percent paid by the next dollar earned—giving citizens the incentive to work, save, invest and produce *more*. His experience made him receptive to conversion.

However, he was not a committed supply-sider. His frequent reversions to traditional GOP economics bothered Wanniski and others in the movement. In 1978, Reagan supported the GOP National Committee's endorsement of Kemp-Roth as party policy. Yet he horrified supply-siders by telling a group of newsmen at his Pacific Palisades home, "Frankly, I'm afraid this country is just going to have to suffer two, three years of hard times to pay for the binge we've been on." Similarly, in early 1979, Evans and Novak reported, "Reagan talked as one dedicated to the deep root canal school of economics: if it hurts you, it must be good for you. In private, he endorsed recession as the antidote to inflation."[22]

———

John Sears became the supply-siders' patron in the Reagan camp. He believed a presidential candidate needed a big idea to run on, and in Reagan's campaign against Ford in 1976, he instructed Jeff Bell, then a policy adviser, to come up with that idea.[23] Bell devised a plan to transfer responsibility for federal programs worth $90 billion to the states. This proved a political disaster, assailed by Ford as requiring tax increases in New Hampshire, a state without sales or income taxes.

Four years later, Sears again sought a dominant, positive theme for Reagan, and supply-side economics seemed to fit. Meanwhile, Kemp's office had been regularly sending texts of his speeches to Reagan's political organization, the Fund for the Republic. After reading a reprint of Kemp's speech to the Longshoremen's union in his favorite publication, *Human Events,* Reagan wrote Kemp a note congratulating him.[24]

Heading into the 1980 race, Reagan made supply-side speeches, but also conventional "Herbert Hoover" speeches advocating budget cuts and austerity. Kemp remained eager to support Reagan, but his allies insisted that Reagan was unreliable and kept urging Kemp to run for president. He withheld any public endorsement.

In the summer of 1979, Wanniski and Laffer concocted a plot to make Kemp Reagan's vice president. Kemp would run for president, but would privately assure Reagan that he'd instruct his delegates at the Republican convention to vote for Reagan, delivering him the nomination. In gratitude, Wanniski and Laffer calculated, Reagan would then pick Kemp as his running mate.

Laffer says Wanniski devised the scheme. Laffer coached Kemp to present it to Reagan at a dinner party at Laffer's home in Palos Verdes.[25] At some point in the evening, Kemp was to take Reagan aside and present the plan to him—without, of course, mentioning the vice presidency.

To Laffer's consternation, Kemp did not follow the plan. He went for a chat with Reagan in Laffer's guesthouse. But when he returned, Kemp told Laffer, "Oh, Art. I couldn't do it. I pledged my support to him totally and said I'd never run against him whatsoever and he's my hero." Laffer responded, "Oh, my God. You just lost the vice presidency. You just lost the vice presidency."

What undid the plot—not that it ever had much chance of success—was that Sears had arranged for Jack and Joanne Kemp to have lunch with Reagan earlier that day.[26] Kemp quizzed the former governor about his dedication to supply-side policies and talked about how a tax-cuts-and-growth message could help the GOP win working-class voters.[27] Reagan's responses won Kemp over. In Laffer's guesthouse Kemp merely renewed his allegiance to Reagan. This time it stuck.

As Reagan approached his official announcement of candidacy, his public statements moved increasingly in Kemp's direction. In an October 1978 speech in Maryland, he touted "the tax-cutting ideas of a young Congressman from New York, Jack Kemp."[28] And he appeared in Buffalo with Kemp sitting as his side. In his column, Novak speculated their closeness hinted at a possible Reagan-Kemp ticket.[29]

When Reagan announced, Kemp was named the campaign's "chairman of policy development and chief economic spokesman." Reagan sounded like a supply-sider. He said that "the key to restoring the health of the economy lies in cutting taxes" and praised Kemp-Roth. He called for cutting wasteful spending and for smaller government, but in contrast with other Republicans, he did not declare that the budget must be balanced before tax cuts could be considered. "A punitive tax system must be replaced by one that restores incentives for the worker and for industry; a system that rewards initiative and effort and encourages thrift," he said in his announcement. Kemp couldn't have said it better.

The next day, Reagan did a "fly around" to various cities, picking up endorsements as he went. In Washington, D.C., where Reagan got the support from thirty House members and six senators, Kemp introduced him at a news conference as "the oldest and wisest" of the GOP candidates "who has embraced the youngest and freshest of ideas."[30] Kemp's line caused Reagan's entourage to wince, but delighted the traveling press corps. Reporters soon began to refer to Reagan in pool reports as "the Oldest and Wisest," later shortened to "the O&W."[31]

———

Kemp's status in the Reagan campaign involved elements of intrigue—and tomfoolery. Sears envisioned making Kemp more than just chief economic and policy spokesman. He wanted to make him at least campaign cochairman along with Reagan's best friend in the Senate, Paul Laxalt of Nevada.[32] David Smick, who became Kemp's chief of staff in 1979, at age twenty-six, on Wanniski's recommendation, says that in one meeting in Kemp's office, Sears even floated the possibility that Reagan might fire his chief policy adviser, Martin Anderson, or persuade Laxalt to step aside as chairman and give one or the other post to Kemp.[33]

Sears wanted Kemp as cochairman because his liberal views on race would encourage moderate Republicans to support Reagan. As Sears tells it, Reagan and the rest of his high command were not let in on his design. So when he talked to Kemp about it, he told him to keep it confidential because "there were a lot of people around [Reagan] who didn't like Kemp."

The effort collapsed because Kemp could not keep the proposal to himself. Smick recalled that moments after Sears left Kemp's office, Wanniski called. "How long do you think it took before the contents of this meeting got to Jude? Twelve seconds! I counted." Wanniski couldn't keep the secret either, and Novak revealed in his column that Anderson and Laxalt were leaving the campaign. The fallout was explosive. Smick recalled, "I have never seen Jack as frightened as he was when he got the call from Sears. . . . I could hear the screaming over the phone. It was so blistering." Sears confirmed that he'd exploded at Kemp over the phone. "I think I started out saying something like, 'You asshole!'" Kemp said he was sorry, "but I wasn't taking any of it."

Once word leaked, thanks to Kemp, Wanniski, and Novak, Nancy Reagan torpedoed Sears's scheme. Reagan assured Laxalt that he would remain chairman, and Kemp remained campaign spokesman. "I couldn't give him the [cochairman] title then. I gave him as big a title as I could under the circumstances," Sears explained. Kemp had a lesser title than he might have had, but he had a bigger role ahead of him: he locked Reagan into the supply-side agenda.

———

In early January 1980, Kemp, Smick, Wanniski, and Kemp's economist, John Mueller, attended a three-day issues-and-policy conference conducted by Reagan and his top staff at the Marriott Hotel at Los Angeles International Airport. Lew Lehrman, Kemp's favorite to be Reagan's treasury secretary, refers to the event as "the boarding party"—like pirates seizing a ship—in which Kemp's team won Reagan's commitment to run on Kemp-Roth tax cuts.[34]

Some Reaganites, including Reagan himself, have disputed the idea that the LAX sessions constituted a "boarding party," contending Kemp & Company were "pushing on an open door." The back-and-forth is akin to, though not as fierce as, the battle among supply-side theorists over credit for supply side's ascendency.

In their memoirs, both Reagan intimate (and future White House counselor and attorney general) Ed Meese[35] and campaign policy chief Martin Anderson[36] dismissed the importance of the LAX meeting and denied that Reagan needed "conversion" to supply-side economics or tax cutting. Meese wrote that "Reagan's interest in lower taxation was spurred not only by his philosophy of limited government and his extensive reading of economic subjects, but by his personal experience. . . . He was a 'supply-sider' long before the term was invented."

Meese specifically rejected an account that Jude Wanniski gave in an ill-advised interview with the *Village Voice* in April 1980. Wanniski asserted that a "battle for Reagan's mind" had raged between supply-siders and conventional Republicans until the LAX meeting.[37]

"All these stories are fantasies," Meese wrote.[38] A three-year phased tax reduction was Reagan policy before the Los Angeles meeting, he said. "The president liked Jack, and Kemp's support was naturally welcome. But far from having to convert Reagan to anything, Jack was basically pushing on an open door." As evidence, Meese cites the Reagan campaign's Policy Memo No. 1, drafted by Anderson in August 1979, which set forth the essence of Kemp-Roth without mentioning the bill itself.

In his own memoir, Anderson declared that Reagan's formal adoption of Kemp-Roth was merely part of a "political deal" to keep Kemp from running against Reagan. "Kemp had a price for supporting Reagan and the price was that Reagan endorse [his] specific tax plan. When Reagan and his advisers heard the terms of the deal, they shrugged and essentially said, 'Why not?'"

Reagan himself, at a black-tie gala in Washington on December 1, 1988, honoring Kemp's retirement from Congress, undercut the idea that Kemp converted him to supply-side economics even as he was praising him.[39] Reagan said that he'd delivered a speech in 1961 saying that tax rates as high as 90 percent "brought the government very little revenue" and advocated replacing progressive marginal rates with a flat tax. "It couldn't be called supply-side economics because that name had not been coined yet," but he implied he had been an early adherent.

Still, Reagan's program had long been an amalgam of supply-side and old-fashioned Republicanism. He did not run in 1976 on a low-tax platform. In 1980, he did—specifically, on the program written and fought for by Kemp. His adoption of Kemp-Roth as a "political deal" was unlikely because Kemp had already endorsed Reagan by the time of the LAX meeting. And Kemp's bill had been introduced years before Policy Memo No. 1 was written.

Either way, Reagan was definitely on board with supply-side cuts, and Kemp was thrilled. He told David Stockman—then a supply-side House ally of Kemp's but later Reagan's anti-supply-side budget director—that Reagan "had an intuitive feel for the Laffer curve" and that the LAX session was "historic."[40] Sears, also at the LAX meeting, confirms that Reagan had not formally embraced Kemp-Roth in November. "We had some things about taxes, but not Kemp-Roth. In January, we embraced it." Kemp was jubilant.

———

But the jubilation didn't last. On Janurary 21, 1980, Reagan lost the initial contest of the presidential campaign, the Iowa caucuses, to Bush, 32 percent to 30 percent. Blame for the unexpected defeat fell heavily on Sears.[41] He was accused of devising a "front-runner strategy" that kept Reagan out of debates and away from the press—a strategy based on his low opinion of Reagan's intellect. Sears also spent lavishly on headquarters staff, a concern for Nancy Reagan. Worst of all for Sears, he'd made ferocious enemies of Reagan loyalists Meese and Laxalt. Laxalt told Reagan bluntly, "You were sitting on your ass in Iowa."[42]

A month later, Reagan won the New Hampshire primary, 50 percent to 23 percent. At Sears's urging, Reagan's New Hampshire advertising emphasized tax cutting and featured Reagan speaking directly into a camera.[43] One spot likened Kemp-Roth to John F. Kennedy's tax cuts and was credited with winning Reagan blue-collar support.[44]

Sears was fired despite setting up Reagan's triumphant New Hampshire finale: the TV debate at which Reagan demanded participation by all GOP candidates, though Bush (and moderator Jon Breen) wanted a one-on-one matchup. Reagan famously exploded on camera, "I am paying for this microphone, Mr. Green!" The line, despite his mangling the moderator's name, clinched Reagan's victory.

Sears was done in by intracampaign intrigue and his attitude toward Reagan. David Smick recalled that Sears and his operatives showed utter disrespect for Reagan behind his back at the Los Angeles meeting. "I remember asking [Sears], 'well if this guy is so stupid, why are you running him for president? What are you doing to the country?'" He added, "Sears would sit at the back, holding his cigarette like Erwin Rommel, and say 'Let me just say something here.' And then would deliver these five minutes of comments [that] basically were disrespectful of Reagan."[45] It's not surprising that the Reaganites did not want to keep that kind of critic around. When Sears was sacked, Kemp kept his lofty title, but functionally he was reduced from policy adviser to a mere surrogate making speeches. He performed with customary zest. And far more important than his campaign role, he had given Reagan his main domestic campaign theme, the chief domestic policy of his administration, and the basis of America's recovery from malaise.

After losing badly in New Hampshire, Bush's campaign introduced a new line of attack, criticizing Reagan for advocating "voodoo economics." "Voodoo" was not originally directed at Kemp-Roth alone, but at Reagan's idea that taxes could be deeply cut and defense spending drastically increased without ballooning federal deficits. Nevertheless, the voodoo label became firmly attached to the Kemp-Roth side of Reaganomics, and critics of supply-side economics occasionally employ the epithet to this day.[46]

Neither the voodoo charge nor any other Bush tactic slowed Reagan's surge toward the nomination. He won the South Carolina primary in March, all but clinching the GOP nomination. He ended the campaign with forty-four primary victories to six for Bush. His decisive win bode well for the general election, especially as Carter was being ferociously challenged for the Democratic nomination by Senator Edward Kennedy of Massachusetts.

———

While Reagan was dealing with presidential primaries, Kemp was making serious decisions about his own future. His political career reached a decisive turning point when he decided not to run for the Senate. Kemp was set to run if Javits, newly diagnosed with Lou Gehrig's disease, stepped down. When Javits called a press conference to announce his decision, Kemp sent a staffer to watch.[47] He was planning to declare his candidacy the same day and preparations had begun for a campaign. To his surprise, Javits opted to run for reelection. Kemp had to decide whether to challenge him in a primary. He declined. In a statement that went through draft after draft, Kemp said that "tempting as I find the prospect of being elected to the U.S. Senate," he believed it his duty to help elect a Republican president and change U.S. economic policy.[48]

Aides[49] describe this as the single most agonizing political decision Kemp ever made. A move to the Senate would have heightened his profile, but international economic aide Richard Billmire said that it wasn't in Kemp's nature as "a happy warrior" to attack Javits.[50] Aides speculated that Kemp would have had a difficult time winning a primary because he represented upstate New York, not the populous New York City area. But Long Island county supervisor Al D'Amato had none of Kemp's qualms, beat Javits, and went on to win the Senate seat. If D'Amato could beat the incumbent, the far more dynamic and appealing Kemp surely could have. And the Senate would have provided a more promising launching pad for the 1988 presidential race than the House did.

———

The 1980 Republican convention proved to be a more propitious event for Kemp than the 1976 convention was. His speech this time was seen by millions—though it nearly wasn't.

At the Detroit convention—the location chosen by Brock to demonstrate GOP concern for urban America—the party platform explicitly endorsed Kemp-Roth. Kemp chaired the platform committee's defense panel. Cheerleading for Kemp, Novak wrote that his deft platform management had helped shed "the image of 'Jacky One-note obsessed with tax reduction'" and enhanced his slim chances of being chosen as Reagan's running mate.[51]

Kemp was assigned a prime-time speaking role at the convention, slotted Tuesday night between 1964 GOP nominee Barry Goldwater and former secretary of state Henry Kissinger. Kemp supporters organized a rousing demonstration for the conclusion of his speech, with Reagan/Kemp signs, banners, and pins promoting him for vice president.[52]

The speech almost did not happen. As Smick recalls it,[53] the seventy-one-year-old Goldwater started speaking and wouldn't stop. Smick watched the clock ticking in a panic, fearing the demonstration he'd planned wouldn't take place. And sure enough "the word comes down from Mike Deaver [the top Reagan aide managing the convention]: 'Kemp's out. Kissinger goes on at 10:20 and that's it.'" Kemp took a phone call from Deaver and assented to being bumped to the next night, not in prime time and after Reagan had chosen his running mate. "Deaver, I'm sure, didn't want the pressure of this 'spontaneous' demonstration. So Kemp says to me, 'Look, we did our best. We'll regroup for tomorrow.'" He walked out of the podium holding area and into the mass of delegates on the convention floor.

But as Smick was walking the other way, he heard over the loudspeakers, "And he played for the San Diego Chargers. . . ." The stage organizer of the convention was a congressman from Delaware, Tommy Evans, a friend of Kemp's. When Deaver ordered Kemp cut from the program, Evans said, "The hell we are" and told the woman making introductions from the podium, "Introduce Kemp, Introduce Kemp. Do it!"

But Smick couldn't find Kemp to call him back to the platform. "It's like finding somebody at a football game. But that hair. I see Kemp's big shock of hair." Smick raced through the crowd and told Kemp he was next up. "You know, that guy lived a charmed life. He runs back. He climbs the steps. Talk about adrenaline, right?

"He goes out, he doesn't even look at the TelePrompter after the first two lines. . . . He gives the speech of his life. And after it's over the 'spontaneous demonstration' takes off and it was spectacular. It was his introduction as a national figure, which almost never happened."

The speech was a triumph, a concentrated statement of everything Kemp believed about politics and its purpose. It distinguished him from nearly every other speaker at that convention in that Kemp showed the opposition the respect of calling it by its name, the Democratic Party— not, derisively, "the Democrat party." But most of all, the speech was an ode to his guiding philosophy, the American Idea.

"Our party was founded on the irresistible idea that the Declaration of Independence applies to everyone," Kemp said.[54] "Mr. Lincoln inspired our party with the conviction that the ultimate source of progress and prosperity is the equal freedom of all Americans to fulfill their hopes and dreams for a better future." He continued: "The American idea never was that everyone would be leveled to the same position in life. The American idea was that each individual should have the same opportunity to rise as high as his effort and initiative and God-given talent could carry him. If you were born to be a master carpenter, a mezzo soprano—or even a pro football player—here in America you could make it."

Under Democratic government—particularly under Jimmy Carter— the country had gotten off the track, he said. "We feel our strength ebbing, our sense of national purpose waning. . . . Even President Carter senses this. But somehow he has persuaded himself that the *people* are to blame." Kemp cited Carter's 1979 "malaise" speech—delivered a year to the day earlier—in which Carter said too many Americas "now tend to worship self-indulgence and consumption."

"He told us we are demanding too much, expecting too much, and are too unwilling to give," Kemp said. "His solution is to impose limits on us, to shrink our opportunities for personal and national growth . . . Again and again, in word and deed, Jimmy Carter has clearly stated that . . . people are the problem and that austerity is the answer."

Kemp continued: "Ladies and gentlemen, austerity is not the answer.

Austerity is the problem. The American people are not the problem. They are the answer.... You cannot help America's poor by making America poor. But the policies of this administration are making the whole country poorer...."

The choice Americans faced in 1980, he said, was that "we can have growth, expansion, hope and opportunity.... Or we can have contraction, suffering and austerity—with the bitter social divisiveness that these conditions bring. Which will it be? An era of limits, or an era of expansion? An era of despair or one of hope?"

As he finished, the Reagan-Kemp demonstration erupted, many delegates eager for Kemp to fill the VP slot. Kemp knew there was little chance he would be tapped. Yet he was in the running. Reagan pollster Dick Wirthlin had taken surveys testing twelve potential running mates.[55] Kemp was one of eight Republicans whose names were leaked to the media as being on Reagan's short list.[56] Some reports said Kemp was the personal favorite of Reagan and his wife, Nancy. But the only candidates seriously considered were Gerald Ford, who polled best, and Bush.[57]

The behind-the-scenes central drama at the Detroit convention was the possible emergence of a Reagan-Ford "dream ticket." Supported by party chairman Brock, it was proposed to Ford by Reagan himself. But the ticket collapsed when Ford appeared on CBS News with Walter Cronkite and declined to rule out the possibility of a "co-presidency." That notion was unacceptable to Reagan, who turned his attention to Bush. Once Bush agreed to support Reagan's agenda, Reagan chose him. Meese called Bush's abandonment of voodoo and acceptance of supply-side "an exorcism at Detroit."[58]

Bush had multiple advantages over Kemp. As a moderate, he was party unifying. As a former CIA director and U.S. emissary to China, he had the kind of foreign policy experience Reagan lacked. And he had run for president and beaten Reagan in six primaries. A Reagan-Kemp ticket would have paired a former movie actor with a former football player—not the image of gravitas the Reagan team preferred in challenging an incumbent president.

Reagan's acceptance speech at the convention delighted Kempians.[59] "I have long advocated," he said,[60] "a 30 percent reduction in income tax rates over a period of three years," beginning with "a 10 percent 'down payment' tax cut in 1981, which the Republicans in Congress and I have already proposed." He was referring directly to Kemp-Roth. Reagan also endorsed the essence of Kemp's Jobs Creation Act—faster depreciation allowances for corporations.

And Reagan made a direct appeal to minorities, with lines Kemp and Jeff Bell inserted into the speech:[61]

"When those in leadership give us tax increases and tell us we must do with less, have they thought about those who have always had less—especially the minorities? This is like telling them that just as they step on the first rung on the ladder of opportunity, the ladder is being pulled up. That may be the Democratic leadership's message to the minorities, but it won't be ours. Our message will be: we have to move ahead, but we're not going to leave anyone behind."

Kemp, despite being left off the ticket, couldn't have been more pleased with the speech.

———

Challenges to Reagan's supply-side platform instantly came from the left, and fears that Reagan would stray from supply-side orthodoxy sprang up on the right. A month after Reagan's address, Carter declared at the Democratic National Convention that Reagan's policies would bring on "a future of despair." Democrats, he said, "grapple with the real challenges of a real world"; Republicans live "in a world of tinsel and make-believe . . . a world of good guys and bad guys . . . no hard choices, no sacrifice, no tough decisions—it sounds too good to be true, and it is."

Carter characterized Reagan's tax plan as "the biggest tax giveaway in history. They call it Kemp-Roth. I call it a free lunch that the American people cannot afford." Six days after denouncing Reagan's individual rate cuts at the Democratic convention, Carter proposed a package of business cuts, and Democrats on the Senate Finance Committee voted out a tax reduction bill of their own. The measure was a pathetic alternative to Kemp-Roth, reducing the top income tax rate from 70 percent to 67 percent and the bottom rate from 14 percent to 12. It lowered the corporate rate from 46 percent to 44 percent and liberalized depreciation rules for business. The hastily mustered Democratic bill went nowhere in Congress. Meantime, supply-siders worried about Reagan's depth of commitment to their cause.

Though the GOP platform—and Reagan too—had explicitly endorsed Kemp-Roth, "Reagan's ambivalence, or perhaps confusion, about supply-side theory continued through the campaign and up to his election," John Brooks reported in the *New Yorker*.[62] Each time Reagan reverted to demand-side rhetoric, Kemp, Laffer, Mundell, and Wanniski—"the high priests of the faith"—would "react with terror and outrage." Wanniski said, "We would call Kemp and scream 'Deviation, Deviation!' and he would call people and scream, 'Deviation!'"

Raising further concerns, after the convention, Reagan's economic high command held a meeting at an estate in rural Virginia to which no supply-siders were invited. The group rejected Laffer and Kemp's idea that lower rates would increase revenues.[63] At the meeting were businessmen and economists who had served in the Nixon and Ford administrations: George Shultz, Caspar Weinberger, William Simon, Paul McCracken, Alan Greenspan, Murray Weidenbaum, Charls Walker, Walter Wriston, and James Lynn—as well as Martin Anderson. All were suspected by supply-siders of being conventional Republican deficit hawks who'd lead Reagan toward "deviationism."[64] The meeting was a precursor of "battles for Reagan's mind"—or, at least, policy—that would continue into his presidency.

———

Reagan was projected by the media to be at a disadvantage in two presidential debates prior to the election, one with Independent candidate Representative John Anderson of Illinois on September 21 in Baltimore, the other with Carter in Cleveland a week before the election.

Anderson, number three leader of House Republicans, once had been one of the most conservative members of the House. But egged on by the media, he had moved steadily leftward and entered the 1980 GOP primaries as the most liberal candidate in the field. He called for gun licensing, supported (in Iowa) Carter's grain embargo against the Soviet Union, and advocated a fifty-cent-per-gallon gasoline tax. He won no primaries, but finished a close second in Massachusetts and Vermont. When he quit the GOP and ran as a third-party candidate, his poll numbers were impressive. In one survey, he got 26 percent of the vote in matchups against Carter and Reagan, enough to qualify for participation in presidential debates.

Carter refused to appear with Anderson, so Reagan debated him alone. Reagan's sparring partner in debate prep was Representative David Stockman of Michigan, then one of Kemp's closest allies. Before running for Congress in 1976 (at age twenty-nine), Stockman had served as executive director of the House GOP Conference under Anderson. He was savage in debate prep, charging that Reagan would "allow the 19th Century philosophy of rape and ruin to be re-established" against the environment.[65] After that thrust, Reagan joked, "Well, John, sounds like I better get a gas mask." On the strength of his performance as Anderson, Stockman was asked to play Carter as well. Reagan later said, "After Stockman, Anderson and Carter were easy."

In the first debate, Anderson said a tax cut would be "irresponsible" and quoted Bush saying it would cause 30 percent inflation. Anderson showed himself to be a traditional Republican in economic policies. "I'm going to bring federal spending under control first," he said, then consider tax cuts.

Reagan unmasked Anderson as having backed Kemp-Roth in 1978 and said, "I don't see where it is inflationary for people to keep more of their earnings and spend it, and it isn't inflationary for government to take that money from them and spend it on things it wants to spend on."

When asked about urban poverty, Reagan made a pitch for the

low-tax enterprise zone concept that Kemp had developed along within Heritage Foundation scholar Stuart Butler and Democratic representative Bob Garcia of New York. He said, as matters stood, the government derived no revenue from nonexistent businesses in poverty areas, or from people on welfare. "Why don't we offer incentives for business and industry to start up in those zones?" he asked. "And individuals . . . give them a break that encourages them to leave social welfare programs and go to work."[66] It was pure Kemp.

Reagan and Kemp had communicated previously about urban policy. Smick said he prepared a pamphlet on enterprise zones and disseminated it widely. "One day we get this thing in the mail from Reagan. He had written all over our pamphlet in the margins. . . . It wasn't [just] 'great line' or 'important point.' I was amazed at how detailed it was. 'In California I did this. . . . Have you thought about this?' He must have known a lot about urban policy. I was amazed." Smick said he tried to make off with the original as a souvenir, but Kemp said, "No, the advantages of incumbency, Dave," and kept the original, allowing Smick simply to make a copy. "He was jumping around the office with it, showing it to everybody and he said, 'Look! He signed it 'Ron!'"[67]

Between his answers on Kemp-Roth and on urban development, Reagan soundly defeated Anderson, but the stakes in the Carter debate were higher. When Reagan and Carter met, Reagan held a small but hardly insurmountable lead in polls. Anderson had dropped to 8 percent support, so the League of Women Voters, then the sponsor of presidential debates, didn't invite him. Carter attacked Reagan for opposing arms control treaties and for advocating nuclear weapons superiority over the Soviet Union, "an extremely dangerous and belligerent attitude." He accused Reagan of wanting to privatize Social Security and opposing Medicare (which he once had). That assault prompted Reagan's famous more-in-sorrow-than-in-anger response, "There you go again."[68]

Along the way, Carter attacked "Reagan-Kemp-Roth" as "one of the most highly inflationary ideas that has ever been presented to the American people." It was "completely irresponsible and would result in inflationary pressures which would destroy the nation." He also claimed that "this ridiculous proposal" would require spending cuts of $130 billion to balance the budget, which Reagan said he could do "by 1983 if not earlier."

Reagan barely defended Kemp-Roth, launching a broader attack on Carter's economic record, especially high inflation and unemployment. In 1976, he recalled, Carter had pointed to a misery index of 15.5 under President Ford. "He said that no man with that size misery index has a right to seek reelection to the presidency. Today . . . the misery index is in excess of 20 percent and I think this must suggest something."

Reagan's debate performance was a triumph, and seven days later he won the presidency in a landslide, with 50.7 percent of the vote and 489 electoral votes to 41 percent and 49 electoral votes for Carter. With 6.6 percent and no electoral votes, Anderson was not a factor. Republicans captured control of the Senate, gaining twelve seats, the largest shift since 1958. Republicans picked up thirty-five seats in the House, still leaving Democrats in control, 243–192. Kemp was reelected with 81.5 percent, though he rarely campaigned in his district as he toured the country as a Reagan surrogate.

The supply-side revolution sparked by Kemp scored its most dramatic political triumph that Election Day, but it had yet to be translated into national policy. In that endeavor—and its defense under unremitting attack—Kemp was also a leader.

Four

REAGAN REVOLUTIONARY

N o sooner was Reagan elected than discord broke out among his advisers about economic policy, and a scramble began for the posts that would influence it. Reagan would win historic legislative victories in his first year in office—notably passing a revised version of Kemp-Roth—but ideological struggles between supply-siders and Republican traditionalists dogged the process. Kemp, largely relegated to a secondary role during the 1980 campaign—and also a congressional backbencher—became a key player for the rest of the Reagan presidency. He'd won Reagan over. Now he would help wage the Reagan revolution.

In Congress, he moved from being leader of the supply-side faction of young House conservatives to the number three leadership position among House Republicans: chairman of the Republican Conference. That gave him regular access to Reagan and the rest of the White House staff. He was also ranking Republican on the foreign operations subcommittee of the Appropriations Committee, overseeing foreign aid, and a member of the subcommittee on Defense and International Affairs of the House Budget Committee.

As Reagan prepared to take office, Kemp was an attendee at crucial early economic policy-making sessions. And he successfully lobbied for allies to take significant positions in the new administration—notably Representative David Stockman to be director of the Office of Management and Budget, one of the top economic posts in the administration. Stockman had convinced Kemp and others that he was a committed supply-sider, but he swiftly turned into one of the leaders of anti-supply-side, deficit-hawk, tax-raising, and budget-balancing conventional Republican forces. Supply-siders, including some Kemp allies who got jobs in the Treasury Department, considered Stockman a turncoat and a traitor. Kemp was more generous, but—remaining loyal to his ideas—constantly fought him and his powerful allies in the White House and Congress. For eight years, the press delighted in writing stories about the "battle for Reagan's mind" as Kemp and his team tried to persuade Reagan to stay on a supply-side course.

———

Kemp became an official House GOP leader after the former number three, Representative Sam Devine of Ohio, was defeated for reelection. Kemp's staff doubted he would have bid for the job had it not fallen open. His friend and supply-side ally, ranking House budgeteer John Rousselot, ran too. Kemp won easily, 107–77, mainly with the support of the first- and second-term members he'd worked hard to elect. He was opposed by Old Guard Republicans[1] who criticized him for spending too little time on the House floor and too much traveling on behalf of his tax cut bill—whose merits many of them still doubted even though it had led to GOP electoral gains.

Kemp, the ex-quarterback, developed a strong inner circle of allies—the "backfield" he could count on to receive his handoffs, catch his passes, and move policy down the field toward the goal line. One member was Vin Weber of Minnesota, who over time became one of his closest allies. Weber got elected to Congress in 1980, at age twenty-eight, literally reciting the Kemp message from memory to campaign audiences. He'd first met Kemp the year before at a weekend retreat he organized to energize young Republicans in his state. Kemp had given his customary upbeat, progrowth, antiausterity speech, and Weber recorded the presentation. When he ran for Congress, he played a tape cassette of it in his car as he drove around his rural district. "So for years after that, when I'd introduce Jack, as I did countless times, . . . I'd say, 'In 1979-80, I ran around my district playing Jack Kemp tapes and by the end of it, I couldn't speak for less than 45 minutes.' He always liked that joke."[2]

Weber said that Kemp's influence on the new generation was powerful. "You'd listen to Jack's speech and then you'd say, 'I've got to go off and read Jude Wanniski's *The Way the World Works*. Oh, that's interesting, I've got to find out who this Jean-Baptiste Say[3] guy is, and Robert Mundell.'"[4]

Still, in the ongoing battles with conventional Republicans in Congress and the White House, Weber said, Kemp could never count on consistent majority support for his ideas among House Republicans—partly because most Republicans were traditional budget balancers, partly to hew to White House policy, partly out of personal jealousy, and partly out of what Weber called "the minority mindset." Democrats had controlled the House almost continuously since the 1930s and Republicans developed the attitude, he said, that they couldn't score touchdowns or win back power, but had to get along with Democrats and perhaps make small-yardage gains.[5]

Dan Lungren was another member of Kemp's inner circle. At age thirty-two, he was elected in the 1978 tax revolt election, a beneficiary of Bill Brock's Kemp-Roth fly around. "Jack made it cool to be conservative," Lungren said. "It wasn't the green-eyeshade, rigid Republicanism of the past."[6] Opposite a politician who "sucked all the oxygen from a room," Lungren said, Kemp "gave you all this oxygen. . . . [He] built you up. Like a very good football or basketball player, the playmaker makes everyone around him better." Lungren served with Kemp from 1979 to 1989, then was California attorney general for nine years, losing in a run for governor in 1998. He returned for another stint in Congress from 2005 to 2013.

Dan Coats, who served in the House from 1981 to 1989 and in the Senate from 1989 to 1999 and returned in 2011, also became a backfield stalwart. He was thirty-six when he met Kemp in 1979 in Fort Wayne,

Indiana. Kemp came down a hall of the Marriott Inn—"a whirlwind of a person"—and pulled a gold coin out of his pocket. "Gold, gold—the gold standard!" Coats recalls Kemp shouting. "We'll never be back where we need to be as a country until we get back on the gold standard!" Coats stayed close to Kemp for thirty years. "Once you're introduced to Jack Kemp, you never forget him. He becomes a part of your life and he makes you a part of his life," he said.[7] Coats was elected to the House the following year, and he and his wife, Marsha, became two of Jack and Joanne's closest friends.

Ultimately, the most prominent member of Kemp's backfield was future House Speaker Newt Gingrich. He was thirty-five when Kemp, then forty-three, spoke at a Georgia GOP convention where Gingrich was preparing for his third (and successful) bid for Congress, in 1978. At the conference, the two men spent an hour talking about ideas, and Gingrich adopted Kemp's supply-side platform as the basis of his campaign.[8] When he got to Washington, he immediately became one of Kemp's key ball carriers, though they later had differences over both political style and policy substance.

"I am very deeply shaped by Kemp," Gingrich says.[9] "Of all the people I've known who really affected me, he would be right after Reagan in terms of genuinely getting me to think differently. . . . I'm much more passionate about a solution-oriented, empowerment-oriented, inclusive party that aggressively takes responsibility for helping people solve their problems than I would have been." Gingrich, a historian with a PhD, said that Kemp was "the most important Republican since Teddy Roosevelt," and equally possessed of "endless energy" and "cheerful persistence." "This will sound goofy," he said, "but in a real sense Jack brought love into the Republican party. He loved people. He loved life. He made people happy. He was a genuine comrade. You were companions on a quest."

Connie Mack III, grandson of the Baseball Hall of Famer (also the grandson and stepson of two U.S. senators and later a senator himself) came to the House in 1982, at forty-two, and immediately became part of Kemp's backfield. He got elected to the Chowder and Marching Club and recalls how Kemp, never self-effacing, got under the skin of Old Guard Republicans.

"The rule was, members speak in the order in which they arrived each Wednesday. But Jack would always burst into the room halfway through and immediately seize the floor. . . . And he would always have a confrontational issue or question to pose." Sometimes members would yell at him, telling him to wait his turn, Mack said, but Kemp would say, "I don't have time to wait my turn. You've got to hear this."

One day, Mack recalled, Jack lectured the C&M that the Reagan revolution policies he'd inspired would send the stock market rising from 1,200 to 3,000, then 10,000. Then he exited the room. "You should have heard the rumbling. 'This guy is crazy.' 'What the hell does he know?' 'He's a quarterback, what does he know?' But Jack did know and made sure you knew he knew."[10] Kemp was essentially right—and made a killing on his insight. Putting his money where his beliefs were, he took his entire savings of $50,000 and invested in the stock market when Reagan was elected. He made a lot of money,[11] by one estimate, $500,000.

One of Kemp's strongest allies was not newly elected. Trent Lott of Mississippi became one of Kemp's closest friends despite Kemp's liberal attitude on civil rights and Lott's conservative past. Lott arrived in Congress in 1972, two years after Kemp. Ten years before, as a student at the University of Mississippi, Lott led the way in defeating a move by his national fraternity, Sigma Nu, to eliminate a racial discrimination clause in its national charter—about the time that Kemp was siding with black teammates against discrimination in American Football League cities.[12] Once a Southern Democrat, Lott changed parties as part of the accelerating migration of southern whites to the GOP.

Kemp and Lott talked about race. "He urged me to reach out to African-Americans, include them in our meetings and on my staff. . . . And he had an influence—not necessarily on my views, but on my understanding and agreeing that we could do better there," Lott said. "I explained to Jack that he didn't understand how difficult it is sometimes in the South, or was, and he didn't even understand how we grew up. . . . We grew up playing together, living together, and Jack didn't quite understand any of that."[13]

They agreed on economics and on the need for Republicans to adopt a growth-and-opportunity message to appeal to workers. And they had an easygoing personal relationship deepened by the friendship of their wives, Joanne and Tricia. As Lott describes it, he and Kemp both debated and joshed with each other. Once an Ole Miss cheerleader, Lott claimed to Kemp that he'd actually spent more time on a football field than Kemp, and he called Kemp "one of the slowest quarterbacks with the biggest feet I'd ever seen."[14]

Lott admired Kemp's leadership style. "He worked us. When we'd have a vote on the floor, he was always harassing somebody like me or Vin Weber . . . or Dan Coats. We were all his acolytes, you know." Kemp's excitement inspired him too: "I like to think my nature is like Jack's. I like to be for things. I like to be positive. I like upbeat. So all his messages and his ideas were right down my alley. I loved it."

Lott supported Kemp to be Reagan's vice presidential candidate in 1980, and the two were elected House GOP leaders at the same time— Lott in the number two minority whip's position, Kemp as the number three. They were a strong team; as Lott put it, "Kemp was an undisciplined leader and needed someone to count votes," which was a Lott specialty.[15] Nicknamed "House snits" by older House members and senators unimpressed with their enthusiasm and economic views, they made a dynamic team. And though both were House leaders and Reagan loyalists, they often resisted White House policy when it strayed from supply-side principle.

————

Paul Craig Roberts, Kemp's former aide who was appointed assistant secretary of the treasury for economic policy, wrote in his 1984 history, *The Supply-Side Revolution,* that the long-standing struggle between supply-siders and traditional Republicans played out with a vengeance in the new administration. He put Reagan, Kemp, and himself in one camp, along with much of the Treasury Department and a few White House aides, including Martin Anderson, Reagan's chief domestic policy adviser. Evans and Novak, and the *Wall Street Journal* editorial page, were their principal media allies.[16] Wanniski was an outside force, but he'd publicly labeled himself and fellow supply-siders as "wild men,"[17] giving ammunition to the traditionalists.

On the other side were Reagan's top White House staff: the chief of staff, James Baker; his deputy, Richard Darman; the communications director, David Gergen; and the supposed supply-sider David Stockman. In Congress, Senator Bob Dole, the new chairman of the Senate Finance Committee, and Senator Pete Domenici, chairman of the Senate Budget Committee, were among the staunch traditionalists. The mainstream press, notably the *New York Times* and the *Washington Post,* served as outlets for the traditionalists—or "pragmatists," as they labeled themselves.

The battle unfolded swiftly—before Reagan was even inaugurated— with Kemp unwittingly playing a supporting role on the traditionalist side. President-elect Reagan assigned then-Los Angeles headhunter Pendleton James to collect policy recommendations from prospective cabinet appointees. Lew Lehrman, Kemp's choice for treasury secretary,[18] and Stockman both submitted papers.

Both documents sounded alarms about the deteriorating state of financial markets and the economy in general, blaming the problems on surging inflation. Their fears were well founded. Unemployment stood at 7.4 percent. Food prices were expected to rise by 10 percent and energy prices by 20 to 40 percent.[19] The Federal Reserve under Paul Volcker had loosened the money supply during the fall. Republicans thought that as a Democrat, he was trying to get Carter reelected. Now he was again raising interest rates. He brought the prime lending rate to a record-high 21.5 percent in December 1980.[20] Many economists predicted the economy was headed back into recession.

Lehrman's memo forecast the imminent collapse of the stock, bond, and loan markets unless the administration immediately implemented a policy of tighter money, tax cuts, relaxed regulations on business, and deep budget cuts. He called for Reagan to declare a "national economic emergency" akin to Franklin Roosevelt's in 1933.

Lehrman's paper reached Kemp and Stockman, and the latter used it in writing his own memo. Kemp carried Stockman's paper to the first postelection meeting of Reagan's economic advisers in Los Angeles on November 16. The twenty-three-page document contained recommendations similar to Lehrman's and even more alarming rhetoric. "In all," wrote Stockman, "President Reagan will inherit thoroughly disordered credit and capital markets, punishingly high interest rates, and a hairtrigger market psychology poised to respond strongly to early economic policy signals." He suggested that a policy of tax cuts without "decisive, credible elements" to balance the budget would result in further inflation and a recession. Stockman did not directly call for abandoning Kemp-Roth in the name of deficit control—as he would later—but declared "severe [reduction] of entitlement and new obligational authority" (that is, spending) to be "critical."[21]

Kemp seemed unaware that his friend was betraying the supply-side cause even though Stockman's paper forecast "coronary contractions among some and . . . an intense polarization among supply-side tax cutters and the more fiscally orthodox." It predicted that "an internecine struggle over deferral or temporary abandonment of the tax [cut] program could ensue." And that could lead to "severe demoralization and fractionalization of the GOP and an erosion of our capacity to govern and revive the economy before November 1982," the midterm elections. All of that occurred, with Stockman at the center.

Ever positive, Kemp wanted the memo to call for an economic "Inchon landing," imitating the bold offensive by Douglas MacArthur that changed the course of the Korean War. Stockman, more pessimistic, chose as his historical reference the massive British retreat from mainland Europe at the start of World War II, titling the memo "Avoiding a GOP Economic Dunkirk."

Carrying Stockman's report, Kemp was the only attendee at the Los

Angeles economic gathering with a paper to pass out.[22] He also was the only noneconomist and the only supply-sider present. And his supply-side ideas were put on the chopping block. Before the meeting, the media speculated—some citing Reagan economic advisers—that the Kemp-Roth 30 percent tax cut would not survive as Reagan policy. George Shultz,[23] the chairman of Reagan's advisory committee, argued in favor of keeping the individual rate cuts, but the committee backed away from other elements of Kemp-Roth, suggesting the elimination of the capital gains tax cut for the top tax bracket. The committee also suggested dropping the idea of indexing incomes against inflation[24] to eliminate bracket creep. And it rejected the idea of declaring an economic emergency.

Kemp surprised members of the committee by agreeing to Stockman's deep spending cuts.[25] Why he did so is unclear. Evans and Novak wrote later that he "harbored misgivings" and even privately said, "I fear there may be blood on the floor" over the cuts."[26] But he did not raise objections at the meeting. It may be that he trusted Stockman, as Novak wrote that he himself still did. It may be that he was simply flattered to be included in the first meeting of Reagan's top advisers. Regardless, his compromise encouraged deficit hawks to think they could elevate a balanced budget to Reagan's top economic priority even though he had been elected on a tax cut platform. Kemp evidently trusted Reagan, most of all, to stick to his guns.

―――――

David Stockman was a brilliant workaholic and intellectual wanderer. He grew up a Republican in Michigan, then became an anti–Vietnam War activist at Michigan State. Following graduation in 1968, he attended Harvard Divinity School and served as a live-in babysitter for Daniel Patrick Moynihan, then a Harvard professor and, in 1976, U.S. senator from New York. In 1970, at Moynihan's recommendation, Stockman got hired as an aide to John Anderson. Two years later he became executive director of the House Republican Conference, chaired by Anderson. Moynihan later lampooned Stockman as "everything you could dream of in a mole" and "the best boob bait for conservatives ever to come out of the Midwest."[27] Anderson protested that while working for him, Stockman wrote an article savaging federal programs Anderson supported.[28]

Stockman was Anderson's aide when he first met Kemp, who then introduced him to Laffer and Wanniski. He seemed such a faithful member of the House supply-side cabal that by 1977 Wanniski entrusted him with galley proofs of his book *The Way the World Works*.[29]

Even before Stockman was sworn in as budget director, however, Wanniski began seeing Stockman as an enemy, though he had helped select him. When Stockman's Dunkirk memo was leaked to the press—possibly by Wanniski—its call for a declaration of national emergency caused tremors on Wall Street and aroused fears of Roosevelt-style bank closings. So Stockman and Kemp went separately to New York to calm the waters. Stockman assured top investors that budget cuts would be Reagan's top priority.[30]

After reassuring the financial titans, Stockman wrote in his memoir, he went "from no-free-lunch to a free dinner that evening at the Century Club hosted by Lew Lehrman." Kemp and other supply-siders were present, and they were none too happy. Wanniski attacked him for apostasy, alleging "Stockman spent the whole day selling root canal and threatening to heave widows and orphans into the snow." Wanniski insisted that "the battle for marginal tax rate reduction, the gold dollar and supply-side prosperity will be lost. We'll end up with Republican austerity as usual." Wanniski was expressing the view that Kemp had advanced for years. What Kemp said at the dinner is not documented, but Evans and Novak wrote that "almost from the beginning, Kemp experienced misgivings about what he had wrought" and said he feared Stockman did intend to balance the budget "by throwing widows and orphans into the snow."[31]

———

Always upbeat, Kemp didn't let harbingers of conflict depress him. The Kemps attended dozens of balls, receptions, and parties over inaugural weekend, bringing along Kemp's former Buffalo Bills teammates. Delighted with Reagan's inaugural address, Kemp told his hometown newspaper that Reagan would restore the economy.

On Inauguration Day, the *Washington Post*'s editorial page editor, Meg Greenfield, featured a long interview with Kemp on her op-ed page.[32] In it, Kemp predicted a Reagan-Bush reelection because inflation and interest rates would be reduced and economic prosperity restored. "I don't want to sound like an economic determinist," Kemp said, "but I'm convinced that the needs of all of the American people, if not the needs of the rest of the world, are inextricably linked to economic opportunity and social mobility and what we used to call the American Dream."

Kemp *was* something of an economic determinist, always under-playing the role of culture, history, and geography in setting the destiny of peoples. "I really think the social fabric of the nation is based upon good will and when the pie is shrinking, when you perceive that your gain must come at my expense or that my gain is coming at your expense, then this whole special interest environment builds up," he said. Even social issues like school busing, abortion, and birth control would be less fractious, he said, if debated in a growing-pie economy.

As Kemp told Greenfield, all he feared was "timidity, trepidation, defeatism." On the basis of his experience in Congress, Kemp expected "timidity" from fellow Republicans as well as Democrats, and his con-cerns were well founded. President Reagan might have been an instinc-tive tax-cutting supply-sider, but—wittingly or unwittingly—he'd packed his White House staff with skeptics. Congress would not be much help either. Afraid of deficits, six GOP members of the House Ways and Means Committee told Stockman and Treasury Secretary Donald Regan that they wanted the proposed January 1 effective date of Reagan's tax cuts slipped to July 1.

There was an added problem: Reagan himself was unsure whether he had promised during his campaign to reduce tax *rates* or merely reduce taxes. Laffer said he was at a meeting in the Oval Office with a dozen or so top Reagan aides and outside advisers when Reagan asked which he had promised.[33] His pollster, Richard Wirthlin, and his communications guru, Michael Deaver, convinced him he'd only promised overall tax reductions, not an across-the-board rate cut for everyone. To the horror of the supply-siders, the confusion led to the watering down of Kemp-Roth. By the time Reagan's cuts were enacted, Kemp's (and Reagan's) original 30 percent proposal was cut back to 23 percent and its effective date was postponed until October 1981. By then, the economy was plunging into recession.

It was pushed there by Fed Chairman Volcker. To crush inflation, he kept the prime lending rate above 15 percent through the summer of 1982 and above 10 percent until 1985. The result was the deepest recession since the 1930s, with unemployment reaching 10.8 percent in late 1982. As Volcker slammed the brakes on the U.S. economy, supply-siders wanted tax rate cuts to push the accelerator, fostering growth to prevent a downturn. Reagan both supported Volcker *and* sought tax cuts. But tax compromises defeated supply-siders' hopes. Amid the deep economic trough—which also swelled budget deficits—both Republican and Democratic critics of "Reaganomics" illogically put maximum blame on the tax cuts.

Reagan announced his economic program on February 18, 1981, to a joint session of Congress. Compromises began being made in the run-up. Though Reagan and his advisers had agreed in Los Angeles to three years of across-the-board 10 percent tax cuts, it was decided that the program would not apply to high-income taxpayers. And there would be no cut in capital gains taxes.

Kemp rebelled and went to the press. The day before Reagan's speech, the *New York Times* carried a front-page story headlined, "Reagan Is Lowering Extent of Tax Cut for the Affluent." A subhead read "Kemp Asserts Move Is Timid."[34] The article said Kemp "broke today with the White House and said he would pursue his own tax plan." It quoted Kemp as saying, "I am no longer bound. Obviously I support the president, but I will pursue my own program."

Maverick though he was, Kemp probably hadn't meant to cause so much of a splash. The *Times* story led him and Reagan to go into overdrive to repair their public unity. Kemp called Reagan and talked with him for twenty minutes. Nancy Reagan also called Joanne Kemp to invite her to sit with her in the House gallery to watch the speech.[35] Afterward, Kemp said he'd used the word "timidity" referring to the Treasury's analysis of the cost of the measure. The Kemp-Reagan relationship was healed, but not his standing with the White House staff.

———

Before long, another controversy involving Kemp erupted, this one mostly out of public view. In the administration's explanation of its economic strategy in a report by the Council of Economic Advisers, the White House trashed a Treasury-commissioned draft introduction by best-selling supply-sider George Gilder. They replaced his work with an introduction identifying budget cutting as "the centerpiece of our program" and tax rate reduction as "the second element."[36] Reporters calling Treasury for comment, Paul Craig Roberts wrote, "let it be known that unnamed White House officials were describing the final draft as a rebuff to supply-siders," specifically including Kemp. "And it was."

The intrigue was interpreted by some supply-siders and the media as an early outbreak of presidential succession politics.[37] If supply-side economics succeeded, Kemp would be in a better position to run for president than George Bush when Reagan left office—possibly, given his age, in 1985. Accordingly, supply-siders suspected that their leading foe was James Baker, Bush's best friend and 1980 campaign manager. Baker flatly denies that any position he ever took as Reagan's chief of staff was based on helping Bush emerge as Reagan's successor. "That's crazy," he said.[38] "I bent over backwards to make sure that everybody knew where my loyalties lay. They were to Ronald Reagan. Now, if seeing Reagan succeed enhanced Bush's opportunities, so much the better. But to say that somehow we were [acting] to defeat the hopes of Jack Kemp running for president, that's crazy." He said his job was to get Reagan's program enacted and this involved making compromises with Congress that Kemp, as a "purist" and "ideologue," didn't appreciate.

—

Reagan's initial tax cut proposal was a disappointment to the "ideologues." Substantively speaking, Reagan's nationally televised February 18 address called for Kemp-Roth rate cuts in each of three years, as well as liberalized depreciation rules for business. He was calling for the biggest single tax reduction ever requested by a president—$53.9 billion for 1982. Supply-siders were unhappy because the effective date of the cuts was postponed from January 1 to July 1, 1981; the proposal did not contain an immediate rate cut for dividends and interest income; and indexing incomes against inflation had been dropped.[39] Kemp had hoped for an immediate lowering of the capital gains rate from 28 percent to 20 percent to stimulate the moribund stock and bond markets.[40]

In early March, a liberal Democrat, Representative William Brodhead of Michigan, introduced an amendment to accomplish what Reagan's plan did not. It gave equal percentage tax cuts to wages and "unearned" income (dividends and interest) by dropping the top capital gains rate from 28 percent to 20 percent over three years—and doing so immediately for capital gains. Reaganites had shied away from this bold step for fear they'd be accused of "favoring the rich," but Brodhead was not queasy. "I am not a supply-sider," he said, ". . . but we have to reduce taxes on wealthy people to have more investment." Kemp, unsurprisingly, cosponsored the measure, as did the Democratic chairman of the House Ways and Means Committee, Chicagoan Dan Rostenkowski.[41]

As Reagan's economic program of budget and tax cuts was beginning its journey through Congress, it was greeted skeptically in the press and on Capitol Hill—and was undermined even inside the administration. Then on March 30, Reagan was shot by would-be assassin John Hinckley Jr. The assault instantly extended his honeymoon period and suppressed partisan rancor. His approval rating soared to the high '70s—but it was not clear whether this would revive prospects for his economic plans. Budget cuts were certain to pass, but tax cuts were under relentless attack. Rostenkowski, House Democrats' leading tax writer, declared in mid-March that Reagan's tax cut was dead and that he would develop his own alternative. For his part, House Speaker Tip O'Neill announced that "all factions of the Democratic party agree they are against Kemp-Roth."

As Reagan recovered, his program suffered heavy blows on Capitol Hill. The House Budget Committee rejected his plan and adopted Democratic chairman Jim Jones's weak alternative calling for just one year of tax cuts skewed to the middle class, as well as more generous business cuts than Reagan had called for. Republican Senate budget chairman Pete Domenici of New Mexico joined three other Republicans to defeat the president's budget in his committee, 12–8. The *Wall Street Journal* labeled the chairman "John Maynard Domenici." But Baker and Stockman—top Reagan aides formally pledged to enact his policies—wrote a letter to the editor defending Domenici.[42]

During both House and Senate deliberations, Democrats exploited Kemp's response to questions about Reagan's projected deficit of $50 billion to $70 billion for fiscal 1982. "We don't worship at the shrine of the balanced budget," Kemp had said. One House Democrat said, "Put me down as one who does worship at the shrine of a balanced budget."[43] An unidentified western Republican senator told the *Buffalo Courier Express* that "Kemp's quote has given the Democrats words to unite around. They are chanting it in the House and the Senate. I think they have us in a hole." He added, "We can't possibly have a balanced budget if we continue to support Kemp-Roth."

————

While Reagan recuperated, stories flew through the media that his aides were determined to "compromise" with Jones—even to the extent of accepting a meager one-year, 10 percent cut,[44] which would amount to surrender by the White House. Kemp allies wondered if the president read the newspapers, and if he did, why he did not clean out the "White House officials" who were whittling away at his program.[45]

Kemp strenuously opposed compromise. In a speech to the Electronic Industries Association in Washington,[46] Kemp expressed shock "that there aren't more business groups speaking out for [Reagan's] program." He defended his "shrine" statement: "I don't worship at that shrine. I want to balance the budget, but the important point I was making was that a balanced budget was not the be-all and end-all of government economic and fiscal policy. Seventy-five percent of the deficit is not caused by liberal spenders, but by high interest rates, high inflation and excessive taxation. We may have to take a short term deficit this year and maybe next year to get the economy revived," he said.

To Kemp's relief, Reagan from his bed sent an order to retract any compromise offers.[47] Less than a month after nearly being killed, he addressed a joint meeting of Congress to defend his budget plan. He downplayed the size of his tax cuts, arguing they would merely reduce "gigantic" tax increases built into existing law. He added a Kempian argument: "Our across-the-board cut in tax rates for three years" will give "the small, independent businessman or woman [who] creates 80 percent of all the new jobs . . . the incentive and promise of stability they need to go forward with expansion plans calling for additional employees."[48]

That same day the Senate Budget Committee reversed itself and approved Reagan's program, but the Democratic House still needed to be convinced. Reagan set to work on it. The Democrats' rival proposal, he charged, was "an echo of the past rather than a benchmark for the future" and would maintain "our present misery": double-digit inflation, mortgage interest at 15 percent, and eight million unemployed. "Isn't it time we tried something new?" he asked.

Reagan's appearance generated an avalanche of messages to Congress and turned the tide. House Majority Leader Wright wrote in his diary, "We've just been out-flanked and out-gunned."[49] Reagan's budget plan—named Gramm-Latta for its Democratic and Republican sponsors, Representative Phil Gramm of Texas and Delbert Latta of Ohio—passed the House May 7 by a lopsided 270–154 vote as 80 Democrats joined all 190 Republicans. A week later, it passed the Senate by a 78–20 margin. House Speaker Tip O'Neill lamented: "We can't argue with a man as popular as he is."[50]

But these early victories didn't end the battle. They enacted a budget *framework* for Reagan's tax and budget cuts. The actual cuts had to be enacted as laws. That would be harder. And the combat continued inside the administration and on Capitol Hill over whether Kemp-Roth would survive or be watered down and delayed. The *New York Times* quoted "a senior White House official," probably Stockman, as saying that Reagan "is prepared to accept less than the full amount of his proposed tax cut but wants Democrats in Congress to make the first move toward compromise."[51] In Congress, Senate Finance Committee chairman Bob Dole "was telling everyone, particularly the press, that he did not have the votes . . . to report out the full Kemp-Roth bill."

Kemp and his "backfield" kept pushing for full Kemp-Roth, but Dole did not want the 10 percent reduction of personal income taxes for three years (known as 10-10-10) not only because it was Kemp's bill, but also because the members of his tax committees had lots of "Christmas tree ornaments"—special interest tax breaks—that they wanted to hang onto the bill. Dole wanted to create "revenue room" for them by cutting back the president's plan.[52] Though Reagan wanted "a clean bill," the press kept reporting that a compromise was in the works. The *Washington Post* quoted Reagan as saying, "I have not changed my mind one bit," but the same day White House spokesman Larry Speakes, instructed by higher-ups, said that "compromise is no longer a dirty word."[53]

Roberts wrote that "impetus for a compromise was coming from within the administration and from Senate Republicans, not from House Democrats or the bond market. Part of the problem were feelings of rivalry toward Jack Kemp, who was seen in some quarters as being too successful in providing political leadership."[54] Stockman was eager to change 10-10-10 to 5-10-10 and delay the first installment until October 1, which "would leave the economy struggling along without supply-side benefits until the second half of the president's term."

In mid-June, Reagan defeated O'Neill again on spending. Conservative Democrats helped Reagan pass a bill dubbed Gramm-Latta II, 217–211. As it turned out, the bill actually decreased spending by only $16 billion from its scheduled level, though newspapers and television carried story after story about widespread suffering under Reagan's "draconian cuts."[55]

To Kemp's dismay, the campaign for tax compromise finally succeeded when Reagan accepted a 5 percent first-year cut effective October 1. He was persuaded on the basis of the need to secure the votes of Southern "boll weevil" Democrats concerned about growing deficits. The estimated cost of the bill for 1982 dropped from $53.9 billion to $37.4 billion.[56] Reagan acknowledged it would "not quite do the job, but will have generally the same effect" as the full 30 percent reduction.[57]

The watered-down bill—a 23 percent across-the-board cut over three years, not 30 percent—became "Conable-Hance," introduced by top Ways and Means ranking Republican Barber Conable (NY) and Democrat Kent Hance of Texas. To gain support from business groups, tax advantages for corporations were enhanced.[58]

In late June, the Senate Finance Committee approved the bill, 19–1, with only freshman senator Bill Bradley (D-NJ) voting against it on grounds it insufficiently aided middle- and lower-income taxpayers. In the process of passage, the bill picked up numerous further tax breaks for special interests, but Kemp's friend, Senator Bill Armstrong of Colorado, succeeded in adding an all-important amendment to index incomes against inflation and end bracket creep. The administration initially—and unwisely—opposed the provision, but Reagan later accepted it and used it to dramatic effect. The Senate passed the bill by a vote of 89–11, with thirty-seven of the Senate's forty-seven Democrats supporting it and just one Republican, Charles Mathias of Maryland, voting against it.

The House Ways and Means Committee produced its version a month later. In synch with Reagan, it reduced the corporate income tax from 46 percent to 34 percent, allowed businesses to write off their equipment purchases in the year they were made, and lowered estate and gift taxes. But Rostenkowski added so many breaks for special interests that the Democratic budget chairman, Jim Jones of Oklahoma, told the *New York Times*: "We're in a bidding war. Any economic foundation for the tax bill has been abandoned."[59]

The chief difference between House (Democrat) and Senate (Republican) bills was that Democrats dropped the third year of individual tax cuts and made it a 5-10 package skewed to earners under $50,000. This allowed Democrats to continue their nonstop campaign to cast Reagan as generous to the rich and callous toward working people. And it did not include indexing, which Democrats claimed would lead to larger deficits and higher inflation. The bill provided more total tax reduction than Reagan's, but for two years only. Over three years, Reagan's bill lowered rates more and kept them down with indexing.

Reagan made much of these differences in a nationally televised speech from the Oval Office on July 27, quipping that the Democratic tax cut was larger "if you're only planning to live two more years." He said Democrats had put together their tax program "for one purpose only: to provide themselves with a political victory." He again urged viewers "to contact your Senators and Congressmen. Tell them you believe this is an unequaled opportunity to help return America to prosperity and make government again the servant of the people."[60]

Again, the response was overwhelming. Phone calls and telegrams poured into Capitol Hill at ten times the normal rate, running twelve to one in Reagan's favor.[61] A chagrined O'Neill admitted, "We are experiencing a telephone blitz like this nation has never seen. It's had a devastating effect."

The crucial House vote came on July 29. Kemp took a limited part in the floor debate, though his name and his Kemp-Roth bill were often referred to, admiringly by Republicans, critically by Democrats. One Democrat, Elliott Levitas of Georgia, said he'd been a sponsor of Kemp-Roth since 1976, but "both the Ways and Means Committee bill and the Conable-Hance substitute contain sweeteners and boondoggles and provisions that have no business being in a responsible bill. Provisions which favor the commodity trader, oil producers, carry-back provisions on corporate investment tax credits—provisions put in by each side to gain votes in a bidding contest." Levitas was right, but his criticism was ignored.

With his wife and his three younger children—teenagers Jennifer and Judith and Jimmy, nine—sitting in the gallery, Kemp took the floor near the end of the debate[62] and delivered a speech that grew in passion and partisanship as he defended his bill. "If you think it is time to get the country moving again, you will vote for President Reagan's bipartisan bill. . . . The Democratic leadership does not have a plan to revitalize the American economy. They have a plan to revitalize the Democratic leadership. But they are wrong in thinking that they can do that by pitting one class of taxpayers against another instead of treating everyone alike."

The House voted after O'Neill himself made a final pitch,[63] asserting that "if the president has his way this could be a great day for the aristocracy of the world." This was the day Prince Charles and Lady Diana were married in Great Britain. "This morning there was quite a royal wedding. This afternoon President Reagan is proposing a royal tax cut."

The vote for the Hance-Conable amendment, Reagan's bill, was 238–195, with forty-eight Democrats joining all but one Republican (Representative Jim Jeffords of Vermont) in the majority.

After the vote, Kemp received a standing ovation from colleagues in the House chamber.[64] And he received a call of congratulations from Reagan. He told Reagan, "I want your support for my next tax bill—a 30 percent rate reduction in your next term." Kemp said Reagan replied, "Gee, Jack, I thought we'd go for 40 percent next time."

"The thing I am happiest about," Kemp told reporters "is that this is a promise I made a long time ago to the people of Buffalo. I promised I would try to do what President Kennedy did in the 1960s."

———

The night the Reagan tax bill passed the House, David Stockman and Richard Darman reportedly sat in a car and talked about how to unwind the cuts and raise the rates. That story, perhaps apocryphal, spread quickly

through Washington, as rumors about curbing the president's conservative inclinations often did.[65] But if Stockman and other White House officials didn't begin conspiring that night to boost taxes, they did soon
afterward. Indeed, taxes went up in 1982 and several times after that, with
Kemp in opposition to all of them despite his official position in the House
GOP leadership.

The final tax bill, known as ERTA (Economic Recovery and Tax Act
of 1981), was processed by a House-Senate conference committee and
passed the Senate, 67–8, on August 3 and the House, 282–95, the next day.
Its cost had grown to $920 billion over five years, according to the Joint
Committee on Taxation.[66] Hayward noted that "because of all the sweeteners added to the bill to win votes, the revenue loss in . . . the final tax
package was about twice the amount of Reagan's original tax cut proposal."[67]

Kemp was hailed by his colleagues and congratulated by Reagan,
but not by White House "pragmatists." Reagan signed the bill August
13, but not in a White House ceremony surrounded by its supporters.
Roberts observed that "the president was whisked off to California in
order to avoid a White House bill-signing ceremony necessitating our
participation along with Jack Kemp's." And when he returned to Washington, Reagan held a reception for congressional staff members who
had worked on his economic program—dominated by those who had
tried to water it down. Omitted from the invitation list were conservative staffers from both houses who had fought for the Kemp-Roth tax
bill before it became Reagan's and then went all out for the president's
program.[68] Roberts and other administration supply-siders were not invited either.

———

The economy officially fell into recession in July 1981, even before the
tax bill was passed.[69] Treasury Secretary Regan, sharing Kemp's view,
blamed it on the Federal Reserve's holding money supply growth at zero
beginning in March. But Lawrence Kudlow, later an ardent supply-sider

but then Stockman's chief economist, declared it "inconceivable to intelligent observers that monetary policy can be accused of excessive restraint." A recession "if there is one, should not be pinned on the Fed."[70]

Stockman and other White House officials blamed high interest rates not on Fed policy, but on the budget deficit—that is, excessive government borrowing—and recommended the administration launch a "September offensive" consisting of deep new budget cuts and tax increases. "Austerity with a vengeance," Roberts called it. "A throwback to the policies of the 1930s and a far cry from the supply-side policy of balancing the budget through economic growth."[71]

The fiscal 1981 deficit came in at $79 billion, exceeding Carter's worst.[72] Press accounts, some citing White House officials, faulted Reagan's tax cuts even though they had yet to take effect.

On September 24, only a month after signing his tax cut bill, Reagan went on national television to propose additional 1982 spending cuts of $13 billion and tax increases of $3 billion (rising to $22 billion in 1984). In the speech, Reagan made no mention of the Fed and, in effect, blamed high interest rates on his own fiscal policy. Republicans in Congress, having just battled for that policy, rejected Reagan's proposals, as did Democrats not eager to cut spending at all.

Kemp was with the opponents, writing two letters in a row to Reagan, cosigned by fellow New York Republican Barber Conable and boll weevil Democrat (soon to be Republican) Representative Phil Gramm of Texas. They wrote that giving in to "the political panic . . . would undermine the economic growth on which we are depending to balance the budget in 1984."[73] They also argued that if House Democrats got hold of a new Reagan bill, they could cause "serious political mischief" by substituting a measure to reverse some of the cuts passed in August.

Stockman's "September offensive" went nowhere in Congress, but the *Wall Street Journal* opined that "a few more flip-flops like that and President Reagan will have himself a credibility problem." The *Journal* fingered Stockman as "the main malefactor in this misplayed game" and said he'd succeeded in making "the public and the Congress more doubtful about the administration's confidence in its own program."[74]

Stockman was undeterred. He pushed next for excise taxes on tobacco and alcohol and defense cuts. The media echoed Stockman, repeatedly asserting that Reagan would (or should) do as he recommended. The *Washington Post's* veteran economics columnist, Hobart Rowen, claimed "the time has come for the Reagan administration to abandon supply-side economics."[75] Jonathan Feuerbringer reported in the *New York Times* that Stockman "is implicitly acknowledging that the original Reagan economic program cannot work."

Reagan dropped his just-issued endorsement of tax increases in a speech before a group of New York Republicans, declaring in Kempian language that "a balanced budget has never been an end in itself justifying any means" and that "we never agreed to balance the budget on the backs of tax payers."[76] It was a victory for supply-siders, but a temporary one.

———

On November 10, Stockman's thirty-fifth birthday, Democratic senator Gary Hart of Colorado read into the Congressional Record an article set to appear in the December issue of the *Atlantic Monthly* magazine.

"The Education of David Stockman" by *Washington Post* editor William Greider. Presaging an avalanche of jubilant attacks from Democrats, Hart said, "it is a fascinating story about what the Director of the Office of Management and Budget knew about "supply-side" economics and when he knew it. For anyone who has had any doubts about either the darker philosophic underpinnings of the administration's economic proposals, or the faulty logic behind them, this article will prove extremely enlightening."[77]

Stockman had been talking into Greider's tape recorder in breakfast meetings at the Hay Adams Hotel since December 1980. Greider, well known as a liberal, used his words to write a devastating piece embarrassing the supply-siders and Reagan. He quoted Stockman as

saying, "It's kind of hard to sell 'trickle-down,' so the supply-side formula was the only way to get a tax policy that was really 'trickle down.'
Supply-side is 'trickle-down theory.'"[78] He also said: "Kemp-Roth was
always a Trojan Horse to bring down the top rate."[79, 80]

Kemp was traveling with Novak in upstate New York when the
Stockman story broke.[81] To Novak's surprise, he didn't react angrily.
When they arrived in Washington that evening, Kemp called Stockman
(celebrating at a Washington restaurant) to wish him a happy birthday.
Then Kemp handed the telephone to Novak. "'Bob, say hello to Dave and
wish him a happy birthday,'" Novak wrote. "After I did so, Stockman told
me, 'you must think I'm Judas. We've got to get together soon.' We never
did. That was the last conversation I ever had with David Stockman."

But it wasn't the last conversation Kemp had with him. Indeed,
Kemp continued to consider Stockman a "friend," though Kemp allies
say he was "disappointed" in him. Some shared Novak's opinion that
Stockman was a traitor.[82] Wanniski, though, told the *New York Times* that
Stockman was "more of a Doubting Thomas—not Judas Iscariot."[83]

Laffer, a member of the president's Economic Policy Advisory Board,
thought Stockman was "finished" as budget director and would have to
leave within six months. "He has lost his credibility." Laffer still believes[84]
that Stockman was "an opportunistic slime ball." White House aide Martin Anderson called Stockman's action "perfidy." Michael Deaver and Ed
Meese wanted him fired.

According to Reagan biographer Lou Cannon, Baker protected
Stockman. After a forty-five-minute lunch with Reagan at which Stock-
man profusely apologized and offered to resign, Reagan kept him on.[85]
Baker now says Stockman wasn't sacked "because we needed him.
Nobody else knew all that stuff. So I prevailed on Reagan not to fire him."

———

Despite some measure of victory with the tax cuts, for Kemp 1981
had not been a complete success. He'd lost Stockman as an ally, and his

tax cuts—which had barely gone into effect—hadn't boosted the economy. Reagan's first year ended with the economy diving into deep recession. The GDP growth rate for the last quarter of 1981 was minus 4.9 percent. And it was minus 6.4 percent for the first quarter of 1982 and minus 1.9 percent for the year. Critics duly pronounced his economic policy a failure.

But Kemp had faith that the years of plenty would come if Reagan and Congress didn't reverse course. Kemp took a group of conservatives to meet with Reagan in mid-December to argue that the president should cut, not increase, taxes by speeding up the effective date of 1982 tax cuts to January 1 instead of July 1 to stimulate the failing economy. Official White House spokesmen rejected the idea, however, so Kemp was back twice in December to argue the case. To no avail.[86] Though Reagan all but ruled out raising taxes at one news conference, James Baker sent White House spokesmen to tell reporters immediately afterward that he hadn't meant what he said.

Stonewalled by the administration, Kemp found himself in frequent conflict with the president over the next seven years, despite his personal loyalty to Reagan and his official position as a GOP leader in Congress. He was vilified for the conflict, but he persisted, believing that lower taxes fostered growth and tax increases deepened the recession. Fortunately, he had the charisma to attract a backfield to support him in his fight—and the wisdom and good luck to put together a front line to protect him.

Five

FRONT LINE

Kemp was in his office, watching the closed-circuit feed from the House floor on May 3, 1983, as the House debated how to help the United States compete to host the 1986 World Cup soccer finals. Suddenly he bolted. One aide yelled to another, "Catch him!" but by then he'd run out the door and into an elevator headed for the floor. There he proceeded (with only "some tongue in cheek," he said) to denounce soccer as a "European socialist" sport, as opposed to football, which "is democratic capitalism."[1]

"Football is football and soccer is soccer," he said. "Soccer does not have a quarterback. Only football has a quarterback." He said he wished that the World Cup's sponsor, the International Football Association, would change its name, lest young people confuse the event with "the Super Bowl, the world's greatest spectator event, with all due respect to soccer and baseball." When he got back to the office, he told his aides he'd get his remarks expunged from the Congressional Record, as members often do when they say something ill considered. But he didn't.[2]

Kemp thought a football team was nothing if not led by a good quarterback, but he appreciated that he needed a strong line to open holes for his backfield and protect him from getting sacked. In his congressional battles, his backfield consisted of his fellow politicians. His line was composed of two parts—first his family, who grounded and inspired him.

Second was his staff—person for person, one of the ablest on Capitol Hill. Together, his team supported a scrambling quarterback who was always in motion—overbooked, multitasking, chronically late, impatient. Kemp's family loved him, and his staff shared his sense of mission, respected his leadership—and loved him too, really. But his quirks—and refusal to be managed—could also drive them to distraction.

———

In 1986, when Jeff Kemp was playing backup to Hall of Fame quarterback Joe Montana for the San Francisco 49ers, he got a call from his father after a game. Jack Kemp said, "Jeff, I saw you today. You looked great!" Jeff said, "Dad, I didn't even get in the game." Jack said, "Yeah, I saw you warming up. You looked great."[3]

As a father, Kemp motivated his four children by encouragement, not enforcement. He didn't pressure his two sons to follow him into professional football, though they did; he inspired them. He left notes of praise—"JFK-grams," the family called them—under his children's pillows. He followed the pattern of his mother, making dinner an educational experience for his children and saying to them every day as they left home, "Be a Leader" or "You know what 'Kemp' means? It means champion."[4] His children, though they note his faults, say he was fundamentally loving and affectionate. And when he rated his life's accomplishments, he put his family at the top of his list.

Like his father, Kemp left the management of his home to his wife, the "glue" of the family. "The division of labor between them was, the house was Mom's responsibility," said his younger son, Jimmy. "Dad controlled his chair and his bedside. She controlled everything else in the house and outside the house."[5] Joanne Kemp had abundant outside activities too: prayer and study groups, congressional and international wives' groups, Prison Fellowship, the National Conference on Soviet Jewry. And she was wise on what was happening in Congress. According to his children and friends, Kemp could be irascible, sexist, selfish, even narcissistic. Joanne Kemp lived with it—when she didn't calmly set him straight.

Unlike many members of Congress today who work and bunk weekdays in Washington, but head home to their families and districts every weekend, the Kemps made their home in Washington—actually, Bethesda, Maryland. Early in his congressional career, Kemp went to the district on weekends and the family spent summers there. As he became a national politician and his district became more safely Republican, he and his family visited less. In 1974, they sold the house in Hamburg, New York, where they'd lived during Kemp's football career, and bought a duplex they rented out.

Joanne chose Bethesda because it was close to Fourth Presbyterian Church, her spiritual home. The family moved once because Churchill High School had a better football program for Jeff than another school, but they lived in the same house from 1975 on. Jeff, born in 1959, got to see his father play football in Buffalo and got to know players—rookies sometimes led the games at his birthday parties—before the move to Washington.[6] Jennifer was eight when Kemp got elected to Congress and Judith, five. In Buffalo, they'd stayed at home when their father was on the field.[7] They—and Jimmy, born in Maryland in 1971—basically grew up as suburban Washington kids. Despite Kemp's celebrity, they lived a normal childhood because congressional children were nothing special at their schools.

Except when he was traveling, Kemp made it a point to be home for dinner. It was late, 8:00 or 8:30, by the time he got back from Capitol Hill, and Joanne sometimes had to give the kids cereal to tide them over. Over the meal, the family would talk. "The conversation just kind of flowed," said Jennifer (Kemp) Andrews.[8] "Whatever was going on in anyone's day. And . . . about what went on in Congress." Joanne was "a wonderful sounding board for him. . . . She really knew his business . . . knew what was going on in Congress, what vote was up," said Judith (Kemp) Nolan.[9] When Kemp expressed dismay at some colleague's behavior, she'd say, "Well, remember, he's the one who helped you pass that other piece of legislation."

Kemp often used dinners to educate his children about the issues he cared about. He tossed out articles and books for them to read on current events and history. He also took them on some foreign trips—his daughters, once to Central American countries during the Contra war and more than once to the Middle East.[10] A lasting memory of theirs from the Latin trip was Kemp playing Debussy's "Clair de lune" on an ambassador's piano—something he hadn't forgotten from childhood lessons.[11]

He brought visitors home for dinner, sometimes on a last-minute basis. "Macaroni and cheese was not beneath serving to senators at the Kemp house," said Jeff,[12] "and there was always garlic bread and there would always be a conversation that Dad would not let be adults-only. He would include the kids." Reagan's United Nations ambassador, Jeane Kirkpatrick, was a frequent guest—and a favorite of the children. "A sweetie," Kemp's daughters call her. When Jeff was barely a teenager, Kemp said, "Hey, Jeane, could you explain détente to Jeff and the kids?"[13] "What 14-year-old was interested in détente or could even pronounce it? We weren't. But he was bringing us into the world of ideas, the adult world."

One of Jeff's most memorable dinners occurred when Kemp invited Chuck Colson over. He challenged the former ruthless Nixon aide turned born-again Christian and Prison Fellowship founder on his entire worldview. "Jack, I thought you believed in my ideas," Colson said afterward. "Why did you do that?" Kemp replied, "That was awesome. It was awesome for the kids having you defend your ideas. It was a great lesson."[14]

Often the guests would be congressional colleagues—Gingrich, Mack, Coats, Lott, Weber, and Stockman, though after his supply-side apostasy, Stockman was dropped from the guest list.[15] The Kemps also entertained journalists, including the *Wall Street Journal*'s Al Hunt and his wife, Judy Woodruff, then of NBC; columnist Chris Matthews and his wife, Kathleen, a local TV anchor; and Brit Hume and his wife, Kim, both of ABC News and, later, the Fox News Channel. Other notable guests included Benjamin Netanyahu, who was number two at the Israeli embassy in Washington when Kemp was in Congress; Irving Kristol and his wife, Bea (Gertrude Himmelfarb); Kemp's old teammate, Cookie Gilchrist; and Arthur Laffer, who drew his curve for the girls.[16] And, of course, Jude Wanniski. Judith Nolan remembers being surprised at the way Wanniski could dominate Kemp. "It was very unique to have someone that Dad yielded to as much as he had to. . . . If Jude wanted to change the subject, he would. And if he wanted to cut Dad off and say, 'You're absolutely wrong about that,' he got away with it, whereas other people wouldn't have dared." Wanniski persuaded Judith to change her college major.[17]

At dinners, Jeff Kemp sometimes did dead-on imitations of his father, mimicking Kemp's voice and adapting his favorite clichés: "Here we are at dinner, in America, where a rising tide will lift all our boats to be anything God calls us to be, a mezzo soprano, a quarterback of Churchill High School or perhaps a B student at Dartmouth College. . . . But, remember, I am a Lincolnian, Churchillian, O. J. Simpsonian, Art Lafferian Republican. . . ." Jeff said, "He was very good at laughing at himself when I made fun of him."[18]

Besides hosting dinners, the Kemps also entertained at their house in Vail, Colorado. Dan Coats and his family often joined the Kemps there, and he remembers Kemp's enthusiasm and competitiveness, even with his family:

"If you ski with Jack, it's a race to the bottom and you'd better not win. Jack will catch you in the last 20 yards no matter where you are. . . . You go up the chair lift, Jack's the first one off. It doesn't matter whether it's his kids, his wife, his guests, the head coach, whatever, [he's not] waiting. He's 'Come on, come on, come on, come on!' As soon as he gets there he's got to be the first one off the lift and then it's hell bent for leather all the way down. . . . He's yelling at Joanne, 'Come on, hurry up, hurry up!' It's like this was a football game and the clock was ticking and if you don't get in enough ski runs, you lose."[19] Once home, Kemp would ice his knees, which had been hurting him all along. He'd yell for Joanne to get him more ice and bring him a Diet Coke.

Kemp called Sundays "religious holidays," said Jimmy,[20] "and it wasn't only because we went to church every Sunday, which we did. . . . We'd go to church in the morning, come home and Dad—you'd find him in front of the TV set, in his chair. He'd have books surrounding him and the football games would be on. . . . Often Mom and Dad would have people over, but other people were not the focus of the afternoon. You were there to watch football with Kemp." After church, Judith said, "Mom would make amazing food." Sundays were "great smells and football on TV."[21] Judith said, "At some point, there were two TVs, and they had to put extra satellite [dishes] on top of the house that looked ridiculous because they had to be able to get the Canadian Football League [where Jimmy was playing], which didn't come on network TV. That was fun." During games, he'd multitask, watching football, talking with guests, reading Sunday newspapers and tearing out articles, leaving a pile on the floor for Joanne to clean up.[22] Joanne had a special recipe for snacks—Triscuits garnished with mayonnaise, green onions, Worcestershire sauce and parmesan cheese, browned in the oven—and Kemp would bark at her, "Hey, Joanne, do you have any more Triscuits?" Or "Joanne, get the phone." Judith said, "He used to be more barky at Mom, and I noticed, at least as we got older, that softened, I think."[23]

At halftime, Jimmy said, "I'd run out and play my own football game by myself. We didn't live in a neighborhood with a lot of kids my age, so I played a lot of fantasy football. . . . I'd be the offense, the defense and the coach."[24] Joanne Kemp says he never pressured his sons to be football players.[25] He taught them how to throw a pass and they grew up in a football-infused environment, but they say they came by their ambitions themselves.

He did, however, want them to win their games and would not brook interference with their concentration. Dan Coats recalls[26] attending a high school football game where Jimmy was playing quarterback. The high school band leader had his minions playing music between each play in the style of the University of Southern California, and it interfered with Jimmy's signal calling. Kemp yelled at the band director to stop, but he couldn't hear him. "I was watching the game and all of a sudden Jack is gone," Coats recalls. "And I look around, he's down there in the face of the band director saying, 'Stop playing in between the plays.' That's Jack."

Jimmy, like his father, was a sports junkie from the get-go, learning to read by studying the sports page. He watched a VHS cassette of his father's football highlights, but when he played imaginary football, he imitated Roger Staubach of Navy and the Dallas Cowboys, and his brother, Jeff, of Churchill High School, Dartmouth, and the pros. He was a good athlete and just assumed he'd become a pro.[27]

Kemp went with Jeff to talk to Atlantic Coast Conference college coaches he knew, but Kemp was happy that Jeff got into an Ivy League college. Jeff said he hid his ambition to become a pro quarterback, lest he not make it. But when he was scouted and then signed as a free agent by the Los Angeles Rams, his father "was thrilled. . . . He was surprised that I had that much passion in me."[28]

In his ten seasons in the NFL, Jeff Kemp was usually a backup quarterback, not a starter. His star season was 1984, when he started in all but one game for the Los Angeles Rams and led the team to the divisional playoffs. In 1986, Joe Montana was injured and Kemp started in six games for the San Francisco 49ers, throwing eleven touchdown passes. In his five seasons with the Seattle Seahawks, he was assigned his father's old Buffalo jersey, number 15. Whatever his status, his father told him, "God has a plan. You're in your right place. You may be third string now . . . [but] the end of the story hasn't been written yet. Your day's going to come." And, "Think like a starter. Act like a starter. Your day's going to come. Hang in there. You'll be a great starter."[29] Jeff called his father "the ultimate encourager."

The encouragement came verbally and on paper in the "JFK-grams"— notes handwritten with a felt-tipped pen on heavy 7-by-4.5-inch cards embossed with a congressional or other official seal. Kemp routinely used that stationery to send notes to colleagues and friends congratulating them or referring an article to them—sometimes regretting some slight. For his children, they got used instead of birthday cards, occasionally for apologies, but mostly for inspiration. If the girls got good grades, there might be "a lovely note, a JFK-gram, sometimes on your pillow, absolutely telling you that the hard work was worth it and . . . encouraging you to keep going," said Judith.[30] When she got called for bad grades and protested she'd tried as hard as she could, she got a JFK-gram saying, "I'm so sorry. I know you're trying." She said, "So sometimes, he was too encouraging. He should have come down a little more. He didn't enjoy being the bad cop." He also sent JFK-grams to his sons- and daughters-in-law, congratulating them on their devotion to their spouses and successes as parents. And he wrote to one grandson, "You're a born leader, so never forget that the example you set is critically important to others. . . . Just remember that as you shine your light, make sure it is to glorify God and not yourself."

Kemp had his quirks at home. He never did chores around the house. Jeff said, "Dad talked and Mom worked. Dad would read papers, watch all the news shows simultaneously, and Mom would run the household. I mowed the lawns." Jimmy also raked and mowed and the girls did dishes. Kemp never joined in. When Jeff brought his future wife, Stacy, to the house for the first time, a thunderstorm flooded the Kemps' basement. She, Jeff, and the other Kemp kids bailed the water like sailors. Kemp walked in wearing tennis shorts, complaining his game had been rained out. "What are you guys doing?" he asked. "Bailing water." "Oh," he says, and goes upstairs and starts reading the *Times* and watching games."[31] "He'd chuckle and say, 'Somebody's got to concern themselves with saving the world. Someone has to handle the big things. That's what I'm doing.'"[32]

It was selfish, "narcissistic, even," said Jeff. "But accepted in the dynamic of our family. He'd do other things that we thought compensated for it. The affirmations, the hugs, the kisses, the love, the desire to be with us, the big efforts he'd make to leave political events . . . to be home."[33] Also accepted, at least then, was a sexist streak. When the boys turned sixteen, they got cars as presents and got to choose the model. The girls did not, with Kemp explaining that the boys needed to drive themselves to football practice—as though the girls did not have tennis matches and piano lessons. Jennifer said that when her father was near death, she whispered to him, "Hey, Dad. I forgive you about not getting cars when we were sixteen." She finally did get a car because she was graduating from college and needed it to drive to her student-teaching assignment. She got it, though, only after beating her father in a tennis challenge. A Honda Civic appeared in the driveway, wrapped in a huge red bow, with a note from him: "You Win!" But she hadn't chosen the car.³⁴

Joanne Kemp had a huge circle of close female friends in Washington, including the wives of people he didn't get along with. She was close to Susan Baker, for example, founder of a group that regularly prays for the well-being of first ladies. That connection helped heal rifts that developed between Kemp, as HUD Secretary, and Secretary of State James Baker during the first Bush administration. After the 1996 election, her friendship with Elizabeth Dole helped close a rift with Bob Dole over Kemp's poor vice presidential debate performance against Al Gore.

In 1995, Kemp wrote Jeff a long letter, which he called "JFK-gram #300 . . . the longest JFK-gram in history,"³⁵ explaining why he was not going to run for president the following year. In it he also retraced his life and values. "Looking back to my childhood, my dream was to play pro ball and, as you know, I was single-minded about being a pro-football quarterback. But as soon as I made it, family, children and grandchildren became an even more important aspiration.

"As Congress and a political career replaced pro football, I began to realize how ego and pride were inextricably bound up in what I was doing, but as long as I thought I was helping 'save the world' or at least 'make a difference,' it seemed to be the only thing to do and the right thing to do. Last summer, standing with Mom as we reaffirmed our vows in Vail Bible Church in front of you and your family, Jen, Judith and their precious families . . . I realized what C. S. Lewis had written in *Mere Christianity* on pride. I had put too much of my ego and pride into football and political accomplishments.

"Family is by far my (our) greatest accomplishment. Mr. Churchill said to his friend that 'a man's greatest monuments' were his children. In no small way, looking at you all, my monuments were my children and that you all stand taller in life than the Washington Monument."

His love for his family, clearly communicated, made up for many of his failings. His staff experienced his impatience and quirkiness too, but also respected him and believed in his mission.

———

Kemp wasn't a control freak, dictating every office detail. But determined to avoid being manipulated, he refused to let his aides or political advisers control him. He often assigned more than one aide to the same task—and not out of absentmindedness. David Smick, his chief of staff from 1979 to 1984, believes he did so to maintain control. "I thought of him like a stallion. He did not want any kind of structure that said, 'here's where you're going.'" Arriving for one of eight negotiating sessions before he was hired, Smick found Kemp reading a book about how Franklin Delano Roosevelt manipulated his cabinet. "He repeated to me on a number of occasions, 'I hate the way Reagan allows these guys to control him. I'm never going to allow that.'" Kemp also told him he had observed Reagan aides and business supporters in California mocking him behind his back, and he wanted to avoid the same fate. "I'm never going to allow them to say that about me—you know, that I'm just the front man," he told Smick.[36]

The staff worked around his quirks. They conferred among themselves and sorted out the work. When he needed Kemp to do something, Smick would call someone Kemp trusted—Irving Kristol was always a favorite—and try the idea out. Then he'd tell Kemp, "I think we should do blah, blah, blah. Irving thinks we should. Or, John Sears thinks we should. Make your call, but we've got to make a decision quickly." Smick said he'd make up numbers to get Kemp to sign off on fund-raising letters: "'Jack, you're losing $10,000 a day [delaying this].' It's a good thing he never asked how I figured that."[37]

Smick calculates[38] that Kemp rated "an 8 ½–9" on a scale of ten for intelligence. He was "quick, very quick." At the same time, "he had . . . a deliberate bravado that kept people at bay. They couldn't get too close." Smick thinks it was insecurity—that Kemp thought, 'I'm just a PE major.' The reality is that he read a lot of books, was very inquisitive and he knew a lot.

"But I think he needed that bravado to keep you off-base a little. Jokes, barbs, this and that. That's 'I don't want you to get too close because you'll find out I don't have a PhD in nuclear physics.' He didn't really need to worry about that. He had all the brain power he needed." But Smick thinks Kemp lacked the self-confidence of, say, Ronald Reagan. Smick thinks this was Kemp's "biggest flaw."[39]

———

Sharon Zelaska, Kemp's longtime office manager, also believed Kemp kept his staff off guard for control purposes. "It was not a malicious thing. He had a saying, he would check on you with minutiae. He would give you ten things to do. My way of doing things would be to prioritize on the basis of what was most important. But in his mind he was going to ask you about the one that was least important because he knew that if you did that one, the other nine were taken care of."[40] But Zelaska found her own ways to manage—she had a "three-time rule" with Kemp. If he asked for something done that she thought was unnecessary, she'd wait till he asked about it three times to make sure that he truly wanted it done.

Zelaska was one of Kemp's most important hires. She was the center of his front line, running his office, mothering his staff, and keeping the Kemps out of tax trouble. But even Zelaska couldn't control Kemp. Happily working at the American Enterprise Institute until recommended by Jude Wanniski, she got a call from Kemp personally on April 16, 1977. "The date is important," she said, "because it was the day after income tax day and he'd gotten a call from his accountant saying that if he didn't do something about his records, he'd be in trouble with the IRS. I was totally happy with my job, but I'd always wanted to work on the Hill or the White House. I didn't know him except from watching football. He'd been to AEI a few times to do one of our TV shows and the girls there always went gaga.

"So I went to the interview . . . and I walked out of there accepting his job. It was, like, 'how did this happen?' It was that he was just so upbeat and positive and said 'I need you.'"[41]

When Zelaska joined him, Kemp already had an office in the Rayburn Building, the biggest and most imperial of the three House office buildings. Previously, during his early years in the House, he'd occupied tiny quarters in the Cannon Building, where junior members are crammed. In each new Congress, he'd go into the office lottery hoping for a bigger space, eventually moving to 2235 Rayburn and finally a senior suite, 2252. Still, the space was crowded. Kemp had an inner office to himself, but Zelaska and various aides—his chief of staff, press secretary, and top legislative assistants—were all crowded into one room. When he was chairman of the House Republican Conference in the 1980s, he could house staff there.

Zelaska stayed with Kemp for twenty years, organizing his schedule and staff, serving sometimes as his conscience, making sure he knew where he had to be and that he got there. In Congress, she answered his phone, paid his office and personal bills, kept his checkbook balanced, made his plane and hotel reservations, made sure someone would meet him—and forced him to make decisions. She was nicknamed "Mother Superior" both because of her devout Catholicism and her care for everyone in the office.⁴²

Kemp's schedule was not easy to manage. He customarily came in at ten after having breakfast at home with his family, went to committee hearings, had a tuna sandwich with a Coke—or a hot dog bought from a vendor off the House floor—and (when he didn't have to travel) went home after congressional business for a late dinner with his family. He also went religiously to his sons' high school, college, and professional football games—though not so much to his daughters' dance performances or tennis matches.⁴³ Despite his overcrowded schedule, he always told Zelaska to keep Monday nights free for watching football. She thought that was crazy, but tried to do it.

Kemp hated saying no to anyone, so he overbooked himself. And speaking requests would pile up because he refused to make decisions. Zelaska carried stacks of them into his office and forced him to do so. Then he would run into a fellow Republican who'd ask him to his district for a fund-raiser, and he rarely said no or even "Let me check."

Zelaska then had to insist he sort out sometimes competing requests—much to his discomfort. "I was always the last person he wanted to talk to because he knew I wanted him to make decisions he didn't want to make," she said. "So I would wait until very late at night. I'd be the last person in the office but him. . . . He'd talk to everybody else but me for as long as he could."

Besides speaking requests, Kemp dawdled before signing all the photos and footballs that political fans requested of him. Fans either sent Kemp footballs or bubblegum cards to sign, or asked for signed footballs that Zelaska would order from the NFL and get the requester to pay for. "It'd take him months to get them back. All this stuff would back up in my office. . . . People would call me up and say, 'when are you going to get it done?' I'd tell them, 'Trust me, I have it.' And then one day I'd say, 'Jack you've got to do this. . . .' That's probably when he would yell at me, but he knew it was for his benefit and it was his image I was concerned about, not mine."

Once the schedule was arranged, Zelaska still had to figure out how to get Kemp where he was supposed to be. In the era before cell phones, keeping track of Kemp was an issue. When members got beepers, he wouldn't carry one. So he called a special number at Zelaska's desk. She also had the number of a House floor aide who could grab him.

Kemp's inner office was a mess. His pattern was to pick up a legal-sized manila folder on Monday mornings and carry it around all week. Everything anybody handed to him would go into the folder. At the end of the week, he would lay the folder on a credenza behind his desk never to pick it up again. Zelaska would beg him to let her organize the stack, but he would have none of it. "He thought it was going to Never Never Land if someone touched them. But I realized that if something hadn't been touched in six weeks, I'd pull it from the bottom of the stack and see if there was anything important in there. The staff knew I was doing it."[44]

Zelaska was also Jiminy Cricket, Kemp's conscience. "I found myself in the role of stopping Jack from doing things like taking corporate jets."[45] When he was HUD secretary, Zelaska talked Kemp out of flying on corporate aircraft, and days later the *Washington Post* carried a front-page story exposing White House chief of staff John Sununu for riding on one. "He came into the office when I was talking to some staff and I said, 'we were just talking about Sununu. Sure glad you didn't take that jet, aren't you?' He gave me a look like he wanted to kill me, but he knew I was right."[46] Zelaska's management also kept him out of the trouble other members got into for kiting checks at the House bank—a scandal exposed when he was at HUD. "He read about it in the paper and said, 'This article is a testament to you.' Because his name was not in it."

Not surprisingly, Zelaska was overburdened. Kemp knew he'd put too much stress on his staff when she and two other Catholics on his staff—his later chief of staff, Dave Hoppe, and economics expert John Mueller—disappeared at lunchtime to attend Mass.[47] "He called us 'the incense burners,'" Zelaska said. She finally got an assistant to handle his scheduling after she once booked him to Springfield, Illinois, when he was supposed to fly to Springfield, Missouri.

Kemp's staff depended on Zelaska for the word on Kemp's mood. And sometimes for food. "I'd save up the non-perishable food that came to our office at Christmastime and then at the end of January, when everybody was poor because we hadn't been paid for six weeks, I'd bring it out and we'd share it."[48]

———

Zelaska served under five chiefs of staff during Kemp's time in Congress. Randy Teague, David Smick's predecessor as chief of staff, was an aide in the Nixon White House when he joined Kemp in 1973—hired for his expertise in tax policy. Teague said Kemp's mind was "frenetically organized. I mean, he was a sponge. His brain was always absorbing these inputs." He also told Zelaska, "There will be days when he'll do something really stupid and you'll wonder, why in the world is he doing that? But he will always land on his feet. . . . He was very disorganized himself.

He had papers everywhere. You wondered, what was in that stack? But he knew what was there. And he knew exactly what he wanted to do."[49] Teague served until 1979, then made a career as a trade attorney and is now chairman of the conservative Fund for American Studies.

Mueller, hired as a speechwriter, served briefly as chief of staff in 1979. Like Zelaska, he was recruited by Jude Wanniski. Mueller originally got Wanniski's attention by favorably reviewing *The Way the World Works* as an editorial writer for the newspaper in Wanniski's home town, Morristown, New Jersey. Once hired, he developed into a sophisticated student of economics, going so far as to learn French in order to translate the writings of the French theoretician Jacques Rueff, a classical liberal opposed to Keynesianism.

Mueller said: "Jack did have his foibles, but I've always been struck by how he chose the people to work for him as if actually to counteract those weaknesses." He said Kemp "had a great relationship with the people that he trusted. . . . He took the big picture and I think his sense of tactics from the football field translated very well into the Congress, which is a very fluid situation. Every Member of Congress has to be his own Secretary of State, his own Secretary of Defense, and so you could find yourself doing almost anything. Jack was great at seeing changes on the field, as it were."[50]

Smick, a young Senate policy staffer, was chief of staff from 1979 to 1984—also recommended by Wanniski. He helped steer the staff and Kemp through the Reagan campaign and Reagan's first administration, then left to run for Congress (unsuccessfully). He went on to become a multimillionaire investor. Economics staffer Joe Rogers headed the staff briefly in 1984 before becoming U.S. ambassador to the Asian Development Bank. David Hoppe, House Leader Trent Lott's top aide, took over in 1984 to prepare for Kemp's run for president in 1988. After the campaign, Hoppe went back to serving Lott, who became Senate majority leader. When Kemp became HUD Secretary, Zelaska was his personal assistant, working under chief of staff Scott Reed.

Kemp had one of the best staffs on Capitol Hill. "It was the quality of the people that he hired—that's what made him so intimidating, particularly to people in the White House," said Richard Billmire, Kemp's international economics expert. "I'm not saying everybody was a genius. But it was hard to prevail against him in debate because, well, Jack once said to me, 'I'm smart enough to hire people who are smarter than I am.'"[51]

———

One of the benefits of working for Kemp was seeing a parade of stars coming through his office: his many football pals, some Hall of Famers; NFL Commissioner Pete Rozelle, one of Kemp's best friends; Nobel laureates; anchormen; anti-Marxist rebel leaders; prime ministers; cabinet officers; publishing tycoons; union presidents; philosophers; and, of course, other big shot politicians.

One of the oddest visits ever was from future California governor Arnold Schwarzenegger, movie star and body builder. As Dave Hoppe recounts it,[52] Kemp was eager to meet the Terminator, but had to be on the House floor when he arrived. Heading back to the office, Hoppe said, "You could tell he was excited. His whole body shook as he walked back.

"He bursts through the door and Schwarzenegger is there wearing a suit. Jack throws off his jacket and lays down on the floor and says, 'Schwarzenegger, let's wrestle!' Schwarzenegger was dumbfounded, had no idea what to say. Jack said, 'Come on, let's wrestle!'" The Arnold was not biting, "so finally Jack got up and shook his hand. It was the strangest meeting I've ever seen in my life. But it was quintessentially Jack."

———

Many of Kemp's specific issue positions were developed through a memo- and speech-writing process and meetings that amounted to all-staff seminars. When Wanniski advocated ideas, they generally got sent to Mueller if they were about policy or directly to Kemp if they were about politics. To keep up with Kemp, Mueller had to learn the history of economics. "I had a six-foot shelf of books from the Library of Congress because there was just a wide range of things that he was interested in."

Ever the autodidact, Kemp was always reading two or three books at one time. Teague[53] said, "He did what very few Members of Congress do . . . go back to the primary source. He would be carrying around the great classics." Kemp listed those most influential on his economic thinking as Friedrich von Hayek's *The Constitution of Liberty* and *The Road to Serfdom,* Ludwig von Mises's *Human Action,* and Milton Friedman's *Capitalism and Freedom.*[54]

Kemp also read six newspapers a day, three of which he got at home, the *Wall Street Journal,* his favorite; the *Washington Post;* the *New York Times.* And (before it folded) the *Washington Star* was delivered to the office, along with the *Buffalo Evening News* and the *Buffalo Courier Express.* He also read a supply of news magazines and specialty publications including *Commentary,* the *New Republic, National Review, Human Events,* and Kristol's the *Public Interest.*

Kemp's pattern was to tear articles out of the paper that he wanted staff to pay attention to, find out more about, and get back to him on. He'd often circle an article in red, put a staffer's name on it and drop it in Zelaska's in-box. Press secretary John Buckley said he challenged his staff to stay as up-to-date as he was, but he also relied on them to know details he didn't.[55]

———

Once Kemp settled on an issue stance, he and his staff disseminated it in multiple forums. They integrated his views into floor speeches, wrote op-eds, gave media interviews, and held persuasion sessions with colleagues. Kemp, ever a proselytizer, loved sharing his ideas and was eager to bring people around to his point of view.

Unfortunately, he was notorious for being unable to make a short speech. No one could curb his habit of giving speeches with numerous ending points. Hoppe said, "Jack never finished a speech before the third time he said, 'this is my last point.' At 20 minutes he would say it, at 30 minutes and at 45 and then at 50 or 55 minutes he would be done. So he meant it. He just meant it a half an hour later."[56]

Kemp staffers weren't the only ones begging Kemp to shorten his talks. His foreign policy adviser,[57] Michelle Van Cleave, accompanied Kemp to Tel Aviv at the 1986 rollout of the Lavi fighter plane he had pushed the United States to help Israel build. She traveled back with Senator John Tower (R-TX), who said, "You know, you really should tell Jack not to talk so long. Really, it is not necessary to recite to the Israelis their entire history."[58]

Kemp didn't only run long. He also was notorious among staff members for rarely delivering the speeches they'd prepared for him. Kemp thought he could detect what audiences were interested in and would stray from the plan at the least hint that he saw a better way to reach a crowd. His extemporaneous talks sometimes went awry. Van Cleave once gave him talking points for a speech to the midshipmen at the U.S. Naval Academy and went along to take notes. Also along was Kemp's younger daughter, Judith, a beautiful sixteen-year-old, sitting in the front row. Kemp talked about policy issues, but "mostly inspiration, the importance of taking leadership in life. It was wonderful and they were eating it up, and he gets to a point where he's trying to express something and he started saying, 'It's important to be all that you can be.'

"Back then the U.S. Army slogan was 'Be all that you can be,' so this groan goes up. So he realized that this was not the right refrain to use and he starts working it around a little more. And he said, "I believe in life we should aspire to do great things. That's what I tell my son, Jeff. When he's on the field. I say, 'Just get out there and give it your all. Go all the way. And I tell my younger son, Jimmy, when he's out there, 'Go all the way.' And I tell my daughter, Judith, 'Just go all the . . .' Then he stopped and realized. And she's bright red. It brought down the house."[59]

Richard Billmire, his international economics expert, was another writer whose work Kemp frequently used merely as a point of departure. Billmire would prepare statements and questions for Kemp for foreign policy hearings only to have Kemp say, "Greetings, Mr. Secretary"—then go off on his own and use nothing more that Billmire had written. One day he decided he had had enough: "I actually gave him a speech which said, 'Good morning, Mr. Secretary' and the rest [of the page] was blank. Jack [said to me], 'What's this?' [Secretary of State] George Shultz is sitting there. 'What's this?' I said, 'You only use [what I write] for notes. Now you have room for them.' I'll never forget, he told me to get into his car afterwards. I got into his Thunderbird and we started driving and he just stopped. 'What was that about?' he said. And I said, 'Well, Jack, am I fired?' He said, 'No. Maybe you get a promotion for that!'"[60]

———

As Kemp's fame increased, so did the work his staff members had to do to keep him protected and on track. Zelaska and other staff members called Kemp Pigpen behind his back—referring to the *Peanuts* cartoon character with flies always buzzing around his head.[61] "Wherever he went, there was a stir of activity all around him. Because of his being a football player and . . . then his name being bantered around for president, everyone wanted to be around him," Zelaska said. "People would walk down the hallways and you could hear them whisper, 'That's Jack Kemp's office.'" Crowds followed him asking for autographs, favors, speaking engagements, whatever they could get.

Sometimes Kemp's staff worried he was too kind. Zelaska said, "He'd let people walk all over him. I'd say, 'Not everyone is out for you, Jack. They've got their own agendas.' He didn't see through that sometimes. The more popular he got, it seemed like the less he realized it. . . . He just liked people liking him, I guess. He had an ego, that's no secret. He had an ego."

Aides and family members say that constantly involved as he was with other people, he had few truly close friends and did not cultivate intimacy. "He'd say, 'So and So? He loves me!' 'That guy? He loves me!'" one family member said. "It was all about him." He maintained a distance from most other people during most of his career—possibly from self-absorption, possibly as an outgrowth of his quarterbacking career, where the team leader (at least in his mind) can't be entirely intimate with his players.

On the other hand, he'd go around the office and ask young people what they were up to. One of them told Kemp, "I'm just an intern." He replied, "Nobody around here is just an intern."

———

The men who traveled with Kemp—known in the office as "aides de Kemp"[62]—were often those who came to know him best. They tried to keep him on schedule, looked after his luggage (including his alligator-skin hair-dryer bag), took scary auto and aircraft rides with him, and watched him make overlong speeches and visit housing projects. Along the way they got screamed at and blamed when things went awry, but they also talked to him about policy, screamed back at him, ate meals with him, and watched *Monday Night Football* with him. Many came to consider him a friend for life. "We were never bored, never bored," said Rick Ahearn, who worked for Kemp for ten years, beginning at HUD. "Never a dull moment. You loved him, but he drove you crazy."[63]

On trips, Kemp's traveling aides knocked on his hotel door at 7:05 a.m., delivering him coffee and newspapers. Wherever he was, even in Nome, Alaska, he expected the *Times, Post,* and *Journal* and complained if he couldn't get them. The aides had them faxed if they weren't available. They constantly checked with Zelaska about where he was supposed to be and when—and had to make on-the-spot corrections if a plane was canceled or fog prevented a helicopter trip. They were responsible for checking Kemp's room to look for left-behind clothing, counting the bags going into airplanes, and teaching him how to use cell phones when they came along.

If Kemp was attending a black-tie event, his aides had to know where to find bow ties and cuff links he might have forgotten, sometimes buying them from waiters. Sometimes he harangued his aides for perceived errors; other times, he joked with them about it. Ed Brady, an aide who started as a campaign volunteer in 1986 and became a close family friend, remembers being blamed for the loss of Kemp's AFL championship ring: "In the back of the plane, Jack would always take off his rings just to relax and put them in the cup holders. And sure enough, [he said] I lost the ring because he didn't pick it up out of the cup holder."[64]

Kemp's chronic tardiness didn't make life easy for his aides. A procrastinator, he was frequently late because he felt it necessary to shake every hand in a room, especially those of waiters, kitchen staff, and policemen. J. T. Taylor, who began with Kemp at HUD and worked with him closely until his death, said,[65] "You could look at your watch all you wanted, you could give him the high sign, it would never matter. He would want to stay and connect with every single person in that room." Michael O'Connell said, "The less important the people, the more important they were to Jack."

Another reason Kemp was chronically late was that he never shaved before coming to work in the morning. Instead, he'd always shave in his office bathroom right before leaving for the airport, frustrating his waiting staff. "Jack, you've got a plane in half an hour and you're in there shaving. Why don't you do it in the morning like everyone else?" Zelaska would ask. He'd respond that he had a thick beard and didn't want to have to shave twice.[66] His late shaving often resulted in mad-dash "white knuckle" trips to the airport.

Aides competed to see who could travel the five miles from Rayburn to Washington National Airport (now named for Ronald Reagan) in the shortest time. "I got to be able to do it in eight minutes. The record was seven and a half," remembered O'Connell.[67] Michael Castine, who started with Kemp as an intern in 1976 and worked full time from 1978 to 1981, said, "You would literally leave the office 10 minutes before the plane was leaving in those days. Sharon would call ahead [to the airline] and they would hold the plane." Kemp was proud that he'd discovered the flight attendants' entry door at Reagan that he could enter. When Kemp drove, "he'd pull up, throw it into Park and the car would jump."

When Kemp was late or delayed or an item was lost, it was inevitably his aide's fault. Ahearn said,[68] "We were having arguments with

Jack on a daily basis. So finally we drew up a sheet and had it typed by the scheduler. It [listed], 'Drive time from [Kemp's home] to Dulles' or '[Home] to National' and two or three other locations. And we walked into his office and said, 'Would you please read this and sign it?' Because every day he would argue with us about how long it took to get somewhere. . . ."

In one celebrated episode among Kemp's staff, planning ahead didn't work. While serving as HUD secretary, Kemp was invited to the country home of Britain's Prince Charles, who had an interest in urban policy. Ahearn, Kemp's advance man, went to the estate ahead of time to understand where it was and how long it would take to get there. Buckingham Palace had told him lunch was scheduled for noon, and the U.S. embassy had confirmed it. Kemp and Ahearn drove to Highgrove House, arriving before noon and finding no one waiting for them. Kemp told Ahearn to go into the house and find somebody. Ahearn was understandably reluctant to invade the home of Prince Charles, but Kemp insisted, increasingly irritated. At first Ahearn couldn't find anyone. Kemp insisted he go farther inside. As it turned out, when he did find a British marine officer, he learned that the prince's schedule had lunch for 12:30, not 12:00. It was a palace-embassy mistake, "but Jack was on my case. 'How could this happen? How could this possibly happen?' I said, 'Jack, this is an English screw up,'" not his. Finally, the prince arrived and they had their lunch. "But it was a classic Kemp moment, where Jack insisted that I walk into the house of the Prince of Wales."[69]

Kemp also often insisted that he knew best with travel directions. He knew Los Angeles so well that if his car got stuck on an interstate, he knew how to make time on back streets. But he also backseat drove in places he'd never visited before. He'd complain about being stuck in traffic, and Ahearn would respond, "Jack, I told you it would be rush hour. That's why I tried to get you to leave the hotel on time, but we're 20 minutes late. . . . It's rush hour, there's nothing we can do about it, that's life." Kemp would relax for a bit, but then he would start pestering the driver: "Are you sure you know where you're going? By the way, is there any factory air in this car? Turn up the air conditioning." They'd turn it up and in a couple of minutes, "It's freezing in here. Turn down the air conditioning."[70]

If Kemp felt his driver wasn't moving fast enough, he would take matters into his own hands. "I remember vividly he would step on my foot on the gas pedal," said Ed Rutkowski, his former teammate and district chief of staff in Buffalo. Kemp once took the wheel and drove on a sidewalk and then into the oncoming traffic lane to make a plane. Another time, he grabbed the steering wheel while Rutkowski was driving, and instead of heading into a road, yanked the car into a clump of bushes. "I was sure there was a road there," he said.[71]

The speeding trips were made both more and less complicated by Kemp's high profile. Were Kemp's vehicle to get in an accident while speeding or breaking a traffic law, Kemp knew he might be in trouble. He once ordered his Buffalo office manager, Marie Shattuck, to run a red light, covering his face with a magazine so constituents in the crosswalk wouldn't recognize him. But he had ways of getting out of trouble. Rutkowski said, "If we got stopped by the police, he said, 'tell him I'll get him an autographed football. Tell him I've got to get to the airport.'"[72] After being stopped more than once, he carried signed footballs in the back of his car to avoid tickets.[73]

As frustrating as driving him was, his aides preferred that to having him drive them. Zelaska had personal experience. "I was scared to death because he would just go so fast and seemed so reckless, zipping in and out of lanes, running red lights."

———

Aides got into screaming matches with Kemp about more than schedules and speeding. Ever a fan of competition, Kemp routinely pitted his aides against each other. Brady said,[74] "It was his game. It was his way . . . to vet ideas in order to make a right decision." But at one point, Brady felt Kemp had gone too far and intervened when Kemp was pitting two aides against each other in Iowa. Kemp got furious with him, but he came back a few hours later to say "You doing okay?" Neither man apologized, but he'd smoothed things over and both men moved on.

Similarly, Ahearn recalls that Kemp frequently ejected him from his hotel suite in an argument. But "the next day or in a few hours we would talk it over and he'd laugh and I'd laugh and we'd patch everything up."[75] He shouted at Zelaska too. "Oh, he could be irritating sometimes . . . so irritating. But the thing about Jack, he never ever held a grudge. He could yell and scream at you one minute and the next minute . . . he'd make it up to you."[76]

———

Kemp's screaming included profanity—except when Joanne Kemp was present. The aides describe her as "a saint," "unbelievable," "calming," and "his ground." Usually a word from her would calm him. "The minute he would start to act up, she didn't even have to say anything other than, occasionally, 'Jack,'" one aide recalled.[77] J. T. Taylor, who eventually became Kemp's business partner, said that during his 1996 vice presidential campaign, he got into a furious argument with Kemp that began on his plane, with aides watching, and continued through a motorcade. "After the event, we got back into the car. A little bit more screaming. Back into the plane, again the eruption started, with advisers present. Joanne and I took Jack back into this very private area in the front of the plane. I left the two of them alone for about 10 minutes. He came back and apologized to everyone for his behavior."[78]

Besides relying on Joanne Kemp, staff members employed various tricks to calm Kemp down. One was to act hysterical themselves with airport employees or others—whereupon Kemp would intervene to calm them down. And Zelaska advised them: if you want him to do something (or not), suggest the opposite.

———

Despite the difficulty of working with a nearly uncontrollable force of nature, Kemp's former staff members loved him. They grew to be like a close-knit family. "We still keep up after all these years. We meet for parties and are godparents to each other's kids. . . . It was a tone that Jack set, really," Mueller said.[79]

Kemp's staff members uniformly still admire him and think of their time with him as high points of their careers. Ahearn said,[80] "It's true that we always recognized that we were his staff, we were not his co-equals, but he treated us in many respects as equals. . . . Once you became a friend of Jack Kemp's you were a friend for life, as I think all of us were blessed to be." Van Cleave added, "I think we all felt that it was a privilege to work for him, not because he was perfect and not because he didn't have his foibles and not because there weren't lots of times of frustration, because there were all of these and then some. But working for Jack was a deep privilege. And it was easy because I knew what he thought and how to work for him . . . because there was a clarity of this thinking about what was important and his values and the ideas he thought were important. . . . Being a member of the Kemp staff trans-lated into being a member of a Kemp community that endured well beyond the campaigns and very much became part of our lives."[81]

By running the office like a quarterback runs a team, Teague said, "he expected the players on his team to do what they were supposed to do. . . . The quarterback can't do it all." He did change his mind on the fly, but for a reason: "What a quarterback does is, he releases the ball to whomever is open, based on a hundredth-of-a-second decision. You don't make decisions in advance. You make them at the last moment."[82] Ulti-mately, Kemp would listen to all of his dedicated staffers, brilliant advis-ers, and smart colleagues, but then the quarterback would do it his way.

Six

COURAGE

Kemp's staff couldn't control him, and neither could House colleagues, including his best friends. When Kemp was running for president in 1988, Trent Lott set up a fund-raiser for him in Jackson, Mississippi. Heading into the dinner, Lott told Kemp, "Jack, I love you. But for the next hour, shut up about opening the party for African Americans," not a favorite topic in the southern white GOP. Kemp listened, nodded "uh-huh, uh-huh, uh-huh." "Then he went in and spoke for the next 35 minutes about opening the party to African-Americans," press secretary John Buckley said. "I was proud of Jack all the time I worked for him, but I think that was the proudest moment of all."[1]

In a similar performance, Kemp went to speak at arch-conservative Bob Jones University in South Carolina. Kemp's state chairman said, "Okay . . . don't talk about Lincoln. Don't talk about labor. And, whatever you do, don't talk about the Pope." John Paul II had just been in the United States. "That's all Kemp talked about the entire time," aide Mary Brunette Cannon said. "He started out by quoting the Holy Father. There was something delightfully perverse about Jack's willingness to do exactly what he was told not to do, out of conviction."[2]

His devotion to conviction didn't always endear him to Reagan or many of his fellow congressmen in the continuing battles over supply-side economics.

As much as Kemp revered Reagan, he was anything but a rubber stamp for his president on domestic or foreign policy. Even though he was the number three leader of House Republicans, he opposed Reagan when he raised taxes, as he did eleven times after 1981.[3] And Kemp repeatedly called for replacing inflation-fighting Federal Reserve chairman Paul Volcker, though Reagan supported him.

When Kemp went "off the reservation," he took heat for it. In his diary, Reagan declared Kemp "unreasonable" and "a purist" when he opposed the nearly $100 billion tax increase that Reagan was persuaded to back in 1982. At another point, Reagan wrote that Kemp "knows I'm mad at him" when he worked against a Reagan international finance policy.

Reagan's private barbs were mild compared to the vituperation heaped on Kemp by Reagan insiders, who leaked story after story to the media accusing him of rank disloyalty and of putting his own political interests ahead of the president's.

For sure, he had ambition. He was planning to run for president in 1988. But mainly he was holding true to his beliefs. He did not always get it right, but he acted on principle. He believed he was keeping true to Reaganism when he thought Reagan aides were systematically undermining it. Kemp said what he thought regardless of the flak he took. He was not disloyal. He was courageous.

———

The recession of 1981–82 was brutal. Between Reagan's taking office and November 1982, the unemployment rate surged from 7.5 percent to 10.8 percent, the highest ever since the Great Depression. It stayed above 10 percent through May of 1983 and above 8 percent until February 1984. Eleven million people were out of work in 1982.

Who and what was to blame? Democrats insisted it was Reagan and supply-side economics. They said the tax cuts produced huge budget deficits, and the deficits sopped up available capital, causing interest rates to rise and depressing business activity. Old-school Republicans accepted this analysis, including many on Reagan's White House staff. They favored tax increases and spending cuts to reduce the deficit. Supply-siders like Kemp, on the other hand, believed that Volcker's tight monetary policy caused the recession. And they regarded it as madness to raise taxes during hard times.

As soon as the 1981 tax cuts were signed into law, battle lines were drawn. Democrats and many Republicans wanted to raise taxes immediately. Kemp's camp held strong, and Reagan struggled in the middle. In December 1981, Reagan wrote in his diary, "My team is pushing for a tax increase to hold down the deficits. I'm being stubborn. I think our tax cuts will produce more revenue by stimulating the economy, I intend to wait and see some results."[4]

James Baker would later recognize that Kemp was right about the cause of the recession. He called himself a "reformed drunk," a convert to supply-side economics.[5] But as White House chief of staff, he and other aides, and Nancy Reagan, pushed Reagan to roll back some 1981 cuts.[6] Baker felt that tax increases were a political necessity. He praised Reagan as a "principled pragmatist" and "a good negotiator . . . willing to take 80 percent" to get a deal. Kemp, though, was a "purist" and "a loose cannon."[7] Baker said compromises were necessary to get Reagan's program through Congress. Baker & Company didn't only work on Reagan behind closed doors. They constantly leaked stories to the media, saying that whatever Reagan might say and believe, tax increases were coming.

Leading up to Reagan's January 26, 1982, State of the Union address, speculation centered on Reagan's calling for excise taxes on tobacco, beer, liquor, and gasoline, as well as closing business loopholes opened in the 1981 bill. Baker was pushing those measures as a way of reducing David Stockman's deficit projections. Kemp, though, said Stockman's deficit estimates of $152 billion for fiscal 1983 and $162 billion for fiscal 1984 were overstated. He declared that "the forces of timidity and defeatism are having their hour, but I have hope that the president will decide the right thing in the end."[8]

Kemp spared no effort to persuade Reagan to hold the course, but Reagan's plans were surprisingly vague. After a fifty-five-minute session with the president on January 11, Kemp and other House Republican leaders left with opposite impressions of what he might do. GOP leader Bob Michel said Reagan appeared to be "facing reality" and was inclined toward tax increases. Kemp predicted that Reagan would reject his advisers' advice to raise taxes.[9]

That same week, Kemp and Lott wrote a populist letter to their former ally, Stockman, accusing him of advocating tax increases on "the little guy"—beer and gasoline—while keeping secret a list of corporate subsidies worth as much as $40 billion a year.[10] "At a time when the world is awash in oil, the federal government is spending over $3 billion to build synfuel plants for Exxon, Gulf and Union Oil of California," they wrote. "Dave, why are Food Stamps, AFDC, Medicaid and Head Start touchable, but not Exxon, Boeing and Gulf Oil?" They said there was no reason to raise taxes, least of all taxes that would hurt ordinary families.

To Kemp's dismay, on January 20, Reagan yielded to his aides. He wrote in his diary: "First anniversary [of inauguration]. A budget meeting and pressure from everyone to give in to increases in excise taxes. . . . I finally gave in, but my heart wasn't in it."[11] The news was leaked instantly to the *Times*. Its story the next day declared that Reagan, "in a rebuff to supply-siders," had decided to announce excise tax increases on gasoline, whiskey, and wine.[12]

The leak infuriated Reagan. And the day after he yielded, he reconsidered. After meeting with business leaders assembled by the U.S. Chamber of Commerce, Reagan wrote in his diary,[13] "They made an impassioned plea that I not raise any taxes. They were touching a nerve when they said I would look as though I were retreating from my own program. That's exactly how I feel." Also that day, Kemp organized fifteen Reagan-for-President campaign state chairmen and cochairmen to write Reagan advising against raising taxes.[14]

Reagan repaired to snowy Camp David to work on his State of the Union speech, recording in his diary that beforehand "I told our guys I couldn't go for tax increases. If I have to be criticized, I'd rather be criticized for a deficit rather than for backing down from our economic program."[15]

And sure enough, in his speech to Congress January 26, Reagan declared, "I promised the American people to bring their tax rates down and keep them down. I will stand by my word." Unnamed "doubters" wanted to undo the 1981 cuts, he said, but "raising taxes won't balance the budget. It will encourage more government spending and less private investment. Raising taxes will slow economic growth, reduce production and destroy future jobs, making it more difficult for those without jobs to find them and more likely that those who now have jobs could lose them."[16] Kemp was pleased, and at the next day's White House briefing, reporters misled by leaks demanded to know if Baker still had his job.[17] He certainly did.

Kemp had won a temporary victory on the tax front, but on monetary policy, he lost. Kemp wanted Volcker replaced, but on February 14, 1982, Reagan met with the Fed chairman for a widely publicized "public embrace." A few days later Reagan explicitly endorsed the Fed's tight-money, high-interest, anti-inflationary policies.[18] Further confirming that Reagan backed what Kemp called "pain economics," Stockman appeared at a Chamber of Commerce breakfast March 4 and declared unemployment "part of the cure, not the problem."[19] This was policy Kemp had charged Jimmy Carter with pursuing.

Matters only got worse for Kemp. Despite the president's State of the Union vow, the Stockman-prepared budget Reagan submitted on February 6 called for $20.7 billion in tax increases.[20] Then in late February, Senate budget chairman Pete Domenici produced a proposal raising taxes $122 billion over three years, five times Reagan's level. Despite this gross reversal of 1981 policy, White House spokesman Larry Speakes labeled it "a good faith effort to come up with a comprehensive alternative."[21]

Most senior Republicans in Congress sided with the White House tax raisers. Senate Finance Committee chairman Bob Dole compiled a list of tax increases totaling $105 billion. Contemptuous of supply-siders—ex-quarterback Kemp, in particular—Dole went to the U.S. Chamber of Commerce and delivered a famous jibe: "The good news is that a bus loaded with supply-siders went over a cliff. The bad news is that there were three empty seats." Dole claimed he didn't know who was absent, but added "the bad news is that they are huddling with the president. That's an inside joke."

Despite Reagan's allergy to tax increases, he authorized Baker to negotiate with congressional leaders on the budget and taxes. The "Gang of 12," as the negotiators became known, met in secret at Baker's home. Reagan's flip-flopping led to press accounts that the president was being manipulated by his staff. Reagan wrote personal letters condemning those reports: "There has not been one single instance of Jim Baker doing anything but what I settled on as policy," he wrote.[22] It remains a mystery to this day whether Reagan was dissembling or expressing his real views when he denounced the idea of raising taxes—right before raising them.

The maneuvering by Senate Republicans and White House staffers emboldened Democrats to push for even bigger changes in Reagan policy. House Ways and Means chairman Dan Rostenkowski proposed $165 billion in tax increases, including cancellation of rate cuts scheduled for 1983. To the frustration of the supply-siders, the president actually accepted $122 billion in new tax increases over three years and agreed to consider a ninety-day delay in the third year of his tax cuts— if Democrats agreed to serious spending restraints.[23]

If Reagan was conflicted on taxes, Kemp was not. Far from agreeing with the president's compromises, Kemp said he'd like to see more tax cuts. "I'm not going to stop until the top rate is 25 percent and the bottom is 5 percent." He wrote "Dear Colleague" letters to fellow House Republicans opposing White House policy, yet expressed confidence Reagan was firmly on his side, despite the evidence. He said in one speech in Chicago,[24] "Republicans who are worried about the president's strong leadership, they'll come around." He referred to businessmen and bankers who called for defense cuts and tax increases as "trepidatious" and said it was the Fed's "impossible, flawed, mistaken" policies that caused the recession. But Kemp was unable to make his case to Reagan one on one—only in group sessions with House GOP leaders.[25]

Reagan finally agreed by telephone with members of the Senate Budget Committee to a compromise consisting of $98 billion in tax increases and $22 billion in defense cuts. According to Baker, he capitulated reluctantly when Baker, Meese, and Deaver told him there was no other way: "All right, goddammit. I'm gonna do it, but it's wrong."[26]

Despite his qualms, Reagan defended the plan to business groups as necessary to contain deficits, which Senate Republicans claimed would top $180 billion in 1983 if Congress failed to act. The Senate Budget Committee promptly approved the $98 billion tax increase, as well as spending reductions of $319 billion and Social Security "savings" of $40 billion over three years.[27]

In the House, Republican leaders made the budget vote a test of party loyalty. Kemp, though a member of the GOP leadership, maintained his opposition, though he did avoid embarrassing the party. He voted no, but kept quiet and saved his vote to the end, explaining, "I did not want my vote to defeat Reagan's budget. I fought for the last six months, inside the administration and the leadership meetings on Capitol Hill and I lost."[28] He was one of only fifteen Republicans to vote no. Most Democrats also voted no—but because they wanted bigger tax increases. The budget resolution passed, 219–206.

The fight was not over. The budget resolution only laid down the parameters of policy—legislation still had to be passed to put the measures into effect. Accordingly, Dole's Senate Finance Committee voted $98.3 billion in new taxes, a minimum tax on individuals and corporations, tax withholding on dividends and interest, and repeal of nearly 95 percent of the business investment breaks in the 1981 tax cut bill.[29] The measure—the Tax and Fiscal Responsibility Act of 1982 (TEFRA)—passed the Senate, and the House voted to go directly to a conference on a final bill.

A new Kemp-led rebellion ensued. Kemp wrote Reagan a letter with fifty-nine House cosigners warning that the GOP was "in danger of making a U-turn back to its familiar role as tax collector for Democratic spending programs."[30] Kemp assembled a group of "New Right" leaders in his office to work against the bill, including the Reverend Jerry Falwell of the Moral Majority.[31]

Reagan and his aides moved aggressively to crush the rebellion. Kemp was at the White House and saw Reagan twice in a day in early August. Reagan wrote in his diary after the meetings, "Met with Jack Kemp [alone] and then in the leadership meeting. He is adamant that we are wrong on the tax increase. . . . He is, in fact, unreasonable. The tax increase is the price we have to pay to get the budget cuts."[32]

White House aides targeted Kemp with a campaign of press leaks over the following days, some of them savage. One story reported he had "clashed" with Ed Meese at the "tempestuous" first meeting, then was "assailed" at the GOP leadership meeting by Senator Paul Laxalt of Nevada. "You are talking about leadership, but the question is whether you want to lead or the president should lead," Laxalt reportedly told Kemp.[33]

One leak quoted unnamed officials as saying that Kemp had been "taken to the woodshed" and told "he should not attempt to be a leader of a minority within a minority." Meetings were dubbed "a verbal slugfest" and "a shouting match."[34] Sources said Kemp was chewed out not only by Laxalt, but also by Dole and Senator Strom Thurmond (R-SC).

The *Los Angeles Times* reported on August 6 that a White House official said of Kemp, "We've had enough. . . . This is supposed to be a team, and he's gotten off of it."[35] White House aides suggested Kemp's opposition might be an effort to "position himself for a presidential run or disassociate himself from the administration's troubled economic policies."[36] Dole piled on with a *Washington Post* op-ed on August 9 asserting that he was more consistently loyal to Reagan than Kemp.[37] He identified TEFRA as tax reform, a tack Reagan soon adopted.

Fighting back, Kemp immediately organized a closed-door "urgent conference" of more than a dozen conservatives, including Wanniski, Kristol, and Kemp's congressional allies. They were joined by four recently departed administration officials also against the increases: ex–White House economist Martin Anderson and political operative Lyn Nofziger, as well as ex-Treasury officials Paul Craig Roberts and Norman Ture. One participant was quoted as saying, "You can't have the largest tax cut in history and turn around and have the largest tax increase in history."

Anderson and Nofziger had worked for Reagan going back to his years as California governor. White House officials were desperate to lure them back into the Reagan fold. Anderson held out, but Reagan and Baker turned Nofziger around almost immediately. He attacked Kemp on August 9 for opposing the bill.[38] "I don't want to charge Jack with sabotage," Nofziger said. "I think he's sincere. I think that maybe he's a bit fanatical on this. I think he is, in spite of himself, hurting the president and hurting the presidency."[39]

Kemp returned to the White House August 10 for another Reagan persuasion session, after which Reagan said, "Jack sincerely believes—is a purist in supply-side economics. . . . We'll continue to talk and reason together." Asked by reporters if he thought—as others were charging—that Kemp was running for president, Reagan joked, "I didn't know the job was up for grabs."[40] Reagan said the bill "is being dishonestly tagged as the largest tax increase in history. It may be the greatest tax reform."

Kemp responded to White House pressure with a series of op-eds, asserting that he was working in Reagan's and the country's best interests. In one, he called the tax bill both "economic folly" and "political folly"—economic, because it would deepen the recession; political, because it enabled Democrats to claim the GOP was inconsistent and not to be trusted.[41] The White House hit back by leaking more negative stories. The *New York Times* reported,[42] "Key White House officials are convinced that Mr. Kemp wants to build a presidential campaign on the ashes of the Reagan economic program." Kemp expressed outrage at the idea, saying Reagan had personally told him, "I'm sorry that these stories have come out because I know them to be unjust."

Reagan may have thought the attacks unfair, but he was unhappy with Kemp, twice criticizing him at cabinet meetings—once for assailing the Federal Reserve and once for opposing tax increases.[43] This "flashed a green light for personal assaults on Kemp by the White House staff," Evans and Novak reported. Defending Kemp, the columnists accused Baker of orchestrating attacks in "the copyrighted style of Dick Nixon, not Ron Reagan."

More than thirty years after the 1982 events, Meese said the press-leak campaign against Kemp was conducted by Baker or someone on his team.[44] Baker all but admitted as much.[45] "Probably was, probably was. . . . It was probably retribution for Kemp opposing the President. . . . Here he was No. 3 in the leadership and he wouldn't support the president's policy. . . . So, you take a shot at him, right? That's what happened." Implausibly, Baker added, "I'm not saying I did it, because I don't think I did."

Reagan himself denied hard feelings. The *Washington Times*'s Jeremiah O'Leary[46] wrote August 13 that he'd asked whether Kemp was "now out of your coalition." "Oh, no." Reagan replied. "I don't bear grudges or anything, no." Reagan said Kemp was "you might say, a purist to the extent that he just can't see the difference between reform and increase. . . . I am just hard put to understand how he can continue to believe that this in some way represents a turn in my direction or philosophy, because it doesn't." Asked about allegations that Kemp was opposing Reagan to buttress his presidential ambitions for 1984,[47] Reagan said, "No, I'm not going to make any suppositions of that at all. . . . I'll just accept it as a legitimate disagreement."

At 2 a.m. on August 15, House-Senate conferees completed work on the tax bill. The measure doubled taxes on cigarettes, created a 10 percent withholding requirement for dividend and interest income, ended the practice of "safe harbor leasing" whereby unprofitable companies could sell their tax-loss benefits to profit-making companies, and established a minimum tax for upper-bracket taxpayers. Because of Kemp's rebellion, Baker predicted that fewer than half of the 192 House Republicans would vote for the bill, so the conferees added an extension of unemployment benefits to win over Democratic voters. Dole, appearing on *Meet the Press*, again denied the bill represented a total reversal from the 1981 tax cuts, instead suggesting it was a retreat from Kemp's excess: "Maybe we went too far last year with some of Mr. Kemp's ideas. I never really understood all that supply-side business."[48]

Reagan knew that passing the bill would be a challenge. He invited thirty-two House Republicans to Camp David on Sunday to work on them, and he scheduled a national TV address to sell the tax bill to the country.

Speaking from the Oval Office August 16, Reagan observed that "some in my own party object to this bill—and strongly. I am told by many that this bill is not politically popular, and it may not be. Why then do I support it? I support it because it's right for America. I support it because it's fair. I support it because it will, when combined with our cuts in government spending, reduce interest rates and put more Americans back to work again."[49] After the speech, Kemp said he was "disappointed that the president has used his considerable eloquence and influence to support a tax increase I believe will harm the economy."

TEFRA passed both the House and Senate—226–202 in the House, with 123 Democrats and 103 Republicans voting for it and 89 Republicans against, including Kemp. In the Senate, the vote was 52–47, with 9 Democrats and 43 Republicans for it. House GOP leaders credited Reagan's last-minute lobbying for getting his party's House "Aye" total over 100.

Kemp addressed the House for five minutes toward the end of a day of debate. He had fought hard and lost, weathering attacks along the way. Addressing the leaked charges against him, he said, "This is not really a clash of purism versus pragmatism or party or personality. It is a historic clash of ideas." He likened raising taxes in the 1982 recession to Congress's choices in the 1930s: "There was high unemployment, there was a huge deficit, the president wanted a tax increase and the Congress went blindly along with it. Interestingly enough, interest rates did not go down; they went up. Unemployment did not go down; it went up, the deficit grew and recession deepened into the Great Depression."

Kemp had lost a crucial battle, but he wasn't entirely defeated. Despite the White House's enmity, his profile had risen. In a postmortem on Kemp's fight, the *Wall Street Journal*'s Albert Hunt said it had "transformed him from an interesting young lawmaker with political promise into a man in the big leagues of Republican party and presidential politics."[50]

Kemp reiterated that he was not acting out of political calculation, the proof of which is "I have been arguing against tax increases for years." Newt Gingrich confirmed that it was not a smart political move; as a result of the fight, Reagan probably would undercut Kemp in his succession fight with Bush. "Jack's actions were courageous," he concluded. [51]

———

With unemployment at 10.8 percent in November and December 1982 and the economy shrinking by almost 2 percent for the year, Reagan's approval rating fell from a high of 68 percent early in his presidency to 43 percent at the time of the 1982 midterm elections. Republicans lost twenty-seven seats on November 2, though they gained one Senate seat. Kemp campaigned for sixty-five GOP candidates in twenty-nine states during the year. Out of Buffalo constantly, Kemp nevertheless was reelected with 75.3 percent of the vote in a newly redrawn, more Republican district. Appearing on CBS's *Face the Nation,* Kemp said that the GOP theme of the year, "Stay the Course," was bland and misdirected. Postmortems on the election were mixed. The *Washington Post*'s David Broder wrote[52] that the voters "struck at the heart of the rigid, doctrinaire element of Reaganomics," defeating sixteen Republicans who'd voted with Kemp against the 1982 tax bill. The *Wall Street Journal* editorialized that 1982 was just "a fairly typical midterm election" but delivered "a warning shot toward the White House" not to mention raising taxes for the rest of Reagan's term. [53]

———

In the lame duck session after the 1982 House losses, Newt Gingrich launched a project to seize control of the chamber after fifty years of nearly uninterrupted Democratic rule. He founded the Conservative Opportunity Society (COS). It was composed of many members of Kemp's backfield, but its purpose was not only advancing ideas, but exposing Democratic misrule. Gingrich was an originator of modern-day polarization politics, which Kemp lamented. COS activists brought ethics charges against Democratic Speaker Jim Wright and succeeded in ousting him in 1989. Five years later, they captured the House and Gingrich became Speaker.

"Conservative Opportunity Society" was a name carefully selected to counter what its leaders called the Democrats' "Liberal Welfare State." Weber was one of Gingrich's first recruits.[54] Others included Lungren, Mack, Walker, and Coats, though Coats quickly dropped out. Kemp and GOP whip Trent Lott, as members of the House leadership, were not in COS. They "didn't want to get branded [with] a group of junior mavericks," Weber said,[55] and felt they needed to stay on reasonably good terms with Democratic Speaker Tip O'Neill and then-majority leader Wright. Gingrich was a challenge too to moderate GOP leader Bob Michel of Illinois, a popular figure.

While Kemp served as leadership liaison to COS and sent staff to COS meetings, Weber[56] said that he was "never entirely comfortable" waging war against Democratic leaders. "He was very excited about us because we were enthusiastic about all of his issues, but I don't think he was enthusiastic about us going after Jim Wright. Jack was never a negative person."

One COS technique was to make speeches at the end of a day's House session—so-called special orders—vilifying Democrats. The House floor was virtually vacant, but COS members reached the public via C-SPAN, which began full-time cable coverage of the House in 1979. Weber said,[57] "We were always trying to get Jack to do special orders. You have to give Newt Gingrich credit for that—he understood the power of C-SPAN. He said to me, 'Jack listens to you. Go tell him he needs to do more Special Orders. Tell him he might have half a million people watching him.'" Weber told Kemp, "We're educating the country. This is what you're good at. You've got half a million people watching." Kemp responded, "'Yes, but I can't hear them cheering.' I've thought that said a lot about the kind of energy he would get from a crowd that just wasn't there. That was not what he was going to do."

Bob Walker was the COS member whose fiery C-SPAN speeches

led Democratic House Speaker Tip O'Neill in 1984 to order cameras to show GOP speakers were addressing an empty chamber. His speeches were so effective that Kemp was approached by a citizen in Puerto Rico who asked, "Aren't you Jack Kemp, a Congressman?" When Kemp said he was, the voter responded, "Well, then you know Bob Walker!"[58]

In founding COS,[59] Weber said, "Newt had the conceptual framework that you needed a set of magnet issues that would attract [followers] and . . . a set of wedge issues that would divide the Democratic party and divide you from the Democrats.

"There was no such thing as a wedge issue in Jack Kemp's vocabulary. Everything was a magnet issue. And if he couldn't convince you, he'd just keep trying. But the notion that we were going to have divisive issues that might [work politically], even if they were dividing the country in our favor, that really wasn't a part of Jack Kemp's mentality."

Gingrich agrees he had an attitude toward conflict opposite Kemp's. "I agreed with Mao. Politics is war without blood. War is politics with blood. And I'd seen my party fail." He said he didn't discuss his differences with Kemp. "It wasn't worth the effort. Jack was tremendous at being Jack. But you'd be asking him to do something so outside his experience and realm of behavior. As long as he didn't get in my way, I didn't care."[60]

———

Unlike Gingrich, Kemp had a strong bipartisan streak. And he had close Democratic friends. He worked on Buffalo-area projects with Representative Henry Nowak, who served in Congress from 1975 to 1993. Nowak was often at dinner at the Kemps' home, as was Senator Sam Nunn of Georgia, who shared many of Kemp's foreign policy views. Another Buffalo Democrat was John LaFalce, who said "Jack was unbelievably generous" in including him at press conferences announcing Reagan projects benefiting the region. "Jack embodied everything that was positive about politics, not negative, and he would hate the negativism that has existed in politics these past many years." LaFalce got consulted in 1996 by Representative Tom Downey (D-NY), who was tapped to play

Kemp as Vice President Al Gore prepared for their debate. Downey asked how Kemp would attack Gore. LaFalce replied, "He will not attack Al. . . . Jack Kemp is constitutionally unable to go negative."[61]

Speaker Tip O'Neill clearly detested Kemp-Roth and Reaganomics, but his press secretary, now MSNBC anchor Chris Matthews, said he can't think of O'Neill's ever saying anything negative about Kemp himself.[62] Similarly, the liberal scholar on Congress, Norman Ornstein of the American Enterprise Institute, says[63] that Democrats never suspected that Kemp was anything other than "the real deal compassionate conservative." Ornstein thinks that "if Kemp had prevailed, we would be looking at a majority Republican party today" because a Kempian GOP could win 40 to 50 percent of the Hispanic vote and 15 to 20 percent of the African American vote (versus 27 percent and 6 percent, respectively, for Mitt Romney in 2012).

Kemp often cosponsored legislation with Democrats—enterprise zones and establishment of the Martin Luther King Jr. holiday with Robert Garcia of the South Bronx, job-training bills with Representative Bill Gray of Pennsylvania, voting rights for the District of Columbia with D.C. delegate Walter Fauntroy, and a measure to curb the independence of the Federal Reserve with Byron Dorgan of North Dakota. Julian Dixon of California told the *Washington Post*'s David Broder, for a piece likening Kemp to Hubert Humphrey,[64] that Kemp was the Republican best liked by members of the Congressional Black Caucus. Kemp's bipartisanship and advocacy for poor people and minorities would hurt him as a GOP presidential candidate. He persisted in them out of conviction.

———

Officially, the Reagan-Volcker recession ended in November 1982, according to the National Bureau of Economic Research. What proved a robust long-term recovery began in 1983. But that was not clear to Kemp or any other major political actor until well into the year. In what seemed like an urgent fight to save the economy, Kemp spent most of 1983 fighting on two fronts—on fiscal policy and monetary policy.

On fiscal policy, he battled his usual adversaries in the White House and Congress who wanted to raise taxes. Despite Reagan's early agreement and a budget resolution calling for $73 billion in new revenues over three years—as well as a last-minute effort by House Democrats to pass an $8 billion tax hike—no income tax increase legislation actually passed in 1983. As Congress was on the verge of enacting one, Reagan threatened a veto.[65] However, Congress did pass—and Reagan did sign—a $24.6 billion annual increase in payroll taxes.

Kemp especially fought against a plan to enact what was variously called a "trigger tax," a "standby tax," or a "contingency tax" that would take effect if the budget deficit exceeded two percent of GDP. To Kemp's disappointment, Stockman convinced Reagan that deficits were heading toward $277 billion by 1986, cajoling him into signing off on a $50 billion tax in his fiscal 1984 budget. Reagan was reluctant to approve the tax but couldn't see any other way. "Oh, darn. Oh, darn, it can't be," Stockman said Reagan lamented as he initialed the document. "I never thought it would come to this."[66]

Kemp believed Stockman was cooking the books by underestimating potential growth, overestimating deficits, and advocating policies that would hurt the economy. Stockman called this allegation "ludicrous" and "mumbo-jumbo."[67]

Kemp, not Stockman, was correct about economic growth. It averaged 4.5 percent for the next five years. But Stockman was not far off about the size of Reagan deficits. They averaged over $200 billion a year for the next five years, 5 percent of GDP, and added more than $1 trillion to the national debt.[68] What accounted for that? Not falling revenue. Accounting for population growth and inflation, tax revenue stayed at its twenty-year average.[69] Rather, it was spending that went up, especially for defense, as advocated by Reagan (from under 5 percent of GDP during the Carter years to an average of 5.8 under Reagan). Domestic spending declined from 20 percent of GDP under President Carter to 18.3 percent in 1988.

But the major reason was the collapse of inflation. Because U.S. debts had to be paid back in noninflated dollars, interest payments on the debt went up from 1.6 percent of GDP during the Carter years to above 3, costing $840 million during the Reagan years. Inflation was a double-edged phenomenon. It had hurt savers, investors, and workers, but it helped the Treasury. Paul Volcker conquered inflation, but caused a hair-curling recession. Kemp feared he would never let the economy recover.

————

So Kemp's second big fight in 1983 was with Volcker. Volcker's first term as Fed chairman was up in August 1983, and Kemp urged Reagan to "dump" him.[70] Bravely challenging conventional wisdom, he criticized not only Volcker's decisions on money supply and interest rates—which, he argued, crippled growth—but also the whole basis of U.S. monetary policy. Kemp wanted the United States to return to the gold standard—not just for the value of the dollar to be pegged to a fixed price of gold, but actually to be exchangeable for gold by U.S. citizens and foreigners. He believed the United States should lead the world back toward the system that had prevailed for most of the nineteenth century and early twentieth century, when international accounts were settled in gold. During that era, prices were stable (except in wartime) and economies boomed, he argued. Kemp's dream was for the United States to convene an international conclave like the 1944 Bretton Woods Conference, where leading nations would agree on a stable exchange-rate system.

At Bretton Woods, nations pegged their currencies to the value of the dollar, which in turn was valued in gold. The system fell apart in 1971. Due to the inflationary effects of the Great Society and the Vietnam War, the value of the dollar weakened and foreigners held more dollars than the United States had gold. President Nixon responded by decreeing that dollars would no longer be convertible in gold. As a result, currencies "floated" against each other, their value determined either by their central banks (in the U.S. case, the Fed), by trade balances or by foreign investors' willingness to purchase their debt.

Kemp, self-taught in economics, had become an expert in the difficult fields of monetary policy and international finance. He staged several high-profile conferences promoting fixed exchange rates and reducing third world debt. He made the argument that U.S. workers were losing jobs because floating money values allowed other nations' products to undersell America's. He also argued that floating rates resembled a situation where a yardstick was thirty-six inches long one day, thirteen the next, and forty-five the day after. "Money cannot be a useful standard of value unless it keeps its value," he wrote.[71]

Though he didn't have a problem explaining the importance of fixed exchange rates, Kemp always had a hard time explaining clearly why the country needed the gold standard. Sometimes he altered his terms, arguing for "a dollar as good as gold," but the idea never got traction with policy makers, voters, or the media. Indeed, his quest seemed quixotic and his efforts to sell "gold" as a policy became almost a laughingstock. He was serious about a serious subject, but his efforts didn't strengthen his stature as a national leader.

Why could Kemp not make the case? For one thing, twentieth-century Americans, most politicians, and the media found the whole subject of monetary policy abstruse. That was in contrast to the eighteenth and nineteenth centuries, when "hard" versus "soft" money was the central argument of popular politics, as demonstrated by William Jennings Bryan's 1896 "Cross of Gold" speech. Moreover, most leading economic thinkers, notably Milton Friedman, were against the gold standard. As a monetarist, Friedman believed price stability and prosperity could be maintained if the Fed—or even a computer—calibrated the nation's money supply needs, expanding to combat deflation, contracting to counter inflation.

In the face of such opposition, Kemp couldn't gain traction. Reagan occasionally listened to progold arguments, but he never acted beyond appointing a commission to study the issue in 1981. The panel had only two members, out of sixteen, who supported gold, and it was led by Friedman intimate Anna Schwartz. As expected, the panel's 1982 report basically ended serious debate on the issue. When Kemp introduced a gold standard bill in 1984, he had just six House cosponsors. and the measure went nowhere.

Unable to change the essence of monetary policy, Kemp constantly criticized Volcker for his management of it. After he had crushed inflation (from 13.3 percent in November 1979 to below 2.3 per cent in mid-1983), Volcker began to expand the money supply and lower interest rates, with the prime rate descending from its all-time high of 21.5 percent in December 1980 to 10.5 percent in mid-1983. His actions helped the economy grow. But Kemp and administration officials worried that a strengthening economy might lead Volcker to tighten again to contain inflation, thus weakening the recovery. In a letter Kemp wrote Volcker in March 1983,[72] he declared that "no one knows what to expect from the Federal Reserve," that there were "ominous signs of a return to the disastrous policy of mechanical monetarism abandoned last fall," and that the United States and the world "must be wracked by the appearance of confusion, inconsistency and indecision."

A consummate bureaucrat, Volcker placated worried White House aides, who were considering Alan Greenspan as a possible replacement chairman. And he invited Kemp to address the Fed Board of Governors. But Kemp, unappeased, mounted a late campaign for Fed vice chairman Preston Martin to become chairman. On June 18, though, Reagan announced he was reappointing Volcker.

Kemp didn't give up. At the time of Volcker's Senate confirmation hearings, Kemp urged Reagan to drop the nomination if the Fed made "a widely-predicted decision to tighten the money supply." He said such a move would "threaten aborting the recovery."[73] Volcker was confirmed by the Senate on July 28, 1983, by a vote of 84–16.

Kemp's feuding with Volcker continued into 1984. Reagan shared Kemp's concern that tight money would stifle the recovery as he faced reelection,[74] but Kemp went beyond the White House's short-term attempts to alter Fed policy. He proposed to reduce the institution's political independence.[75]

His legislation called for the treasury secretary to be a member of the Fed's Federal Open Market Committee, giving the administration some say over interest rate policy. He also called for minutes of FOMC meetings to be promptly made public. The legislation went nowhere. Democrats feared passing it would signal that the Fed, not Reagan, was to blame for an economic slowdown.

Volcker defended himself against Kemp's charges of mismanagement:[76] "We certainly have no desire to see real GNP decline or the unemployment rate to rise," he wrote, "and we believe that our policies are consistent with continued growth . . . sufficient to bring about a lower jobless rate by the end of the year." Indeed, the politically sensitive unemployment rate dropped from 8 percent in January to 7.3 percent in November.[77] Inflation stayed in the 4 percent range, giving Reagan the opportunity to claim that he'd turned the economy around. And the economy kept growing until 1990. The upshot is that Volcker knew what he was doing and Reagan appreciated it. Whether the economy could have grown sooner and faster—as Kemp believed—is unknowable.

———

As the 1984 election season began, Kemp's political courage was put to the test again over the future of U.S. tax policy. The debate caused conflict among Republicans at the GOP National Convention, pitting supply-siders against the Reagan White House in "the battle of the comma." Because it was a key issue in Reagan's presidential race against Democrat Walter Mondale, the issue had added political potency.

Democrats held their 1984 convention first, in San Francisco. In his acceptance speech, Mondale declared, "Let's tell the truth. It must be done. Mr. Reagan will raise taxes and so will I. He won't tell you. I just did." Rostenkowski, on the convention floor, told a reporter Mondale had made a political blunder even though Democrats (including Rostenkowski himself) had long favored tax increases.[78]

As the GOP platform was being drafted before the Republican convention in Dallas, Kemp and Gingrich sought an explicit "no-tax-increase" pledge to sharpen Reagan's contrast with Mondale.[79] The White House staff preferred not to make a binding promise. Dole, not surprisingly, declared that "it would not be responsible to put into the platform that we won't raise taxes."[80]

A week before the convention, Reagan issued a statement saying that while Mondale planned to raise taxes as "a first resort," he would raise them only as "a last resort."[81] Draft language on the tax plank was faxed back and forth between Dallas and the White House, where Deputy Chief of Staff Richard Darman was insisting on language giving the president options. Kemp & Company—including the platform chairman, Trent Lott, and the economic policy subcommittee chairman, Senator Bob Kasten of Wisconsin—were insisting on no-tax-increase language. The dispute boiled down to a comma—in or out. Kemp's side wanted the platform to read that the GOP opposed "any attempt to increase taxes, which would harm the recovery and reverse the trend to restoring control of the economy to individual Americans." Without the comma, taxes might be raised which were deemed not to inhibit recovery.

The back-and-forth got so heated that Lott called Baker and said, "I don't want Dick Darman in Dallas. I don't want him near Dallas. I don't want him on the phone with anybody in Dallas. If you've got something to say, you say it to me."[82] Kemp and Lott won and the final platform contained the comma. The platform also condemned the Fed in Kempian language and suggested a return to the gold standard. Kemp characterized the platform as "a very populist document, not a right-wing document," as it was being described in the press, mainly for its strong antiabortion language.[83] He also described it as "the most radical platform in the history of any party."[84]

At the convention, Kemp again had a prime-time speaking slot. Any disputes he may have had with Reagan policy disappeared. After beginning, "What a difference a president makes!" he continued, "What a difference leadership makes. Our economy is expanding again without inflation. The United States is respected again. Our adversaries are on the defensive. America is once again a model for other countries. And Ronald Reagan actually seems to be getting younger!"[85]

With the misery index reduced from 20 percent to 12 during Reagan's first term, he won 58.8 percent of the popular vote and carried every state but Mondale's Minnesota and the District of Columbia. Kemp won reelection with 75 percent of the vote, and Republicans picked up 16 House seats, though Democrats remained in control, 253 seats to 182. Republicans lost 1 Senate seat, but retained control.

––––––

The election results did not settle any disputes within the GOP or between the parties over deficit cutting versus growth. Stockman left the White House in August 1985. The next year he hit the administration (and Kemp) with his book *The Triumph of Politics: Why the Reagan Revolution Failed.* He called Kemp "a serious man" who fell "completely in the thrall of Wanniski and Laffer."[86] Kemp's battles with Dole continued, with both aspiring to the presidency in 1988. They publicly traded barbs before a group of college Republicans. Dole said Kemp wanted to include in tax reform a deduction for hair spray. Kemp told the group that a fire had occurred in Dole's library. "Both books were lost and Sen. Dole hadn't finished coloring them." After the back-and-forth appeared in print, Kemp called Dole to urge they cool their attacks on each other.[87]

As the candidates and parties fought over tax rates in 1984, a movement was building to reform the entire system—what Jimmy Carter had once called "a disgrace to the human race."[88] Comprehensive tax reform wasn't an issue in the presidential race, but it developed into the number one domestic achievement of Reagan's second term. Kemp played a key role in it—and demonstrated yet more courage by bucking fellow conservatives who wanted to kill it.

Seven

TAX REFORMER

On a warm evening in August 1983, the Kemp entourage gathered for dinner around his swimming pool in Bethesda, Maryland—twenty supply-side intellectuals, politicians, and policy advisers. Their purpose was to map strategy to dominate the 1984 GOP platform and develop ideas to inject into President Reagan's second-term agenda. They wanted to counter the constant pressure from the White House and members of Congress of both parties to increase taxes. Kemp and his allies wanted to *lower* them. The only way to do it was to reform the entire tax code.

What emerged from the session was a decision that Kemp would sponsor a plan to reduce rates, simplify the tax code, and close special interest loopholes. Drafting the measure would be a challenge. Passing a tax reform act would require monumental effort.

———

The road to tax reform actually began in December 1981 with an op-ed in the *Wall Street Journal* by Stanford University academics Robert Hall and Alvin Rabushka. The two proposed that both businesses and individuals should pay the same 19 percent tax rate, with allowances made to shield the poor.[1] The idea provoked intellectual conversation about tax reform, but no legislation. Reagan later tried to sell TEFRA, the 1982 tax hike, as "tax reform," but the bill didn't lower rates, an essential part of true reform, though it did close newly widened business loopholes. George Shultz talked to Reagan about reform during a golf game that year and may have got him thinking.[2] And a congressional committee looked into a flat tax. But as actual administration policy, reform was dropped amid Stockman and Darman's scheme to enact a "standby tax" in 1983.[3]

In Congress, Senator Bill Bradley (D-NJ) became the father of tax reform in the spring of 1982, unveiling a proposal to create a tax code—as he put it to a group of journalists—that treated all persons of equal incomes equally. "We should have a tax code which allows taxpayers to make their economic decisions on the basis of real value in the marketplace—with little, if any, regard for tax implications," he said.[4]

Bradley, the former Princeton and New York Knicks basketball star and Rhodes Scholar, was opposed to Reaganomics and voted against the 1981 tax cuts. Like Kemp, he had spent much of his travel time as a professional athlete reading economics. He read Milton Friedman, who argued that a flat-tax rate of 20 percent could raise as much revenue as then-current high rates. And he read the work of Harvard law professor Stanley Surrey, who'd coined the term "tax expenditures" to refer to breaks and loopholes for special interests.[5] Like Reagan, the movie actor, he disliked the tax code, though not so much for its high marginal rates as for the gyrations he and other athletes went through to avoid taxes.

As a senator, Bradley was determined to draft a tax bill providing "the lowest possible rate to the greatest number of Americans" by shutting loopholes. In August 1982, he introduced his bill with Representative Dick Gephardt (D-MO), slashing the number of individual tax brackets from fourteen to three. The top rate would fall from 50 percent to 30 percent. Eighty percent of taxpayers would pay the lowest rate of 14 percent. That was higher than the 1981 level of 11 percent, but they added benefits for lower-income persons through expanded personal exemptions and an enlarged standard deduction.

Bradley proposed to limit deductions for mortgage interest, charity, and state and local taxes to no more than 14 percent of gross income, a move that would affect only high-income taxpayers. He raised the rate on capital gains from 20 percent to 30 percent and lowered the corporate tax rate from 48 percent to 30 percent while eliminating most business breaks and reducing allowances for depreciation of buildings and equipment.[6] The measure was "revenue neutral," neither raising nor lowering the estimated amount of money going to the Treasury.

As the 1984 elections neared, some of Walter Mondale's advisers suggested he adopt Bradley-Gephardt as a device to demonstrate fairness and growth-orientation at the same time. Mondale mentioned it once, got bad reviews from Democratic groups benefiting from tax breaks, and gave up on it. Bradley was unable to secure an audience to sell Mondale on the plan until after the 1984 Democratic convention, at which he'd promised to raise taxes. Bradley made an impassioned plea for his proposal,[7] saying it appealed to voters he'd addressed around the country. But his argument was lost on Mondale, a liberal who favored high top rates for the affluent. Mondale was preoccupied with the deficit problem. And tax reform represented the antithesis of his campaign's basic structure as a collection of interest groups.

Then came the poolside dinner at Kemp's house. Among those present were Lew Lehrman, Jeff Bell, Alan Reynolds, Richard Rahn, Norman Ture, Jude Wanniski, David Smick, and Irving Kristol. Kristol stunned the group by suggesting Republicans simply adopt and cosponsor Bradley-Gephardt. At first there was silence, then discussion went well into the night. Some in the group didn't know what was in the bill. But several participants—including Kemp, Bell, and Wanniski—argued that adopting a Democratic idea would draw attention. "It would have thrown the Democratic Party into a real state of confusion," Kemp said.[8]

Others opposed the bill. Rahn, chief economist for the U.S. Chamber of Commerce, disliked its attack on business incentives. It was Lehrman who convinced the group that Republicans should craft their own bill and that Kemp should sponsor it.

It became John Mueller's job to design it. First he had to remove the parts of Bradley-Gephardt that didn't work for the Republicans. He found that supply-siders didn't like Bradley's eliminating indexation that held incomes constant against inflation and protected taxpayers from bracket creep. And they opposed his disallowance of deductions above 14 percent of gross income, which struck them as differential treatment of different taxpayers,[9] violating a key attribute of tax reform.

With the offending provisions removed, Mueller and the team added their own designs. The new reform plan sought to enhance incentives for business investment by allowing rapid write-offs for equipment purchases. The Kemp plan contained a $2,000 personal exemption to help families with children, retained the full deduction for mortgage interest and charitable contributions, and kept capital gains rates low.

For Senate cosponsor, Kemp enlisted Wisconsin Republican Bob Kasten, partly because he'd demonstrated his ability to defeat Dole on tax issues, having successfully fought to end IRS withholding of interest income. Kemp and Kasten introduced their bill—the Fair and Simple Tax, or FAST—in the spring of 1984. On the floor, Kemp said, "This bill is fair to everyone. But it is especially fair to families with children, to the poor, to working men and women, to homeowners and givers to charity and to those who face discouragingly high tax rates. It is also fair to taxpayers who now spend countless hours trying to figure out an unnecessarily complicated tax code."[10]

The bill attracted minimal press coverage. The *Wall Street Journal* gave it ten paragraphs on page five, predicting the bill would go nowhere despite "the political clout of Rep. Kemp."[11] The *Journal* followed up with an analysis of the political difficulties tax reform would encounter.[12] A jaded Treasury official said of the plan, "At best, there will be a lot of losers and a lot of winners. The winners will say, 'Thank you, I appreciate that. Goodbye.' The losers will raise hell." The implication: tax reform would never make it. The *Journal's* editorial page was more upbeat, speculating that the flat tax might prove "the sleeper of this election year."[13] In fact, it was barely discussed by any presidential candidate.

Because of the Kemp plan's generosity in retaining tax breaks curbed by Bradley, his bill faced a serious substantive problem. The original version was not deemed revenue neutral by the Treasury Department or Congress's Joint Committee on Taxation. If enacted into law, it would add tens of billions to the nation's budget deficit. At least that's how "static analysis" calculated Kemp-Kasten's impact. Kemp maintained that "dynamic analysis"—accounting for its incentive and growth effects—would balance losses. Regardless, the Kemp-Kasten tax bill helped make the quest for tax reform bipartisan, and only a bipartisan effort stood any chance of passage, little as that seemed.[14]

The Reagan administration couldn't completely ignore the issue. As it prepared for Reagan's January 25 election-year State of the Union message, supply-siders urged the president to advocate reform. The White House was reluctant, convinced (wrongly) that Democrats would adopt Bradley-Gephardt and steal the issue.[15] And presidential pollster Richard Wirthlin warned that the public thought "tax reform" meant "higher taxes"—not a banner Reagan should carry into the campaign. The White House decided to defuse the issue by having Reagan order a "study" of it. In his speech to Congress, the president said, "Let us go forward with an historic reform for fairness, simplicity and incentives for growth. I am asking Secretary Don Regan for a plan of action to simplify the entire tax code, so that all taxpayers, big and small, are treated more fairly. . . . It could make the tax base broader so personal tax rates could go down, not up." Then Reagan added, "I have asked for specific recommendations consistent with those objectives to be presented to me by December 1984." Derisive laughter arose from the House chamber. Democrats understood he was kicking the issue past the election and assumed he wasn't serious. Treasury's Regan, enthusiastic about reform, was disappointed at the decision. But he proceeded with the study as ordered.[16]

Movement on tax reform was frozen during 1984 while Treasury was doing its study. But Kemp and Bradley, as the concept's leading proponents, made numerous joint appearances—not acting as rivals, but as collaborators. In September, they sat for a joint interview with the *New York Times*[17] in which Bradley said, "I've believed for a long time that the key to prosperity is a new tax system with low rates and fewer loopholes.

There's a wide perception out there that the system is unfair, that equal incomes don't pay equal tax, that the rates are much too high—that it is extremely complex. . . . The country is ripe for fundamental reform." Kemp responded: "I couldn't have said it better myself. Welcome to the supply-side of the tax debate."

Kemp explained that Kemp-Kasten would reduce the top rate on personal income from 50 percent to 25 percent and remove many of the loopholes that were preventing the tax code from doing what it was designed to do: raise revenue without hurting incentives. At the same time, the bill retained "socially as well as economically desirable middle-class deductions" such as interest on mortgages, large medical expenses, charitable contributions, IRAs, Keoghs, "things that encourage savings."

He said the bill modified the flat-tax concept by including a tax credit of 20 percent against the first $40,000 of wages "to keep the working poor and the middle class taxpayer from being pushed up into the same brackets that are being paid by a wealthier individual." And it removed many low-income people from the income tax rolls. Under then-current law, he said, "the woman who leaves welfare and gets a job in the private sector faces such a high marginal rate that it's an impediment to keeping families together." His plan would keep her from paying taxes at all.

Bradley and Kemp agreed that an alternative tax reform idea under academic discussion—a consumption tax—was undesirable because it would, as Kemp said, "be regressive and hurt. . . . the families of the poor." They also both opposed Mondale's call for tax increases. And asked "if the alternative before the House of Representatives next year was Bradley-Gephardt, would you vote for it?" Kemp answered, "Oh, sure. . . ." Bradley, less definitively, said that if Kemp-Kasten were before the Senate, "We ought to head in the same direction. I'm going to look at getting one bill."

———

Before the tax bill, Kemp and Bradley had interacted very little. Even though they had both been star professional athletes, the two had very different backgrounds. Bradley had gone to Princeton, was a Rhodes Scholar, an All-American basketball player, and a gold medal Olympian. He'd led Princeton's basketball team to the NCAA final four, a feat never achieved before or since by an Ivy League team. He was touted in articles and books as a phenomenon even in college, then became a pro Hall of Famer. Kemp, by contrast, was a phys-ed major at Occidental College, was not even a first-string Little College All-American, and had scrambled his way to a position as All-Star pro quarterback, but not one in line for the Hall of Fame. They did have in common, though, the fact that they'd been leaders of their respective sport's players' unions. At the early stages of tax reform's progress, the two were allies, but hardly knew each other.[18] "We know *of* each other," said Kemp. And Bradley said, "I have no greater distance from him than from any other House Republican." After working together on tax reform, though, they become experts in international finance, appearing together on panels in the United States and abroad organized by Kemp's former chief of staff investor, David Smick.

Nearly thirty years later, two years after Kemp's death, Bradley said he admired Kemp's conviction, indefatigability, and character. "I think there's something to the experience of competitive sports at the highest levels, team sports, that creates a bond. . . . It was almost nonverbal. He knew what I was thinking and I knew what he was thinking in terms of what was important and how you behaved, how you treated a teammate. In a sense, we were on the same team. And, besides, he was just fun to be with. I never saw Jack say a bad thing about anybody, and to me, that's the mark of his character. It's always easy to take a pot shot at somebody, but I never saw him do that."[19] He said Kemp might start out "ripping on some economic idea that we disagreed about, but he would always end up saying, 'Well, yeah, but we agree on more than we disagree.'"

Years afterward, Bradley conceded there was a supply-side element to his tax reform proposal—specifically, reducing marginal tax rates and tax rates generally. But he said he never bought Kemp's notion that tax cuts alone would produce higher revenues—hence, the need to close loopholes—and he still thinks Volcker's conquest of inflation and Reagan's spending programs had more to do with the Reagan economic boom than his tax cuts. But he liked debating Kemp. "When you have an opponent who really is arguing on an intellectual level, it's really kind of an exciting thing. . . . It was never personal, it was always on an intellectual level. It was always a dueling set of ideas."

Bradley also said he admired Kemp's stance on race—and his willingness to take on fellow Republicans over it. In sports, "I lived in a black world. He lived in a quasi-black world. We recognized how superficial somebody's skin color was. You either caught the pass or you dropped it. You either hit the shot or you missed it. You either passed when you should or you kept it and were selfish. So I think that was a real bond. And I think there was a common assumption that if either one of us could in our own way move our collective humanity a few inches forward, that we'd feel really good about what we had done." Bradley recalled especially his last encounter with Kemp, in 2008, when the two were jointly interviewed by a conservative talk-show host.[20] The host, he said, was hammering on the Reverend Jeremiah Wright, Barack Obama's radical black pastor in Chicago. "And Jack just called him off. It was like he hit him almost. . . . He basically said that day, 'Hey, cut it. This is not the issue. Get beyond this. Don't keep playing this card.' I sat there, [listening on] an earpiece. I think I was in Texas or someplace. I actually got tears in my eyes and thought, 'That's a real guy.'"

———

At the Treasury Department, Donald Regan took Reagan's directive to simplify the tax code seriously. By Election Day 1984, his team had developed a proposal more radical than any contemplated at such a high level of government. It eliminated hundreds of special interest tax breaks—sure to offend countless Republican constituencies—including the investment incentives that were championed by Reagan in 1981. Treasury 1, as the plan was dubbed, actually proposed raising the corporate tax rate, which Reagan wanted to eliminate. It ended lower rates for capital gains (though indexing them against inflation); cut back business entertainment allowances; and eliminated breaks for oil and gas companies, timber interests, and real estate developers. On the individual side, it established rates of 15, 25, and 35 percent; increased the personal exemption to $2,000 to aid the poor; restricted mortgage interest deductions to first homes; and capped charitable and other deductions.[21]

Treasury 1 was tax reform in a pure and idealistic form, but it was politically toxic. When it was presented to Reagan and the White House staff, acting chief economic adviser William Niskanen declared, "Walter Mondale would have been proud."[22] Baker, responsible for getting Reagan's agenda passed, didn't like it either. He arranged for it to be unveiled at Treasury instead of at the White House. Reagan issued a bland statement saying he'd have to study it.[23] Treasury 1 was so filled with political land mines that when Regan unveiled it—noting that "this thing is written on a word processor. It can be changed"—tax reform looked dead.[24]

Both the AFL-CIO and the National Association of Manufacturers opposed it, along with representatives of charitable groups, the electronics industry, real estate developers, and top politicians in high-tax states—in fact, practically every special interest group. Businessmen were outraged by the $150 billion increase in corporate taxes. Oil and gas drillers, heavy contributors to the Reagan campaign, angrily sent back the "Eagle pins" they'd earned for annual contributions of $10,000 to the GOP. The Knights of Columbus launched a telephone blitz to protest the taxation of its insurance plans. Veterans paraded in protest of the taxation of their disability benefits.[25] Irving Kristol flatly declared tax reform "a dead issue."

But it wasn't. In January 1985, Regan and Baker switched jobs, putting a skilled politician in charge of Treasury and what had become Reagan's top domestic priority. Baker had no personal interest in reform, but Reagan's program became his program.[26] As his deputy secretary, he brought with him the brilliant, abrasive Richard Darman, who would play a crucial role in enacting the 1986 reform.

Shortly before Reagan's 1985 State of the Union address, the Tax Reform Four—Kemp, Bradley, Gephardt, and Kasten—held a joint press conference to announce reintroduction of their bills. Kemp, ever optimistic, said they were "very, very close" to cosponsoring a joint measure. In truth, they weren't. He also said that "chances were good" it could be melded with an administration bill when it was introduced. But Bradley and Gephardt let it be known that no negotiations were yet under way, and the White House said that no work had yet been done on its measure.[27]

To cool tax reform fever still more, senior Republicans in the Senate—notably Majority Leader Bob Dole—said deficit reduction should be Congress's and the administration's first priority for 1985, ahead of tax reform. Several conservative Republican House members, led by Kemp and Gingrich, pushed back with a letter to Reagan urging him to "reject the counsel that deficit reduction should be the top priority of the new Congress." They vowed not to "support further social spending cuts" until the White House presented its tax reform plan to Congress. At his confirmation hearings, Baker said tax reform and deficit reduction had equal priority for the administration.[28]

Reagan didn't agree. He made tax reform the lead proposal of his 1985 State of the Union address and instructed Baker to start working with Congress to produce bipartisan legislation. Kemp said of the speech, "It was music to my ears."

Baker's task was not easy. He had to retain enough tax breaks to keep mighty special interests from torpedoing the entire effort and at the same time repeal enough preferences to make reform meaningful. Baker and Darman initially consulted a broad swath of legislators— Kemp and Bradley, and their cosponsors, as well as the chairmen and ranking members of the congressional committees of jurisdiction, especially Dan Rostenkowski of Ways and Means and Robert Packwood (R-OR) and Russell Long (D-LA) of the Senate Finance Committee. They held secret meetings with the legislators, some on Capitol Hill, others at Baker's home, as they tried to gauge where the political center of gravity on tax reform might lie.

But broad participation in consultations fell apart because

Rostenkowski balked at negotiating with junior members of Congress like Bradley, Gephardt, Kemp, or Kasten. More important, he feared the entire administration effort was a Republican trap. He wanted to make sure that tax reform, if it happened, bore a Democratic stamp. Baker and Darman pushed to pass a bill in 1985, but Rostenkowski regarded that as impossible. Moreover, the U.S. Constitution requires that revenue bills originate in the House, where Rostenkowski was the leading tax writer. And he was jealous of his prerogatives. So Baker and Darman abandoned the multilegislator negotiating strategy and decided to write their own bill, send it to Rostenkowski, and let him work his will.[29] Tax reform was headed for another near-death experience.

Kemp contributed to Rostenkowski's displeasure by telling the *New York Times* that tax reform could be "a basic realignment issue" causing millions of Democrats to become Republicans. With polls showing that large majorities of voters believed the existing tax system unfair, and with Brookings Institution tax scholar Joseph Pechman declaring that the biggest changes in tax law since World War II might be in the offing, Rostenkowski expressed his partisan anxiety. "I don't think Democrats can allow Republicans to take all the credit for this," he said.[30]

The Reagan administration unveiled its new proposal in May, dubbed Treasury 2. It called for three individual rates (15, 25, and 35 percent) with a personal exemption of $2,000. It restored business tax breaks that Treasury 1 had eliminated. It also proposed lowering the capital gains tax from 20 percent to 17.5 percent. Kemp's reaction was, "I'm opposed right now to Treasury 2."[31] He thought the 35 percent top rate too high. "I say it's got to be 30 or below," he said. But he promised not to fight Reagan's plan in Congress. "I want to amend it," he said.[32]

Once Reagan's plan was public, Rostenkowski declared restructuring of the tax code was "now a matter for Dutch [Reagan] and Dan." Rostenkowski said writing the fine print would be up to him. It would be Reagan's job to sell the concept.[33] When asked who'd get credit if tax reform passed, a White House aide recalled that the 1981 tax bill was originated by Kemp, but became Reagan's. "Jack Kemp had a great idea," the aide said, but "it's the famous Reagan tax reform now."[34] Kemp's initial lack of enthusiasm for the Reagan bill was deemed a political error by, among others, Evans and Novak. But Kemp reversed himself in a New York speech, saying he heartily endorsed it while still planning to push for a lower top rate. And alone among New York politicians, he came out against the deductibility of state and local taxes—notoriously high in New York—because to maintain it would require raising the top rate.[35]

When Rostenkowski released his tax reform draft, Kemp and Lott led a group of thirty-seven House Republicans in asking Reagan to reject it. And if necessary, they said, he should give up on reform rather than accept the Chicagoan's proposal. Their main objection was Rostenkowski's raising the personal exemption, then $1,080, but only for the minority of taxpayers who itemized their deductions, and, for them, only to $1,500 instead of the $2,000 proposed by Reagan and Kemp. "A flawed tax reform measure would do our nation and your administration more damage than no tax bill at all," the members wrote. "Compromises on details are acceptable and expected. Capitulation on the goals and principles of your historic reform are not."[36]

Doubling the personal exemption—the level of income excluded from taxation for each member of a family—became a GOP rallying cry and litmus test for House Republicans. It was not for Baker and Darman or for Rostenkowski. Politically, it was favored by Christian Moral Majority Republicans who wanted the tax code to be more "family friendly" by helping parents with large numbers of children. Kemp saw the issue as one of fairness for lower-income taxpayers. He accepted the sophisticated analysis of his aide John Mueller, who argued for reversing the tendency of Republicans to tax labor and favor capital and encourage investment in plant and equipment over human investment. "Jack got the argument that people are just as important as machines—in fact, that investment in people provides about two thirds of our economy and investment in property, only about one third. So he saw it as a pro-family issue but also as a fairness issue. Under the tax code then, you were taxed even if you were below the poverty line, and you were not made whole if you raised children."[37]

There was an important political element to Mueller's analysis that Kemp understood. James Madison declared that "the most common durable source of factions is the various and unequal distribution of property," Mueller observed.[38] Eighty percent of American families get about 80 percent of their income from labor, and voters' party affiliation tracks with income. This puts Republicans at a disadvantage when, in tax proposals, they favor capital over labor income. Kemp wanted to help those earning labor income, whether they were Republicans or Democrats. But paying for it in tax reform was a problem.

Mueller recalled, "Baker and Darman came to Jack's office once and Secretary Baker sat sideways on his couch with his cowboy-booted feet up, and Darman sat next to him and tried to explain to us that it was impossible to raise the personal exemption to more than $1,300 without a value-added [sales] tax to pay for it. So I set the task to figure it out, but every step of the way, they were always trying to reduce the [exemption] and they kept the rate too high."[39] Mueller figured out a solution: the cost and income distribution of the $2,000 personal exemption and the use of deductions for interest on consumer loans were roughly the same. "It suddenly made sense why this is. If you're going to pay for your kid's college tuition, you can borrow against your house or car or boat and write off the interest on your taxes. You can't borrow against your kid. So, the answer seemed to be: double the personal exemption and get rid of the consumer-interest deduction."[40]

Kemp wasn't a member of the Ways and Means Committee, but Representative Henson Moore (R-LA) was, and he promoted the Kemp case in the committee. But Moore's amendments to raise the personal exemption and lower the proposed top rate were defeated. Democrats voted to raise the standard deduction allowed for married couples from $3,600 to $5,950 and for single parents from $2,500 to $4,775, but Republicans were committed to benefiting families with children.[41] As Mueller recalled, "House Republicans became more and more disaffected with the whole process. And they didn't trust Darman as far as they could throw him. So by the time the committee got through, there was a 38 percent top rate and a reduced personal exemption, and it was just too much for them."[42] Mueller wrote a memo to Kemp telling him "there are no two ways about it—the $2,000 exemption was sandbagged by the Treasury." Darman and Baker persuaded Reagan to endorse the Rosten-kowski bill as a "good start" that could be improved in the Senate, but White House aides held up the announcement for ten days because of House GOP sensitivities.[43] During the hiatus, GOP members got steadily angrier. They were convinced either that Reagan didn't really want tax reform or that Baker and Darman had done "a devil's deal" with Rosten-kowski.[44] When Ways and Means voted on the Rostenkowski bill, only five of the committee's thirteen Republicans voted for it.

Now a GOP revolt was fully under way. The House Republican Conference, chaired by Kemp, voted overwhelmingly to oppose the bill. The entire GOP leadership was bucking the wishes of its president on his chief domestic priority. Various Republicans had various reasons. Some opposed the measure to protect special interests. Many were mad at the White House for ignoring them. Others, like Kemp, pronounced the Rosten-kowski bill "anti-family, anti-growth and anti-investment."[45] The Rosten-kowski bill was opposed by the U.S. Chamber of Commerce, the National Association of Manufacturers, the Business Roundtable, the National Association of Home Builders, the American Bankers Association, and a host of other lobbies that regarded the bill's loophole closings as bad for the economy (and their members). The White House's premise was that the bill could be "fixed" in the Senate, but House Republicans doubted it because Chairman Bob Packwood and members of his Senate Finance Committee were lukewarm about tax reform. Many, in fact, were cold.

The weekend before the bill was to be voted on in the House, Reagan used his weekly radio address to call for a "vote yes" to "allow the Senate to consider, debate and to improve this important measure." He also sent a letter to each House member with the same message. A vote was set on the "rule," which needed to be adopted before debate on the bill could occur. A 435-member body can't engage in Senate-style open debate and amendment, so the House Rules Committee—controlled by the Speaker—sets the parameters for floor action, in this case, five hours of debate and three amendments. Rules usually are routinely approved, but one of the amendments, slipped in by Rostenkowski, would have retained a tax break for members of Congress and their staffs that would be canceled for other federal employees. Democrats rebelled against that, encouraging Republicans to think they might beat the rule and kill Rostenkowski's bill. Packwood helped their cause by announcing on the morning of the vote that he doubted the Senate would make any changes in the Rostenkowski bill.[46]

With GOP whip Trent Lott directing GOP rebels to work the floor, all but fourteen Republicans opposed the rule and it was defeated, 223–202. In his speech, Kemp said, "I stand second to none on behalf of true tax reform . . . But unfortunately, this is not it." The Rostenkowski bill, he said, "is 1,737 pages of complication, obfuscation and tax increases. It takes out incentives for growth and leaves in loopholes that create tax shelters." Though he'd sought to introduce a "true tax reform" amendment, this was denied by the Rules Committee. So Kemp told his colleagues, "If you care about tax reform, vote down this rule. It will not kill the reform movement in America. Tax reform is too powerful an idea."[47]

As the votes were being tallied, Bradley put in an exasperated call to Kemp to find out why he was opposing the rule. Kemp said his purpose was not to kill reform, but to get the president's attention. But Bradley feared the vote could spell the death of tax reform. He thought Kemp, the top GOP reformer, was helping to wield the murder weapon.[48]

The vote did get Reagan's attention. The day of the vote he wrote in his diary[49] that he'd met with twenty Republicans in three separate sessions to solicit their votes, "but up on the Hill our Republicans led an attack that prevented the bill from coming to the floor. I saw them gloating on TV. Tip O'Neill on TV said they had 'humiliated the man who led them to victory' (me) & d—n they had." He began intense lobbying to turn the tide. But since a majority of Democrats had supported the

Rostenkowski bill and because he was of two minds about reform, Speaker O'Neill demanded that Reagan produce 50 to 75 GOP yes votes before he'd bring the measure back.[50] Kemp was eager to revive reform and so was GOP leader Bob Michel, but Lott and other Kemp allies were not. They wrote talking points for fellow Republicans to defend their vote against the president.

With no assurance that they could round up 35 to 60 more votes, Michel and Kemp urged Reagan to come up to Capitol Hill to address the entire GOP conference. It was a risky move on both sides. Kemp and Michel were bucking the overwhelming sentiment of their colleagues. And Reagan might well fail to turn them around, suffering humiliation in the process.

The president arrived at 2:15 p.m. on Monday, December 16, to a private session, the press barred. Going into the meeting, the administration had rounded up only 38 votes for the bill, and many of those were iffy. The Speaker had given the president until 8 p.m. that night— less than six hours—to produce his quota. Kemp introduced Reagan: "Mr. President, we all appreciate your gesture in coming here, and we would like to respond by being equally gracious and candid. As you know, all of us revere your leadership." But, he said, House Democrats had given Republicans a choice "between a bad bill and no bill." The Rostenkowski bill "fails to fulfill the pro-growth, pro-family promise of your original proposal." Democrats would not allow Republicans a vote on an amendment to provide a $2,000 personal exemption, he said, and Packwood had signaled that the Rostenkowski bill would not be changed in the Senate. Republicans were eager to hear how Reagan would keep the tax reform process alive "and wind up, not with just a tax bill, but substantive changes which will result in a true pro-family, pro-growth tax reform for the American people."[51]

In classic Reagan style, the president tamed his angry followers. He'd just returned from a memorial service at Fort Campbell, Kentucky, for 248 soldiers killed when their transport plane crashed in Newfoundland. Visibly moved, he called for a moment of silent prayer. "That took the sting out of our bite," Lott said. "That changed the whole mood of the conference."[52]

The sting was gone, but the complaints still flooded in—about the 38 percent top rate, the personal exemption, oil and gas provisions, the effect on heavy industry. The president was sympathetic on each issue, but he said if tax reform died now, there might never be another chance to resurrect it. But if the bill passed the House, he promised he would veto a final product that did not meet GOP concerns. And he promised to write a letter to that effect.[53]

The first break came from Representative Henry Hyde of Illinois, who'd been an outspoken foe of the rule. "Mr. President," Hyde said, "if you say you'll fight for the $2,000 exemption, the rate reduction, effective dates and a lower capital gains rate, I don't need a letter. I'll vote for it." Reagan had shifted the tide and members began applauding his answers.

At the end of the session, a secret ballot showed only forty-eight members willing to vote for the rule—still short two, and even the forty-eight were not locked in. Baker and Darman horse-traded for the remainder of the day, finally letting O'Neill know they were ready for a vote the next day. And Reagan sent a letter to Michel and Kemp—made stronger with Kemp's editing—promising "I will veto any tax bill" that didn't contain the $2,000 personal exemption and depreciation allowances for business, though he did not stipulate a top rate.[54]

Even Kemp's chief of staff, Dave Hoppe, was against what his boss was doing—as were conservative colleagues like Lott, Dick Cheney, and Newt Gingrich. Going up a stairway in the Capitol to a near-midnight meeting of the Rules Committee, Hoppe told Kemp: "You can't vote for this. You cannot vote for this rule. This bill is just as bad." Kemp was ahead of Hoppe on the stairway, with Mueller trailing them. Standing above the two, Kemp yelled, "I am going to vote for this bill. Nothing will stop me. We must move this forward. We can't stop tax reform. Now, shut up. I don't want to hear another word out of you!"[55] The Rules Committee set three votes—on the rule to proceed with debate, on a

Republican motion to recommit the bill to Ways and Means, and on the Rostenkowski bill itself, essentially unchanged.

On the floor, Kemp said he was glad he'd helped lead opposition earlier and, while the Rostenkowski bill was not changed, "what has changed is that the president is now directly involved in shaping the substance." He said, "We will have another chance to vote on tax reform when it comes back from the Senate. Some of you think it would be impossible to make a change. I do not think we should rule that out tonight." If it did come back as a "bad bill," he said he would lead a fight to defeat it.

On the rule vote, 70 Republicans (out of 182) voted yes, and it passed 258–168. The GOP substitute duly failed. On final passage of the bill, Speaker O'Neill declared that the ayes had it on a voice vote. Republicans forgot to ask for a roll call, and O'Neill pronounced the bill passed.

In press coverage of the events, Kemp took heat from the White House for (at first) leading opposition to the rule. He had "lost all chance for the (1988) presidential nomination" for abandoning Reagan, one aide said.[56] After his reversal, he got the same criticism from House colleagues who "whispered betrayal" that would undermine his conservative support for '88. "Jack has been all over the ballpark," Lott said, and "fell for" Reagan's assurances of Senate changes. "The board rooms of America are not going to like it."[57] An unnamed Republican leader said, "The feeling is, Kemp was elected by the conference to represent them, but he let his own national aspirations interfere with that."[58] Evans and Novak concluded[59] that Kemp's switch represented his transition "from congressional politician to presidential candidate." It was also the action of a "conviction politician" who wanted to see his (and Reagan's) great second-term project survive. The columnists said Kemp showed he knew how to manipulate the political process to achieve results.

Tax reform was assumed to be dead when it reached the Senate. In fact, it all but died several times there, particularly when Finance Committee chairman Robert Packwood scheduled committee votes on amendments on April 18, 1986. Fearing victories by almost every special interest lobby, he canceled the vote. Some lobbyists cheered.[60] But

Packwood underwent an epiphany. He and his top aide, William Diefenderfer, repaired to their favorite saloon, the Irish Times, and over a "two pitcher lunch" decided to go back to the drawing board and adopt a "radical approach"—a bill with a 25 percent top individual rate and a 33 percent corporate rate. Packwood decided that Kemp and Bradley were right: if rates were low, special interests might be willing to forgo their loopholes and the economy would work more efficiently.[61] His first post-lunch proposal eliminated even deductions for mortgage interest, state and local taxes, and charitable contributions.[62]

After two weeks of complicated maneuvering and negotiation, the Senate Finance Committee unanimously approved a measure on May 7 with a top rate of 27 percent, a $2,000 personal exemption, keeping the mortgage interest and charitable deductions, a 33 percent corporate rate and accelerated depreciation for plant and equipment, and a hike in the capital gains tax from 20 to 32 percent. It accepted Mueller's idea of eliminating deductions for consumer interest.

Floor debate lasted more than twenty days, but on June 24, the Senate passed tax reform by a vote of 97–3. Bradley was instrumental as Packwood's guide and was included on the House-Senate conference on the final bill. Kemp was not on Rostenkowski's House team. The conference approved the bill on August 16. The House adopted it, 292–136, on September 25, and the Senate passed it and sent it to President Reagan for signature on September 27. In his closing speech, O'Neill spoke like a convert, calling the vote "the decision of a political lifetime. . . . We have come too far to waver now, accomplished too much to give up now, struggled too long to fail now." Kemp said afterward, "I don't want to ruin Tip's day, but I agree with him."[63]

Reagan signed the Tax Reform Act of 1986 on October 22 in a ceremony on the White House lawn attended by 1,500 people, the largest audience for a bill signing during the Reagan presidency. Kemp was on the podium, along with other major players, including Rostenkowski, Baker, Regan, and Dole. Packwood was in Oregon campaigning for reelection. Bradley, too, was in Oregon, caught by a fog and unable to return to Washington. Reagan called the measure "the best anti-poverty bill, the best pro-family measure, the best job-creation program ever to come out of the Congress of the United States."

The 1986 tax reform stands even now as a model for leaders of both parties who hope to make the tax code simpler, fairer, and more economically efficient. It needs to be revisited because, as Bradley said, "politics and . . . legislation [are] often like building a castle of sand near the water, near the waves. Over the next couple of years, the waves came in and washed away the castle."⁶⁴ Within months of its passing, "the guys who wanted a differential rate for capital gains were back, pushing, pushing, pushing." Kemp was one of those pushing, in the belief that a capital gains tax rate lower than that for ordinary income spurred investment and job creation. The differential actually came about because rates on ordinary income were raised in 1990 and 1992. Other special interests drilled new loopholes into tax law year by year, such that tax expenditures rose 44 percent from 1986 to 2013, to $1.3 trillion annually.⁶⁵

Tax reform was clearly a triumph for Reagan and Kemp, bringing the top individual tax rate from 70 percent in 1980 and 50 percent in 1981 down to 28 percent, and dropping the corporate rate from 46 percent to 34 percent. Six million lower-income workers were freed from paying any income tax. GDP growth jumped from 4.9 percent in 1986 to 7.6 percent in 1987 and 7.76 for 1988. In press postmortems on the political effects of tax reform, one of Kemp's 1988 campaign aides said the bill's passage "is proof that Kemp is one of the pioneers of the Reagan revolution." Bush's campaign manager, Lee Atwater, countered that "no one will ever be able to get any credit for anything that comes out of the Reagan administration more than George Bush."⁶⁶ Though Kemp deserved the credit, Atwater was proved basically correct in the 1988 primaries.

———

Reagan's Gallup approval rating achieved its highest level, 68 percent, in May 1986 and was at 63 percent when he signed the tax reform bill days after returning from the Reykjavik summit with Mikhail Gorbachev and days before the November 4, 1986, midterm elections. Thanks to Reagan, in the sixth year of his presidency—historically difficult for the incumbent party—Republicans lost only five House seats. The Senate Republicans were not so fortunate; loss of eight seats turned control over to Democrats for the first time since 1980.

Despite deserving almost as much credit for the Tax Reform Act of 1986 as he did for Kemp-Roth in 1981, Kemp won reelection with just 57.5 percent of the vote—his lowest margin since 1970—after the Democratic Congressional Campaign Committee decided to make him spend time and money defending himself rather than helping other GOP candidates and advancing his presidential prospects. His opponent, James Keane, a Buffalo city councilman and former firefighter, charged that Kemp for years had ignored the district in favor of national politics. He got 42 percent of the vote.

The Republicans were lucky to have passed tax reform early in 1986, because the end of the year and early 1987 were fraught with foreign relations scandals and other woes. The day after the election, a Lebanese newspaper broke the news that the United States had been selling arms secretly to Islamic-revolutionary Iran to secure the release of U.S. hostages held in Lebanon. It soon developed that money from the arms sale was diverted to assist anticommunist "freedom fighters" in Nicaragua, unleashing the greatest political crisis of Reagan's presidency. By March, Reagan's approval rating had sunk to 43 percent, its lowest level since the 1981–82 recession. By the end of his presidency, it would bounce back to 63 percent, but that would have been too late to drum up support for tax reform.

Kemp was a Reaganite through and through, but he was more loyal to his idea of Reagan's basic beliefs than to particular policies Reagan might be advancing. When he thought the president was being misled, he opposed him—and got harshly criticized for it. When he thought the president was right—as in the tax reform fight—he was willing to take criticism from some of his closest colleagues. It's the mark of leadership, and he exhibited that leadership in foreign as well as domestic affairs.

Eight

FREEDOM FIGHTER

I n 1983, Kemp visited Russia with Joanne and fellow members of Congress. To his frustration, Soviet officials wanted to talk only about arms control and trade. When Kemp insisted on bringing up human rights and the plight of Soviet Jews, the Soviets told him, "Don't mix the flies with the soup." Disgusted, Kemp reported back in the States, "You see, to them, people and human rights are flies!"[1]

Kemp's passion for human rights was a key basis of his foreign policy, along with fierce anticommunism and a dedication to free markets. And he wasn't afraid to speak his mind, even undiplomatically. He once asked China's ambassador to the United States how many children he had. When the ambassador produced pictures of three, Kemp said, "Now, which one would you give up under your country's one-child policy?"[2]

Whether asked to or not, Kemp intervened forcefully on foreign issues he cared about—which were many. He was nearly as sophisticated about nuclear strategy, international finance, economic development, and regional conflicts as he was about tax, fiscal, and monetary policy. And he was always vociferous. He supported Ronald Reagan's "peace through strength" foreign and defense policy, but when he thought Reagan was being led astray, he opposed him just as he did on domestic policy. And, as in domestic policy, Kemp was not always correct in the foreign policy stances he took. But, as in domestic policy, he did what he thought was right.

————

Though Kemp made his mark in Congress as an advocate for lower tax rates and growth economics, and as an exponent of "bleeding heart" conservatism, his status in foreign policy was also significant. In the 1980s, Kemp was the ranking Republican on the foreign operations subcommittee of the House Appropriations Committee, the panel that funds foreign aid and the State Department. He was one of the Budget Committee's leading experts on defense issues. As chairman of the House Republican Conference, he was a top party spokesman and regular visitor at the White House. He served as chairman of the defense and foreign policy subcommittees of the GOP National Convention platform committees in 1980 and 1984. In the 1970s, he was on the official congressional delegation observing negotiations on the second Strategic Arms Limitation Treaty.

Kemp used his role on the foreign operations subcommittee to push for the spread of free market supply-side economic policies and democratic politics around the globe. He initially sought to curtail U.S. support for international institutions such as the World Bank, International Monetary Fund (IMF), and regional development banks. He argued they fostered "statism" rather than private enterprise in developing countries and austerity rather than growth. The United Nations and the World Bank—and the U.S. government by supporting them—failed to encourage individual initiative and entrepreneurship in third world countries, he said.[3] "We told them that roads, steel mills and power plants are the secret of wealth and strength [as opposed to the resourcefulness of their people]. So we advised them to turn over their economies to planners who would direct massive taxation and spending . . . and supervise the tremendous burden of debt which would be necessary to build their infrastructure. . . . The tragic results can be seen around the world." To repay their debts, he charged, the IMF demanded that countries raise taxes and devalue their currencies, further stifling development. And the U.S. government was making its aid contingent on their obeying IMF demands.

This stance put him at odds with both the Reagan administration and Democrats led by his antagonist, foreign operations chairman David Obey (D-WI)—until Kemp devised a strategy to shift U.S. policy in a supply-side direction.

In 1983, Kemp aggravated Reagan by opposing increased U.S. funding for the IMF. Reagan wrote in his diary, "Jack Kemp, who told me he couldn't vote for it but wouldn't actively oppose is working his head off to torpedo it."[4] A day later, Reagan wrote, "Jack Kemp now knows I'm mad. He's against us on the IMF increase but promised he wouldn't work against us. He's working his head off."[5] And a few days after that, "Jack Kemp now knows I'm teed off at him."[6]

Their breach made it into the media. *Newsweek* reported[7] that "the stock of Jack Kemp . . . has hit a new low at the White House." Lobbying congressional leaders on IMF funding, Reagan reportedly looked directly at Kemp and said, "I understand that some members feel they have to vote against this bill as a matter of conscience—but their conscience is as wrong as hell," then wouldn't speak to him. Earlier in the week Reagan reportedly had fumed, "I was elected president, not Jack Kemp." That year, the IMF measure passed the House.

In 1984, House Republicans voted en masse against IMF funding though Reagan favored it. Then the campaign arm of House Republicans took out ads attacking Democrats who'd supported Reagan, citing loans to Communist Poland. Obey, enraged, vowed that Democrats would not be put in such a vulnerable position again and would oppose the president until he got his party in line. That produced near-unanimous bipartisan opposition to IMF funding in 1985, and Kemp cleverly used it as leverage to change administration policy toward the multilateral banks. Henceforth, the administration would instruct U.S.-appointed bank executive directors to encourage private-sector growth. The new policy was known as the Baker plan after James Baker, the treasury secretary who unveiled it. But actually it was Kemp's plan.[8]

Obey claims that Kemp was single-mindedly focused on the banks but was otherwise too preoccupied with national politics to concentrate on subcommittee business.[9] In truth, Kemp used his position to protect aid to Israel, fight China's mandatory "one child" population policy, and effect smaller changes important to various countries. He formed a coalition with members of the Congressional Black Caucus, all Democrats, to threaten the Inter-American Development Bank with defunding unless it stopped forcing Haiti to import pigs from Iowa, which died from sun exposure. And he put similar pressure on the banks to ensure that schools funded in Honduras actually got built and water projects actually produced potable water.[10] He was anything but inactive.

———

Kemp got involved with individuals as well as policy. He and Joanne became activists on behalf of Soviet Jews denied permission to emigrate. He urged Reagan and Secretary of State George Shultz to make human rights and the cause of Soviet "refusniks" a key item in negotiations with the Soviets and to make special appeals on behalf of jailed individuals such as activist Anatoly Shcharansky, the pianist Vladimir Feltsman, and Nobel Prize scientist Andrei Sakharov.

Kemp also personally took up the cases of obscure dissidents, such as Edward and Tatiana Lozansky. The couple married in 1970 against the wishes of her father, a Soviet general, who relented only after she attempted suicide. Edward, a Jewish physicist, became a human rights advocate and applied for permission for both of them to leave the Soviet Union. In 1976, he got an exit permit after his father-in-law demanded he agree to officially divorce his wife, though he promised she could join him later. Then he reneged, and Tatiana and their daughter were denied exit visas for six years, during which Edward appealed for help in Washington. Two members of Congress stepped up: Kemp and his frequent foe on economic policy Senator Bob Dole.

Kemp took up the Lozansky cause in 1979, appealing unsuccessfully to Soviet authorities for Tatiana's release. In 1982, Dole served as best man and Kemp as witness at a long-distance remarriage ceremony in the U.S. Capitol designed to call attention to the family's plight while Tatiana staged a hunger strike in Moscow. She lost sixty pounds and was deemed near death when her father again relented, allowing her departure. After the Soviet Union collapsed, they returned home, Edward becoming president of the American University in Moscow. He retold the story in 1996 when Dole and Kemp were GOP running mates, defending Dole against charges he was hostile to Jewish interests.[11]

Kemp also backed dissidents in Eastern Europe, notably the Solidarity labor union in Poland. He urged Reagan to impose economic sanctions on the Soviet Union when its client, the Wojciech Jaruzelski regime, declared martial law in Poland in 1981. Reagan did so. In 1986, he inserted an amendment into that year's foreign aid bill imposing sanctions on Poland, declaring that Solidarity was still being oppressed. He also pushed assistance to Solidarity through the Appropriations Committee after Kemp's aide, Richard Billmire, embarrassed Obey by telling a Polish language newspaper in Milwaukee that Obey opposed it.[12]

———

Kemp's anti-Soviet views, his dedication to democracy, and his longstanding affinity for Jews[13] came together in unswerving support for Israel. This, too, occasionally put him in conflict with the Reagan administration. In 1981, he opposed Reagan's decision to go ahead with the sale (negotiated under Jimmy Carter) of Airborne Warning and Control System (AWACS) ground-surveillance aircraft to Saudi Arabia, arguing on the House floor[14] that the Saudis were "calling for holy war against Israel." In June 1981, Kemp was on a trip to Israel when its air force destroyed Iraq's Osirak nuclear facility. He announced he was "troubled" by the administration's criticism of the attack.[15]

Reagan considered himself a staunch ally of Israel. "No conviction I've ever held has been stronger than my belief that the United States must ensure the survival of Israel," he wrote in his autobiography. Yet "this tiny ally was a source of great concern to me when I was president."[16] After the

AWACS controversy (which Reagan won after "one of the toughest battles of my eight years in Washington"),[17] Israel invaded Lebanon on June 5, 1982. Responding to Palestinian rocket attacks from Southern Lebanon, tanks commanded by General Ariel Sharon[18] drove all the way to Beirut with the aim of expelling eight thousand Palestine Liberation Organization (PLO) fighters from the country. Reagan appealed to Israeli prime minister Menachem Begin to withdraw, and the United States supported a UN resolution calling for a cease-fire and withdrawal.[19] Reagan wrote that the Israelis were "shelling [Beirut] with a savage ferocity that was killing more and more civilians."[20] Reagan told Begin "to stop or our entire future relationship was endangered. I used the word 'Holocaust' deliberately." Reagan wrote that the Israelis were "winning the war, but plunging . . . into a quagmire."[21]

Lebanon became a quagmire for the United States too. Under terms of the cease-fire, PLO fighters, Israeli troops, and Syrian forces were to leave Lebanon (the PLO did, to Tunisia), while U.S. Marines arrived to act as peacekeepers. But before Syria or Israel departed, civil war broke out in Lebanon. Israeli forces stood by as Christian militiamen killed more than a thousand Palestinian refugees and Shiite Lebanese in the Sabra-Shatila neighborhood. As the civil war escalated, U.S. involvement deepened: Iranian-backed Shiite terrorists bombed the U.S. embassy on April 18, 1983, killing sixty-three people; U.S. planes and warships in the Mediterranean hit targets on the mainland, and four U.S. Marines were killed by snipers.

U.S. involvement provoked a furious debate in the United States and in the Reagan administration. Defense Secretary Caspar Weinberger and National Security Adviser William Clark, usually hard-liners, called for a U.S. withdrawal. Shultz favored continued commitment, which Reagan approved.[22] In most policy disputes, Kemp sided with Weinberger, but in this case, he was strongly with Shultz.[23] On October 23, 1983, Iranian- and Syrian-backed Hezbollah suicide bombers killed 241 U.S. Marines in their barracks in Beirut, which Reagan referred to as "the saddest day of my presidency, perhaps the saddest day of my life."[24] U.S. forces were first withdrawn to ships offshore, and U.S. operations ended the following February.

When Reagan was pushing for a swift Israeli withdrawal, Kemp sent him a telegram on June 11, 1982, urging the opposite. "Israel," he wrote, "has given us the opportunity to set back Soviet/Syrian advances in the Mideast."[25] He told the *Jerusalem Post* four months later that "by putting an end to PLO territorial control and by removing Syria, the Israelis have dealt a defeat to two Soviet allies, and now the potential exists for the transformation of Lebanon into a stable, independent and sovereign country at peace internally and with its neighbors."[26] This did not happen, but Kemp maintained his position. After Sabra/Shatila and outbreak of the civil war, Kemp said that "one need not be callous or indifferent to the suffering and loss of life brought about by the war in Lebanon to recognize that, as a direct result of Israel's military success . . . America's opportunity to exercise influence and counsel in the region is at an all-time high."[27]

Reagan, too, hoped to exercise influence by proposing a Mideast peace plan. On September 1, 1982, after the PLO's departure from Lebanon was complete, he called for Israel to freeze settlement activity in West Bank territories captured in the 1967 war and to commence negotiations on Palestinian autonomy (but not statehood) in return for Arab recognition of Israel's right to exist. Begin promptly rejected it, asserting that "the West Bank" was historically "Judea and Samaria" and would not be relinquished.[28] Kemp had "some problems" with the Reagan plan, though he welcomed Reagan's rejection of an independent Palestinian state.[29] As late as 1991, Kemp said that Israeli settlements in "Judea and Samaria" were not a barrier to peace and that Israel "should not give up a single inch of territory until . . . Arab nations make their peace with Israel."[30]

In 1979, on a trip to Israel, Kemp met Benjamin Netanyahu, then director of a public policy institute named for his brother, Jonathan, who was killed leading an Israeli mission to free Israelis on a hijacked airliner in Uganda. The two became fast friends and remained in close touch as

Netanyahu moved to Washington to be deputy chief of mission at the Israeli embassy (1982–84), ambassador to the United Nations (1984–88), leader of the Likud Party and, ultimately, Israeli prime minister. Netanyahu called Kemp "a great, great friend" and "a totally reliable" and "rock-solid" ally of Israel, especially effective in persuading him and other Israelis to institute tax reform and otherwise move away from a socialist economy.[31]

Asked if Kemp had views about Palestinian nationalism, Netanyahu said,[32] "He pretty much left it to us. I think his view was, 'It's your fate. It's your future. You're the ones who should make the decision.'" Netanyahu said he didn't think Kemp ever stopped regarding the PLO as a terrorist organization.[33] In 1987, Kemp worked with Netanyahu to pass a bill calling for the closing of PLO offices in Washington and New York—"terrorist outposts on U.S. soil," Kemp called them.[34] Reagan closed the Washington office, but a federal judge ruled that Kemp's anti-terrorism law could not be applied to the PLO's UN observer mission in New York.[35]

———

Kemp passionately supported the Reagan Doctrine,[36] the policy that, contrary to Soviet doctrine, no country under communist rule was condemned to remain so. And he backed U.S. aid to anti-Marxist "freedom fighters" around the world. In some cases, his stances were more absolute than Reagan's.

He supported arms aid for the mujahideen fighting Soviet occupation in Afghanistan, little suspecting (along with other U.S. officials) that some of them would take over the country as the Taliban and harbor Al Qaeda. He was relentless in pushing for aid for the Contras in Nicaragua and for UNITA (National Union for the Total Independence of Angola) forces fighting the Cuban-backed government in Angola. Afghanistan was a bipartisan cause, but Kemp's hard-line stances on Africa and Central America led to constant conflict with Democrats and splits between Kemp and the administration.

When the Marxist Sandinista National Liberation Front overthrew Nicaragua's corrupt forty-year Somoza dynasty in 1979, the Carter administration offered it economic aid. Reagan canceled it, showing evidence that the new regime was shipping Soviet and Cuban arms to communist-led insurgents in neighboring El Salvador.[37] Carter and Reagan both backed the Salvadoran government headed by Christian Democrat José Napoleón Duarte, who'd been cheated out of election as president by the military in 1972, then installed as leader of a civil-military junta in 1980. Reagan kept aid going to combat the Marxist insurgents, but Democrats soon turned against the government, accusing it and unofficial right-wing "death squads" of atrocities worse than those committed by the Marxists.

The Reagan administration itself was bitterly divided over Central America. Shultz and most State Department diplomats advocated a two-track approach: covert aid to the Contras (plus open military assistance to El Salvador) combined with efforts at regional peace negotiations. Reagan's first national security adviser, William Clark, along with CIA director William Casey and UN ambassador Jeane Kirkpatrick, deemed this "appeasement." They wanted overt U.S. support for the Contras and a military victory over the Sandinistas. Reagan sided with Shultz.[38] Kemp opposed nearly every effort at negotiation, denouncing the State Department in the process. But his major fight was with Democrats, who called the Contras terrorists and worse, neglecting the Sandinistas' ties to Cuba and the Soviet Union.

El Salvador became a less-partisan issue after Duarte was elected president in 1984. Kemp had a hand in suppressing death squad activities by telling right-wing leader Roberto d'Aubisson that no party in the United States would tolerate them.[39] But through the Reagan years, Democrats constantly fought to cut off aid to the Contras. Tip O'Neill branded them "marauders, murderers and rapists" and accused Reagan of wanting to send U.S. troops to fight with them, a policy he had specifically ruled out.[40] A pattern developed: Democrats in Congress would vote down aid. Then the Sandinistas would commit some blatant excess:

rig an election, reject a negotiating proposal, suppress the Catholic Church, import Cuban and Soviet arms and military advisers, or invade Honduras. They built up their military forces to sixty thousand men. In reaction, Congress would approve an aid package—sometimes military, mostly merely humanitarian—until the memory faded or the United States committed an error such as the CIA's installing (nonlethal) mines in Nicaraguan harbors in 1984. Then the aid would plummet again. When they were getting funded, the Contras made military progress. When they weren't, they retreated to Honduras, whereupon the Sandinistas overstepped with cross-border raids and human rights crackdowns.

Kemp was a vigorous participant in every congressional debate. Before one vote, he wrote an op-ed comparing the Contras to American revolutionaries.[41] In another debate, he compared those opposed to Contra aid to U.S. isolationists of the 1930s who "encouraged Hitler . . . encouraged the Holocaust."[42]

In October 1984, Congress passed its third amendment sponsored by O'Neill's Massachusetts colleague Representative Edward Boland forbidding any military assistance to the Contras, direct or indirect, from the Pentagon or the CIA. The administration said it would participate in regional peace talks, but decided to find foreign funding for the Contras, which led in 1986 to the Iran-Contra scandal. White House National Security adviser Robert McFarlane and his aide, Lieutenant Colonel Oliver North, secretly secured Contra funding, first from Saudi Arabia, then by illegally diverting money from arms sales to Iran. When the scheme was revealed, Congress cut Contra funding to a trickle.

Throughout this period, the State Department pursued various peace initiatives offering suspension of Contra aid in return for political reform in Nicaragua. Kemp opposed them and once called for the ouster of the U.S. negotiator.[43]

Kemp especially opposed a peace plan fashioned by Costa Rican president Óscar Arias in 1987, which required that the Contras disband in return for Sandinista promises of political reform. Arias received the Nobel Peace Prize, and Reagan gave the plan a lukewarm endorsement after the Senate endorsed it 97–1. It collapsed, owing to Honduran and Salvadoran objections.⁴⁴ Kemp also vigorously opposed the administration's agreement to join House Speaker Jim Wright in fashioning a settlement. Wright began personally negotiating with the Sandinistas, angering Shultz and Reagan.⁴⁵ But the administration backed the regional peace plan Wright was seeking to advance. In his diary⁴⁶ Reagan wrote, "It seems Jack Kemp is blasting our peace proposal & even went so far as to call Pres. Duarte of El Salvador & try to persuade him to oppose our plan."

Hoping a Democrat would be elected in 1988—all the Democratic candidates promised to end Contra funding—the Sandinistas agreed to a cease-fire allowing the Contras to keep their arms and Congress voted humanitarian aid to keep them intact. Once Republican George H. W. Bush became president, the Sandinistas agreed in negotiations to hold an election. They lost, and remained out of power from 1990 to 2006.

———

On November 3, 1986, the Lebanese magazine *Ash-Shiraa* revealed that the United States had been selling arms to Iran, precipitating the Reagan administration's worst scandal. Not only was the administration trying to buy the release of Americans held hostage by Iran-allied Hezbollah terrorists in Lebanon, but proceeds from the sale were being diverted to support the Nicaraguan Contras in violation of Congress's will. The scandal led to years of investigations, indictments, trials, convictions, conviction reversals—and six pardons at the close of the Bush administration in 1992. Immediately, the scandal precipitated a 31-point drop in President Reagan's approval ratings, the largest one-month fall for any U.S. president in history.⁴⁷

"Ollie" North was a central figure of the scandal. Kemp knew North well. He took a trip with him to Central America and talked frequently with him on the phone.⁴⁸ But it's unlikely Kemp had any knowledge North was financing the rebels with proceeds from weapons sales to Iran, though it was common knowledge that "private" money was being raised on the Contras' behalf after Congress cut off support.[49] Three weeks after public disclosure of the arms-for-hostages deal, Reagan fired North, National Security Adviser John Poindexter resigned, and Reagan appointed a three-member commission headed by former senator John Tower of Texas to investigate the scandal. That day, Kemp praised Reagan for conducting his own investigation and said, "If any illegalities took place, then appropriate action should be taken by the Justice Department."[50]

In July 1987, when it was revealed that Reagan had told his top aides a week after the scandal first broke, "Don't talk specifics" and say there had been "no bargaining with terrorists," Kemp defended the president on CBS's *Face the Nation*. Kemp said Reagan was rightly interested in improved relations with Iran and with the fate of U.S. hostages held by Hezbollah—and that informing Congress would have led to leaks. By this time—well into the 1988 presidential campaign—Kemp was on the warpath against Shultz. When Kemp was asked about Shultz's testimony that he'd threatened to resign three times because he opposed selling arms to Iran, Kemp said, "I wish the president had accepted his resignation."[51]

In December 1987, with North and Poindexter facing possible indictment—both were convicted on various charges, but cleared on appeal—Kemp said in a GOP candidates' debate that he'd pardon both. He added he "didn't mind being lonely" when he was the only candidate to say he'd pardon the pair. "The others don't have the courage to say what ought to be said."[52]

———

In December 1986, as the Iran-Contra scandal was unfolding, Kemp published a long op-ed in the *New York Times,* titled "Trust the President's Foreign Policy."[53] It stands as a pure expression of Kemp's own foreign policy. Reagan, he wrote, had reversed not only America's post–Vietnam decline in military preparedness and world influence; he had also cured deeper weaknesses: a "steady erosion of clarity and confidence in Western ideas and values," widespread acceptance of "moral equivalence" between East and West, and acquiescence to the Brezhnev doctrine. This mind-set had led to the notion that détente, economic concessions, and unilateral restraint were the only ways to tame Soviet belligerence. But Reagan, along with Britain's Margaret Thatcher and West Germany's Helmut Kohl, "jarred us from this complacency, ended our long retreat and sparked the revitalization of the West," Kemp wrote.

The three leaders had a "clear-eyed understanding that the Soviet Union remains a ruthless, dangerous enemy" and understood that "the West must always summon the will to deal with totalitarians from a position of strength." During the détente era, the "ever-expanding Soviet empire captured nine nations and more than three million innocents died at the hands of brutal dictatorships," but under Reagan, "we have not only prevented any nation from falling to Communist conquest, we have overturned the Brezhnev doctrine by welcoming the first country in post-war history, Grenada,⁵⁴ back into the family of 'free nations.'"

———

As a Reagan supporter, Kemp took a leading role in opposing the "nuclear freeze," a misguided effort by U.S. liberals, leading Democrats, and the international peace movement (elements of it Soviet sponsored) to stop Reagan's nuclear weapons buildup. At the same time, Kemp misjudged Reagan's willingness to negotiate with adversaries where possible.

In 1979, NATO authorized deployment of U.S. Pershing II intermediate-range ballistic missiles and cruise missiles to counter a Soviet force of six hundred nuclear missiles aimed at Western Europe. In November 1981, Reagan proposed a "zero" option whereby the United States would forgo its deployments if the Soviets dismantled their arsenal. Reagan also proposed new U.S.-Soviet talks on long-range weapons to be called Strategic Arms *Reduction* Talks, replacing the Nixon-Carter era Strategic Arms *Limitation* Talks. The name change signified Reagan's desire that nuclear arsenals be diminished, not merely capped. At the same time, he decided to deploy one hundred long-range MX missiles, each with ten warheads. He also proposed a new class of missile submarines and a new strategic bomber. He intended to negotiate to reduce weaponry, he wrote in his autobiography,[55] "but I knew I had to begin with an *increase* of arms" because "if we were ever going to get anywhere with the Russians . . . we had to bargain with them from strength, not weakness." Reagan doubled annual defense spending during his eight years, increasing its annual share of GDP over Carter levels by 23 percent.[56]

The international "peace" movement was apoplectic, assailing Reagan's entire program as a menacing "escalation of the arms race." The "peaceniks," in line with Soviet policy, especially opposed the Pershing IIs for Western Europe. Marchers paraded in every European capital. In the United States, Democrats in Congress and the party's presidential contenders in 1980 and 1984 advocated a "negotiated, verifiable freeze" on nuclear weapons, naively hoping it would lead to arms reductions. In a House debate that went on for four weeks in 1983, Kemp argued the Reagan case. He said the freeze would simply entrench the Soviets' monopoly in INF weapons.[57]

At the time, U.S.-Soviet talks in Geneva on intermediate nuclear forces (INF) were going nowhere. In November 1983, the Soviets walked out in protest of Reagan's decision to deploy Pershing IIs. As Congress considered a new "freeze" resolution, Kemp argued it would undermine the NATO alliance, one of whose key members—West Germany—had just held an election in which Pershing deployment was a major issue. Christian Democrat Helmut Kohl won despite Soviet threats his victory would bring on a "nuclear Auschwitz."[58] With major U.S. religious leaders and "good government" groups like Common Cause backing the freeze (along with street demonstrators), it passed the Democratic House 278–149. But a similar proposal was defeated in the Republican Senate, 58–40.[59]

Those resolutions were nonbinding, but in late 1983, "freeze" advocates tried to cancel Pershing II funding. They lost on a voice vote. Their timing was bad. In the previous week, terrorists had killed the 241

Marines in Beirut, and U.S. forces invaded Grenada. In an emotional floor speech, Kemp said, "I have been here on the floor and heard the United States called outlaws. I have heard the United States and this administration called provocateurs. I can't stand it anymore. Don't undercut your country at a time of international crisis. It would be a terrible mistake to do this. I beg of you: don't send this signal" to U.S. allies and the Soviets.[60]

But Democrats didn't give up. Next they sought to deny funding for the MX missile, the new land-based centerpiece of U.S. strategic nuclear forces. Reagan infuriated Democrats by dubbing it "Peacekeeper." After MX funding was blocked in the House in December 1982, Reagan announced—in a letter to Kemp—he would suspend arms talks with the Soviets if the funding was not restored.[61] Reagan's hardball worked, and the House reversed itself in May 1983, which Kemp said would strengthen the hand of U.S. arms negotiators.[62] Kemp, along the way, called himself not a hawk, but "a well-armed dove."[63]

———

Reagan's aim was to rebuild American strength—military, moral, and economic—then bargain. The American left and allied Democrats considered the arms buildup "provocative." And they were outraged when Reagan labeled the Soviet Union "an evil empire" and "the focus of evil in the modern world" in a March 1983 speech. When he proposed the Strategic Defense Initiative two weeks later, they were further alarmed. SDI would add an antimissile shield to the nuclear mix and, if deployed, end the era of nuclear deterrence or "mutually assured destruction (MAD)," as it was called. Foes dubbed SDI "Star Wars," as though it were science fiction. Democrats repeatedly sought to cut SDI funding. Reagan was trashed as a "warmonger" and a "cowboy" in the U.S. and European press—and as Hitler by the Soviets,[64] who claimed he intended SDI to be a shield behind which the United States could launch a nuclear "first strike" on the Soviet Union without fear of retaliation. Even Shultz was disturbed by the "evil empire" speech and opposed SDI as "destabilizing."[65]

What Reagan said about Soviet "evil," Kemp totally agreed with. He became one of the leading congressional advocates of SDI. He sided with Defense Secretary Caspar Weinberger against Shultz's attempts to delay SDI testing on the grounds that it would violate Richard Nixon's 1972 Anti-Ballistic Missile Treaty. And he opposed using SDI as a "bargaining chip" in nuclear negotiations—an idea Reagan repeatedly rejected as well.[66] Kemp was so pro-SDI that he advocated its deployment on a more accelerated schedule than even Reagan thought possible. Kemp believed that elements of an antimissile system could be put in place in the early 1990s. In a letter to Reagan, he mentioned as possibilities surface-to-air missiles, high-energy lasers in space, and infrared warning systems mounted on Boeing 767s.[67] Reagan felt research and development of a workable SDI system might take "decades,"[68] and he offered to abide by the 1972 Anti-Ballistic Missile Treaty and not deploy for ten years.[69]

———

Kemp misjudged the depth of Reagan's personal commitment to negotiate with adversaries. Three months into his presidency, Reagan began sending private handwritten letters to Soviet leaders. He hoped to find someone in the Kremlin who realized that the United States and the Soviet Union were "like two cowboys with guns pointed at each other's heads [posing] a lethal risk to survival of the Communist world as well as the Free World."[70] At that early point, he wrote, "I doubted I'd ever meet anybody like that." And through four years and three Soviet leaders, he didn't. But after Mikhail Gorbachev came to power in March 1985, Reagan began to change his mind. For one thing, his defense buildup and rallying of the West, his SDI proposal, America's economic success—plus Soviet economic weakness—had altered the balance of power (or "correlation of forces," as the Soviets called it) decisively in America's favor. Reagan believed that Gorbachev saw this and "was trying to turn things around [in the USSR] but is having a hard time."[71]

Reagan bargained hard on arms control. He refused to trade away SDI, as Gorbachev proposed, walking out of the 1986 Reykjavik summit when Gorbachev demanded giving up SDI as the price for an INF agreement.[72] He called the Soviets out for cheating on past commitments, and constantly brought up human rights. And this tough-minded approach ultimately led to the agreement he'd first proposed in 1981 to eliminate intermediate-range nuclear forces from Europe. He signed the INF treaty in a Washington summit with Gorbachev in December 1987. A total of 2,692 weapons were destroyed, 846 by the United States and 1,846 by the Soviet Union, substantially achieving Reagan's 1981 "zero-zero" goals. As Reagan wrote, "Not only did the INF treaty provide for the elimination of an entire class of nuclear weapons, it contained teeth to assure compliance"—intrusive, on-site inspections by each side of the other's installations.

Kemp did not accept any of this. Gorbachev, he said in a 1987 speech at the Heritage Foundation, was a "student" of Stalin and was continuing his policy of world domination, "using arms control as a wedge to break up NATO and neutralize Western Europe." "If Gorbachev truly were sincere about reducing international tensions," he said, "then we should see change reflected in Soviet foreign policy. Instead Soviet aggression continues. Soviet espionage has become more brazen and Soviet terrorism and subversion more widespread." In another speech, he declared, "Mikhail Gorbachev is no mellowed Marxist, he is a hardcore communist."[73]

He called Reagan's INF treaty "a nuclear Munich"[74] and urged senators not to ratify it. He argued that the Soviets couldn't be trusted to live up to any commitment, that the pact couldn't be verified, and that it would weaken NATO. It was signed amid "arms control euphoria," Kemp charged, that would lead to "moral disarmament" and public pressure to cut the defense budget and abandon SDI.

Some of Kemp's specific objections to the treaty had merit and had useful effects. He wrote to Shultz in January 1988, a month after the signing, that the Soviets had failed to supply photographs of the SS-20 missile they were pledged to dismantle. In March, the Senate postponed consideration of the treaty because, as Senate Intelligence Committee chairman

David Boren (D-OK) put it, the Soviets were "backsliding and reneging" on the treaty's verification provisions. These objections led to further negotiations in which the Soviets largely acceded to U.S. demands. Kemp's allies in the Senate, led by Jesse Helms of North Carolina, waged a last-ditch effort to block the treaty's ratification with "killer amendments" and delaying tactics. But the treaty was ratified, 93–5, in time for Reagan's final summit with Gorbachev in Moscow in May 1988.[75]

––––––

Kemp first called for Shultz's ouster in January 1986. His main ground was State Department opposition to openly aiding anti-Marxist rebel groups in Angola and Mozambique, though fellow conservatives such as Helms were already attacking Shultz on arms control and Central America policy. Kemp said the State Department was not supporting "the causes of fundamental freedom" in the two African countries. "I think getting a good Secretary of State would be a step in the right direction. . . . Having the right Secretary of State is essential for the right kind of change." He said that if he were president, he would name Jeane Kirkpatrick, then former U.S. ambassador to the UN, or Donald Rumsfeld, Gerald Ford's secretary of defense.[76]

Marxist governments took power in both Angola and Mozambique when they gained independence from Portugal in 1975. Both faced armed resistance from anticommunist rebels—UNITA in Angola, RENAMO in Mozambique—and imported Cuban fighters and Soviet arms to aid them. Rebel groups received assistance from the white regime in South Africa. Kemp, Helms, and other conservatives thought both UNITA and RENAMO deserved U.S. support, but Reagan chose to lure Mozambique out of the Soviet orbit with carrots instead of sticks.[77] From 1976 to 1985, the United States was legally barred from aiding UNITA by the Clark Amendment, named for its chief sponsor, Senator Dick Clark (D-IA). UNITA's charismatic leader, Jonas Savimbi, made frequent trips to the United States and was lionized by conservatives.

Shultz favored covert aid to Savimbi and it began flowing at the rate of $15 million a year.[78] But Shultz opposed a bill sponsored by Kemp and Democrat Claude Pepper of Florida in 1985 to provide $27 million in overt nonlethal aid. Shultz argued that open support would undermine U.S.-brokered negotiations under way with South Africa and Angola to grant independence to Southwest Africa (Namibia) and secure removal of Cuban troops. Kemp wrote to Reagan protesting the Shultz position, arguing that "we need to make it clear to the rest of the world that . . . the US intends to support those people in Angola and Namibia who share our commitment to democratic government." Kemp's position had the backing of the Pentagon, CIA, some National Security Council staffers, and White House communications chief Patrick Buchanan.[79]

But Reagan was on Shultz's side. He wrote in his diary[80] that in a GOP leadership meeting at the White House "Jack Kemp kicked up a fuss when he challenged the St. Dept. about not supporting $27 mil. Aid to Savimbi in Angola. George replied that our objection was to Cong. making the aid overt. We want a covert operation for real. Our problem is Cong. interference in what should be exec. office management of international diplomacy. Things got hot for a while." Shultz described[81] having "a stinging set-to" with Kemp. "The president turned pale at our harsh exchange, as Kemp harangued for an open vote for an open program and I tore into him, warning all the reasons why an open program would be a disaster. 'Why don't you try thinking, Jack,' I snapped. 'How are you going to get aid delivered? Zaire and Zambia can't openly support insurgents in another African state. And the aid has to go through there. If the aid isn't delivered, it's worthless to Savimbi.'"

In December, Buchanan arranged for Kemp to make his case directly to Reagan, hoping the president would match his strong rhetorical backing of Savimbi with policy backing UNITA to the hilt. But Reagan demurred and Pentagon and NSC participants remained silent. Shultz prevailed.[82]

After thirteen years of warfare and repeated failures of the Marxist government to defeat UNITA, Assistant Secretary of State Chester Crocker produced an agreement for gradual withdrawal of Cuban troops and Namibian independence in 1988.[83] Kemp wrote Reagan a letter, along with twelve colleagues, questioning whether the agreement would be adhered to and complaining it failed to guarantee UNITA's inclusion in Angola's politics. Reagan responded that getting Cuban troops out would strengthen Savimibi's hand and that implementation of the Crocker deal should not be delayed.[84] Though Cuban troops did leave, combat in Angola did not end until after Savimbi was killed in battle in 2002. UNITA's foe, the Popular Movement for the Liberation of Angola (MPLA), headed by José Eduardo dos Santos, still rules the country. Dos Santos has held elections and the economy is no longer Marxist.[85]

––––––

The Reagan administration was wracked by internal differences not only over Angola, but almost across the board—Central America, U.S.-Soviet relations, and arms control. And Shultz was at the center of the disputes, which were often personal. "While Reagan settled into his role as chief salesman for the freedom fighters," Reagan biographer Lou Cannon wrote,[86] "his principal advisers battled one another with a ferocity rarely equaled by the Contras in combat." Casey, Clark, many White House speechwriters, Weinberger, and Kirkpatrick distrusted Shultz. Baker and Casey bluntly called each other liars. Reagan hated disharmony, but wouldn't tell his subordinates to stop their warfare. "This went on endlessly," Jeane Kirkpatrick said.[87]

Conservatives believed Shultz had been co-opted by the State Department's bureaucracy, which would abandon U.S. vital interests in the name of diplomacy. They thought Shultz, who met privately with Reagan once a week, was misleading the president and undoing his policies. White House chief of staff James Baker, leader of Reagan's "pragmatist" faction, called the conservatives "the crazies" and his allies called Weinberger and Casey "the war party," appealing to Reagan's "dark side."[88]

On almost every issue, Kemp sided with the hard-liners. It caused him personal anxiety in the case of South Africa. Kemp's antiracist instincts led him to support economic sanctions in the summer of 1985, contrary to Reagan policy. He was joined by fellow conservatives Newt Gingrich, Vin Weber, Dan Coats, and Bob Walker. They took a battering from right-wingers who supported South Africa's apartheid regime and who argued that its black opposition, the African National Congress, was a communist-dominated terrorist organization. Howard Phillips, president of the Conservative Caucus, said, "Jack Kemp has badly damaged his presidential prospects by being to the left of George Bush on this issue."[89]

Kemp quickly modified his stance, writing to a supporter in October 1985 that the measure he voted for was "very mild" and that he intended merely to "send a signal" with "a deliberate protest vote" against suspension of civil liberties by the white government. He insisted his position was "wholly consistent" with Reagan's. If Reagan vetoed an antiapartheid bill, Kemp said he would vote to sustain it. And he did in September 1986.[90] Gingrich, Weber, and Walker stuck to their position and voted with 87 other Republicans and 218 Democrats to overturn Reagan's veto.

Kemp had difficulty[91] squaring his domestic civil rights views with his South Africa stance. But he tried. In a speech on the House floor in opposition to sanctions in 1986, he argued that "apartheid, in every form, must end and is demonstrably evil," but "we do not improve the future of South African working people by destroying their jobs. . . . There are many of my colleagues and good friends who will not understand a vote against sanctions. I am profoundly sorry, but I sincerely have the common goal of . . . the release of Nelson Mandela. . . . Let's eradicate apartheid, not the economy."[92]

Another factor in Kemp's stance was that "our highest national interests dictate that South Africa's strategic importance, its alliance with the West and its mineral wealth must receive the highest priority in formulating US policy."[93] Despite favoring Mandela's release, Kemp regarded the ANC as a terrorist organization. He listed Shultz's proposed 1988 meeting with ANC president Oliver Tambo among the reasons he ought to resign.

———

Kemp's attacks on Shultz thrilled conservatives. His splashiest call for Shultz's resignation came at the annual Conservative Political Action Conference in 1987. He accused Shultz of purging Reaganites from the State Department, dragging his feet on deployment of SDI, and opposing full support for foreign "freedom fighters." He said Shultz "personally rolled out a red carpet for Oliver Tambo."[94] The crowd hissed when Kemp first mentioned Shultz's name and said, "Let's face it, the Shultz Doctrine is not the same thing as the Reagan Doctrine." Kemp admonished them. Then he got a standing ovation when he hit his key lines: "When the question is whether the president will conform to his Secretary of State or the Secretary of State will conform to the president, it is time for Mr. Shultz to do the only correct thing. It is time for George Shultz to resign."[95] In a straw poll of 268 activists who filled out ballots, Kemp was the 1988 favorite of 68 percent, followed by Buchanan. Bush, who did not attend and got few votes, had previously said that Shultz had his full confidence.[96]

Kemp's call for Shultz's ouster wasn't an easy stance to arrive at, said David Hoppe, his chief of staff. It was "substance-driven, not personal. He just went down the line and on issue after issue, he thought the advice Shultz was giving the president was wrong."[97] John Buckley, Kemp's 1988 campaign press secretary, said Kemp's policy differences went all the way back to Shultz's presence at Camp David in August 1971, when Richard Nixon decided to take the U.S. dollar off the gold standard. "You have to remember, today Shultz is seen as a statesman. Back then, he was looked upon by conservatives as a technocrat who was bamboozling Reagan in his talks with Gorbachev. He was the conservatives' bogeyman."[98]

———

Kemp's basic disagreement with Shultz and Reagan was their approach to the cold war. He certainly agreed, as Reagan said in his first press conference, that the Soviets were dedicated to establishing a "one-world Socialist or Communist state" and, to do so, "reserve unto themselves the right to commit any crime, to lie, to cheat." And that "so far, détente has been a one-way street that the Soviet Union has used to pursue its own aims."[99] However, as future CIA director and defense secretary Robert Gates wrote in 1996,[100] "Reagan, nearly alone, truly believed in 1981 that the Soviet system was vulnerable, not in some long-range historical sense, but right then. . . . So he pushed—hard."

Reagan was confident, as he said at Notre Dame in 1981, that "the West won't contain communism; it will transcend communism. . . . It will dismiss it as some bizarre chapter in human history whose last pages are even now being written."[101] As optimistic as Kemp generally was, he did not share Reagan's confidence about the demise of the Soviet Union. But after communism collapsed, he praised Reagan's foresight: "Can you believe that President Reagan saw that this was possible, that the Soviet Union could be ended? I never believed that, but President Reagan did. He had the vision."[102]

Like most foreign policy experts, right and left, and even the CIA, Kemp thought the Soviet system was at least capable of sustaining itself. Liberals and Republican "realists" thought coexistence, even mild appeasement, was necessary. Kemp feared arms control might lead to "a Soviet Union potentially far more powerful, more menacing, more dangerous than before."

Reagan agreed with Kemp that Soviet ambitions had to be countered. Nonetheless, he saw "the futility of the arms race and the hair-trigger risk of annihilation it posed to the world." He tried, he wrote, "to send signals to Moscow indicating we were prepared to negotiate a winding down of the arms race if the Soviets were also sincere about it—and proved it with deeds."[103] In his first handwritten letter to a Soviet leader—to sick and aging Leonid Brezhnev in 1981—he vowed the United States would resist communist advances. But he also asked, "Should we not be concerned with eliminating the obstacles which prevent our people from achieving their most cherished goals?"[104] He repeatedly sought summit meetings with Brezhnev, then Yuri Andropov, then Konstantin Chernenko. "They kept dying on me," he said, half jokingly. Reagan finally succeeded with Mikhail Gorbachev.

Shultz and Reagan agreed on who was in charge of foreign policy. It wasn't Shultz. "I did not have my own foreign policy," he said. "I knew who I was working for—President Reagan."[105] And Reagan knew whom he wanted as secretary of state. Reagan wrote that Shultz "proved again and again that he was one of the finest and most distinguished secretaries of state in the history of our country."[106] He refused to let him be ousted—and his confidence in Shultz was justified.

Shultz insisted he had no personal dislike of Kemp, but in March 1988, Shultz had something of a last laugh on him. He was testifying before the House foreign operations subcommittee when then-ranking Republican representative Mickey Edwards of Oklahoma, a Kemp '88 campaign supporter, apologized for having to leave to take part in Kemp's announcement that his presidential campaign was over. Shultz remarked: "That's what happens when you base your campaign on calling for my resignation."[107]

Kemp was wrong about Shultz and he was less visionary about foreign policy than Ronald Reagan. But he does deserve credit for holding the idealistic view that the freedom and prosperity enjoyed by Americans should be available to people all over the world, and trying to put that belief into action. And, by fostering prosperity in America through tax policy, he helped make democratic capitalism, not statism or socialism, the model that most people in the world aspire to live under.

Nine

ALSO RAN

The year was 1975 and the scene, a hallway in the Cannon House Office Building, where mainly junior members of Congress have their offices. Kemp was a third-term backbench Republican. Pro-football stardom was six years in his past and he was still a year away from discovering supply-side economics, which would make him a political star and historic force. Vin Weber, later a close congressional ally and a key player in Kemp's 1988 presidential campaign, was twenty-three years old and holding his first job out of college: working for a newly elected Minnesota congressman.

This day a small clutch of conservative young staffers was huddling near an elevator—their numbers and spirits devastated after their party's forty-nine-seat "Watergate election" defeat in 1974. An elevator door opened and the staffers began to buzz about one person who emerged. Weber had no idea who it was or why the buzz. He asked the staffer next to him, who said, "You don't know who that is? That's Jack Kemp. He's the next Ronald Reagan." As Weber recalls it, "Reagan was still five years away from being elected president and we're talking about who the next Reagan is going to be!"[1] Over the next decade, the group of those who thought Kemp was indeed the "next Reagan" continued to grow.

Beginning in 1984, when it was clear to all but ideological adversaries that Reagan was on his way to a historically successful presidency, the identity of Reagan's successor became a dominant subject of political discussion, especially in the GOP. Kemp seemed a clear choice: he'd been for Reagan in 1980. He was the original author of Reagan's most important domestic achievement, the 1981 supply-side tax cut, followed by the most important domestic achievement of his second term, the 1986 supply-side tax reform law. He was the guardian of Reaganomics, doing constant battle with "Herbert Hoover," "green-eye-shade" "deep root canal" Republicans in Congress and the White House staff. Kemp defended Reagan's foreign policy—as he understood it—more faithfully than Reagan himself. In fact, so fierce was he in his protectiveness of supply-side ideas, he once charged that if either of his major rivals—Vice President George Bush or Senate Republican leader Bob Dole—was nominated, "the Reagan revolution is over, gone, dead."[2]

Kemp had forgone running in 1980, at age forty-five, deferring to his hero and deeming himself not ready. He believed 1988 would be his moment, and so did much of the conservative movement. Little did he know what a jarring route the campaign trail would be.

————

Reagan stayed formally neutral throughout the 1988 GOP primaries, writing in his autobiography that "I had to follow the Eleventh Commandment"[3]–not to speak ill of another Republican. And White House aides were under instructions to say Reagan "was not engaged in 1988 politics."[4] Still, whenever the subject came up, Reagan was full of praise for his loyal vice president, calling him more than once "the best Vice President in history"[5] and saying at a 1986 press conference that Bush "is part of every decision . . . heart and soul in support of everything that we're trying to do."[6] He seemed to be grooming Bush for the presidency.

Reagan's presidential approval ratings fell from the 60s in 1986 to the low 50s in 1987 and 1988 because of the Iran-Contra scandal, but unemployment was still declining and the economy was growing at more than 7 percent per year, so his popularity did not stay low. Despite questions about Bush's role in the scandal, he managed to avoid the blame that fell on Reagan, instead reaping the benefits of Reagan's economic and diplomatic successes.

Bush went from being a critic of Reagan's to a total loyalist. He had run against Reagan in 1980 and had pilloried Reagan's program as "voodoo economics." Reagan was unimpressed with Bush's campaigning and personal strength, but picked him as vice president (after a dubious flirtation with ex-president Gerald Ford) because Bush was a moderate who'd unite the party and because Reagan pollster Richard Wirthlin said he'd help the ticket.[7] Bush was politically savvy and immediately dropped all his differences with Reagan. Bush never allowed any hint of disagreement to appear in the media and became Reagan's unwavering defender. He rarely spoke at cabinet or National Security Council meetings, rendering his advice at his weekly private lunches with the president and daily conversations.

Already possessed of an impressive résumé—the youngest navy combat pilot in World War II, Texas congressman, Republican National Chairman, CIA director, UN ambassador, envoy to China—Bush burnished it with extensive world travel that included Soviet leader Leonid Brezhnev's funeral, a mission to persuade Europeans to deploy Pershing II missiles, and oil negotiations in Saudi Arabia. As vice president, he had constant dealings with senators. He was the White House's designated envoy to African American and Hispanic leaders. Kemp and Dole also traveled extensively to aid GOP candidates—Kemp, actually, was the most sought-after speaker next to Reagan—but Bush came and went on Air Force Two.[8] And he sent a personal note to almost everyone he met and kept their names on what became an enormous national mailing list.

Bush took hits for his loyalty: Columnist George Will called him a lapdog. *Newsweek* ran a cover story on his "wimp factor." And the *Doonesbury* comic strip lampooned him for having "put his manhood into a blind trust."[9] Still, when the *Dallas Morning News* polled delegates to the 1984 Republican National Convention, 47.7 percent favored Bush as the party's 1988 nominee. Kemp was second, with 25.6 percent. Outgoing Senate GOP leader Howard Baker of Tennessee got 16.2 percent, and Dole and his wife, transportation secretary Elizabeth Dole, combined for 11.1 percent.[10]

Baker and Mrs. Dole did not run. Senator Dole did, announcing with typical acerbity that he was offering America "a record, not a resume."[11] Like Bush, he was a war hero, his right arm shattered and rendered useless by machine-gun fire in Italy. He was a man of Kansas and of Congress, but with burning national ambition—a House member from 1961 to 1969, then a Senate heavyweight: chairman of the Finance Committee, minority leader, and majority leader. Also, he had been chairman of the Republican National Committee, Gerald Ford's 1976 vice presidential running mate, and a 1980 candidate for president. He'd shepherded Reagan programs through the Senate, both tax cuts and (more often) tax increases designed to reduce federal deficits, his abiding concern. He was Kemp's political nemesis, a die-hard enemy of supply-side economics. "Tax collector for the welfare state," Kemp's friend Newt Gingrich called him. To Kemp, Dole was the ultimate "root canal" Republican. Dole considered Kemp a lightweight, preaching "painless solutions . . . while some of us do all the dirty work."[12]

In August 1985, as the candidates were getting organized to run, the *Washington Post*/ABC Poll showed that 59 percent of all voters and 87 percent of Republicans had a favorable view of Bush, who also enjoyed 87 percent name recognition and garnered equal levels of support from all groups in the party. Dole had a national favorability rating of 36 percent and was unknown to 49 percent of the electorate. Kemp was unknown to 69 percent of voters, and only 21 percent had a favorable view of him. He scored well among "strong Republicans" and conservatives. Disconcertingly, for a self-described populist, he scored well among the highest one third of income earners, but was favored by only 11 percent among the lowest third.[13]

———

Announcing his candidacy on April 6, 1987, the first priority Kemp mentioned was "like the Good Shepherd, America must reach out to the weak and to those who have been left behind." He pledged to "oppose any plan, from any quarter, to raise taxes on the American people" and called for Congress to overturn *Roe v. Wade* by statute. He said the 1988 campaign should be "a national referendum . . . on deployment of SDI as soon as possible."[14] On his postannouncement campaign stop in Buffalo, he was joined at the podium by presidents of the Buffalo AFL-CIO and NAACP.[15]

Jude Wanniski was thrilled with Kemp's candidacy. He argued that Kemp should be "Alexander [the Great] to Reagan's Philip"—an "international good shepherd" bringing supply-side prosperity to the world rather than conquest.[16] Weber was also enthusiastic, if a bit more measured, becoming one of the first members of Congress to endorse Kemp after the 1984 convention. "I understood that an incumbent Vice President was going to be difficult [to beat], but I really believed that the movement that had carried Reagan to the White House was still in full force, and that Jack was the logical recipient of that movement's support."[17]

More realistic was Charlie Black, the veteran political operative who signed on as Kemp's campaign manager in December 1986. "Kemp was the best political leader of his time, but he knew and we knew that his nomination was a long shot. No sitting Congressman had been nominated since the nineteenth century. . . . [18] [Bush and Dole] had universal name recognition with Republicans. Jack was well known among activists and party leaders, but his name identification among Republican voters was about 25 percent."[19]

Weber and Black thought Kemp the best qualified to lead. A major world figure who also thought so—or at least told Kemp so—was British prime minister Margaret Thatcher. Kemp's press secretary, John Buckley, was with him on a 1986 trip to see her and she said to Kemp, "By God, you've got to win because our ideas depend on your winning." She was dismissive of Bush and said, "You have to stop him from being the nominee." But, well informed about U.S. politics, "she also was pretty realistic that he was a long-shot candidate."[20]

Kemp's strategy for winning centered on the February 16, 1988, first-in-the-nation primary in New Hampshire. Starting in third place behind Bush and Dole, he hoped to move past Dole into second place in a state where antitax conservatives predominated and voters historically were friendly to come-from-behind candidates.[21] The Iowa caucuses February 8 would be dominated by social conservatives, while Kemp's strengths were in economics. So his campaign focused on New Hampshire. If he won there, he could concentrate on debating Bush and consider the race a two-way contest.

The New Hampshire plan came close to succeeding, only to fail embarrassingly. Two crucial factors upset the strategy—Kemp's misguided decision to spend precious time trying to score an early victory in Michigan and the unexpected entry, in force, of televangelist Pat Robertson.

In an effort to elevate their state's importance in the GOP nominating process, Michigan's governor and state party chairman created a Byzantine delegate-selection process starting with precinct elections in August 1986—eighteen months ahead of the Iowa caucuses and two years before the New Orleans nominating convention. Hoping to attract the strong conservative working-class base in the state, raise money, and conduct a surprise early strike, Kemp's team quietly began to campaign there.[22]

In September 1985, Treasury Secretary James Baker spoke to a state GOP gathering on Mackinac Island, Michigan, and noticed that Kemp supporters had put literature touting him on every seat in the audience. Baker, Bush's best friend and later his campaign manager and secretary of state, called Bush and told him he had to accelerate his campaign planning.[23]

Then Robertson got into the race, organizing the state's evangelical voters. By May 1986, Robertson had signed up 4,500 supporters to run for precinct delegate, nearly a thousand more than Bush's and Kemp's teams. Kemp strategist John Maxwell said that "we've had an organizational success, but a public relations disaster" because press accounts focused almost entirely on Robertson.[24] Evans and Novak reported that Kemp was caught in an "oozing quagmire" in Michigan because he was still running for Congress, had not formed a presidential exploratory committee, and couldn't campaign in his own name. Moreover, his backers were distributing literature implying that President Reagan was urging support for his slate, which White House political director Mitch Daniels declared "misleading and deceptive." The columnists predicted Kemp would come in third on August 5.[25]

He actually came in second to Bush in delegates, 26 percent to 12 percent, with just 9 percent going to Robertson. But a *Wall Street Journal* poll of Michigan Republicans taken on caucus day showed Bush favored by 40 percent and Robertson, Dole, and Kemp all tied at 9. Those numbers received more attention than the precinct count.[26] Kemp press secretary John Buckley said that Michigan was a "tremendous trap" for Kemp—a waste of time and resources in a large state that produced little.[27] After August, Kemp's backers formed a temporary alliance with Robertson's to freeze out Bush in county delegate selection. That pact fell apart acrimoniously; then Black arranged an alliance with Bush, ultimately getting thirty-two delegates for Kemp to Bush's forty and Robertson's nine—but long after the primary process had moved on to other states.

The Michigan defeat was devastating—and boded ill for the future. Buckley, who traveled constantly with Kemp from early 1985 through the primaries, believes that "the moment Michigan didn't happen, Jack was running not because he thought he could win, but to make sure his ideas had a voice."[28]

―――

Another aide, Mary Brunette Cannon, thinks an even heavier psychological blow came on September 14, 1987, at the Ames, Iowa, straw poll. Two months earlier, Kemp's young Iowa organizer, Scott Reed, had engineered a Kemp victory at Polk County's small straw poll in Des Moines. The victory gave Kemp national exposure and put him on weekend TV talk shows,[29] but it also raised dangerously high expectations for the bigger Ames event. "I still have nightmares about Ames," says Reed, who arranged for Kemp supporters to buy 1,800 of the 5,000 tickets purchased for the event by the Thursday before. "We thought we were in the hunt." They weren't.

On the Saturday of the straw poll, Robertson brought in "bus after bus after bus" full of energized evangelical supporters, buying up 5,000 tickets and doubling the size of the event. Robertson swept the poll with 33.6 percent of the ballots to Dole's 24.9, Bush's 22.4—and 13.5 percent for Kemp. "I think that was the moment," said Cannon, "when there really wasn't a path to victory because we couldn't out-conservative Pat Robertson."[30]

Kemp tried, however. To match Robertson and Moral Majority leader Jerry Falwell, who backed Bush, Kemp took on author-evangelist Tim LaHaye as a "national cochairman" of his campaign—only to have to drop him in the wake of disclosures that he'd made anti-Semitic remarks and declared Roman Catholicism a "false religion . . . that is more dangerous than no religion."[31] In an attempt to recoup among evangelicals, Kemp said that, if elected, he would renominate defeated conservative judge Robert Bork for the U.S. Supreme Court. He emphasized his pro-life record, including his sponsorship with Senator Orrin Hatch (R-UT) of a bill to deny federal funding to Planned Parenthood. He declared right to life a "human rights issue" on a par with the American Revolution, the writing of the Constitution, and the abolitionist and civil rights movements.

But Robertson went negative on Kemp, running radio ads in Iowa charging, "You can't trust Kemp on the right to life issue. You go listen to him speak. He never mentions it." Weber confirms that Kemp was "not completely comfortable" appealing to religious conservatives, partly because he preferred "unifying themes" to divisive ones and partly because he had strong Jewish supporters who were put off by talk of school prayer and abortion.[32]

Kemp also sought to win hard-line conservatives by being the most hawkish candidate on foreign policy, winning the Conservative Political Action Conference's (CPAC) 1987 straw poll of 287 attendees with 68 percent of the vote after calling for Shultz's ouster.[33] In the first all-candidates' debate of the campaign, he criticized Bush for support-ing Reagan's Intermediate Nuclear Forces treaty with the Soviet Union.[34] A poll of Republican debate watchers in primary states, though, showed Bush favored afterward by 43 percent, followed by Dole at 18, Robertson at 16, and Kemp, ex-Delaware governor Pierre Du Pont and former White House chief of staff Al Haig in single digits.[35]

Kemp had as supporters such hard-line conservatives as Eagle Forum founder Phyllis Schlafly and direct mail fund-raiser Richard Viguerie.[36] He also got the endorsement of right-wing senator Jesse Helm's North Caro-lina political organization, the Congressional Club. Bentley Elliott, Rea-gan's hawkish chief speechwriter, quit his job to join Kemp. Right-wing commentator and former Reagan communications director Pat Buchanan did not endorse Kemp, but announced he would not run for president in 1988 so as not to "mortally wound" Kemp's chances.[37]

Though Kemp's hawkish credentials were impeccable, Kemp was suspect among some conservatives for his outreach to minorities, his opposition to right-to-work laws and a balanced-budget constitutional amendment, and for his failure to deliver "red meat" to campaign audi-ences. He was not in favor of cuts to Medicare or Social Security, food stamps or Head Start. He was one of the first Republicans to endorse the Voting Rights Act and full voting rights for the District of Colum-bia. He supported the Martin Luther King Jr. holiday. He opposed farm subsidies, but advocated low-tax enterprise zones in inner cities.[38]

Kemp almost never attacked an opponent personally—only on pol-icy grounds—leaving the zingers to Buckley, whose barbs so got under the skin of Bush and his wife that he was banned from any administra-tion job after Bush was elected.[39] In truth, Buckley's one-liners weren't savage. When 65 of 176 House Republicans endorsed Bush in 1987, Buck-ley cracked, "That means that 110 refused to endorse the Vice President of the United States. If you ever wanted evidence of what a weak front-runner he is, that's it."[40] When he finished third in the Ames straw poll, Bush was quoted as saying that his supporters were playing golf or attending their daughters' coming-out parties. Buckley's retort: "Well, Jack would have done better, but his supporters were flipping cheeseburgers or bowling or cleaning their guns."

Unfortunately, Kemp was not delivering those one-liners himself. And often when his campaign staff prepared him to get tough in a speech—and Buckley told reporters to watch for it—Kemp failed to deliver the shots.[41]

As the Iowa caucuses and New Hampshire primary approached, Kemp's campaign did toughen up. It distributed fliers accusing Bush of changing his position on right to life and "promoting abortion" while UN ambassador. At a Catholic high school, Bush said he'd "always" opposed abortion, noted that the flier was marked "Paid for by Jack Kemp for President," and ripped it up with a flourish, saying "Fini!"[42]

Kemp and New Hampshire senator Gordon Humphrey attacked Bush and Dole for supporting cuts in Social Security benefits and for favoring higher heating oil prices. The campaign sent out a flier in an envelope resembling a government document imprinted "Important Social Security Information Enclosed" and without political identification. It drew attention to Dole's favoring a temporary benefit freeze in 1985 and Bush's voting for it to break a Senate tie. Bush made a show of tearing that one apart as well. Kemp's campaign flooded the airwaves with radio ads charging that Dole had supported an oil import fee—Dole asserted oil-dependent states like New Hampshire were exempt—and that Bush had negotiated with Saudi Arabia to keep prices up to help the U.S. oil industry. Dole's campaign charged that Kemp and Humphrey had become "the hatchet men of the 1988 campaign." Buckley said, "Looks like we've engaged the enemy." Kemp said, "They've gone completely wild. And, we're coming up in the polls."[43]

Indeed, Kemp was rising fast in New Hampshire, just as he'd hoped. When Kemp announced his candidacy in April 1987, a *Boston Globe* poll showed him holding just 6 percent support in the state, trailing Dole's 27 percent and Bush's 49.[44] On January 13, 1988, a Gallup poll showed Kemp at 15, Dole at 23, and Bush at 38.[45] On January 24, two weeks before Iowa and three weeks before New Hampshire, the *Los Angeles Times* reported that Kemp and Dole were in a statistical tie with 18 and 22 percent, respectively, with Bush ahead at 35.[46]

In Iowa, though, the influential *Des Moines Register* endorsed farm stater Dole, criticizing Kemp as "rigidly mechanistic . . . as if he believes all human behavior is governed by tax incentives and monetary policy." Its poll the day before the caucuses showed Dole leading in Iowa with 37 percent, Bush at 23, Robertson at 13, and Kemp at 11.[47] The day of the Iowa voting, the *Boston Globe* reported Bush leading in New Hampshire with 39, while Dole had 19 and Kemp, 17.

Then the bottom fell out of the Kemp campaign in Iowa, causing it to crash in New Hampshire as well. Dole won Iowa with 37 percent of the vote, Robertson finished second with 25, Bush (in a shocker) finished third with 19. Kemp got just 11 percent. Kemp immediately launched a thousand-mile, four-day tour of New Hampshire and predicted that "we're going to finish first or second. . . . This is a Kemp state." But it wasn't. Kemp's New Hampshire director, Paul Young, said that after Iowa, "the media just wrote us off. I could have had Jack walk naked down the streets of Manchester . . . and not one reporter would show up. It was as brutal a 10 days in politics as I've ever seen."[48] To make matters worse, the *Manchester Union Leader,* traditionally influential with conservatives, endorsed the libertarian Du Pont even though, in 1980, it had called for Reagan to make Kemp his vice president.[49]

On February 16, Kemp finished a distant third in New Hampshire, with just 13 percent of the vote, barely ahead of Du Pont at 11. Bush won with 38 percent and Dole was second at 28. Robertson got 9 percent. Kemp pronounced the result "a victory for the conservative wing of the Republican Party" and declared "I am convinced as this race goes on it will narrow to a Bush-Kemp race or a Dole-Kemp race and I can beat one or the other." But Kemp's staff went on unpaid "volunteer" status the day of the primary and Black said,[50] "I thought Jack should get out after New Hampshire. I knew that if you didn't make the cut after New Hampshire, if you weren't in the top two, you probably were not going to be covered by the press or be competitive." Bell, Kemp's policy chief, agreed.

Kemp decided to continue, but he began to acknowledge the possibility of losing, discussing with Buckley whom he should endorse. His main concern was to get an advocate for his ideas elected, and he said, "Of course, I'm going to endorse Bush because with Bush at least you've got a chance that these [Reaganite] ideas will be seen through, whereas with Dole, there's no chance."[51]

On March 5, Kemp publicly acknowledged there'd been discussions about ending his candidacy, but he said he'd decided he'd remain in the race through seventeen-state Super Tuesday, March 8. Leading up to that date, he spent $350,000 on a last-minute television blitz in South Carolina[52] but finished fourth with 11.5 percent behind Bush at 48, Dole 21, and Robertson 19. On March 8, Kemp failed to top single digits in a single state and finished with just five percent of the total vote and only 4 of the 712 convention delegates selected. Bush won 55 percent of the vote, Dole 25 percent, and Robertson 13 percent. Bush gained 571 delegates, almost half the number needed to be nominated.[53]

On March 9, Kemp dropped out of the race, having won only 39 delegates. In his Washington press conference he did not endorse any candidate, but did not rule out a future endorsement. A few weeks before, he'd said that the nomination of either Dole or Bush would mean "the end of the Reagan agenda," but he said at the press conference that Bush successfully "ran on the Reagan agenda. . . . We were competing for the Reagan wing of the Republican party and he won."

Kemp closed out his press conference by pulling out a note his daughter, Jennifer, had left under his pillow after his defeats on Super Tuesday. "Typical for a Kemp child," he said, it ended with a quotation from Winston Churchill: "Success is never final. Failure is never fatal. It's courage that counts." He said he did not expect to be picked for vice president, but, if asked, he would consider it "an awesome thought."[54]

On March 28, he endorsed Bush at a joint news conference in Milwaukee and toured with him for three days before the April 5 Wisconsin primary. He said the only thing about the future they'd discussed was that he would have "a strong voice in the Bush campaign in the fall."[55]

———

Kemp wrote a 6,500-word postmortem on his campaign and the state of the GOP in the Summer 1988 issue of the Heritage Foundation publication *Heritage Review*.[56] The article stands as an accurate assessment of why he lost—mainly that Bush's total identification with Reagan policy had trumped Kemp's efforts to portray himself as Reagan's ideological heir. Even the Iran-Contra scandal had worked in Bush's favor, he said, because Bush emerged as Reagan's "loyal defender." Moreover, Kemp had been unable to distinguish himself from other candidates in the race because they all adopted nearly identical policies on issues that mattered to Republicans—abortion, SDI, the need for continued growth.

It mattered little that Kemp was the idea man behind Reagan's signal economic achievements—the 1981 tax bill and the 1986 tax reform. They were seen as Reagan accomplishments, and they were in the past. Kemp had little new to offer, and what he did—monetary reform and the gold standard—was largely unintelligible to voters, or was deemed weird. Foreign policy differences with the administration and with Bush—the INF treaty, early SDI deployment, and weak support for "freedom fighters"—weren't cutting-edge issues.

The most important economic event during the campaign, he said, was the worldwide stock market crash of October 18, 1987, when the Dow Jones Industrial Average lost 22.6 percent of its value. That was also the day, Buckley remembers, when Kemp's "single biggest fundraiser to raise money from the New York financial community took place in a disco on the Upper West Side of Manhattan. . . . All the people who were to come to write their checks, they were showing up looking like their dog had been shot. . . . Sometimes you know when a campaign is just snake-bit."[57]

Kemp wrote that he wanted the GOP to adopt policies attractive to minorities so that "in ten years, one quarter will consist of conservative blacks, conservative Hispanics, conservative Asian-Americans." He campaigned more than any other candidate in minority communities, but it did him little good. White Republicans were unmoved and minorities represented just a tiny fraction of GOP primary voters.

Kemp did not mention it, but he was also defeated by the seemingly iron GOP law of primogeniture—the next man in line gets to inherit the throne.

———

There were other factors, as well, ones that Kemp could not recognize.

Kemp could be energetic and scintillating on the stump, but he was notoriously long-winded and abstruse. On one of his first trips as Kemp's press secretary in January 1985, Buckley said,[58] Kemp addressed a small dinner with wealthy potential donors in Upper East Side Manhattan. "He was delightful—but he gave the same speech three times." Afterward, Buckley told him that John F. Kennedy never gave a campaign speech longer than eighteen minutes and that his regular stump speech was just twelve minutes long. Buckley said Kemp had to start delivering speeches from a text so that the sound bite of the day would not get lost. "Kemp was astounded—and never really got the message," Buckley said.

Once again, in Red Bluff, Iowa, Buckley recalled, Kemp "gave a great speech—and then gave it again and then gave it a third time. And the mayor, at the end, said, 'Well, thank you, Congressman Kemp. Those were three of the best speeches I've ever heard.'"[59] Ed Rollins, who'd managed Reagan's 1984 reelection campaign and, in a public relations coup, joined Kemp in '88 as campaign chairman, wrote in his book *Bare Knuckles and Back Rooms*[60] that aides put Kemp on a "word diet" and gave him a time clock to put on his podium. "Jack would nod his head obediently and behave for a speech or two. Then it was back to the mumbo-jumbo like the gold standard, Malthusian theory, baskets of commodities, T-bill rates, Hannah Arendt and Maimonides, whoever the heck that is."[61] Aides tried posting a list on the door of Kemp's campaign office of things he was supposed to eliminate from speeches—"things we knew were dear to him, but we could see in these forums that eyes were glazing over and people didn't know what he was talking about."[62]

Paul Young, his New Hampshire organizer, remembers[63] driving Kemp to the most Republican county in the state and telling him he should concentrate on guns and Social Security. "I had an hour and a half with him in the car. Anybody who's ever driven with him knows Jack does not like driving. 'Are we there? Are we there?' I've got bruises down my side. . . . I'm telling him, here are the demographics. Here's what to talk about: guns, taxes, Social Security. He says, 'I got it, I got it.' So we go to the place. It's a packed house, a lot of older people and he's three minutes into his speech and he starts invoking [Maimonides.] And I see the audience just deflating."

Kemp may have thought he got through to Iowa farmers talking about the possible beneficial effects of the gold standard on farm price stability—a strong dollar was making U.S. farm goods hard to sell abroad—but aides saw that he wasn't and pleaded with him to stop trying.[64] When he kept it up, the press labeled him "eccentric" and "stubborn."

Reed said Kemp also refused to dress appropriately for campaigning in Iowa. Farmers wore overalls or dungarees, but Kemp insisted on white shirts, blue suits, tasseled loafers, and "these goofy gold tie bars, which he thought were a real fashion statement, but to most people in Iowa you might as well be coming from Pluto."[65]

Rambling speeches and fancy tie bars aside, there was also an issue of gravitas. Kemp had an easygoing, friendly relationship with journalists because he was available, open, and playful with them. Though much of the media was hostile toward conservatism, the dozens of profiles written about him during the campaign were generally favorable. But even with positive coverage, he couldn't develop a strong public image. Possibly because he was just a House member, possibly because he was seemed undisciplined, Buckley said.[66] "I think most reporters thought there was a gravitas issue, that Jack carried himself like a Member of Congress, a former professional athlete, not like a President.

[But] I don't think there's anything any of us could have done to have gotten him to change in any way."

———

The Kemp campaign was plagued with severe organizational dysfunction and conflicts over strategy and money. Problems stemmed from Kemp's inability, as a former play-calling quarterback, to let his managers manage while he campaigned. Dave Smick said that he undermined his campaign fatally by pitting various power centers against each other in an effort to maintain control.[67] Charlie Black was set against Ed Rollins; the two of them were against (House chief of staff) Dave Hoppe; then Kemp's brother, Tom, allied with key fund-raiser Richard Fox of Philadelphia; and Hoppe was against both Black and Rollins.

Jude Wanniski was no help in keeping unity on the campaign team. Kemp was bombarded almost daily with advice—harangues, actually—from his self-described "theologian." He urged Kemp to fire various members of his campaign team. He told Kemp in one letter, "I told you before and I tell you again, you are surrounded by D-W-A-R-F-S! Grown leaders do not have to read polls at the 11th hour to decide what kind of TV spots to run. Only dwarfs do. Grown leaders do not have to hide their Grand Visions of global economic expansion from voters. Only dwarfs."[68] Kemp didn't necessarily follow Wanniski's suggestions, but the suspicions he planted made Kemp even more likely to pit his staff against one another.

When Kemp wasn't sowing discord among his staffers, he was micromanaging. At one point, Smick went to Kemp and said, "I don't think you're going to get elected. I don't see how you can be the performer and also the detail guy. You cannot run for president and be approving fund-raising letters. That's insane." Smick said, "Jack would have been president had he played quarterback in the modern era where the coach called the plays."[69] But Kemp refused to allow anyone to be his coach.

Reed, trying to run Kemp's Iowa campaign, respected Kemp's work ethic, but complained about the disorder.[70] Black and Rollins were con-

stantly contradicting each other and giving different directives to everybody, he said. "There was nobody in charge. . . . I saw bickering. I saw no
agreement. And what I really saw was a lack of controls over how money
was being spent, how time was being allocated."

Recounting a classic example of Kemp's ignoring a dire need, Rollins wrote that in 1987, Kemp asked him to prepare a memo on campaign
problems. Rollins called it the "Apocalypse Now" memo. Kemp read it
over and said, "I've got to watch Jimmy play football. You and Charlie
work it out." Rollins never heard another word about the memo.

Unfortunately for his campaign's finances, fund-raising calls were
something Kemp wanted nothing to do with, according to his office manager, Sharon Zelaska.[71] Kemp's staff would put him in a room at campaign
headquarters in Rosslyn, Virginia, and say, "Okay, you're going to have to sit
in this room and make these phone calls." She said Kemp's brother, Tom,
brought in by Kemp to keep the campaign solvent, would stand over him
and say, "Make this call." Kemp "hated it. He'd maybe get through three or
four calls and then he'd hang it up. . . . Then Tom would make the calls."

Those fund-raising calls, when they happened, brought in the campaign's money, which was then promptly spent. Hoppe[72] worried that the
campaign spent too freely, employed too many people, and rented offices
the campaign couldn't afford. Buckley defended the campaign's management, insisting the headquarters in Rosslyn, were not lush, but "an absolute pit" with four staff members crammed into each room in a building
that shortly postcampaign was torn down.[73] One "lavish expense" was
Kemp's travel by chartered jet—reportedly costing $100,000 a month[74]—
but Black and Reed defend it as saving "wear and tear on his body" and
avoiding the inconvenience of traveling commercially.

Whether Kemp was spending too much or not, his campaign was
certainly financially stressed. In January 1988, Federal Election Commission records showed Bush's campaign with a balance of $11.3 mil-
lion, counting expected federal matching funds. Dole had $6.4 million;
Robertson, $3.4 million; and Du Pont, nearly $1 million. Kemp had a
negative balance of $27,000.[75]

Black and campaign operations chief Frank Cannon insist that Kemp raised enough money—$18 million to $20 million of the $25 million Black originally projected to run the campaign adequately.[76] The press often reported on Kemp's need for bank loans to keep the campaign afloat, but Black and Cannon say that was a planned strategy: donations up to $250, raised mainly by direct mail solicitations, were matched by the federal government beginning in January 1988, and the money owed could be borrowed against. They insist they had enough money to pay the bills, ended up with $200,000 cash on hand, then faced about $500,000 in "clean-up" costs such as legal fees and accountant fees for completing Federal Election Commission audits.

Federal Election Commission audit reports[77] confirm that between November 1986 and May 1988, the campaign raised $18,942,695 and spent $18,821,791, closing out with a $120,903 positive cash balance. However, the campaign had net liabilities of $1,281,054 and owed the U.S. Treasury $103,555 in penalties for overspending state limits.

Zelaska said Kemp was personally burdened by his campaign debt, which took years to pay off. To assist him, Bush later appealed to his own contributor base to help pay Kemp's debts and that Kemp organized several fund-raisers himself.[78] But as late as March 31, 1991, the Kemp for President campaign still needed $213,500 to get out of debt.

———

The minute Bush sewed up the nomination, speculation turned to who his running-mate would be. Kemp was on every "short list," including Bush's own, along with Dole,

Bush periodically asked his top aides and others for their thoughts on his selection, but kept his own thoughts secret from all of them until the last minute. Evans and Novak reported that at one meeting of ten Bush political advisers three weeks before the convention, all but two urged Bush to choose Kemp, arguing he would balance Democratic nominee Michael Dukakis's selection of Senator Lloyd Bentsen of Texas. Kemp would be a nonestablishment "outsider" against a Senate Finance

Committee "insider," a tax cutter and reformer against a tax raiser and loophole opener, a vigorous fifty-three-year-old against a sixty-seven-year-old.[79]

Dan Quayle, a senator from Indiana, was not even mentioned in early speculation that included, besides Kemp and Dole, California governor George Deukmejian, White House chief of staff Howard Baker, Senate minority whip Alan Simpson, former governors Lamar Alexander of Tennessee and Dick Thornburgh of Pennsylvania, senators William Armstrong of Colorado, Pete Domenici of New Mexico, and John Danforth of Missouri, plus Dole's wife, Elizabeth.[80] Quayle, however, was working hard behind the scenes to be tapped for veep. Quayle and his wife, Marilyn, began a stealthy but concerted campaign in February to win the number two spot by raising his profile, ingratiating him with top Bush advisers, and acquainting him personally with Bush.[81] Quayle wrote in his book[82] that "for months" he and his wife talked about his possible nomination and that Bush called him just after the Democratic National Convention ended July 21 to ask if he'd let himself be considered.

From the time he endorsed Bush, Kemp spoke enthusiastically about him, but did not wage a Quayle-like campaign for the number two slot.[83] He didn't even seem to be particularly hungry for the position. Hoppe said:[84] "Did Jack think he could be helpful to the ticket? Definitely. Did Jack think he could help move and strengthen the ideas he believed in a Bush presidency if he was a part of it? Yes. Was he panting after it? I don't get the sense that he was."

But most of his staff members were. Kemp was to deliver a prime-time speech to the convention on Monday, August 15, the night delegates honored Ronald Reagan and the day before Bush was to unveil his choice, and the aides hoped Bush would be impressed. In his speech he praised Reagan, and mentioned Bush a few times—perhaps too few. Mueller, who wrote the speech,[85] said instead of "an encomium to Reagan . . . it should have been sucking up to Bush." Instead, in seventeen minutes, the speech contained nineteen references to Reagan, only four to

Bush, and three to Abraham Lincoln.[86] The speech was well received, but Bush was heading in another direction.

On Tuesday morning, August 16, Kemp conducted a long round of press interviews. One was with David Broder, who arrived saying that the "betting where I am is that you're going to be vice president."[87] Shortly after that, word spread that other candidates were being called by Bush and told they had not been selected. Hoppe said, "It got to be 11 [a.m.], then 12, then 1 and we'd had no call.[88] Journalist gossip had it that the Secret Service was saying there would be a Bush trip to Buffalo.[89]

Buckley added to the suspense. Working at the convention for CBS News, he called Hoppe to report that he'd run into veteran California political operative Stuart Spencer, who would be one of the veep selectee's chief "handlers" for the Bush campaign. Spencer[90] asked him if he could be available after the convention. "The unmistakable message was, 'I think it's going to be Jack.'"[91]

In the early afternoon, at a thank-you event for campaign supporters,[92] Kemp got a call from Bush's office saying he should go back to his hotel to await a call from Bush. Accounts differ as to exactly what happened there. Reed said Kemp took the call in private, emerged from his bedroom and reported, "It's Dan Quayle," shocking staff and family members gathered in the living room. Hoppe remembers it differently: Kemp was sitting by a phone with staff and family present. "I happened to be facing him. And he picked up the phone and said, 'Oh. Thank you, Mr. Vice President.' And then he said, 'It's Dan Quayle.'" Putting down the phone at the end of the call, Kemp said, "I guess I'll be going to every one of Jimmy's games."

An hour after getting Bush's call, Kemp praised Quayle in an appearance before the College National Republican Committee, calling him "a dear friend" and predicting that he would make the GOP "as appealing to young people as it has ever been in our history." He noted that Quayle had been the key sponsor of the 1982 Job Training Partnership Act, which Quayle worked on with Senator Edward Kennedy (D-MA) to reorganize federal programs for the unemployed, and had supported enterprise zones and strategic defense. "He's articulate, a dynamic conservative. He's an activist. He's not satisfied with the status quo," Kemp said.[93]

Many of the college Republicans Kemp addressed were wearing Bush-Kemp buttons and began to chant, "Kemp in '92, Kemp in '92." Kemp chastised them mildly for losing faith in the party and suggesting that Bush would lose, leaving space for him to run the next cycle.[94] "We're going to win in '88 and we're going to win again in '92." He said he did not expect to be asked to serve in Bush's cabinet because others were in line for the two jobs that interested him: State and Treasury.[95]

Kemp was traveling between television interviews at the New Orleans Superdome the night of Quayle's selection when he encountered Barbara Bush, who stopped and whispered, "Jack, I was for you." Hoppe[96] was with him and thought she didn't have to say it, and therefore meant it.

That night, after the convention proceedings, Kemp and his wife went to dinner with Reagan education secretary Bill Bennett and his wife, Elayne. Mrs. Bennett had told her husband that Kemp surely would be dejected and that he should cheer him up. Instead, Kemp did his usual thing, greeting waiters and visiting the kitchen help, telling them, "You've got to support George Bush. He's going to be a great president."[97] Among the staff, said Hoppe, "there was sadness. Absolutely there was. Having said that, [for Kemp it was] 'so it's gone. What's tomorrow?'"

Quayle's nomination came as a huge surprise at the convention—and not entirely a welcome one. Quayle complained in his book that Baker and Spencer made it clear to the media that they'd opposed his selection.[98] Even though Quayle was more conservative than Bush, the right was not elated either. Activist Paul Weyrich said, "I'm calling this NutraSweet Kemp. I think, in the Bush context, this is as far in our direction as you could get."[99]

Numerous accounts of the Quayle selection process make the same point: Bush wanted a vice president who'd behave as he did for eight years toward Reagan, and Kemp did not fit that bill. Robert Novak wrote that Bush aides told him Bush "dreaded the prospect of . . . being second-guessed every day by a Vice President Kemp."[100]

———

Kemp may have taken his nonselection as veep in stride, but not his failure as a candidate. After being a national figure for so long, he was shaken by the sudden silence once he was off the political stage. Kemp's daughters, Jennifer Andrews and Judith Nolan, say it was "devastating" and led him to try to find solace in Christian Science teaching. "You could almost see that he was physically knocked over," Judith said. "I knew he had a faith . . . but to see him wake up at six in the morning and pore through the Bible, I'm like, 'Oh, gosh. He's soul-searching.'"[101]

Kemp had declined to discuss his Scientist background with reporters on the campaign trail, fearing the topic might present a political vulnerability, but now he focused his energy on his faith, reading Mary Baker Eddy and the Bible daily. Kemp took solace in the favorite saying of his Christian Scientist mother—"No door closes but another one opens"—and found that his faith buoyed him up. As Buckley noted, when most candidates are asked, "What happens if you lose?" most say, "I don't intend to lose." But Kemp had said, "If I don't get elected president, something good will happen. Something else will happen."

And after campaigning hard for Bush/Quayle and other Republicans,[102] a new door did open and something Kemp considered good did happen. He got a chance to fight poverty—and remake the GOP into "the party of Lincoln"—as Bush's secretary of housing and urban development.

Ten

POVERTY WARRIOR

n 1965, New Orleans was a divided city. Black diners were barred from many restaurants. Taxicabs were segregated. This kind of racial division was not an entirely new experience for Kemp when he arrived there for the AFL All-Star game. He'd encountered and opposed racism before, but it was a shock to him each time. Kemp's teammate, running back Cookie Gilchrist, yelled for a cab outside a nightclub. "Uh, we don't serve y'all," the driver told him, Bills tight end Ernie Warlick said.[1] "You got to call a colored cab." Gilchrist said, "I don't care what color the cab is. We just want a cab."

The next day, Gilchrist declared he wasn't going to play in the All-Star game. Black players from the 1964 league champion Bills and opposing AFL All-Stars voted unanimously to boycott the game. As captain of the Bills, Kemp was on board with the decision. He stood with the players, and the game was moved to Houston.[2]

Kemp's compassion and belief in human equality had taken root in early childhood. Kemp's grandmother, "Grandma Sunshine," had lived with his family and told stories about feeding and sheltering Blackfoot Sioux in South Dakota. In an age when racism was a normal part of life, she had insisted that her offspring must always help those in need, no matter their ethnicity.[3]

Combining his grandmother's training, his respect for his black teammates, and his background working with unions, Kemp possessed a racial sensitivity unusual in conservatives of his day, as well as a sympathy for the blue-collar workers. A passionate admirer of Lincoln, he believed in an "opportunity society," similar to Lincoln's idea of a "just, and generous, and prosperous system, which opens the way to all—gives hope to all, and progress, and improvement of condition to all."[4]

And like Lincoln, Kemp believed it was the job of government to enable people to achieve their aims—and remove obstacles, especially, in Kemp's view, high taxes. Lincoln favored public support to build roads, dams, and waterways. Kemp believed, with Lincoln, in government's assisting people in improving their lives. So when Bush needed a housing secretary, Kemp seemed a logical choice. But whether the "bleeding-heart conservative" could make a difference would remain to be seen.

———

Although Bush had passed over Kemp in the veep search, not wanting the independent-minded, free-speaking conservative close at hand in the White House, Bush did want Kemp in his administration. Bush's estimation of Kemp rose during the 1988 presidential campaign, said his vice presidential chief of staff, Craig Fuller. During primary debates, Bush appreciated that Kemp "talked about issues" and never got personal or went negative. He liked Kemp's unique ability to communicate with minority communities.[5] And Barbara Bush liked Joanne.

Fuller was in charge of Bush's postelection transition team along with pollster-political adviser Bob Teeter. Eager to see his boss kept relevant, Kemp's 1988 campaign manager, Charlie Black,[6] suggested to Teeter that it would be good for Bush to have former rival and conservative hero Kemp in the administration. Teeter told Black, "Bush is willing to appoint Kemp to HUD, but he's not convinced that Jack is a team player and will be on message with his administration's policies." Black suggested Teeter and Fuller talk to Kemp and ask if he would be loyal and "not spout off about subjects, like taxes, not in your area." After Kemp met with Teeter and Fuller, he told Black he'd reassured the Bush advisers. "I used to be a football player. I called the plays, but I also answered to a coach who was my boss. I can be a team player."

Bush also was impressed by Kemp[7] at the December 1, 1988, black-tie gala marking his retirement from Congress. Among hundreds of people Kemp called out by name was Kimi Gray, the black public housing organizer from Washington, D.C. Kemp said she'd kicked drug dealers out, created jobs for tenants, started a day-care center, and reduced welfare dependency from 83 to 2 percent. She was a model, he said, for his "urban homesteading" idea enabling tenants to own their apartments.[8]

Bush, in his remarks that night, joked about seeing so many familiar faces—"you might call it dejavoodoo"—but he also praised Kemp for bringing "hope into corners of America that had heard too little from Republicans in the past" and thanked him for his "tireless campaigning" for him and other GOP candidates in 1988. Kemp responded graciously. "It's no secret that I thought I should follow Ronald Reagan" into the White House, he said. "But I go by the marketplace and the best man won." He called Bush "the right man at the right time in the history of the country," adding, "He is our leader for the next eight years." Bush was taken. The next day, he told an aide, "Let's get Jack in. I want to talk to him."

Bush and Kemp talked about housing and neighborhoods for forty-five minutes. A few weeks later, Bush named him housing secretary.[9] Before doing so, Bush consulted John Sununu, Dan Quayle, and James Baker, all of whom gave thumbs up. Sununu said[10] that he and Quayle "lobbied hard" for Kemp.

Besides economics and foreign policy, Kemp's principal passion in Congress had been creating opportunity for poor people, chiefly by encouraging job creation in poverty areas, allowing public housing tenants to own their homes, and lowering the marginal cost of moving from welfare to work. He also wanted to make the GOP attractive to minorities. Retired from Congress, Kemp had been scheduled to become a senior fellow at the Heritage Foundation—had set up an office there, in fact. But the prospect of becoming the cabinet officer in charge of urban affairs challenged him, and Joanne encouraged him to accept Bush's offer.[11]

———

From the outset, Bush and Kemp had very different ideas about helping urban America and the poor. Bush's main idea was Points of Light, a program that emphasized voluntary private efforts. He highlighted such projects throughout his presidency. Kemp advocated stronger stuff. Even on the day Bush asked him to be HUD secretary, Kemp talked about waging "a war on poverty." Bush was taken aback by Kemp's reference to Lyndon Johnson's 1960s initiative, saying it conjured up the Great Society and big government.[12] Kemp argued to Bush that he had something different in mind—an activist agenda driven by markets, not bureaucracies: tenant ownership of public housing, enterprise zones that lured businesses to distressed areas through tax cuts, education and housing vouchers, and "radical welfare reform" that wouldn't punish the poor financially when they got a job. Bush told him he had one caveat. "He didn't want me to call it a 'War on Poverty,'" Kemp recalled.[13] He didn't seem to listen.

In Bush's four years in office, the president uttered the words "war on poverty" precisely three times in speeches.[14] Kemp did so constantly, publicly and privately—including on the day Bush announced his appointment, December 19, in the White House briefing room. Bush said he'd appointed Kemp because his "innovative approach" could substitute for big spending in a tight-budget environment, but Kemp didn't follow the spending cut hints. Instead, he was blunt: "I want to wage war on poverty. . . . I don't believe we're going to balance the budget by cutting housing. I don't think we're going to balance the budget . . . unless we have healthy cities." He promised he would "make my case in the Cabinet, not out on the street." But he told the press: "I want it known that you cannot balance the budget on the backs of the poor." He said he had not yet met with incoming budget director Dick Darman—soon to be his nemesis—but did not believe Bush would have appointed him if he planned to have "the budget for housing emasculated."[15]

Some reporters presciently homed in on future sore spots. Could

Kemp stick to his own business? Kemp replied, "I'm not going to speak on foreign policy. I've got my views. If I had a chance to meet [the president] privately, I'll exercise the opportunity. But I'm not going to go in there with a portfolio that includes defense or someone else's Cabinet position." What if Bush broke his 1988 convention vow, "Read my lips— no new taxes"? Kemp said, "The answer is, I read his lips. I believe him." What about Republican weakness with black voters, Bush's "Willy Horton" ads, and the fact that the head of the NAACP, Benjamin Hooks, had labeled Kemp a "Big L Liberal"? Kemp responded that he considered it "a badge of honor" to be called a liberal on race relations. "I think in appointing me, if I may be so bold to suggest, this is something I have a longtime interest in—expanding the party, making it truly a Lincoln party."

———

President Bush did Kemp the favor of appearing at his swearing-in ceremony on February 13 in the cafeteria of the hulking Department of Housing and Urban Development headquarters building. Before a standing audience of HUD employees, whose morale was deflated after eight years of neglect and slashed budgets during the Reagan years, Bush endorsed the full Kemp agenda: growth economics, enterprise zones, urban homesteading, tenant management and ownership of public housing, empowerment of poor people to rebuild blighted neighborhoods, ending the tragedy of homelessness, strong enforcement of laws against discrimination. "These are our goals. And these ideas I have clicked off today—Jack Kemp has been out front for those very principles for a long, long time." Bush did not use the term "war on poverty." And Kemp did him the favor—that one day—of not using it either.[16]

In his remarks that day, Kemp called on HUD workers to "keep our minds, our work, and our hearts focused on those we are meant to serve: not just the homebuilder but the homebuyer, not only public housing authorities but the public housing resident, not just mayors and city managers but the poor and those who live temporarily on the streets or in shelters." He said he wanted to do the work of Dr. Martin Luther King Jr., giving the poor "a stake in the American dream," and he invoked Lincoln as his model.

In his office at HUD, Kemp kept two busts of Lincoln and a portrait on display. If his program was successful, he thought, "the Lincoln party" could attract 80 percent of the Asian vote, 50 to 60 percent of the Hispanic vote, and 30 to 40 percent of the black vote. It was not to be. Bush's support among Hispanics dropped from 30 percent in 1988 to 25 in 1992 and among blacks, from 11 percent to 10 percent. He did win a majority of Asian American votes in 1992.

In 1992, Kemp was asked at a journalists' breakfast where his passion came from.[17] He recalled the years he spent as a professional quarterback and the lessons of racial equality he had picked up in a locker room filled with black athletes. He added: "It is my way of redeeming my existence on this earth. I wasn't there with Rosa Parks or Dr. King or John Lewis, but I am here now and I am going to yell from the rooftops about what we need to do." During the civil rights movement the Republican Party had missed the opportunity to oppose racism, he said. "And frankly," he warned, "to miss this opportunity is to lose what history rarely grants—a second chance."

———

To underscore his dedication to his agenda, on the day after his swearing-in, Kemp traveled to Atlanta, where he met with tenant leaders and low-income housing advocates, visited housing projects and the Martin Luther King Jr. Center, and overnighted at the legendary Paschal's Motor Hotel on the city's predominantly black west side. As residents and city leaders urged more funds for housing and downtown development, he said, "I am here to listen. You have my eyes, ears and attention. You also have my heart." He was accompanied by civil rights–era heroes Representative John Lewis and Mayor Andrew Young, Democrats who expressed optimism about his intentions. He dined with Coretta Scott King.[18] Ten days later, he visited a Baltimore homeless shelter, overnighted at a senior citizens housing project, and met tenant advocates in Philadelphia.

On one of his early trips, Kemp told a reporter that then–Urban League president Vernon Jordan had changed his mind about the role of government in helping the poor. He used to believe[19] that general economic growth was all it took to help the poor, that a "rising tide lifts all boats." But Jordan convinced him that "a rising tide can't lift boats that are stuck on the bottom. . . . And it began to click in my mind that you have a legitimate role for government to help . . . repair the boats that had sunk, or the families that had been injured."

Kemp traveled out of Washington on HUD business more than 250 days during his four-year tenure.[20] Many of the trips were organized by Kemp's long-standing urban mentor, Bob Woodson, founder of the National Center for Neighborhood Enterprise. Woodson advised Kemp to visit housing projects and invite along mayors and governors—many of whom, though politically liberal, had never seen a project. If Kemp visited, say, Chicago's monstrous, dismal Cabrini-Green project, he'd invite residents to accompany him to his downtown lunch or dinner event, seat them at the head table, and reference them in his speech. Woodson arranged for blacks and Hispanics to arrive early for Kemp congressional appearances and take seats behind him where they would be seen in a TV bite.[21]

In a celebrated outing on May 15, 1991, Kemp accompanied England's queen Elizabeth II and Barbara Bush on a tour of inner-city Washington, D.C. They visited the new home of Alice Frazier, sixty-seven, whose purchase was possible through HUD. Frazier had been given full instructions as to the proper etiquette for meeting the queen of England—no one was to touch the queen, even to shake hands. She utterly disregarded them. Saying "Hello, Queen," she walked up to her and hugged her, to the shock of all present.[22] Said Kemp aide Rick Ahearn, "Jack thought it was the best thing since sliced bread. . . . [He] told the story over and over. . . . Jack's line was 'It's her palace. It's her home.'"

For Kemp, his travel was a way to make a statement and create news on his agenda items. He called them "offensive trips," according to his chief of staff, Scott Reed.[23] "After those trips took off, we had a barrage of Members of Congress wanting him to come" and piled up thick collections of press clippings, mostly admiring.

———

Early on, Kemp laid out the strategies for his "war." He had posters and cards printed and passed out to HUD employees titled "Priorities of HUD Under President George Bush and Secretary Jack Kemp: Recapturing the American Dream." The idea was they all would know where Kemp was headed. Its six bullet points were

- *Expand Homeownership and Affordable Housing Opportunities*
- *Create Jobs and Economic Development through Enterprise Zones*
- *Empower the Poor through Resident Management and Home-steading*
- *Enforce Fair Housing for All*
- *Help Make Public Housing Drug Free*
- *Help End the Tragedy Homelessness.*

The original list had just five items. But on one of his trips Kemp saw how ravaged a housing project was by drug dealing. He added "drug free" as a major HUD goal.[24]

Before he could concentrate on his "offensive" agenda, though, Kemp had to clear the "swamp," his term for the morass of scandal, mismanagement, and corruption left behind at HUD by his predecessor, Samuel Pierce. Pierce was a prominent lawyer who had argued the landmark *New York Times vs. Sullivan* free-press case before the U.S. Supreme Court on behalf of Dr. Martin Luther King Jr. He was the first black partner in a major New York law firm, the first black board member of a Fortune 500 company, and had been general counsel of the Treasury Department under Richard Nixon.[25] But he was inept at running an agency and knew nothing and cared little about housing policy.

By the time Kemp arrived, the department had already been the subject of a well-publicized scandal nicknamed "Robin HUD." It involved a Maryland real estate agent charged with and later convicted of stealing $6 million of the proceeds of government property sales, a bit of which she gave to charity.[26] A week before he was sworn in, Kemp wrote Paul Adams, HUD's inspector general, asking for a briefing the following day on pending audits of fraud, waste, and mismanagement in the department.[27] It was an eye-opener.

Adams's reports and subsequent investigations by Congress, media organizations, and, ultimately, the Justice Department revealed that Pierce was nearly a hands-off secretary who spent afternoons watching TV soap operas in his tenth-floor office, regularly left work at 4 p.m., and took five taxpayer-financed trips to Russia. In 1981, he'd been assigned a "brat pack" of young Republican campaign aides with no housing experience. He let them run amok, dispensing HUD grants on the basis of political connections and personal favoritism.[28, 29] Meantime, Reagan's Office of Management and Budget had cut HUD funding by 59 percent: from $35.9 billion in 1980 to $14.7 billion in 1987[30]—but provided little management oversight. HUD personnel dropped nearly 30 percent, from 16,300 to 11,500. HUD's oversight committees in Congress also provided little supervision.

Pierce once had nine hundred lawyers working under him at Treasury, and Kemp had never run anything larger than a congressional office. He quickly set about assembling a team to help clear the mess and begin on his agenda. He brought over Sharon Zelaska, his capable personal assistant, and Mary Cannon, his legislative assistant, from his congressional office. He hired Reed, a young campaign operative, as his chief of staff. Reed, who knew the difference between a House office and a federal department, immediately found an experienced administrator to be Kemp's deputy secretary: Al DelliBovi, who'd run the Urban Mass Transit Administration under Reagan. And he hired Frank Keating, an ex-FBI agent and the former number three in the Reagan Justice Department, to be his general counsel.

Six months after Kemp took office, DelliBovi identified twenty-eight housing programs afflicted by "theft, influence peddling or serious mismanagement," accounting for 94 percent of the money HUD spent or collected.[31] A Senate subcommittee concluded that "Pierce and a handful of political appointees created a culture at HUD whereby programs designed for the poor became programs for the benefit of the politically well-connected."[32] In all, seventeen ex-federal officials, lobbyists, developers, and consultants were convicted, including three former HUD assistant secretaries.[33] The government fined defendants $2 million, though losses from abuse were variously estimated at $2 billion to $6 billion.[34]

In 1990, the House Government Operations Committee unanimously found that Pierce "at best . . . was less than honest and misled the committee about his involvement in abuses and favoritism in HUD funding decisions. At worst, Secretary Pierce knowingly lied and committed perjury during his testimony."[35] But he was not indicted based on lack of evidence that he or his family profited from HUD fraud. He signed a statement admitting that his "own conduct contributed to an environment in which these events [criminal acts] could occur."[36]

After eight years of mismanagement, budget and personnel cuts, virtual invisibility, and then exploding scandal, morale at HUD had collapsed by the time Kemp arrived. His exuberance, positive press, and skill at retail politics turned "the building" around. Immediately, he reversed the Pierce policy that no HUD worker was allowed to ride an elevator with the secretary or speak to him in a hallway. Kemp quizzed and engaged his bureaucrats, sometimes invited them to his office to finish a conversation, and periodically had lunch in the employee cafeteria. He insisted that they call him Jack.[37]

When he arrived, the HUD building itself was, as Mary Cannon[38] put it, "ten floors of basement, really hideous." Kemp ordered brighter lights in the hallways, put decorative art on the walls to replace drab photos of public housing projects, and redid the cafeteria. To observe National Secretaries Day, the department held a lottery whose winners had lunch with Kemp in his private dining room. His fifty-fifth birthday was celebrated in the employee cafeteria with a full house attending—and fifty-five cakes baked by HUD employees. Most of all Kemp changed morale by reforming the agency, then mounting an aggressive agenda and selling it publicly—nonstop. Kemp made it an exciting place to work, said Sherrie Rollins, his assistant secretary for public affairs.[39] "It could be exhausting. He could drive you crazy trying to keep up with him," she said. "But it gave you the feeling that you could really make a difference."

Once he saw what a mess HUD had become, Kemp fixed more than the building. He ordered a team including DelliBovi, Keating, Cannon, and his assistant secretary for policy, John Weicher, to develop a reform agenda he dubbed "Clearing the Decks."[40] Kemp said[41] he "didn't want to be the Secretary of Reform. He wanted to be the Secretary of Empowering People." What emerged was the HUD Reform Act of 1989. In record time—six weeks—Congress passed most of its recommendations and Bush quickly signed it. When Kemp testified before a House Government Operations investigative subcommittee, he was praised by Chairman Tom Lantos (D-CA) for moving "promptly, forcefully and decisively" to deal with the scandal and for demonstrating "hands-on, responsible and energetic leadership."[42]

Praised in the media and (for a time) on Capitol Hill, Kemp immediately ran into trouble with his minders at the White House Office of Management and Budget. Once Kemp got his reform package together, the bureaucratically correct procedure would have been to submit it to OMB, which would then pass it around to other departments, who'd vet it and send it back for revisions. Kemp & Company didn't do that. "We knew that if we did that, it would never get done," Reed said. "They'd nitpick us forever. So we announced the day before that we were going to have a big press conference at HUD at 10 a.m. and informed OMB about it at 5 p.m. They went absolutely bonkers, demanded to talk to Kemp. He had gone home, so we said, 'Well, come over in the morning.'" The morning session was raucous, with OMB officials complaining that HUD was freelancing. But HUD went ahead with its press conference and submitted its reform legislation to Congress intact.

The fast one "haunted us for the next four years," Reed said, "because they didn't like us. They didn't like our style, they thought we were a little off the reservation, Lone Rangers." [43] Kemp had gotten the job done, but at the cost of constant problems in the following years.

————

Among hundreds of Kemp speeches, articles, and interviews during the period, it was a sweeping address to the conservative Heritage Foundation on June 6, 1990,[44] that best illuminates his outlook. It had a grandiose title—"An Inquiry into the Nature and Causes of Poverty in America and How to Combat It"—borrowed from Adam Smith's "An Inquiry into the Nature and Causes of the Wealth of Nations."

The speech came at the time when communism was in its death throes, and Kemp seized on that moment. He likened the sclerotic economies of the East Bloc to those in impoverished communities throughout America. "If we are to present the example of democratic capitalism and the rule of law to the rest of the world, we've got to make it work for the low-income people and distressed neighborhoods and communities right here in our own country," he declared. "It is not only Eastern Europe looking to us for market oriented answers. It is also East Harlem, East St. Louis and East LA." He said that helping those left behind was not only a moral imperative, but a winning political strategy. "Whether it's called bleeding heart conservatism, capitalism with a social conscience or populist conservatism—it's the right thing to do, the right time to do it, and we're the right people to help lead it."

He disputed the notion of "America as two cities, one rich and one poor, permanently divided into two classes." That had been the crux of New York governor Mario Cuomo's keynote speech to the 1984 Democratic National Convention. "With all due respect to Gov. Cuomo, he got it wrong," Kemp said. "America is not divided immutably into two static classes. But it is separated or divided into two *economies*. One economy—our mainstream economy—is democratic capitalist, market-oriented, entrepreneurial and incentivized for working families whether in labor or management." It produced the widespread prosperity and high standard of living of the Reagan years.

"But there is . . . a second economy that is similar in respects to the Eastern European or Third World 'socialist' economy," Kemp said. "It is almost totally opposite to the way we are treated in our mainstream economy and it predominates in the pockets of poverty throughout urban and rural America. This economy [denies] entry to Black, Hispanic and other minority men and women into the mainstream, almost as effectively as hiring notices 50 years ago that read 'No Blacks (or Hispanics or Irish or whatever) Need Apply.'"

If someone *wanted* to create poverty and make people dependent on government, he said, he would do what liberal policy had done. Among other things, reward welfare and unemployment at a higher level than working and tax the entrepreneur who succeeds in the legal capitalistic system much higher than in the illicit underground economy. Also, reward people who stay in public housing more than those who move to private housing and home ownership. Reward the family that breaks up rather than the family that stays together. Encourage debt, borrowing and spending rather than saving, investing and risk-taking. And, "most of all . . . weaken and in some cases destroy the link between effort and reward."

Then Kemp turned to what he called the "good news." Government policies "can change and . . . good policy can lead to good results. . . . The poor don't want paternalism. They want opportunity. They don't want the servitude of welfare. They want to get jobs and private property. They don't want dependency. They want a new declaration of independence."

He reiterated his agenda: to encourage investment, cut the capital gains tax rate to 15 percent (from 28 per cent), and eliminate it altogether in enterprise zones. The capital gains tax reduction, he said, wasn't intended to help the rich or secure old wealth, but "to free up or unlock old capital and old wealth to help new business, new risk takers, job-creation and economic growth." He advocated resident management and purchase of public housing units, a policy pioneered in Britain by

Conservative prime minister Margaret Thatcher. And he proposed housing vouchers to allow poor people to choose their own housing, plus "a
new version to tax reform to remove low income families from the tax
rolls and dramatically increase the after-tax income of welfare mothers
and unemployed fathers who go to work."

In 1948, at the median income, he said, "a family of four paid virtually no income tax and only $30 a year in direct Social Security taxes.
This year, the same family's tax burden would be over $6,000. To be
comparable to 1948, the personal exemption—the tax allowance for nur-
turing children—would have to be well over $6,000 today. Instead, it is
only $2,000." To achieve this, he advocated "dramatic expansion of the
earned income tax credit, a $6,000 exemption for children under 16 and
[President Bush's] child care tax credit to roll back this tax burden on
low income families and unemployed parents."[45]

The elements of the speech, taken together, constituted the most
comprehensive antipoverty program—and the most compelling critique of existing policy—ever offered by a conservative American politician. But Kemp didn't stop there.

———

Justifying Bush's reluctance to choose him as vice president, Kemp's
agenda went well beyond his HUD portfolio—and miles beyond Bush's
program. Kemp persistently assumed that his goals were Bush's and
seized on every positive Bush statement as an in-cement endorsement of
the "empowerment" agenda. In the blizzard of memos he sent Bush urging more action on poverty and economic growth, he invariably couched
his case in terms of advancing "your program." Aides like Mary Cannon
and Scott Reed insist that Kemp sincerely believed that Bush supported
what he sought to do and that others in the administration—notably
Darman—were obstructing him.

Unfortunately, this was not the case. In reality, Bush was focused
mainly on international affairs and was uninterested in urban policy. Weber
told the *Washington Post*[46] that Kemp's initiatives always were included in

Bush's announced program and sometimes in Darman's budgets, "but the only one who wanted to push them was Jack Kemp." For Bush and Kemp "a critical decision point" came in March 1991, just after the Gulf War had been won and Bush's approval ratings approached 90 percent. "George Bush had enormous political capital to spend, and he decided to spend it on the Middle East peace process, rather than on domestic programs."

Reed acknowledged that Kemp created problems for himself at the White House: "Jack would occasionally overstep, write a confidential memo that we'd leak to [columnist Robert] Novak and then they'd go crazy. Jack would never tell me in advance that he was going to do something that would create controversy. He would just do it. . . . It got to a point that we were really ostracized from these guys [at the White House]."[47]

Not surprisingly, Kemp was frustrated his entire tenure at HUD, Cannon said,[48] especially over "the missed opportunities." Yet privately and publicly, he continued to believe that Bush was on his side, despite the evidence.

Bush's enthusiasm for Kemp's agenda can be measured by his references to it in State of the Union addresses to Congress. He made no reference whatever to enterprise zones in 1989 or 1990, though he did, briefly, in 1991 and 1992. He addressed "homelessness" in 1989, but not again. He referred to tenant ownership in one line or paragraph in 1990, 1991, and 1992. In no address did Bush use Kemp's favorite word, "empowerment."[49] It was not until the 1992 Rodney King riots in LA—exploited by his Democratic opponent, Bill Clinton, as evidence of Bush's "neglect" of the cities—that he got serious about the urban agenda.

———

Kemp's strongest opponent in the administration was Richard Darman. Serving in four administrations, six cabinet departments, and two White Houses, Harvard-educated Richard Darman was a brilliant, tough, abrasive, and manipulative technocrat. Kemp was a problem for him for two reasons. First, there was his bold and expensive agenda. Second, Kemp was a rarity in the Bush administration, a politician with star quality. This meant the media would cover any hint of friction between Kemp and the White House. And Kemp was not afraid to use the leverage this gave him. He was, among other things, a persistent leaker when he thought it would help his agenda.

The dislike went both ways. In his last weeks at HUD after Clinton won the 1992 election, Kemp gave a blistering assessment of Darman's influence to Jason DeParle of the *New York Times*. "Darman not only cost those of us who believe in the War on Poverty," Kemp said. "I believe in no small way he is responsible for the President losing the election." He called Darman "the Prince of Darkness" and a "pencilneck." Darman "dropped poison" on new ideas to maintain his own power, Kemp charged, and brought "a really sick attitude" to the poverty debate. "He didn't care about poverty; he cared about what the budget looked like . . . [and] opposed everything I tried to do."[50] Darman later wrote that he and Kemp became "friends" during the Reagan administration and that he urged Kemp's HUD appointment. He thought Kemp "had a combination of positive vision, idealism and inclusiveness." But "what I failed to imagine was that future differences would put a strain on this and many other relationships."[51]

Conflicts between Kemp and Darman over HUD budgets and policy arose fundamentally because Darman's staff persistently estimated that tax cuts central to enterprise zones would cost massive amounts of revenue. This was implausible. "Those poverty areas were not producing any revenue to lose," Mary Cannon said, and wouldn't need to be offset by "draconian cuts in the HUD budget."[52]

Also, Darman figured—correctly—that congressional Democrats would never cut traditional HUD programs like public housing construction to fund Kemp favorites like home ownership for public housing tenants. If they funded Kemp's schemes at all, it would be with added money, busting Darman's budget. So he nixed Kemp's money appeals from the get-go. Or if a Kemp request did get in the president's budget, the White House didn't fight for it in Congress. What's more, Darman doubted that Kemp's ideas would work. And during the Bush era, they didn't. Of 1.3 million public housing units in the nation, only 135 were sold to tenants on Kemp's watch, all but 16 of them in Washington, D.C.[53]

Kemp suffered his first bureaucratic rout on June 29, 1989, when he visited Sununu's office with an inch-thick folder outlining his proposals.[54] Kemp sought first-year funding of $1 billion for HOPE, his tenant-purchase plan. Darman distributed a single-page handout tallying up the program's costs as three to five times higher than Kemp's. "It just blew apart Kemp's ideas, before they ever got started," said Kemp aide Thomas Humbert.

When Sununu suggested there might be no money for HOPE (Home Ownership for People Everywhere) at all, Kemp leaped up from his seat and threatened to resign. "Sununu got up and said, 'Jack, you're getting overheated. Sit down.' Kemp left the meeting with a $250 million pledge for HOPE, a quarter of what he'd asked for.

During 1989 and 1990, a cabinet staff committee suggested Kempian ideas for fighting poverty, but each time the cabinet itself found the cost too high, the politics wrong, or the promise of success too thin.[55] When the cabinet decided to recommend more studies, Kemp exploded. "Meanwhile, what's going on in our neighborhoods and on the streets?" he wrote in a memo. He accused the White House of "bureaucratizing the effort and sending it into oblivion."

Their biggest difference was the 1990 deal in which Bush agreed with Democrats to raise taxes, thereby breaking his unqualified 1988 election pledge. Like Reagan budget director David Stockman before him, Darman was consumed with controlling federal deficits and debt. The annual deficit when Bush took over in 1989 had fallen from a Reagan-era high of 6 percent of GDP in 1983 to 2.9 percent. But the cumulative public debt had climbed from 26.1 percent in 1980 to 40.6 percent in 1989.[56] Darman was convinced that Republicans would have to raise taxes to persuade Democrats to control entitlement spending.

In 1988, Darman had fought with speechwriter Peggy Noonan to keep Bush's signature "Read My Lips" line out of his 1988 convention address.[57] In her memoir, Noonan[58] credits Kemp with putting the line in her head: "Jack Kemp told me [to] hit hard on taxes. Bush will be pressured to raise them as soon as he's elected, and he has to make clear he won't budge. In Bush's speech, this became: 'The Congress will push me to raise taxes and I'll say no, and they'll push and I'll say no, and they'll push again. And all I can say to them is read my lips; No New Taxes.'" Kemp won out then, but the promise didn't keep Bush from agreeing to the budget deal that broke his promise and split the GOP.

On June 26, 1990, after months of negotiations with congressional Democrats conducted by Darman and Sununu, Bush posted a three-paragraph statement in the White House press room saying it was clear to him that "tax revenue increases" would be needed to bring down the federal deficit and achieve a budget agreement. Also needed, he said, were entitlement reforms, defense and domestic spending cuts, and growth incentives. The release made no mention of "new taxes" or "higher taxes."[59] But both Democrats and Republicans knew that this was a breach of his campaign promise. The next day's New York Post front page blared: "Read My Lips. I Lied."

Kemp had spent months opposing the deal[60] and his immediate reaction was to consider resigning, Reed said.[61] But he quickly decided this would kill any chance for poverty fighting. "He moved on. But there was a lot of heat from his friends in the House and Senate [urging] 'you've got to make a statement about this.'"

Bush's action divided the GOP. House minority whip Gingrich led opposition to the White House. After more negotiations and a brief government shutdown, Bush agreed to a final deal raising the top tax rate on individual income from 28 to 31 percent and limiting deductions for high earners. The deal hiked payroll taxes; imposed excise taxes on autos, boats, airplanes, and furs; and increased taxes on gasoline, tobacco, and alcoholic beverages.

Bush asked Kemp to support the deal, but he declined, then went out of his way to praise Gingrich.[62] The agreement drove down Bush's presidential job approval rating from 79 percent to 56 percent by October 1990. It soared back to 89 percent with the U.S. victory in the war with Iraq a few months later. But the deal inspired right-wing TV commentator Pat

Buchanan to challenge Bush in the 1992 primaries, weakening his bid for reelection. Bush apologized for the deal in his GOP convention speech. And Darman became a pariah among conservatives, but not before subverting another of Kemp's plans.

———

When Kemp proposed[63] that a cabinet officer be appointed to head anti-poverty planning, Darman and other cabinet officers opposed it. Sununu surprisingly went along and persuaded Bush to sign a memo on August 6, 1990, creating a new Empowerment Task Force with Kemp as chairman. It took a month, though, for the White House to disclose its existence.

Darman played a complicated game with Kemp's concept of "empowerment." Kemp attracted support from a group of young White House conservatives led by James Pinkerton, a reed-thin, six-foot-nine former campaign operative, that dubbed itself "the perestroika group."[64] In the winter of 1990, Pinkerton made speeches advocating a "new paradigm" for government policy emphasizing market forces over bureaucracy. Like Kemp, he often used the word "empowerment."

Darman loathed the term, which had originated with 1960s "New Left" radicals. Some Kemp allies said that was the point—conservatives were stealing an idea from the left. Darman wasn't mollified. He asserted that his budget deal already was doing more for the poor with $18 billion in new tax credits than Kemp's tenant program could with a maximum appropriation of $256 million a year. Darman was also furious at Pinkerton's vocal opposition to the budget deal.[65]

On the day that Kemp had breakfast with the "perestroika group,"[66] Darman delivered a scathing speech on what he called "neo-neoism." He attacked the "incipient faddism" of unnamed Washingtonians bandying about terms like "empowerment" and "new paradigm."

"Hey, brother, can you paradigm?" he mocked.

The "paradigm" fight was seen briefly as a major split in the administration and the GOP, with conservatives in Congress siding with Pinkerton because they detested Darman's budget deal. Amid this flurry, Kemp's task force produced a set of mostly familiar proposals that included a $50 billion increase in the personal tax exemption. His cover letter disparaged "green eyeshade thinking"—clearly a barb aimed at Darman.[67]

Suddenly Darman reversed field, announcing he'd decided to put some of Kemp's proposals (though not the $50 billion) in the next year's budget, including enterprise zones and HOPE. The budget document released in early 1991 said the administration's goal was to "empower low-income individuals." At the same time, Darman instructed other White House aides not to use the word *empowerment*. When Kemp heard that, he called it "a sick thought."[68] He persuaded Bush to make an antipoverty speech, but he could not get him to deliver it to an audience of poor people. Instead Bush spoke to a hotel ballroom full of lobbyists who sat on their hands. It was delivered on the day Bush declared victory in the Iraq war. Bush later told aides, including Pinkerton, that he never wanted to make another poverty speech. And when he went before a joint session of Congress on March 6, Bush said the postwar domestic agenda would emphasize transportation and crime.[69] Kemp had lost again.

In May 1991, Kemp did get Bush to visit the Cochran Gardens, a St. Louis housing project run by its tenants. But the presidential tour did nothing to bolster Kemp's bureaucratic position. During June battles over a congressional appropriations bill, Kemp was left alone to fight for his HOPE program. He won a slight increase only after standing in a Capitol hallway and accosting his former House colleagues as they filed in to vote.[70]

Kemp suffered periodic humiliations at the White House. When he arrived at a cabinet meeting, White House aides stopped him from distributing a printed report from the task force. Cabinet rules required prior clearance. When Kemp tried to deliver its contents orally—with customary verve—Sununu told him to "keep the speechmaking to the campaign trail."

When Kemp was presiding at a meeting of his task force in the Old Executive Office Building, Darman walked in. Declining to sit down, he listened to a few minutes of Kemp's proposing that welfare recipients be allowed to keep eighty-five cents of each dollar of new earnings without having their benefits reduced. Darman, an expert on welfare policy, quickly calculated that people would be able to collect welfare while earning as much as $70,000 a year. He curtly suggested that Kemp and his colleagues examine the extensive technical literature on welfare policy. The following year, even after the LA riots, Kemp's Economic Empowerment Task Force was abolished.

While Bush suffered politically from the impression that he did not care about urban policy, Kemp was judged as an idealistic warrior who fundamentally failed. Two headlines captured this: in the *Wall Street Journal* on July 31, 1991: "Bush Seen as Uncaring on Domestic Issues"[71] and in the *New York Times* when he was selected as the GOP vice presidential candidate in 1996: "Kemp's Legacy as Housing Secretary: One of Ideas, Not Accomplishments."[72] Despite Kemp's efforts, the number of Americans living below the poverty line rose from 31.7 million in 1988 to 38 million and the poverty rate rose from 13 percent to 14.8 percent.[73]

Congress, as well as the Bush White House, stifled Kemp's agenda. His 1989 reform bill was a hit on Capitol Hill, but some of his reforms got him into serious trouble with his chief funders. Senator Barbara Mikulski (D-MD), who chaired the Senate Appropriations subcommittee overseeing HUD and twenty-one other federal agencies, became a nemesis for Kemp almost on a par with Darman. She denied Kemp money for new programs, criticized his management, and threatened to cut his travel budget and legal staff and eliminate his entire public relations division. For two years running, Kemp urged Bush (unsuccessfully) to veto the funding bills she produced. HUD official Bill Dal Col[74] said Mikuski "would do whatever she could to screw us. Jack treated her with respect and tried to soft-pedal their differences." But not always. At one cabinet meeting[75] Kemp started talking about how he'd seek better relations with Mikulski, then "leaned back and stuck a finger down his throat, as if gagging at the very thought."

Their differences were political, institutional, and philosophical. Kemp and his staff saw Mikulski for what she was—an old-style urban liberal wedded to programs created in the New Deal and Great Society, including public housing. A diminutive, combative Polish American social worker and community organizer, she was elected to the Baltimore City Council partly on the strength of a much-publicized 1970 speech defending ethnic whites as "sick of being stereotyped as racist and dullard(s) by phony white liberals, pseudo black militants and patronizing bureaucrats."[76] Elected to the House in 1976, she went on to become the first woman elected to the Senate from Maryland, the longest-serving woman in Congress, and chairman of the Appropriations Committee. She was deeply leery of Kemp's "empowerment" agenda.

Kemp's first big battle unfolded when Kemp unilaterally eliminated his own use of the Department Secretary's Discretionary Fund. He insisted that Congress quit using it too. The common practice of appropriators was to tap the fund to pay for "special projects"—aka "earmarks" or "pork barrel"—for their and their colleagues' districts. Their directives were laid out in a House-Senate conference report, not in law. In November 1989, Congress directed $93 million in spending in this way. Kemp refused to spend it.

He went on NBC's *Meet the Press* to denounce the practice, saying it was "disgraceful . . . for Congress to take those monies that ought to go to helping homeless people or fighting poverty and distributing them without any competition, without any merit other than influence." Kemp charged that Congress was ordering by appropriation the same kind of influence-based funding that he'd wiped out after the bad old days of Sam Pierce.[77]

In 1990, when Kemp similarly refused to spend money for twenty-eight special projects, Mikulski punished him in the Senate funding bill by threatening to close down his Office of Public Affairs and forbidding him to travel first class, which he said he needed to do to stretch his football-battered knees.

After two years of skirmishing, Congress won the earmark fight. In 1991, Mikulski publicly defended the size of that year's special projects account—$150 million for 133 projects—as reflecting public needs and the process as a fast way of fulfilling them. When Kemp again threatened to refuse to spend the money, her subcommittee forced him to comply by pulling the special projects out of the committee report and writing it into the law.[78]

While Kemp objected to his or Congress's using the discretionary fund, he did exercise the common bureaucratic practice of "reprogramming"—shifting funds from one program in his department to another. Specifically, in 1990, he tried to fund tenant "empowerment" programs with money designated by Congress for building, rehabbing, and tearing down public housing projects. Mikulski fought back, forbidding HUD (and only HUD) to reprogram. And Mikulski embarrassed Kemp by nearly torpedoing a ceremony at which Kemp planned to use "reprogramming" to distribute assistance funds to prospective homeowners at Kimi Gray's Kenilworth-Parkside project in Washington. She granted permission only at the last minute. At the ceremony, attended by D.C.'s mayor and other dignitaries, Kemp proceeded to criticize Congress for failing to support his overall "empowerment" plan.[79]

In late 1990, Congress passed the National Affordable Housing Act, also known as Cranston-Gonzales after its two principal Democratic sponsors, Senator Alan Cranston of California and Representative Henry Gonzales of Texas. Besides the HUD Reform Act, Kemp counted it as his other major legislative accomplishment. But it, too, led to continuing skirmishes with Congress.

Among other things, the bill authorized Kemp's HOPE initiative, which embodied his tenant-ownership and "empowerment" visions. The bill called for spending $4.2 billion over two years. However, it was merely an authorization. When appropriators produced a HUD funding bill in 1991, they designated $504 million less than Kemp wanted. For a second year in a row, he asked Bush to veto the entire $23.8 billion bill funding HUD and twenty-one other federal agencies. Bush refused, mainly because the bill increased money for the NASA space station.[80, 81]

Along the way, Mikulski told Kemp she had "great reservations" about his whole tenant-ownership plan.[82] She contended that most public housing tenants were too poor to purchase their units and that the cost of rehabilitating units to make them purchase-worthy was prohibitive. Rehabbing units at Kenilworth-Parkside under a bill Kemp had managed to pass as a congressman cost an average of $75,000 per unit.[83] (Woodson claimed it was because D.C. government officials cut overly expensive deals with favored contractors.)[84]

Kemp wanted to match here Margaret Thatcher's privatization program in Britain. It worked there, with 1.25 million units sold in the 1980s. But occupants of British council housing were mainly middle class. One study showed that U.S. tenants who were able to buy had incomes averaging $16,000 a year, but that the average income of all tenants averaged just $6,500.[85]

Mikulski was no fan of Kemp's management of HUD and he made things worse in 1990 by a miscalculation of $1.2 billion in his estimate of the next year's needs. That required her to tear up months of work and threw her spending decisions into disarray.[86]

At one point, Kemp talked of resigning if Congress failed to fund tenant ownership. "I was born to be HUD Secretary, but they've got to give me the resources," he said.[87] Budget authority for Kemp's department actually rose during his tenure, from $14.3 billion in 1989 to $24.9 billion in 1992. But Kemp felt too little was devoted to "empowerment" of the poor and too much to "pork barrel" benefiting developers, public housing authorities, and politicians. Nevertheless, he did not resign.

———

And he did not mind only HUD's business. It was said of him that "Kemp had his fork in everyone else's plate." Kemp joked during his lifetime that he was "the only HUD Secretary in history with his own foreign policy." Secretary of State James Baker did not appreciate Kemp's forays into his area of responsibility. Baker said other cabinet members "used to call [Kemp] High School Harry because he'd come into these Cabinet meetings . . . full of ideas and ebullience and he wanted to be a combination of chairman of the Federal Reserve, Treasury Secretary, Secretary of State and Secretary of Commerce. . . . It became the subject of some mirth."[88]

And, more than once, of anger. In 1990, as the Soviet Union was nearing collapse, Lithuania declared its independence. Baker told the cabinet that U.S. policy was to negotiate with Soviet leader Mikhail Gorbachev and his foreign minister, Eduard Shevardnadze, on a broad range of issues—a policy that would be disrupted if the United States recognized Lithuanian independence. Kemp urged immediate recognition and continued to do so to Bush in the Oval Office after the cabinet meeting.

As Press Secretary Marlin Fitzwater wrote in his book, *Call the Briefing!*[89]—and Baker confirmed[90]—Baker, standing at one Oval Office doorway, overheard Kemp working on Bush. Unable to contain himself, Baker shouted across the office, "Fuck you, Kemp." Fitzwater wrote, "Kemp started running through the furniture, sidestepping the couch, dodging the end table, breaking into the clear near the door. He chased Baker down the hallway, catching him just outside my office door. They were nose to nose when [National Security Adviser Brent] Scowcroft caught up" and ended the confrontation.

Kemp also entered into public disagreements with Bush-Baker Mideast policy, one time setting up a meeting with Ariel Sharon to discuss housing, even while Baker was trying to dissuade him from building settlements. Kemp aides heard regularly from White House minders when Kemp was "off the reservation," but Kemp continued to misbehave, at one point reporting to ex–New York mayor Ed Koch that Baker had said "Fuck the Jews—they don't vote for us." Koch promptly wrote about it in his column in the *New York Post* and the *Post* blew it into a page one headline: "Baker: F— the Jews!" Baker flatly denied making the alleged remark, saying he had said "Screw AIPAC," the American Israel Public Affairs Committee, the leading pro-Israel lobbying group in the United States.[91] It remains in dispute exactly what Baker did say, but the incident damaged Kemp's and Baker's relationship. Baker said he and Kemp had a conversation about the episode later and "he indicated that he regretted it. . . . It was a trashy thing to do, a really bad thing to do." Fortunately,

Baker's wife, Susan, was a good friend of Joanne Kemp's, and the two worked to repair the damage after the two men left office. Eventually, Baker referred to Kemp as "a friend."

———

Kemp trod not only on Baker's turf, but intervened in Bush economic policy, not only to oppose the 1990 budget deal, but to push capital gains tax cuts as a means of boosting the economy. When Bush became president, the top capital gains rate was 28 percent, raised from 20 percent as part of 1986 tax reform legislation. Kemp initially accepted the increase, but Congress persistently drilled new loopholes into the tax code, reigniting Kemp's advocacy for supply-side cuts.

Kemp's campaign for capital gains cuts accelerated as the U.S. economy slowed, then slipped into a mild recession, ending six years of sustained growth and falling unemployment. GDP growth dropped from 5.4 percent in the fourth quarter of 1988 to 0.1 percent in the third quarter of 1990. Kemp had feared an impending recession while the administration was still officially optimistic about the economy. At a cabinet meeting in August 1990, he urged Bush to drop plans for a tax-increasing budget deal with Congress, call for a capital gains reduction, and blame Democrats for blocking one in 1989.[92] Evans and Novak reported that no one at the meeting agreed with Kemp's analysis.

After the Iraq war, Kemp hoped that Bush would use his mighty political capital not just to wage war on poverty, but to reinvigorate the economy with capital gains tax cuts. Bush did not. Indeed, the day before the war ended, his advisers agreed that Bush should "solidify the capital" earned by the victory by concentrating on foreign, not domestic policy. Their argument was that Bush's polls would stay high if the public was reminded of his signal triumph—and Democrats' near-unanimous opposition to the war—and not about the unpopular 1990 tax increase.[93]

In speeches, Bush did mention the desirability of capital gains cuts,[94] but could not decide whether to lobby Congress for them because his advisers were deeply split. Brady, Sununu, and Darman were opposed to a cut. Brady feared Bush would be accused of favoring the rich. He once told Kemp ally Vin Weber that it was permissible for Reagan, a poor boy from Dixon, Illinois, to cut them, but not a rich senator's son from Connecticut. Brady also asked Weber how it was that Reagan could get away with repeatedly raising taxes when Bush couldn't. "Because he never admitted it," Weber replied.[95]

On November 4, 1991, in an interview with the *Wall Street Journal*, Darman ruled out a tax cut in the budget for 1992 "unless the economy is sputtering."[96] The interview—plus a handwritten note from Bush on November 5—caused Kemp to send what he called an "eyes only" two-page letter on November 7 to the president, insisting that a tax cut measure could pass and warning that Darman's opposition to tax cuts was putting the administration in political danger.[97]

Later in November, 81 (of 166) House Republicans wrote Bush urging that Kemp be appointed the administration's domestic policy czar. "We must declare war on our domestic ills. Jack Kemp is the man to lead that war," they wrote. Bush might have saved his presidency had he done so, but he did not.

Kemp would not keep quiet about his tax ideas even under direct instructions that he do so. "Jack had his own agenda," then-chief-of-staff Sununu said.[98] "I would call Kemp after every speech and poor Joanne would answer and she said, 'What did he do now?' Towards the end, Jack was playing . . . to history instead of the President."

Finally, in his election-year State of the Union, Bush called for tax cuts, overruling Darman and Brady. He directed federal agencies to end regulations that might hinder growth, directed the Treasury Department to alter income tax withholding tables to give taxpayers $25 billion more to spend over the next year. He called on Congress to enact a 15 percent investment tax allowance, give tax breaks to real estate developers, allow savers to tap their IRAs for first-time home purchases, and raise the personal exemption by $500. And he again called for a cut in the capital gains tax to 15.4 percent. "This time, at this hour, I cannot take no for an answer," he told Congress.

As the State of the Union address was being drafted,[99] incoming White House chief of staff Sam Skinner and Bob Teeter, Bush's 1992 campaign director, persuaded Bush to include Kemp ideas like IRA withdrawals and an increase in the personal exemption. For the moment, Kemp was back in favor at the White House. And he gave the State of the Union a ringing endorsement—at first.[100]

But when actual details of Bush's agenda came out, those items got low priority. Kemp erupted. He appeared on Evans and Novak's CNN show and said, "It's no secret that I've never liked tax credits. Basically, those are gimmicks." He added: "Clearly, the withholding idea is a gimmick. . . . Frankly, I cannot sit here on your show and retain my credibility and say that allowing people another $30 a month is going to spur economic recovery."

Mary Cannon,[101] Kemp's HUD communications chief, was watching the show when Kemp made the "gimmick" remark. Her instant reaction was, "Oh my gosh. We are in big trouble." She went to her office and got a call from White House press secretary Fitzwater. "You've got to fix this right now," Fitzwater said. "Get something out retracting it, denouncing it, denying it. Do whatever you have to do to say that he's sorry, that's not what he meant, whatever." Meantime, Skinner called Kemp and told him he'd blown it. Kemp issued an instant public apology and called Bush to deliver it personally.

Days later, a banner headline in the *Washington Post* read "Kemp Apologizes to Bush for Remark," but with the subhead "HUD Chief Regrets Context, Not Content of 'Gimmicks' Statement."[102] White House correspondent Ann Devroy reported that Kemp told her it was "not artful" for a cabinet member to publicly criticize his president's program. He added it was a "mistake" to hand Bush critics a weapon to pummel him and it was "wrong" to "wear my feelings . . . tattooed on my forehead." He said he'd told Bush, "I was sorry. I was a loyal soldier and I would not do it again. He was very gracious. . . . I am not going to leave the administration because of this."

While Bush may have accepted Kemp's nonapology apology, Bush aides told Devroy that Kemp should be sacked—especially for giving ammunition to Pat Buchanan in the New Hampshire primary just days away.

In his 1994 book, *Standing Firm: A Vice-Presidential Memoir*, Dan Quayle wrote that he and Kemp were long-standing friends with similar views and that he'd urged Kemp's selection to the cabinet. "Sadly, he disappointed me during the Bush administration," he wrote. "Many, I know, questioned Jack's loyalty to Bush, and there were times when the President would have been justified in letting him go."[103] Quayle wrote that "Jack was constantly at war with Darman and Brady, and meetings where the three of them were present (without the President) turned into a mud fight of words. . . . Kemp periodically opposed the president publicly—only to meekly claim he was misquoted. This didn't do the president or Kemp any good."[104]

———

Kemp's position in the administration changed radically after April 29, 1992. At 3:15 p.m that day in Simi Valley, California—6:15 p.m. in Washington—a mostly white jury acquitted four white Los Angeles police officers on charges of using excessive force in subduing black fugitive Rodney King. An eighty-one-second video of the officers beating King had been played thousands of times on television before the verdict, and the verdict itself was carried live. Rioting began in LA within two hours and lasted six days, until May 5. Fifty-four people were killed, 2,800 injured, and $1 billion in property was lost to fires and the sacking of businesses and homes. Among the vivid images carried throughout the nation were signs reading "Black-owned business. Do not burn," a savage mob nearly beating truck driver Reginald Denny to death, cars being trashed by shirtless youths, and fires consuming wrecked stores.[105]

The Los Angeles riots marked a turning point for Kemp. After three years of frustration at having his "conservative war on poverty" either thwarted or ignored by both Congress and the Bush high command, he was singled out in the media as "the only . . . vocal advocate in the administration for a strong urban policy,"[106] and as "the only high administration official who had expressed any interest in the plight of the poor."[107] Some White House aides continued to disparage Kemp, especially when he accompanied Bush to the riot zone and, alone among the presidential party, doffed his coat and chatted with citizens along the route. And when he, not Bush, was mobbed by reporters, residents, and local officials, White House aides groused that Kemp was "grandstanding," perhaps building himself up for another run for president.[108, 109]

But after the 1992 LA riots, President Bush—flagging in his race for reelection and widely accused of ignoring domestic policy even amid a recession—had to pay Kemp some attention. Bush tried to advance an urban agenda he'd merely paid lip service to for more than three years and to resuscitate the Kempian tax cut policy he'd promised, then spurned. It was too late.

Kemp was still on the outs at the White House when the rioting began. Instead of consulting his leading urban affairs cabinet officer about what to do, Bush went to his lone black cabinet officer, Health and Human Services Secretary Louis Sullivan. And when he picked a team to head to LA to plan a postriot aid package, he assigned David Kearns, deputy secretary of Education, to lead it, though DelliBovi was also a member. After all his racial advocacy within the administration, Kemp was deeply disappointed not to be Bush's point man.[110]

Still, Kemp was interviewed repeatedly by newspapers and TV stations—and his message couldn't have been further from Bush's. Bush delivered a national television address and said of the violence: "It has nothing to do with civil rights. . . . It's not a message of protest. It's been the brutality of a mob, pure and simple," though he did promise a full federal investigation of the King beating.[111] Kemp called the riots "a cry for help." He said: "I want to say something to people who are Anglo-Saxon watching this because they're listening to a law-and-order Republican say it, a member of Bush's Cabinet. . . . Our system has locked in rewards basically for people who have already made it and it's preventing people who don't have anything but the shirt on their back from getting access to property and the seed corn and the capital and the jobs and the

Jack, at age eight, with his younger brother (and football pupil), Dick, four. It was "all sports, all the time" for the four Kemp boys, including older brothers Paul Jr. and Tom.

The most important event of Kemp's years at Occidental College was his meeting Joanne Main. Here, at a 1957 fraternity dance. When he proposed that New Year's Eve, she said she was "stunned," but accepted. They were married July 19, 1958.

Kemp led the San Diego Chargers to two American Football League divisional championships, in 1960 and 1961, and the Buffalo Bills to two league championships, in 1964 and 1965, and a divisional championship in 1966. He set numerous passing and scoring records, but threw for more interceptions (183) than touchdowns (114) and is unlikely to be inducted into the Pro Football Hall of Fame.

Kemp hung this photo prominently in his office—of him about to be demolished by six-foot-nine, 315-pound San Diego Chargers defensive tackle Ernie Ladd. It reminded him, he said, "that a little guy can compete against a big guy if you've got the spirit, if you've got some courage." He also told visitors it reminded him that, rough as politics might be, he'd been through worse.

In the Buffalo Bills' offseason in 1967, star quarterback (and political junkie) Kemp served as an intern in California governor Ronald Reagan's communications office, establishing a personal bond that led to Kemp's endorsing Reagan for president in 1980, rejecting the entreaties of supporters that he run himself.

A Buffalo football hero, Kemp announced his candidacy for Congress in 1970 with the support of New York governor Nelson Rockefeller. His campaign advisers told him to lose his football-era buzz cut to look more serious.

Kemp habitually grabbed a manila file folder at the start of a week and crammed it full of articles, notes, invitations, and mail. It got stashed on a huge pile of other folders in his office, sometimes to the consternation of his staff. But he always knew where to find things.

As a football star, Kemp was not used to asking fans for favors. As a first-time congressional candidate, he had to learn to ask for votes. Here, he does, outside the Bethlehem Steel plant in Lackawanna, New York.

In 1981, Kemp moved from being a tax-writing backbencher to chairman of the House Republican Conference—number three in the GOP leadership. Here, meeting the press with (*left to right*) policy committee chair Dick Cheney (WY), GOP leader Bob Michel (IL), and whip Trent Lott (MS).

To calm furious partisan debate over Reagan's Central America policy, Kemp introduced legislation in 1983 creating a commission headed by former secretary of state Henry Kissinger. Kemp, a commission "counselor," helped curtail "death squad" atrocities in El Salvador.

The three supply-side "originals," in 1990. In their thirties, they sparked an intellectual revolution in economics (*left to right*): Arthur Laffer, first an academic, then a presidential policy adviser; Nobel Prize winner Robert Mundell; and Jude Wanniski, the journalist-activist who for years was Kemp's closest political and policy adviser.

Kemp and Senator Bill Bradley (D-NJ), both former star professional athletes, were the original sponsors of what became—after many near-death experiences—the revolutionary 1986 tax reform law. They later often debated international finance issues.

Kemp was a frequent visitor to the Oval Office, usually to argue against efforts by Ronald Reagan's budget director, David Stockman (*to Kemp's left*), to raise taxes. Also in this meeting (*left to right*): policy development aide Edward L. Harper, Deputy White House Chief of Staff Richard Darman, legislative affairs director Ken Duberstein, and chief economic adviser Martin Feldstein.

Kemp ran for president in 1988, deeming himself the natural heir to Reagan and the candidate most likely to attract minorities back to the "Party of Lincoln." He finished third.

Kemp was sworn in as President George H. W. Bush's secretary of housing and urban affairs on February 13, 1989, by Supreme Court Justice Sandra Day O'Connor. He swiftly had to tackle a department that was scandal ridden and demoralized.

A budget balancer and tax raiser, Bob Dole for years disparaged supply-side economics and Kemp himself—"the Quarterback," he called him. But he picked Kemp as his 1996 vice presidential running mate to energize the GOP. Temporarily, at least, it worked.

Jack and Joanne Kemp celebrated their fiftieth wedding anniversary at a ranch near Vail, Colorado, in July 2008, with their children: Jennifer Andrews (*to Jack's right*), Judith Nolan (*to Joanne's left*), Jimmy (*back row, far left*), and Jeff (*back row, behind Jack*), plus their spouses and seventeen grandchildren.

ownership of homes." Lacking opportunity, he said, "undermines respect for the law, it undermines respect for property." He added, "I don't believe there's enough federal troops, there's not enough police in the country to solve the problem of restoring peace and harmony."[112]

In a May 3 op-ed in the *Washington Post*, Kemp made clear that "There can be no excusing wanton violence, lawlessness and destruction of life and property" and gave Bush credit for acting "decisively to end the anarchy." But the burden of his article—and all his postriot speeches and action in administration councils—was to call for "a dramatic new agenda for ending the poverty that keeps too many inner city residents locked in hopelessness and despair."[113]

Bill Clinton beat Bush to Los Angeles by three days, and pummeled the president and his party for "twelve years of denial and neglect" of urban problems.[114] White House spokesman Fitzwater had blamed Great Society programs for the rioting and Clinton said, "It's just amazing. Republicans have had the White House for 20 of the last 24 years, and they have to go all the way back to the '60s to find somebody to blame." He said he was advocating a "third way" to fight poverty, which LA community leaders also supported, explaining that people "want basic empowerment at the grass-roots level, which is different from what either party has done in the past. They want to work through community-based organizations instead of through federal bureaucracy." The Democrat's message sounded exactly like Kemp's.

When Bush traveled to Los Angeles, Kemp was with him. Beforehand, Kemp got summoned to three cabinet meetings in three days, plus a session with mayors. "It's nice to be needed," Kemp said at the time.[115] But behind the scenes, Darman warned that Kemp would use the occasion to upstage Bush. Other advisers shared the worry, but also recognized that Kemp was the only political asset they had.[116]

In LA, White House aides watched in wonder as a group of black Democratic mayors, awaiting a meeting with the president, swarmed around Kemp. "Jack Kemp is a beacon of light," one of them said.[117] Bush's aides grumbled anew when the entourage visited a burned-out shopping center and Kemp alone took off his coat and chatted with residents—a point noted on national television by ABC correspondent Brit Hume. A Bush aide was dispatched to tell Kemp to butt out of TV shots that should feature the president.[118]

Bush, though, seemed genuinely moved by what he saw and heard: the destruction, tales of anguish and injury, demonstrations of selfless heroism, and the importuning of mayors and other officials for both immediate aid and long-term opportunity creation. He told aides, "Look, Jack Kemp is saying the right things. He understands what we need to be doing." Almost instantly, the Kemp bashing stopped.[119]

On May 12, Bush announced a renewed push for most of what Kemp had called for: passage of an enterprise zone bill, $1 billion for the HOPE initiative, welfare reform that would lift the savings limit for welfare recipients, and a school choice plan. "Some of these things have been proposed before," he told reporters at a briefing that also featured Kemp, "but we're going to now fight for them to get them passed."[120]

And, at long last, they did. Even Darman worked hard to pass an aid bill in the House that would create enterprise zones. But the effort fell apart in the Senate, which turned the bill into a vehicle for higher taxes and more spending. Kemp denounced it and Bush vetoed the final bill the day after the election, saying that it "contains numerous tax increases, violates fiscal discipline, and would destroy jobs and undermine small business. The urban aid provisions that were once the centerpiece of the bill have been submerged by billions of dollars in giveaways to special interests."[121]

Kemp made two postriot trips to LA, one with the president, one on his own. On the second, he was due to visit a community center, but got a call from Watts congresswoman Maxine Waters warning him he would be met by street demonstrators. Waters used "vile language" and accused Kemp of being a racist.[122] (Her office declined to respond to inquiries on the events.) Kemp called on two legendary football friends, Hall of Famers Jim Brown, formerly of the Cleveland Browns, and John Mackey, the Baltimore Colts tight end with whom Kemp had merged the NFL and

AFL players unions. Brown, then fifty-six and known for wearing an African dashiki, had founded Amer-I-Can, which works with youth-gang members in LA and Cleveland. Brown organized members of the Crips and Bloods into an escort for Kemp, but the protesters threatened by Waters never appeared.

———

As election season approached, Kemp returned to arousing the ire of Bush aides by agitating openly for changes in administration economic policy—and personnel. Meantime, columnist George Will urged that Kemp replace Treasury Secretary Brady and that Weber replace Darman. Will also recommended dropping Vice President Dan Quayle, though he didn't recommend a replacement.[123] Columnist William F. Buckley called for Quayle to be replaced by Kemp.[124]

Fitzwater wrote in his book[125] that on July 23, 1992, Bush got a call from former president Gerald Ford urging him to replace Quayle to save his reelection campaign. Bush told Fitzwater, "I could never get away with taking Quayle off the ticket. But a lot of people are talking about it." The press secretary replied, "Even the right wing is talking about it. Of course, they want Kemp." Bush responded: "I could never take Kemp. Can you imagine how out of control he would be?"

Rather than being called on more, Kemp and his staff were treated to a new set of petty insults as the 1992 Republican National Convention approached in August, in Houston. The administration didn't invite him to attend until late, and then, according to HUD aide Bill Dal Col,[126] convention organizers—at the behest, he thinks, of White House aides—made it difficult for Kemp to bring staffers to Houston. "They squeezed us. We had to go out on our own dime. . . . We were getting hosed. They limited the number of people we could bring and bitched about the number we got." Kemp got his people rooms and passes by agreeing with then-RNC chairman Rich Bond to sign footballs for sale at fund-raisers.

As it turned out, Kemp was given a prime-time speaking role at the convention on Tuesday night. During the day, however, a rumor arose that Kemp might be ousted in Bush's second term. Kemp blew his top. He threatened[127] to use his convention speech to denounce Darman, Brady, and the Bush economic policy.

Kemp's aides—and his wife especially—calmed Kemp down and he delivered his Tuesday speech as planned, with delegates cheering and waving "Jack Kemp" signs. The next day, Fitzwater announced that Bush had called Kemp to "express his concern" about the rumors he might be sacked and said Bush "believes his cabinet is doing an excellent job."[128] That did not end convention conflict, though. Kemp and Darman almost came to blows over notes they passed in the Bush cabinet box at the convention. Dal Col said, "I know Tim Russert [of NBC News] was watching it with amusement."[129]

Bush's acceptance speech was hailed by Evans and Novak as a "supply-side triumph," but it was scarcely a Kempian triumph. Bush admitted that the 1990 tax increase had been "a bad call" and "a mistake." He promised to ask Congress for across-the-board tax cuts (matched with spending cuts) and said he'd "continue to fight" for a capital gains cut and an increased personal exemption. But nowhere in the speech was any mention of cities, the poor, housing, or enterprise zones.

After the convention, Kemp campaigned for Republicans in seventeen states, once with Bush in Missouri. His regular stump speech was described by Timothy Noah in the Wall Street Journal as bearing "a far greater resemblance to his own philosophical compass points than to the campaign themes being enunciated by the Bush-Quayle campaign." Where Bush relentlessly attacked Democrat Bill Clinton's record and proposals, Kemp told a Missouri GOP fund-raising audience that Clinton was "a decent man; he's just got it wrong."[130]

According to Charlie Black,[131] when Bush held his first debate with Clinton on October 11 in St. Louis, he was preprogrammed to announce that a new economic team would take command in his second term, headed by Baker, with Kemp playing a role. But, Black said, Bush "muffed it" with an allusion so vague that no one understood it. And when Bush announced Baker's prospective role the next day, he made no mention of Kemp.

Bush left the convention trailing Clinton by 20 points. On November 3, he lost to Clinton by 6, 43 percent to 37 percent in the popular vote, with third-party candidate Ross Perot, running against free trade and budget deficits, receiving 18.9 percent. Even though the 1990–91 recession was long over, Clinton campaigned as though the economy were still in dire straits. Reagan pollster Richard Wirthlin said that Bush was guilty of "hubris" after his popularity soared following the Gulf War and did not tend to domestic policy.[132]

Kemp blamed "Darmanomics" for the loss. He told the *Washington Post*'s David Broder[133] in an interview embargoed from publication until after the election that with "cynicism," Darman had "undermined the populist economics that Ronald Reagan and George Bush had been elected on." He said that the 1990 budget deal had prolonged the recession and that the failure to provide serious stimulative remedies had left Republicans with "a terrible economic message and an even worse political message." The result, he said, was that "the base we had broadened in the 1980s shrank on us," especially among young and middle- to lower-income voters who then believed "we were the party of expanding opportunities."

Polls of delegates by the *Washington Post* and the Associated Press at the GOP convention showed that Kemp was by far their favorite for the 1996 presidential nomination—by 24 points over Quayle in the AP poll.[134] After Bush's loss, Kemp was anointed by Evans and Novak as the "clear Republican heir apparent" for 1996.[135] But David Broder noted that Senate minority leader Bob Dole, newly reelected in Kansas and Kemp's longtime ideological adversary, would be the "most influential Republican in Washington."

Eleven

VEEP

Borrowing his hero Winston Churchill's description of his time out of power between World Wars I and II, Kemp self-deprecatingly referred to his time after leaving HUD in 1993 as his "wilderness years." Without any official base, Kemp stayed politically active and remained a leading— if controversial—Republican figure. And he was constantly mentioned as a possible 1996 GOP opponent to Democratic President Bill Clinton.

After Clinton's 1992 victory, Democrats held both houses of Congress as well as the White House, causing Kemp to believe conservatives needed a "shadow government" to counter them and influence GOP policy. Before Clinton was even sworn in, Kemp formed Empower America, a tax-exempt advocacy group, with Bill Bennett, former UN ambassador Jeane Kirkpatrick, and himself as principals, and Weber as president.

The group would push "populist politics and progressive conservatism," advocating free trade, an interventionist foreign policy, education reform, and "growth" economics, but avoiding divisive issues such as abortion and gay rights[1]—in other words, the Kemp agenda.

Empower America was not a classic Washington think tank with a collection of scholars. Rather it was an "action tank" made up of just its principals and a small staff of writer-researchers who helped prepare

speeches and churn out op-eds, white papers, and newsletters, and organize forums around the country. One of Kemp's assistants was twenty-
three-year-old Paul Ryan, who went on to be chairman of the House
Budget and Ways and Means committees and the 2012 GOP vice presidential nominee. Another was Mike Gerson, later George W. Bush's
chief speechwriter and a syndicated columnist.

Initial funding came primarily from New York investment banker
Ted Forstmann, who told Kemp, "Why don't you figure out what it costs
and I'll underwrite it for you." Forstmann, as the group's chairman, collected $8.6 million the first year, largely from other rich conservatives.[2]
Of that, $4.8 million was invested in direct mail fund-raising that yielded
a hundred thousand donors, an impressive achievement.[3] After Empower America's first year, Forstmann became founding chairman and
another multimillionaire, magazine publisher Steve Forbes, took over
as chairman. When Weber left the CEO post, he was succeeded by
Kemp's former HUD aide, Bill Dal Col.

Kemp took no salary because he drew $136,000 as a Heritage Foun-
dation fellow and made speeches at $35,000 each through the Washing-
ton Speakers Bureau.[4] Financial disclosure forms showed that Kemp
earned $6.9 million during the three years after leaving HUD, and his net
worth rose from between $500,000 and $1.25 million to more than $5
million.[5] After years of relatively modest income as a quarterback ($50,000
per year in his final contract), member of Congress ($89,500 in his final
year), and $189,900 as HUD secretary, Kemp's "wilderness years" were
quite comfortable financially.

Kemp started out in good shape politically too. Empower America
advertised itself as nonpartisan—it had Democratic philosopher Michael
Novak and Perot adviser Orson Swindle as associates—but it was widely
viewed as a vehicle for Kemp to mount a 1996 presidential run, much as
Clinton had used the moderate Democratic Leadership Council. He'd
left the 1992 GOP convention as the delegates' leading choice for the
1996 nomination, so the position seemed his to lose.

———

Kemp's first foray as a leader of the Clinton opposition was to critique the new president's inaugural address at a forum sponsored by *National Review*. He charged that Clinton put forth the "myths" that Americans needed to sacrifice and were undertaxed, and that government creates jobs. He brought the audience to its feet when he declared that "the purpose of a party that is in the minority is not to oppose, but to become the majority" with "ideas that have consequence."[6]

When Clinton delivered his first economic speech to a joint meeting of Congress on February 17, 1993, proposing tax increases on corporations and high-income individuals, a new energy tax, defense cuts, and $30 billion in stimulus spending, Republicans went into immediate opposition. Empower America waged an all-out campaign against Clinton's tax plan. Kemp called Clinton's "the most liberal of any administration in this century"[7] and predicted his economics would "destroy his presidency" and "elect a Republican Congress in 1994."[8]

Despite fierce opposition, Clinton's plan passed Congress in August— by 218–216 in the House and 51–50 in the Senate, with Vice President Gore breaking a tie. Republicans did take over both houses of Congress in the midterm elections as Kemp had predicted, though the victory had more to do with the collapse of First Lady Hillary Clinton's health-care reform than the tax bill.

Kemp maintained general opposition to Clinton, at one point saying, "I think that the Clinton administration has the most anti-capitalist mentality of any in this century,"[9] though he supported Clinton on the North American Free Trade Agreement originally proposed by Bush. When Clinton proposed empowerment zones as an urban policy, Kemp denounced them as a "weak imitation" of his enterprise zones.[10] Kemp opposed Hillary's health-care reform too, declaring the Clintons intended to "radically nationalize" U.S. health care.[11]

Even as he resisted most of Clinton's policies, Kemp aroused intense opposition from conservatives for taking positions that amounted to apostasy. Grilled by Robert Novak on NBC's *Meet the Press* on March 7, 1993, he came out against term limits for members of Congress and repeated his long-standing opposition to a constitutional amendment requiring a balanced federal budget. He said he might accept individual tax rate increases in exchange for capital gains cuts. He endorsed three funding increases proposed by Clinton—for Head Start, the WIC (Women, Infants and Children) nutrition program, and the earned income tax credit for low-income workers. He came out for outlawing assault rifles despite his "perfect" eighteen-year-year record in Congress as scored by the National Rifle Association. And he declined to condemn welfare benefits for illegal immigrants unequivocally, using the argument "we should control the border at the border."

Novak wrote that "on one issue after another, Kemp abandoned and rejected positions dear to a conservative movement that had enshrined him as the lineal successor to Barry Goldwater and Ronald Reagan. To many, Jack Kemp showed that he had moved left at a pace his supporters had not appreciated." Novak wrote that Kemp "was the runaway Republican choice for president in 1996 with nobody else even close.... He seemed the one Republican who could unite country clubbers and Christian activists and then have a chance to go on to beat Bill Clinton." So it was "worrisome that four years as [HUD secretary] had profoundly changed Jack Kemp."[12]

The *Meet the Press* episode led to reports of conflict at Empower America and a brief flurry of speculation that Bennett might run for president. Bennett and Kemp were actually close friends. Rumors of their division were exaggerated, though they did argue a lot—"spitball fights," Forbes called their spats.[13] Their disagreements were basically intellectual and philosophical, carried on in bull sessions, watching football games, traveling, on policy panels. In Bennett's mind, Kemp was very nearly an economic determinist. "I used to say, 'You're just a Marxist, a good-guy Marxist. You think it's all about opportunity and enterprise and giving people a chance. I'm for that, but if people don't have the wherewithal to take full advantage of the chance, they're going to blow it. They'll default on their loans . . . they'll wreck their property."[14]

They also had different worldviews stemming from their religious origins. "I'm probably chronically, constitutionally pessimistic—Catholic original sin, darkness in man's soul," Bennett said. "Jack was not. We used to joke at Empower America that people came in to the sunny end, Jack's end, and then they'd come down to my end. They'd say, 'what's going on down here?' And I'd say, 'sex, drugs and rock and roll.'" One of Bennett's projects was a recurring "Index of Leading Cultural Indicators," derived from (mostly dismaying) statistics on crime, family structure, popular culture, religious observation, and youth behavior.

———

In 1994, Kemp courageously opposed California's Proposition 187, which would have denied public services to illegal immigrants, including education to children. Bennett originally endorsed Proposition 187 amid cheers from a San Francisco audience in late September 1994. Then Kemp persuaded him to read it. Bennett changed his mind. Together they wrote a *Wall Street Journal* op-ed denouncing the voter initiative as "fundamentally flawed, constitutionally questionable" and charging it would hurt the GOP by suggesting "an ugly antipathy toward all immigrants," notably Latinos and Asians. The party that represented optimism, confidence, and opportunity under Ronald Reagan "will be replaced by an isolated fortress with the drawbridge up," they wrote.[15]

Other Empower America leaders, including Weber and Kirkpatrick, declined to cosign the article.[16] Newt Gingrich phoned California governor Pete Wilson, who was exploiting the proposition to get reelected, to say he favored it. Empower America got more than a thousand angry calls after the op-ed appeared and some protesters sent Bennett back their copies of his best seller, *The Book of Virtues*. But Kemp and Bennett stuck to their guns. It was Kemp's finest hour since his supply-side crusades.

Kemp's strong stand seemed to ensure his time in the wilderness would be prolonged. When the article appeared, Kemp was still considered a leading candidate for the 1996 GOP presidential nomination. His opposition to the so-called Save Our State initiative was praised by President Clinton and leading editorial pages. But it was greeted with outrage by Republicans. California congressman Dana Rohrabacher declared Kemp's step "an act of stupidity that has knocked him right out of the presidential race." Kemp's hint that supporters of 187 were bigots didn't help matters.[17, 18]

———

By the time Prop 187 came around, Kemp had already dropped from his place as the overwhelming favorite for the party's 1996 presidential nominee.[19] By September 1993 he had slipped into second place behind Dole. In March 1994, a USA Today poll had him in fifth place behind Dole, Colin Powell, Ross Perot, and Dan Quayle.[20]

He frequently departed from conservative dogma and focused obsessively on the subjects of race and inequality. At a March 1994 banquet concluding National Review's Conservative Summit, he upbraided ex–New York mayor Ed Koch for delivering a long-winded tirade against black leaders who blamed poverty on white racism and failed to deal with crime, the drug culture, and illegitimacy. Kemp leaped to the podium and declared, "There is racism. How do you explain a young black entrepreneur who can't get a loan? God, Koch, you've got me on fire." He said conservatives will "never be a majority again" until they embrace "that lost lamb who's been left out of our coalition." He insisted that the audience at the following year's summit be a third black and half Latino and Asian. Applause after his speech was not thunderous.[21]

Besides often being at odds with the GOP base, Kemp's polls declined because he had made himself practically invisible on the GOP fundraising circuit for the first seventeen months of Clinton's presidency. He explained that 1993 "was a legislative year. I couldn't possibly compete with Bob Dole, [Texas senator] Phil Gramm and Newt Gingrich. I used the year to raise money for my family, pay off debt and (become) financially secure."[22] In 1994, he was hit with a bill for $120,000 in added penalties from the Federal Election Commission for accepting excessive contributions and corporate donations in 1988, and he needed money to pay it off.[23] As a result, instead of organizing a presidential campaign, he concentrated on well-paid appearances before business groups.

Trent Lott, then in his first Senate term, confronted Kemp at a meeting of his political brain trust in August 1993. He said he needed to assure his allies he would run in 1996. Kemp refused. "I'm not sure he wants it anymore," Lott concluded. Moreover, Kemp was at odds with two of his closest friends, Bob Novak and Jude Wanniski. Wanniski and Kemp broke when Kemp approved Weber's running a consulting business in competition with Wanniski. Miffed, Wanniski signed on as an adviser to Dole. Kemp was furious at Novak for stimulating—then denouncing—his "heresy" on *Meet the Press*.[24]

To repair his political standing, Kemp planned to increase his speaking schedule from 40 in 1993 to 150 in election year 1994. In June 1994, though, he announced he had told GOP office seekers he would only campaign for them if they sought votes in minority areas. He said he did not want the GOP to continue pursuing a "Southern strategy," which he defined as "not even asking blacks to vote for you for fear of losing white votes. . . . That's my litmus test," he said.[25] He wrote his son Jeff that he ended up making 160 speeches, at least partly "testing the waters" for a 1996 presidential run.[26] Weber said he "was a huge draw" for GOP candidates in 1994, but was also "high maintenance," demanding private jet travel and pricey hotels that party campaign committees paid for. "He did not want to go Holiday Inn," Weber said.[27]

Despite a drop in the unemployment rate from 7.4 percent when he was elected to 5.6 percent in November 1994, Clinton's approval ratings were in the mid to low 40s during the fall of 1994, largely owing to the failure of his health-care initiative, his proposal to tax energy, and a weak crime bill. House GOP whip Newt Gingrich unified the party's candidates around the Contract with America, promising to immediately reform House operations grown authoritarian and corrupt after sixty-two years of almost uninterrupted Democratic rule. The Contract called for enactment, in the first hundred days of the next Congress, of a balanced budget constitutional amendment, term limits for members of Congress, more prison construction, tax breaks for small businesses and families, and tort and welfare reform. When the Contract was unveiled in September, Kemp called it "a good start," but said "an agenda for the next 1,000 days" should be set, including repeal of both Clinton's and George Bush's tax increases, Federal Reserve reform, market-based health-care reform, and school choice.[28] After the Contract was assailed by Democrats, however, Kemp called it a set of "banners to be proudly carried into battle."[29]

To almost everyone's surprise, Republicans gained fifty-four House seats in the election. Gingrich was elected House Speaker with former GOP leader Bob Michel's retirement. The GOP gained eight Senate seats, winning control and installing Dole as majority leader. Kemp extolled the victory, but ultimately believed it his duty to critique policies of the GOP Congress.

———

A further shock occurred on January 30, 1995, when Kemp announced he would not run for president in 1996. He told reporters, "My passion for ideas is not matched with a passion for partisan or electoral politics." He said he enjoyed talking about policy issues, but detested raising money. "There are a lot of grotesqueries in politics, not the least of which is the fundraising side."[30] Former Republican National Committee chairman Frank Fahrenkopf had dinner with the Kemps soon after the announcement and said, "Joanne had it all figured out. She said 'We would have had to have raised $65,000 a day for six months and we just were not going to do that.'"[31]

Between the November election and the January announcement, Kemp sent a seventeen-page handwritten letter to his son Jeff exploring the financial, political, and personal reasons why he probably wouldn't run. Campaigning in 1988 was "great fun, challenging and unforgetta-ble, but honestly, it was driven by ego, pride and conceit that I was the only 'true believer.' What nonsense!" He said he was "at peace . . . des-tined to be the idea man of the GOP and not its nominee for president."[32]

In the letter he said he was delighted with the 1994 GOP victory, but added, "I must say I feel somewhat alienated from the current party emphasis on 'austerity' over 'growth' and 'change' over 'equality of oppor-tunity' for all, even those left behind."

Kemp's withdrawal left a field led by Dole that included Pat Buchanan, Lamar Alexander, and Phil Gramm, later joined by Forbes, running as Kemp's stand-in.

———

Two months later, Kemp was named by Dole and Gingrich to chair a fourteen-member GOP commission designed, as Dole put it, "to move beyond tax reform toward a complete overhaul of the federal tax code." Kemp should start with "a blank piece of paper and design a system that is flatter, fairer and simpler—one that will encourage strong economic growth and great opportunity for all people."[33] Kemp's ex-aide, John Mueller, a consultant to the commission, said Kemp wanted to be selected for vice president and thought that producing a new tax plan for the GOP would help.[34]

The commission was supposed to complete its report by October 1995, in time to influence debate ahead of the '96 primaries. But after holding hearings around the country, it didn't finish until January 1996. The campaign was well under way. Kemp said that at the panel's first meeting he had indeed held up a blank piece of paper and said, "This is what we start with."[35] In his own mind, however, Kemp was not starting with a clean slate. He had been advocating a flat tax to replace the exist-ing five-rate (15 percent to 40 percent) graduated income tax structure with a single rate. It eliminated deductions and loopholes and sought to protect the poor with an increased standard deduction.

Originally proposed by Hoover Institution scholars Robert Hall and Alvin Rabushka in 1981, flat-tax proposals became the rage as GOP candidates and members of Congress approached the '96 elections. At one point, Kemp endorsed House majority leader Dick Armey's proposal for a 17 percent rate and the elimination of all deductions, including those for mortgage interest, charitable contributions, state and local taxes, and employee-paid health benefits. That led to charges of bias from senators Pete Domenici (R-NM) and Sam Nunn (D-GA), sponsors of a proposal to tax consumption, not income.[36] Kemp acknowledged he favored the flat tax, but promised a fair hearing for all ideas.

When the commission reported, two Republicans were campaigning hard on the flat-tax theme: Gramm, who advocated a 16 percent rate, retaining deductions for mortgage interest and charitable deductions, but not for state taxes, and Forbes, who adopted the Armey plan and called for eliminating all taxes on dividends, interest, and capital gains. With Forbes spending lavishly to buy TV ads and rising in polls, Gramm charged that it was unfair to tax persons who "earn their living by laboring," but not those who "earn their income by investing in capital."[37] Buchanan, who had a flat-tax plan similar to Gramm's, denounced Forbes's as an idea "worked up by the boys at the yacht basin." Alexander called it "a truly nutty idea." The Clinton Treasury Department estimated Forbes's plan would cost $200 billion a year in lost revenue, Armey's $140 billion, and Gramm's $138 billion. Their advocates disputed the estimates, claiming a flat tax would raise revenue by stimulating the economy.[38]

Dole sought to shed his reputation as "tax collector for the welfare state"—in Newt Gingrich's classic jibe—by "taking the pledge" not to raise taxes if elected.[39] But he was leery of the political impact of pure flat-tax ideas, the possible ballooning of deficits, and their impact on the middle class after popular deductions were eliminated or the flat rate had to be raised to 20 or 25 percent. Dole advisers urged Kemp, in his commission report, to lay out principles for tax reform, but avoid specifics.[40]

That is what he did. The sixty-page report advocated a single-rate flat tax, but no specific rate. It endorsed a generous personal exemption without specifying what deductions might be eliminated and called for corporations to be taxed just once, with dividends and capital gains not taxed. Grace-Marie Arnett, the commission's executive director, explained that the panel lacked the staff or legislative authority "to come up with all the t's and i's of a specific plan."[41]

Kemp personally favored a flat rate of 19 percent, maintaining charitable and mortgage interest deductions, reducing capital gains taxes and indexing the gains, and allowing workers to deduct their payroll tax payments.[42] The accounting firm Coopers and Lybrand estimated that Kemp's proposal would cost the Treasury $200 billion a year.[43] Kemp disagreed. He began his report by quoting John F. Kennedy's December 14, 1962, speech to the Economic Club of New York: "It is a paradoxical truth that tax rates are too high and tax revenues are too low, and the soundest way to raise the revenues in the long run is to cut taxes now." Kemp said his proposal would double the GDP growth rate.

The commission had difficulties. It ran a deficit. And Mueller, Kemp's long-standing loyal staffer, was fired as an adviser when he was mistakenly blamed for leaking internal documents indicating that the flat tax would pile ever-higher tax burdens on middle-income taxpayers.[44] Mueller was fingered because he'd advanced that case in memos and commission deliberations. He later wrote a *Washington Post* op-ed pointing out that the tax system already favored investment in physical capital—buildings and equipment—while treating investment in human capital, such as raising children and paying for college, as consumption. The situation would be made worse, he wrote, if capital investment income were freed of taxation and middle-class taxes went up. And because a majority of voters earn their income from labor, a Hall-Rabushka-style plan would be politically suicidal for Republicans. "This was the only major policy disagreement I ever had with Jack," Mueller said, "but it was a significant one."[45]

———

When Kemp got out of the presidential race, Steve Forbes got in. Son and heir of legendary publisher Malcolm Forbes, Forbes met Kemp through

Wanniski in the pre-Kemp-Roth 1970s. He was a committed supply-sider who wanted Kemp to run for president in 1980 and backed him in 1988.[46] As chairman of Empower America, Forbes "thought it was a given" that Kemp would run in 1996. And after Republicans triumphed in 1994, he thought, "Boy, this is going to be a natural. No way Bill Clinton is going to out-people Jack Kemp. Jack has the right ideas. He's not coming across as Scrooge. We didn't even discuss it. It was a given."[47]

Forbes was "flummoxed" when Kemp told him in December 1994 that he was not running.[48] He told Kemp, "You can't walk away from this," arguing that history required him to run, that he couldn't let Dole inherit the GOP.[49] Wanniski, who'd dropped Dole, wrote Forbes a memo urging that he run and he began thinking about it. Forbes consulted Dal Col, Empower America's president, who told him he was crazy—inexperienced, not facile, unused to being attacked, and forced by near blindness to wear Coke-bottle glasses. But he got continuous encouragement from Wanniski and then Novak and, in August 1995, decided to run in Kemp's stead, on Kemp's economic agenda.[50]

Before he announced, Forbes asked Kemp to back him. Kemp said he was sympathetic, but wouldn't immediately commit. Wanniski harangued Kemp in phone calls and letters, declaring at one point, "You have been our leader for 20 years, not Reagan. When you said you would pass the torch to Steve, it gave him the assurance he needed to believe it was his responsibility to do this . . . You have to see that unless you throw in with us . . . history will record your reneging on your promise to Steve as the primary cause of his defeat. Novak will be the first to write that history."[51] Novak had already pinned Kemp down, eliciting a private promise that if Forbes ran, he'd endorse him.[52] It took six months for Kemp to fulfill the promise, however—during which Kemp twice made it seem impossible he'd ever be selected as Dole's vice president.

———

On January 30, 1996, two weeks before the Iowa caucuses, Scott Reed—Kemp's former HUD chief of staff, now Dole's campaign manager—

arranged a meeting between Kemp and Dole. He assured Dole, "Quarterback's coming on board." At that point, Forbes had spent more than $18 million—all but $1.5 million his own money—buying ads attacking Dole as a tax raiser and touting his own flat-tax idea. He was gaining on Dole in national polls and actually leading by 9 points in New Hampshire.[53] Reed had used his old Kemp connections to clear Kemp's schedule for an endorsement trip to New Hampshire with Dole the following day.

Kemp began the meeting by telling Dole what he didn't like about his campaign: he was attacking Forbes on the flat tax and for advocating allowing younger workers to open private savings accounts in lieu of Social Security, which Kemp also supported. And for favoring an immigration policy like Proposition 187. Reed said negative ads were necessary because Forbes's negative ads had driven Dole's favorable ratings from 80 percent to 50 percent.

Kemp left saying he'd promised Forbes he'd talk to him before endorsing Dole. The next day, he met with Forbes, who also asked for a public endorsement. Kemp told him, "You've got my undying support for the ideas," then proceeded to outline what he didn't like about Forbes's campaign: his harsh negative ads against Dole "were not worthy of the Lincoln wing of the Republican party." This meeting, too, ended inconclusively.

Around 9 p.m., after the Forbes meeting, Kemp called Reed and told him, "I'm not ready to go." Reed replied, "We need you now. We don't need you in two weeks. . . . I'm giving you friendly, sound advice. This is the time to do it. Any other time, it's not going to be important. . . . This is to help you." Kemp said he wasn't going to New Hampshire. When Reed called Dole with the news, Dole said, "Last time we're dealing with the Quarterback."[54]

Dole briefly stopped attacking Forbes, leaving the job to his campaign staff. Then he started again, bashing Forbes as a rich guy trying to buy the election. By the time of the Iowa caucuses, Dole had driven Forbes down to third place. But surprisingly, he barely beat Pat Buchanan after conservatives rallied around him. Dole figured Buchanan's base was too narrow for him to win the nomination, but Lamar Alexander, who'd finished third in Iowa, could win if he finished second in New Hampshire. Dole feared if he finished third in New Hampshire, his campaign would be over. So his campaign began attacking Alexander, who did not have the funds to answer. On February 20, Buchanan beat Dole in New Hampshire, 27 percent to 26 percent, with Alexander at 22 and Forbes at 12.

Dole was still alive. Forbes won primaries in Delaware February 24 and Arizona February 27, narrowly beating Dole. After hiring a new ad team and going positive, Dole went on a roll, winning in North Dakota and South Dakota, South Carolina and Wyoming on March 2 and all nine states on March 5, "Junior Tuesday," with Buchanan a distant second in most places and Forbes, third. The iron GOP law of primogeniture also kicked in: Dole, having been a vice presidential nominee, finishing second to Bush in 1988 and being Senate majority leader, was "next in line."

On March 6, with Dole virtually certain for nomination, Kemp endorsed Forbes, a sure loser. Reed was astonished at Kemp's decision, "The timing is absurd—it's over. I told him I thought he was making a big mistake. We're in the process of unifying the party and Forbes has nothing to add to that."[55] According to Kemp, Gingrich called to tell him he was "finished [in the GOP], that this is the equivalent of Winston Churchill leaving the Tory party in 1903."[56] Novak reported[57] that Kemp's move was triggered by a paragraph he read in the *Journal* citing Dole as saying—in Buffalo, Kemp's former hometown—that Forbes's flat tax would endanger GOP plans for a balanced budget. Kemp campaigned with Forbes in upcoming major primary states including New York, Florida, Texas, and California.[58] Dole won them all and Forbes quit the race just eight days after Kemp's endorsement.[59] After spending more than $25 million, he'd won just two primaries (Delaware and Arizona) and collected seventy-six delegates.

A March 8 *Wall Street Journal* poll showed that Forbes and Kemp had failed to make their tax case to the public. By 54 percent to 39 percent, voters favored a graduated income tax over the flat tax. Among

Republicans, support for the flat tax had dropped from 54 percent to 49 percent. Upper-income and lowest-income voters were evenly split on the issue, but the middle class—the huge majority making $30,000 to $100,000—were against it 58 percent to 37 percent, vindicating Mueller's political judgment.[60]

After Forbes's concession, Kemp told reporters he was back "in my wilderness years." "I'm not seeking anything. I don't expect anything," he said. "I'm not worried about it . . . I like where I'm at right now, being able to speak out with as much candor as I possibly can." Asked about being Dole's vice president, he said, "I don't think that's in the cards."[61]

———

When Dole had the GOP nomination wrapped up, he was trailing Clinton in every national poll by double digits—in some, by 20 points. With unemployment at 5.3 percent in June and the economy growing at a 4 percent clip for the year, Clinton's approval rating had risen to 58 percent from its low of 40 percent in December 1994. Voters blamed the GOP for two government shut-downs, from November 11–14, 1995, and December 16 to January 6, 1996, forced by House Republicans in an effort to compel Clinton to accept a plan for balancing the budget in seven years. Clinton vetoed the plan on the grounds (much overstated) that Medicare and Medicaid recipients would be hurt. Gingrich's disapproval ratings hit 65 percent after he told reporters that his budget stance toughened when he was asked to descend from the back door of Air Force One after returning with Clinton from Israeli leader Yitzhak Rabin's funeral.[62] Dole privately chafed at the House's hard-line stand, but was reluctant to openly oppose Gingrich for fear of losing conservative primary voters to Forbes and Gramm. His ratings suffered too. After the government had been shut for three weeks, Dole did declare, "Enough is enough" and forced a settlement—but the political damage had been done, and the compromise caused him to take heat from conservatives.[63]

Meantime, Clinton's new (and controversial) political strategist, Dick Morris, succeeded in getting the president to "triangulate" between conservative Republicans and liberal congressional Democrats, adopting centrist stances such as his 1996 State of the Union claim that "the era of big government is over." Clinton's strategy also included casting Gingrich as Dole's vice president until Dole actually picked his own,[64] making Dole out to be a heartless Grinch.

In late April, Dole decided to resign not only from his Senate majority leader's post, but from the Senate, running for president as a private citizen. Partly, the move was an effort to take a dramatic, surprising step to shake up the campaign. Partly, it was meant to show that Dole was 100 percent committed to the presidential race. Partly, it was Dole's attempt to escape being identified (in Pat Buchanan's phrase) as "Beltway Bob." And partly, it was to free Dole from being tied to the Senate floor, where Democrats contrived to bog down activity and keep Dole off the campaign trail.[65] Dole delighted in surprising people and insisted on keeping his decision a secret until the last minute. "It caught the White House with their pants down," Reed said.[66] "He pulled it off brilliantly."

Dole's next major move, announced August 5, the week before the San Diego GOP convention, was a plan to cut taxes across the board by 15 percent, an idea first proposed by Kemp's former economic adviser, Bruce Bartlett.[67] Democrats derided him for abandoning his career-long commitment to balanced budgets with a proposal costing $548 billion over six years, but Dole adopted a supply-side argument: "history has shown us that tax cuts, by stimulating growth, bring in more revenue." He said growth would cover a quarter of the tax cut's cost; he did not say how he would make up the rest, but said the budget could be balanced by 2002.[68] A Washington Post/ABC News poll showed that as delegates began to gather in San Diego, Dole had cut Clinton's 15-point lead before his tax speech to 10, though other major polls still had Clinton up by as much as 20 points.[69]

———

Dole's biggest surprise was Jack Kemp. In April, Dole asked his closest friend, former deputy secretary of defense Robert Ellsworth, to begin a search-and-vet process for prospective running mates. Ellsworth recruited former labor secretary Ann McLaughlin to assist. The process was to be conducted in total secrecy. But on June 26, the *Washington Post* published excerpts from Bob Woodward's book *The Choice*,[70] reporting that Reed and Ellsworth had drawn up a first list of fifteen possible veep candidates that included such luminaries as retired general Colin Powell, former cabinet officers Dick Cheney, James Baker, and Donald Rumsfeld as well as Pennsylvania governor Tom Ridge, and senators Connie Mack of Florida and Richard Lugar of Indiana. Dole met with Powell and determined that he wasn't interested in running for vice president any more than he had been for president earlier in the election cycle.[71] Reed traveled to New Jersey to ask Governor Christie Todd Whitman if there was any "give" in her pro-choice position on abortion, opposite the party's position. There was not.[72] Reed also met with Cheney, but "he was overweight, sweating profusely. I called Dole and said, 'This guy's going to have a heart attack.'"[73]

The Ellsworth-McLaughlin team, with lawyers and accountants based in New York, collected detailed questionnaires and did financial and background checks on Mack, Michigan governor John Engler, Oklahoma governor Frank Keating, former South Carolina governor Carroll Campbell, Arizona senator John McCain, and Nebraska senator Don Nickles.[74] Dole asked Bennett to consider it and he took home Dole's questionnaire, but returned it the next day without completing it.[75]

Throughout the campaign, Kemp had been on Dole's radar. Dole regularly teased Reed by asking him, "Talk to the Quarterback lately? What's the Quarterback thinking?"[76] On July 29, three weeks ahead of the convention, Reed informed Dole that polls and his own intuition told him none of the names on the short list would bring needed excitement to the campaign, Dole responded, "Maybe we ought to look at the Quarterback." Reed said, "You sure you want to do that?" Dole said, "Yeah, I think we should."[77]

To maintain secrecy, Reed bypassed the Ellsworth-McLaughlin process. He arranged to meet Kemp at the Westin Hotel in Washington's west end. He brought Kemp up to date on the Dole campaign, told him Dole was getting serious about picking a running mate, and said Dole wanted to see if Kemp was interested. "He acted surprised," Reed said, "but he left me with the impression he would be interested." About the same time, Bennett talked to Dole and recommended Kemp. Dole didn't let on he was considering Kemp and said, "Ah, I'm not going with Kemp. . . . Ah, his ideas. I don't agree with his ideas."[78]

Reed then arranged a dinner between Dole and Kemp at the Watergate apartment of Dole's finance chairman, John Moran. "I snuck him in. There was just the four of us," Reed said. "We talked strategy, not about his being Vice President. Dole told campaign stories. There was good chemistry. Kemp was on his best behavior." Dole talked about his 15 percent tax cut, which Kemp applauded. Reed called Kemp the next day, telling him Dole had enjoyed the dinner and confirmed that Dole wanted to take Kemp's candidacy "to the next level." Reed asked if Kemp was willing and, if so, urged him to keep the process secret.[79]

Then Kemp shocked Reed. "Out of nowhere, Kemp said, 'I'm not willing. It's not the right thing for me.' I was flabbergasted. It knocked me over. 'I said, 'You gotta be kidding! This is your chance to have everything you've ever worked for!'" Reed immediately phoned Joanne Kemp, who said Kemp had reported to her that he'd enjoyed the dinner with Dole. Reed told her Kemp had just told him he wasn't interested in proceeding. She asked, "Interested in what?" "The vice presidency," Reed said. Joanne told Reed—to his amazement—that Kemp had told his wife he was being considered for secretary of the treasury. "I said, 'This is the moment we always looked forward to all these years, what he'd worked toward all these years.' She said, 'Yes, you're right. I'm so happy this is happening.'" I asked her if she'd talk to Jack about it. She said she would.

"Two minutes later, Kemp calls, screaming. He chewed me out, using every word imaginable. Like, 'I can't f—ing believe you called my wife. How dare you!' I said, 'Jack, why are you doing this? This is your chance. This is everything you've lived to do. Talk to Joanne about it.' It was a surreal moment. From the high of the dinner with Dole, then this crash. I thought he was scared to go to the next level."[80]

Joanne recalls[81] Reed asking whether she was aware her husband didn't want to go on with the selection process and whether she opposed it. She told Reed she was not "locked in stone anywhere, but unless he wants to do it, I don't know. There's a lot to think about." After the call, she said she told her husband, "You know, Jack, it could be this is where you're to be. It might be that this is God's plan for your life. So I wouldn't say 'No' absolutely. Just think about it some more." They talked and "there was a point where he said, 'Well, who else is going to be Dole's Vice President?'[82] I just figured, 'Well, we've been amazingly taken care of down through the years of his career, so it was a no-brainer then to both of us and we said, Okay, let's go for it.'"

In 2007, Kemp told presidential scholar Richard Norton Smith,[83] "I was very reluctant" because "I thought [Dole] needed more of a pit bull and I'm not a pit bull politician. . . . [But] Bob said, 'You know, Jack, we're not going to run that kind of race. Bill Clinton's our adversary, not the enemy.' And I liked that. . . . So, once I was assured that I wasn't going to have to rip off the face of Al Gore and Bill Clinton, I decided— my wife and I talked about it and decided to do it."

After Kemp filled out the questionnaire, the campaign spent more than $50,000 in accounting fees to get his complicated financial reports in order.[84] But Dole still wanted to make sure he wouldn't be embarrassed by anything in Kemp's past and ordered Reed and Buckley to confront him directly. With reporters swarming outside Dole campaign headquarters near Capitol Hill, the two hid in the rear of a Chevrolet Suburban to escape for a meeting with Kemp at the Key Bridge Marriott Hotel in Rosslyn, Virginia. "We looked him in the eye and said, 'Is there anything, anything that would be problematical to Bob Dole if you were on the ticket?' and Jack looked us in the eye and said, 'No.'"[85]

The suspense was not over. The Doles, Elizabeth and Bob, and the Kemps had a pleasant dinner at the Doles' Watergate apartment, but the formal offer had still not been made. Kemp had to consult his children and other members of his family about the grueling road ahead. His consultation calls occurred on August 8, the day before Dole was to depart for his hometown of Russell, Kansas, where his choice would be unveiled before the convention. Dole called Reed at 10 p.m. and again at 11 to see if he'd heard from Kemp. He hadn't. Dole went to bed, having to leave at six the next morning. Kemp finally called Reed at 1 a.m. saying it all was a go. Reed told Kemp he and Joanne would be picked up by a plane and secretly flown to Kansas.[86] Stand-by arrangements had been made for Mack if Kemp's candidacy somehow fell through.

The next day, Friday, Kemp had two speeches to deliver in Orlando, Florida, and he kept to his schedule. His name surfaced as the leading contender in some newspapers on August 9, but no one had the story buttoned down, pleasing Dole immensely.[87] Dole personally tracked down Bob Novak in San Diego and told him that Kemp was one of three finalists, which Novak reported on CNN.[88] Campaigning in Kansas during the day, Dole teased reporters asking about Kemp, telling them he knew who his choice was, but had not made a final offer. He was telling the truth. The campaign went so far as to send a decoy plane to Christine Todd Whitman's home airport in New Jersey.[89]

Kemp was at a private holding room at Dallas's Love Field when Dole called him at 10 p.m. to seal his selection.[90] Reed had written talking points for Dole on a yellow pad. "The first thing he said was, 'I want you to join the ticket,' but then he told the story, which I loved, about what Gerald Ford told him when he asked Dole to be on his ticket [in 1976]. Ford said to him, 'You know, I don't plan on you being out there making farm policy for me,' which was a way to say to Kemp, 'You're not going to be out there making economic policy for me.'" Because Dole had basically adopted a Kempian tax cut strategy—though not precisely his flat tax—Kemp said "Great, great, great." And Dole assured him that he would not be asked to take the traditional "attack dog" role of a vice presidential candidate,[91] a reassurance that proved to be untrue.[92]

The Kemps flew to Great Bend, Kansas, forty miles from Russell and spent the night at a Holiday Inn, whose power failed during a thunderstorm, causing Joanne Kemp to wonder if it was an omen.[93] Early the next morning, they were escorted through the back door of Dole's home, then introduced to the throng of reporters and cameras waiting in front. The ticket was formally unveiled at a rally at the Russell County Courthouse, where Dole said Kemp rated "15 on a scale of one to 10"—he'd told reporters he was looking for a "10"—and noted 15 was the number on Kemp's football jersey and that Kemp would be instrumental in selling his 15 percent tax cut. Kemp spoke double Dole's seven minutes, praising Dole's war record, quoting Dr. Martin Luther King Jr., and declaring that "Bob and I are going to be asking for the support of every single American from the boroughs of New York to the barrios of California. . . . We may not get every vote, but we're going to make it unambiguously clear . . . that we want to represent the whole American family, that no one will be left behind and no one will be turned away. That's Bob Dole's vision for America."[94]

Practically every story written about the selection referred to the long history of ideological and personal rancor between Dole and Kemp; current differences over immigration, affirmative action, and prison sentencing; and the ill-timed Forbes endorsement. *Time* magazine and David Broder, among others, referred to them as "the Odd Couple."[95] The *New York Times*'s Maureen Dowd quoted Wanniski as saying, "I think of Darth Vader and Luke Skywalker, father and son," and Ed Rollins as saying, "These guys are like fire and ice." She commented, "Everyone knows Bob Dole is going to lunge for Jack Kemp's throat. The only question is whether it will take weeks, days or hours."[96] Bob Novak wrote that "surpassing even John F. Kennedy's selection of Lyndon Johnson in 1960, Dole's choice of Kemp is the most startling development of any of the 19 national political conventions I have covered."[97]

The candidates made a grand entrance in San Diego at the center of a flotilla of three hundred boats—"a motorcade on the water," Reed called it. That and an ensuing rally were "the highlight of the convention, the highlight of the whole year. It was a wildly enthusiastic crowd where everybody was pumped that Kemp, an economic conservative, was going to be on the ticket, and Dole had done the unconventional thing" in picking his old rival.[98]

Democrats publicly ridiculed Kemp's selection as a "Hail Mary pass,"[99] but top Clinton campaign aides Mark Penn, Ann Lewis, Doug Sosnik, and George Stephanopoulos all admitted later[100] that "it was the best choice they could make at the time," that "we weren't prepared for it. We were flat-footed."

Nominated by his son Jeff, Kemp delivered a rousing acceptance speech at the convention, citing Lincoln, Martin Luther King Jr., Churchill, and Shakespeare and repeating his line that he and Dole would seek votes everywhere. He told Republicans that America could not reach its potential "so long as it tolerates the inner cities of despair, and I can tell you, Bob Dole and Jack Kemp will not tolerate that despair in our nation's cities."[101, 102]

As soon as he was selected, Kemp met Wayne Berman, a future D.C. "super lobbyist" assigned to travel with and manage the vice presidential candidate, whoever it turned out to be. Berman was from Buffalo, had grown up rooting for Kemp on the football field, and had met him at various events where Kemp usually tried out his Yiddish. But when Kemp learned what Berman's role would be, Berman said he put on a look that said, "'This stranger . . . is going to run my campaign?' Jack had no ability to govern his body language or his facial language. You could just tell his attitude was, 'Oh, no, he's not.'" At the outset, Berman said, "Kemp did not regard me as an aide or a friend, [but] as a spy for the Dole campaign." By the end of the campaign, Berman regarded him as "the most inspiring officeholder I ever worked with—and the most frustrating. . . . Jack earned my loyalty and affection as well as my anger—he's probably the only person I ever actively thought about killing."[103]

Attempting to show he would be a "team player" for Dole—"Bob's the quarterback, I'm his blocker," he said—Kemp temporarily reversed his position on Proposition-187-style restrictions on public services for illegal immigrants and on a pending California ballot initiative, Proposition

209, ending affirmative action programs. He said in one interview, "You're watching a metamorphosis."[104] When Democrats and the *New York Times* bashed him for abandoning his principles, Kemp tried to play the change as a compromise, saying his and Dole's formerly opposite positions were "reconcilable." He made it clear, though, that he was still opposed to the constitutional amendment called for in the GOP platform denying citizenship to children born in the United States to illegal immigrants.[105] And on the campaign trail later in California, he distanced himself from Proposition 209, which Dole was strongly backing in an effort to carry California. Kemp said, "There is an old Chinese proverb: 'Don't blow up your old house until you build a new one.' We have to build a new house of opportunity. . . . I think affirmative action was necessary, but I don't think it's necessary in perpetuity. We are in transition. . . ."[106]

The convention gave Dole a big—though temporary—bounce in the polls. He went from 19 points behind in the *Washington Post*/ABC poll to 4 and from 20 to 12 in the CBS/*New York Times* poll.[107]

And Kemp was out of the wilderness. When Kemp came to address House and Senate Republicans in Washington after the convention, he saw his friend and fellow Churchill admirer Senator Dan Coats, and said, "Tell them Jack is back," appropriating Churchill's "Tell them Winston is back," the remark he'd made when resuming his post as First Lord of the Admiralty in 1939.[108]

———

After the convention, Dole and Kemp campaigned together in Denver, where Kemp delivered an introduction of Dole that was supposed to be five minutes long, but lasted twenty. Then Kemp went on to Buffalo, where Kemp endeared himself to Berman by giving him time to visit his old haunts at the University of Buffalo while Kemp waited in a holding room.

But flying out of Buffalo, Kemp called Berman to the front of his campaign plane and said there were three things he wanted: to have the plane repainted Dole/Kemp instead of Dole for President, to have Heritage Foundation founder and president Ed Feulner brought aboard to run his campaign, and to replace his Dole-supplied advance man with his old aide, Rick Ahearn. "He said he had nothing against me . . . but that Feulner was his buddy, his brother, and he would feel more comfortable with him."[109] When they got back to campaign headquarters, Berman was preparing to turn Kemp over to Feulner, but Reed pushed him into Dole's office. Dole told Berman, "'Wally'—for some reason he called me Wally—'Feulner's not for Dole. Feulner criticizes Dole. Feulner says Dole is not a conservative. I don't want Feulner around.'"[110]

Berman went to see Reed, who called Kemp and told him it was all right to have Feulner be a senior adviser and travel. But Berman was running the Kemp campaign—and Kemp wasn't ever to make a personnel change without checking with Reed. Kemp said, "I'm not going to take that kind of thing from you. I'm the vice presidential candidate. I was your boss at HUD." Reed swore and said, "Well, I'm the boss here. You're the running mate," and reminded him that Feulner had not supported Dole. Kemp had to back down.

Despite this conflict, the campaign got off to a good start, with Kemp immediately pulling his weight as a candidate who could appeal to minorities. Three of Kemp's early campaign visits were to South Central Los Angles, Chicago's South Side, and East Harlem. In LA, he said to Latinos, "We covet your support. It's not the same old Republican Party. It's going to be new. We're going to ask for every vote."[111] In Chicago, he denied he had abandoned affirmative action. "Affirmative action are two good words," he said.[112] And, in Harlem, at famed Sylvia's restaurant with Democratic representative Charlie Rangel in the audience, he said, "My goal for America is that by the end of the century, 50 percent of all African-Americans [are] voting Democratic and 50 percent, Republican."[113]

———

The peace was not to last. Evidently egged on by Wanniski, Kemp went seriously off message on the race issue on September 8 in a *Boston Globe* interview, praising Nation of Islam leader Louis Farrakhan's black self-help philosophy as "wonderful" and saying he would have liked to speak at Farrakhan's 1995 Million Man March in Washington, D.C. Despite Farrakhan's alleged anti-Semitism, Kemp called it "a celebration of responsible fatherhood, individual initiative, of not asking the government to do everything for you and getting an opportunity to be the man that God meant you to be."[114]

Wanniski had been lobbying Kemp to serve as a go-between between Farrakhan and white America, suggesting in one letter, "I think it could be one of the most important things you have ever done in your life."[115] Earlier he'd persuaded Kemp to try to broker a meeting between Farrakhan and Abe Foxman, head of the Anti-Defamation League, which didn't occur because Foxman demanded that Farrakhan first apologize for his past anti-Semitic statements.[116] Feulner said he worried every time Kemp was on his cell phone that he was talking to Wanniski and is convinced it was Wanniski who planted praise for Farrakhan in Kemp's head.[117] Berman said Kemp also "was getting these secret faxes from Wanniski—he thought I didn't notice—that were filled with crazy fantasies about the gold standard and abandoning Israel."[118]

In the *Globe* interview, Kemp said his remarks would "set off rockets" if they were taken out of context. They were, and the rockets went off. The day the *Globe* story appeared, Kemp said his views had been "sorely misrepresented," but they were condemned by several Jewish leaders.[119] Berman said, "Jack knew he'd made a mistake, [but] one of Jack's flaws was that admitting a mistake did not roll off his tongue. . . . He used to say to me, 'You know, I need a little sugar with my medicine.' If you were going to give him bad news, you had to give him some praise in there. But that wasn't my default position . . . and with Bob Dole, there was no sugar in anything. He didn't give any and he didn't demand any."[120]

Dole and Berman insisted that Kemp issue an apology. Dole and Kemp were already scheduled to speak, along with Gore, to Jewish leaders a few nights later, and the event seemed like the perfect opportunity to reassure allies that Kemp was not a supporter of anti-Semitism. However, Kemp refused to consider an apology. So Berman enlisted John

Sears, Kemp's old ally, to persuade him to read a statement prepared for him. Kemp agreed. At the Conference of Presidents black-tie dinner, Kemp said everyone present should understand that "I abhor bigotry and anti-Semitism" and called on Farrakhan and his followers to renounce anti-Semitism.[121] Despite his apology and his long-standing support for Israel, the Jewish leaders gave Kemp an icy reception and cheered Gore.[122]

Farrakhan did, in fact, issue a statement renouncing anti-Semitism that October, which Kemp praised, bringing on yet more criticism.[123] When the election was over, Bob Novak, echoing Wanniski, wrote that Kemp's praise for Farrakhan was an "audacious sally" that "horrified Dole's staff," though "Farrakhan is the one major black leader willing to try to lead African Americans off the Democratic plantation. He wrote that "close associates signaled he was eager to do so if Dole was interested. Dole was not."[124]

———

Meantime, Clinton left the Democratic National Convention in Chicago with a huge new lead over Dole, 54 percent to 34 percent, with 8 percent for third-party candidate Ross Perot.[125] A *Washington Post*/ABC poll a week later showed Clinton with a smaller 14 point lead, but it also showed that by two-to-one, voters felt they were better off economically than when Clinton took office.[126]

The Clinton administration, though, was steeped in scandal and rumors of scandal that Dole might have taken advantage of—especially if he'd had a traditional "attack dog" vice presidential candidate. The Clintons' 1970s investment in the Whitewater Development Corporation led to the appointment of Special Prosecutor Kenneth Starr, who had obtained two convictions in the case. Rumors abounded that Clinton might issue pardons (which he did as he left office in 2001). One of Hillary Clinton's former law partners, Associate Attorney General Webb Hubbell, had been convicted of embezzlement and another, deputy White House counsel Vincent Foster, had committed suicide. Former Arkansas state employee Paula Jones had sued Clinton for sexual harassment. On entering office, the Clintons had fired employees of the White House travel office, accusing them (unjustly) of embezzlement. In June 1996, the "Filegate" scandal erupted after a White House employee was found requesting confidential FBI files on past GOP officials. Despite the wealth of material, Kemp and Dole barely mentioned the scandals.

And on September 21, the *Los Angeles Times* published a story headlined "Democrats Return Illegal Contribution,"[127] setting loose an avalanche of allegations that the Democratic National Committee had been systematically collecting illegal contributions from South Korean, Indonesian, Hong Kong, and even Chinese sources. In mid-October, the *LA Times* reported that Al Gore had attended a fund-raising event at a Los Angeles Buddhist temple, where some contributors were found to have made donations to the DNC with money given to them by others. Other papers pursued the story too.[128]

Through September and into October, the Dole campaign avoided any reference to Clinton's ethical problems. The closest Dole came was to identify himself as having "spent a lifetime keeping my word" and as "a man you can trust," and saying of Clinton "Buyer Beware: What you see is not what you get."[129] Kemp, meanwhile, practically avoided any mention of Clinton or Gore, explaining Dole did not want him to be an "attack dog." Gore, though, referred to Dole, with Gingrich, as "a two headed monster" whose election would represent "a radical U turn" for the country.[130]

Dole skipped any mention of Clinton's ethical problems in their first televised presidential debate on October 6 in Hartford, referring only to Clinton's acceptance of contributions from the trial lawyers' lobby and calling for campaign finance reform. At one point, Dole compared Clinton to his own brother, Kenny, whom the Dole family tagged "the great exaggerator."[131]

The campaign's failure to home in on Clinton's ethics got criticized by other Republicans, including Bennett, who said Dole had been "obsessive about not appearing critical . . . as if it was more important to be nice than to win."[132] Buckley said the campaign's plan was for Dole to be "aggressive against Bill Clinton, but he couldn't go and be a hatchet man . . . and couldn't be too mean."[133] Reed said[134] the campaign was receiving information "over the transom, every day" about Clinton campaign finance scandals, but it didn't respond.

Then, abruptly, the campaign decided to switch tactics and go on the attack. On October 8, in Morristown, New Jersey, Dole said that "Clinton's word is no good." A Dole ad began running blaming Clinton for the nation's "moral crisis." By inadvertence, former Senate Whitewater investigator Michael Chertoff appeared with Dole at a rally in Lyndhurst, New Jersey, and declared that "the president promised us the most ethical administration in history. Well, how many members of that administration are in jail now? How many had to resign in disgrace?"[135]

The Dole strategy shift occurred on the day before Kemp debated Gore in Sarasota, Florida, and was reported on in the media that morning, October 9. Reed flew down on debate day and delivered the message to Kemp: "Ethics is going to be the top issue tonight. It is going to be probably the first question. . . . You gotta be tough. You gotta be aggressive. Read what Dole said. Repeat it. You don't have to deviate from it one word. Just say it. Be tough. That's all I'm asking."[136] Unfortunately, Kemp didn't listen.

————

Kemp did not take his debate preparation seriously. Feulner said he traveled with Kemp most of the two weeks before the debate, carrying videotapes of Gore in various past debates. He made sure advance men had a VCR in Kemp's hotel rooms and insisted, "Jack, tonight, we've got to watch that tape." But Kemp always had an excuse: "'Oh, no. It's Monday. I've got to watch *Monday Night Football.*' 'Jack,' I'd say, 'we've got to watch this tape.'" But he didn't.[137]

With days to go before the debate, Kemp and his advisers went to practice at a hotel next to Dole's condominium near Palm Beach. Reid Buckley, William F. Buckley's brother and a speech trainer, was on hand to coach. Senator Judd Gregg of New Hampshire was there to play Al

Gore in mock sessions, and Berman played moderator Jim Lehrer. Feulner said that Kemp listened to Buckley for three or four minutes and lost interest. Kemp told one of Berman's deputies that he didn't want to see Buckley again and the coach was sent away.[138]

In their first mock session, Gregg[139] modeled Gore's aggressive, attacking style. Kemp had difficulty keeping to time limits and, Gregg said, "after 20 or 30 minutes, Jack got totally frustrated with the exercise, gave me the finger and walked off the stage." Their second (and last) session went the full one and a half hours, but Berman said, "Judd just eviscerated Jack time after time."[140]

A day before the debate, the entourage flew across the state to St. Petersburg, where Kemp finally looked at Feulner's Gore tapes. "He watched it for about the first six or seven minutes and you could almost see the blood draining out of his face," Feulner said. "He said, 'Oh, this guy is good, isn't he?'" But still Kemp watched only for fifteen or twenty minutes more and quit. Feulner said he told his wife, "He just wouldn't take it seriously." Feulner thought Kemp's attitude was "Al Gore's smart. He's got to understand why I'm right . . . I'll be able to convince him." Feulner said he tried to tell him, "Jack, it doesn't work that way."[141]

"We blew the debate preparation," Berman said, "and we blew it because—and it was completely my responsibility—I did not discipline Jack. Jack insisted on having . . . this sort of Kemp fan club around. . . . I let this big group start dealing with Jack, and that meant that every exit ramp Jack wanted to take intellectually, we took." Gregg, who later played Gore and Senator John Kerry in preparing George W. Bush for debates in 2000 and 2004, said Bush's preparations lasted months, not days, and hangers-on were severely limited. Kemp, he said, had "roomfuls." Dal Col, one of those traveling with Kemp, said that Wanniski put in a last-minute call to Kemp "that didn't help," but that Joanne Kemp talked her husband out of using whatever lines he was proposing.[142] Jeff Bell is convinced Wanniski did reach Kemp and told him, "Don't be an attack dog."[143]

J. T. Taylor, who'd run Kemp's political action committee and later became president of Empower America, talked to Kemp the morning of the debate. Kemp said, "My mind is mush." Ed Brady, a close family friend, said that in final prep sessions in St. Petersburg, Kemp was "inundated with information and it wasn't what he wanted to say."[144] The truth may be that he resembled a student cramming for a final exam after not studying all semester.

————

As Reed anticipated, Jim Lehrer's first question at St. Petersburg's Mahaffey Theater, directed to Kemp, provided a perfect opportunity for him to be aggressive: "Some supporters of Senator Dole have expressed disappointment over his unwillingness at Hartford Sunday night to draw personal and ethical differences between him and President Clinton. How do you feel about it?"[145]

Kemp responded: "Jim, Bob Dole and myself do not see Al Gore and Bill Clinton as our enemy. We see them as our opponents. . . . People are watching not only throughout this country, but all over the world, [to see] how this democracy can function with civility and respect, and decency and integrity. . . . It is beneath Bob Dole to go after anyone personally." He went on to quote Abraham Lincoln, cite the First Amendment, and say that the issues "will be aired with dignity and respect" and left to the American people to decide. When it was his turn to speak, Gore said, "I would like to thank Jack Kemp for the answer he just gave. I think we have a positive opportunity tonight to have a positive debate about this country's future."

As Kemp and Gore spoke, a collective groan erupted in the holding room where Reed, Buckley, Mack, Weber, Republican chairman Haley Barbour, and others assigned to "spin" the press after the debate were sitting. A phone rang next to Reed. It was Dole. "'What was that?'" Reed recalls Dole asking. "'That wasn't in the briefing book.' Click."

As the debate went on, he said, Dole put in more calls "to the point I couldn't answer it anymore." Dole asked, "'What's going on? Didn't he practice? Wasn't he ready for this?" Reed said, "We had lost the night" with the first answer.[146] "He whiffed. He completely whiffed."[147]

For the rest of the ninety minutes, the toughest Kemp ever got was to say that under Clinton and Gore, "our foreign policy is ambivalent, confusing" and that tax plans put forward by Clinton and Gore "suggest that they'll give a tax cut, but only if we do exactly what they want us to do. That isn't America. That's social engineering." He said, when Gore charged that Dole would cut Medicare to pay for his tax cut plan, "It is disgraceful, the campaign being waged to scare American senior citizens." He also called it demagoguery. He criticized the administration for cutting the defense budget "as a percentage of our national economy to a lower level than it was prior to Pearl Harbor." And, "Their answer—this administration—to every single question is another regulation and another tax."

Gore was tougher. Asked about Kemp's charge of "demagoguery," he pushed a wedge between Kemp and Dole. Kemp, he said, "used much harsher language when he talked about Bob Dole. He said that Bob Dole's solution to every problem was to increase taxes." Driving another wedge, he said "Now, I want to congratulate Mr. Kemp for being a lonely voice in the Republican Party over the years on [race issues]. It is with some sadness that I refer to the fact that the day after he joined Senator Dole's ticket, he announced he was changing his position and . . . was going to adopt Senator Dole's position to end all affirmative action." Kemp leaped to defend himself, mentioning Dole only in passing.

Gore attacked Dole for wanting to abolish the Department of Education, for voting against the creation of Head Start, and opposing the Family and Medical Leave Act. Kemp did not defend him. Gore returned to the Medicare issue repeatedly, pointing out that Dole had bragged in 1996 that he'd voted against the creation of the program. He hit again and again at Dole's "risky, $550-billion tax scheme" that would "blow a hole in the deficit." And he repeatedly touted the Clinton administration's achievements. Kemp had few ripostes, many theoretical, none of them memorable. When Kemp claimed that Dole's tax cuts did not represent "trickle down" economics, but would instead produce a "Niag-ara Falls" of growth, Gore retorted that Dole and Kemp "would put the American economy in a barrel and send it over the Falls." It was the laugh line of the night.

According to one press report, Kemp had been prepped to say, when Gore drove wedges between his and Dole's records, "Al, where are you getting those old votes? Have you been going through my FBI files?" The punch line was never delivered.[148] Bennett said[149] that watch-ing the debate was "one of the worst hours of my life. . . . He didn't take Gore on. He wanted to be friends with Gore." In the holding room, Buckley tried to coach the prospective postdebate spinners on what they could say afterward, but Berman said, "There was no way to spin your way out of it. It was an absolutely horrible performance."[150]

Buckley theorizes that Kemp thought he couldn't do what he was asked—be the "attack dog"—and rationalized his position as "Gore may attack me and may attack Dole, but he's going to look worse and I'm going to be the statesman and . . . get my positions across."[151] If so, it didn't work.

Many press previews of the debate had heralded it as a warm-up for the 2000 presidential race. Reviews afterward were not favorable to Kemp. *Washington Post* columnist Mary McGrory's assessment was headlined "Kemp Gets Gored."[152] In Novak's column, it was "Better Luck Next Time."[153] In the *Buffalo News*, "Quarterback Drops the Ball."[154] Three "instant polls" by television networks indicated that by margins of more than twenty points, viewers judged Gore the winner.[155]

Reed said that when Kemp "got killed" in the media, he became "wildly defensive and tried to blame the guys: 'You didn't prep me right.'" Reed said he responded, "Well, Jack, you didn't want to do prep." Reed acknowledged that Kemp's staff "should have jammed him. I wish I had jammed him. I wasn't around. But they should have done a better job."[156]

The debate severely shook Kemp's confidence. Even worse, it dam-aged his relationship with Dole. Dole and Kemp traveled separately to Cincinnati the next day for a "unity event" with Colin Powell. "Dole didn't want to be alone with Kemp, he was so mad," Reed said.[157] As Buckley remembers it, Dole was most angry that Kemp did not defend him. He said it also poisoned his own standing with Dole. "When he looked at me, he saw Kemp."[158] Berman said, "I've only heard Dole swear twice. . . . One time, on a very personal matter, and the other talking about Jack's debate performance. He said to me, 'You know, that was goddamn disappointing.' I've got to say it was a big thing with Dole, and he really kept his distance from Jack after that on the campaign trail."[159]

———

The job Dole needed Kemp to do he was compelled to take on himself in the second (and final) debate, October 16 in San Diego. He used the first question posed to him—about why Americans couldn't be more united—to go on the attack, "There's no doubt that many Americans have lost faith in their government. They see scandals on a daily basis. They see ethical problems in the White House today. They see nine hundred FBI files, private people, being gathered up by somebody in the White House. Nobody knows who hired this man. So there is great cynicism out there."[160] But that was the only reference he made to Clinton scandals, reflecting differences in the Dole campaign and the GOP over how negative to go.

The differences were played out in the media, with Bennett and other Republicans telling reporters Dole didn't need to raise personal scandals like the Paula Jones case, but that "Filegate," "Travelgate," the possibility of Whitewater pardons, the Asian money connection, and "the ethical climate in this administration" were "fair game."[161] Days after a Dole aide said that Kemp had delivered a "powder puff" debate performance,[162] he did deliver a radio address accusing the White House of "arrogance of power . . . avoidance of responsibility . . . (and a) habit of half-truths"[163] and repeated the theme on ABC's *This Week with David Brinkley*. Gore hit back, accusing Kemp of a "low road attack."[164]

A few days later, in Cleveland, Tennessee, Kemp was back to saying, "I'm an old football player. There was another team on the other side. They were my enemy in an adversarial sense, but my best friends were the guys who beat me up on Sunday." Aides insisted to reporters that while some Dole supporters were criticizing Kemp, Dole had not ordered him to go negative.[165] This is disputed by Buckley, who said, "Poor Jack was in this miserable position of being asked . . . every single day, to do exactly the one thing he isn't any good at, which was attack." Reed says he does not recall any such requests.[166, 167]

As the campaign entered its final weeks with Clinton still leading by 12 to 15 points, Dole sharpened his message. Reed said that the campaign's "closing theme is going to be about trust and telling the truth and Clinton's ethical mishaps. Clinton is on the defensive."[168] In one speech, Dole said, "We've finally got foreign aid coming to America! And it's all going to the Democratic National Committee! India, Indonesia, who knows what country will be next to . . . give foreign aid to this Administration? They're going to need it . . . to pay moving expenses come November 5."[169]

A *New York Times* poll on October 22 indicated that two weeks of Dole attacks had backfired, with 49 percent saying he was "trustworthy," down from 56 percent, and Clinton at 46 percent. Dole's favorability rating was just 28 percent to Clinton's 49 percent. And 63 percent of voters thought Dole was spending more time attacking Clinton than explaining what he would do as president. Only 14 percent thought Clinton was spending his time attacking Dole.[170] Moreover, the NBC/ *Wall Street Journal* poll showed that more voters opposed Dole's tax plan than favored it, by 46 percent to 34 percent.[171] In a Hail Mary move, Reed traveled to Dallas in late October and tried to persuade Ross Perot to drop out of the race and endorse Dole. Perot refused, but did issue a blast at Clinton's ethics.[172]

In the final ninety-six hours before Election Day, Dole launched a nonstop, four-day, seventeen-thousand-mile, nearly sleepless run of campaign visits to nineteen states, with Clinton's ethics as a major theme of his speeches. Reed said Dole knew that his race was lost, but ran the marathon to buck up the party base to save GOP control of Congress.

To the surprise of those who thought of him as an energetic go-getter, Kemp did not participate in or match Dole's final run and instead allegedly told GOP governors that the election was lost. No one could argue Kemp hadn't pulled his weight previously; Kemp's traveling press secretary, Alixe Glen, pointed out that, since his nomination, Kemp had done 140 campaign events in twenty-eight states and raised $2.8 million for GOP candidates. "He has campaigned his heart out," she said.[173] Kemp campaigned during the final days, but not nearly as energetically as the much older Dole, a contrast not lost on Reed.[174] Rick Ahearn said that at the end of one long campaign day, Kemp wanted to play tennis on a lighted hotel court. Ahearn and Joanne Kemp stopped him, warning he'd be filmed by the press while Dole was "going to a bowling alley at 3 a.m. in Las Vegas."[175]

Dole's ninety-six-hour blitz did do him some good, but it wasn't enough. Gallup daily tracking polls showed that Dole closed a 13-point deficit on Nov. 1 to 11 points by Election Day. He lost to Clinton, but the actual final result put Dole behind by 8.5 percent. And Republicans did retain control of both Houses of Congress, losing only three net House seats and gaining two Senate seats despite Clinton's victory. Conceding defeat, Dole graciously said that Clinton "was my opponent, not my enemy," wished him well and offered any assistance he could be. And he said that "I'm very proud of my teammate, Jack Kemp," who, with his wife and family, "did an outstanding job."[176]

No sooner had Kemp delivered his own concession speech—promising to stay active in pushing policies he cared about—than speculation and polling began about the 2000 presidential race. An NBC/ *Wall Street Journal* poll in December showed Colin Powell the choice of 37 percent of Republicans, Kemp of 20 percent, and just-reelected Texas governor George W. Bush at 19 percent. In December, he told one interviewer he was "starting to put the architecture in place to be ready" to run, though Beltway politicians said his debate performance was a permanent handicap. Kemp said he "missed some opportunities" against Gore, but did not think he did as badly as critics claimed.[177]

One who would have been for him had he run was Berman, his daily companion from August to November. Berman said there was "the good Jack" who "worked like a dog when he worked" and loved Q and A town hall session with voters. "And then there was the Jack who decided that Bob Dole's views were interesting, but Jack had his own views and he was going to put those out." The Kemp who frustrated Berman also traveled where he wanted regardless of where the Dole campaign sent him, assembled a "rainbow tour . . . a traveling circus" to travel with him and sometimes decided to skip the final event of a day. Yet he endeared himself to Berman—one, by calling him a "mensch" for taking responsibility for Kemp's debate performance and for having "command of the emotional language of policy that a presidential candidate has to have."[178]

Despite the speculation, though, Kemp did not run again for any office.

Twelve

FOURTH QUARTER

Jack Kemp always saw the best in people. Not believing in evil, only good, his judgment wasn't always sound. Once when Dan Coats and Kemp were waiting to vote, a man in the Visitors' Gallery dressed in clerical garb began shouting in a foreign language. Guards wrestled him to the ground. "Kemp said to them, 'Don't be so hard on him,'" Coats recalls. "He thought he was a man of the cloth. The guards hustled him out, then the vote got under way. The Floor was filled with Members." Afterward, Coats asked the guards what had happened and they said the shouter was trying to detonate a bomb hidden beneath his gown by putting two wires together, but had failed. "If it had worked, what would have happened?" Coats asked. "They would have carried you out of here in a bucket," the guard replied. "This was Jack, always looking on the positive side of things, thinking this was a cleric who just got over-excited. . . . It just didn't occur to him that such things could happen."[1]

Despite his defeats, Kemp's optimism didn't sour as he aged, and his belief in the goodness of others seemed to be rewarded. In the pattern of Kemp's life, when the door closed on the vice presidency, a new one did open: the opportunity to make real money. He walked through it with gusto. He had never before accumulated any real wealth, and he enjoyed being able to spend lavishly on his family. True to his compassionate roots, he served on many nonprofit boards, doing what he could to help others.

Even though he never ran for office again, he did not disappear from the public stage. He campaigned for Republican candidates. He stayed on top of policy issues, especially to push—in a weekly column, interviews, speeches, and Empower America statements—for tax rate cuts, monetary reform, immigration reform, home ownership, and poverty fighting. Surprisingly, he opposed George W. Bush's Iraq war both in public, and more vociferously in private, believing that Saddam Hussein had no weapons of mass destruction and could be "contained" much as the Soviet Union had been. This marked a fundamental shift in Kemp's position on national security—from hawkish critic of Ronald Reagan to dovish dissenter from George W. Bush.

———

In 1989, Kemp had to cash in his entire congressional retirement fund to pay for both his daughters' weddings.[2] His income rose during his four so-called wilderness years, but after 1996, it soared. "He made a lot of money and he spent a lot of money," said his son Jimmy, who became his business partner and helped focus his efforts. He spent most lavishly on his family, flying Joanne, the four children, and (in the final count) seventeen grandchildren on private jets to Vail, where he bought a ski house, and to vacations in warmer places.

Kemp's late financial success had its roots in his years in the House. Raul Fernandez had become an intern in Kemp's office in 1983, when he was just a sixteen-year-old high school student, taken on because he could speak Spanish and he knew about computers, then brand-new on Capitol Hill. He translated documents for the Kissinger Commission on Central America, developed a spreadsheet to save Kemp aide John Mueller from having to calculate tax reform distributional tables by hand, programmed the Kemp family's VCR, and once rigged up a paper reel for a movie projector at a party so Kemp's staff could watch old Super 8 films of his football exploits. He graduated from intern to a part-time job, then a full-time job during college working on foreign aid and Central America, once traveling to the war zone with Kemp. He worked with Cuban Americans in Florida in the 1988 campaign and had visions of a White House post when Kemp was elected president.

That door closed and Raul Fernandez became a tech entrepreneur. In 1991, at twenty-five, he invested $10,000 he'd saved to found a company called Proxicom, which pioneered in developing Web and then e-commerce sites for big corporations. His business prospered after Fernandez came to the rescue of AOL's cofounder, Ted Leonsis, after he overheard him on a plane wondering aloud how to build Web pages.[3] Kemp joined the Proxicom board in 1997. The company soon had a global reach, went public, and later sold for nearly $500 million. Even before the sale, Fernandez, at thirty-four, was listed among *Forbes* magazine's richest Americans under forty, and Kemp was reported as owning $2.3 million worth of Proxicom stock.[4] Fernandez said, "We made a lot of money together. . . . I think he got to see my dream and he got to live my dream."[5] In 2004, Fernandez bought ObjectVideo, a firm making it possible to analyze surveillance camera data. He asked Kemp to join that board too.

Kemp went on Proxicom's board just after he'd run for vice president. Earlier, he'd served on the board of Oracle, the software giant headed by billionaire Larry Ellison. Financial disclosure forms he filed when he ran showed he earned $6.9 million from 1992 through 1995 and his net worth rose from between $500,000 and $1.25 million to more than $5 million.

Among the companies whose boards he joined before 1996 were Columbus Realty Trust, run by former Dallas Cowboys quarterback Roger Staubach, and Miami-based American Bankers Insurance Group, recruited by another football Hall of Famer, Nick Buoniconti, whom Kemp played against when he was with the AFL Boston Patriots. Buoniconti said that Kemp "always talks about the American Dream, and he finally was able to take advantage of it."[6]

Kemp resigned from his boards when he ran with Dole, though he was allowed to keep his options to buy stock in the companies, including Oracle's, which he listed as worth $250,000.[7] He rejoined Oracle's board after the election and added, besides Proxicom, Speedway Motorsports and Sports Authority—plus more than a dozen others, mainly tech companies, some of which died in the 2000 dot-com bust. Kemp's advice was described as "invaluable," his connections "gold-plated," and his networking "indefatigable."

Kemp explained his success by saying, "I introduce companies to people who have access to capital. I'm involved in start-ups, in speed-ups. While I don't consider myself an expert, I can open doors and make connections." He added, "I played football when there was no money in it. I was in Congress when there was not a great deal of income from it. I believe in capitalism and I paid my dues. Now I'm doing very well."

Kemp continued making speeches too, though the number and the size of his honoraria tapered off as he got further from football and politics and closer to business. In 2000, Kemp told *USA Today* that he was then on fifteen corporate boards, was making sixty-five to seventy speeches a year, skiing forty-five days a year, and had been traveling regularly to Canada to watch his son Jimmy play football. He always traveled first class, he said, and he was then considering buying fractional ownership in a private jet company.[8]

When George W. Bush became president in 2001, Kemp knew almost everyone in the top level of the administration, so if a company needed an introduction to a cabinet member or top regulator, Kemp could make it, though he did not lobby. In 2002, in the wake of the dot-com bust and the Enron, Tyco, and other scandals, Congress passed the Sarbanes-Oxley law, which increased the accountability—and the paperwork—of corporate directors. In 2003, Jimmy Kemp and the then-president of Empower America, his old HUD aide J. T. Taylor, convinced Kemp that he needed to bring order to his corporate responsibilities. Kemp had the attitude that if someone seemed to value him, he instantly became a "great guy—loves me" and had a hard time saying no to a request for a favor. "It's a miracle this man did not get in trouble. He was not careful," Jimmy said.

Indeed, his carelessness had gotten him into trouble before. In the 1980s, along with more than a hundred wealthy individuals, Kemp invested with Clifford Graham, who claimed he had a technology that could extract gold, silver, and platinum from mining waste. Graham disappeared after collecting $13 million in investments and later was indicted for fraud.[9] Kemp didn't learn his lesson, though.

In 2003, despite his long-standing opposition to leftist dictatorships, Kemp got involved in a company called Free Market Petroleum LLC, aiming to import crude oil from anti-U.S. strongman Hugo Chavez's Venezuela for the U.S. Strategic Petroleum Reserve. He was warned against it by Jimmy, who did background checks on the participants, but Kemp had struck up a friendship with Venezuela's ambassador to the United States and made business trips to Caracas to negotiate terms, which had the potential of netting $1 billion over three years. Kemp also visited the *Wall Street Journal*'s editorial offices to defend it and argue for improved relations with Chavez. The enterprise came to naught, wasting Kemp's time and nicking his reputation.[10]

In a more successful venture, Kemp connected timber tycoon Tim Blixseth with celebrated ski-movie director Warren Miller, who promoted Blixseth's private ski resort in Montana, the Yellowstone Club. Kemp was given a lot on the property and lifetime memberships for his family. According to Jimmy, Jack and Joanne decided they'd rather have a house in Vail, so they sold the lot and got "a couple million out of it."

In 2002, Kemp, Taylor, and Jimmy Kemp formed Kemp Partners, paring back his for-profit board memberships and organizing his corporate work for maximum profit. (He served on the boards of many nonprofits too, such as Habitat for Humanity and the Martin Luther King Jr. Memorial Foundation.) "He could say 'No' to board requests," said Taylor, and say, "If you want our help, hire Kemp Partners."[11]

How much money Kemp ultimately made is not clear: by one estimate, $60 million to $70 million from the time he left HUD in 1992 until he died in 2009. He marveled at one point that each time Oracle's stock went up $1, he was $1 million richer. How much he spent is also unclear.

By the standards of those with similar incomes, he made no extravagant purchases—no yachts, houses beyond Vail, fancy cars, artwork, or lavish gifts. He and Joanne lived in the same Bethesda, Maryland, house they'd bought when he was in Congress. He evidently spent his money mainly on travel—the fractional jet ownership, trips to Super Bowls and other sports events, all-expense vacations for his large family. He bought books with abandon—to read, not collect. He also set aside money to send his seventeen grandchildren to college.

———

In February 1997, Robert Novak wrote a column indicating that Kemp was seriously considering another run for president in 2000. Novak noted that Republicans were still criticizing Kemp's 1996 debate performance, but he told Novak[12] that "it was not a disaster" and that he'd "learned a lot from it." He explained, "I'm not an Oxfordian debater. I'm a preacher, an evangelist, a coach and a salesman," adding "I will be better next time." Novak wrote it was odd that Kemp, who didn't run in 1996 when he was a rank-and-file GOP favorite, "now contemplates a candidacy at the moment of his lowest popularity in the party." But "it is Jack Kemp's turn more than anybody else's in 2000 and at least he sounds like he could mean business this time."

In truth, Kemp had no plans to run in 2000. He was no longer ambitious politically. But he wanted to continue having political influence, so he kept the 2000 buzz alive—and it did remain alive in political columns, polls, and chatter until April 1999, when he announced that he would not seek the nomination and that his "professional political career" was over. He explained he would focus on "a public mission in philanthropy and public policy," including becoming national chairman of the Rebuilding Our Communities campaign, a project of Habitat for Humanity.[13]

The announcement liberated Kemp from a political system that had become more about fund-raising than ideas. Jack Pitney, a political scientist at Claremont McKenna College, said Kemp "can now say things that active politicians can't. . . . At long last, he can throw the long ball."

Kemp was still a party loyalist, but he said, "I don't feel like I'm a very good Republican. I disagree with so much of what the party is not doing. I'm not in the mainstream of the Republican Party right now. It's too grumpy, too willing to sit on the status quo." He criticized congressional Republicans for failing to slash tax rates in the District of Columbia, which might have set a national trend. "[GOP leaders] were too busy counting angels dancing on the head of a budget pin," he said. And despite the end of the cold war, too many Republicans were "looking for new enemies to replace old enemies."[14] As the 2000 presidential campaign unfolded, he said, he would keep in touch with the contenders and ultimately endorse one.[15]

———

During Bill Clinton's second term, from 1997 through 2000, Kemp was at odds with the president, but he also clashed openly with Newt Gingrich, one of his earliest supply-side allies and, as House Speaker beginning in 1995, the most powerful Republican in Washington.

In January 1997, though, Kemp stoutly defended Gingrich against Democrats who filed eighty-four ethics charges against him and mounted an effort to oust him as Speaker. He said Gingrich was "among the most conscientious men I have known and he possesses a profound devotion to the greater good of the country." Attacking the anti-Gingrich Democrats, he cited the ethical flaws of the Clinton administration that he'd avoided during his 1996 vice presidential run.

Gingrich was narrowly reelected Speaker on a party-line vote. Later in January, he was formally reprimanded by the House by the lopsided margin of 395–28, and agreed to pay $300,000, the cost of the investigation. In truth, the Democratic assault amounted to political revenge for Gingrich's use of ethics rules to oust Speaker Jim Wright in 1989. Ultimately, Gingrich was exonerated of all charges against him by both the House Committee on Ethics and the Internal Revenue Service.[16]

On policy grounds, Kemp repeatedly took Gingrich to task. In March 1997, Gingrich suggested Congress should delay major tax cuts and work instead on a balanced budget deal with Clinton. This provoked a blast from Kemp. "If the Republican Party cannot reach agreement on this fundamental priority, we should break up the party and start over,"[17] he wrote the Speaker. Kemp disputed the notion that balancing the budget was a "moral crusade" and argued, "The moral imperative is to re-establish limited government and to maximize freedom for the American people"—code for cutting taxes.[18]

In June 1997, Gingrich endorsed a proposal that would dedicate two thirds of future budget surpluses to reduce the national debt. He claimed this would address shortfalls in the Social Security system and "build a grand coalition." In a memo to Gingrich, Kemp asked: "Will we become the party of austerity and go the way of the Canadian, French and English conservatives, or will we . . . regain the confidence and vision of Ronald Reagan and Margaret Thatcher?"

Republicans had shut down the government in 1995 and 1996 in budget fights with Clinton and lost the 1996 presidential election partly as a result. But in 1997, when Gingrich and Clinton reached an agreement to produce a balanced budget by 2002, Kemp criticized Republicans for "worrying about the president threatening a veto" and compromising too quickly.[19] And when Republicans and Clinton agreed to lower the top tax rate on capital gains from 28 percent to 20, Kemp declared, "They cut capital gains, but they wouldn't index it. The whole tax code has been made into a worse nightmare than it already was."[20]

Despite criticisms from Kemp and others on the right, in 1998 the Congressional Budget Office produced a report suggesting that the 1997 capital gains cuts had raised $177 billion in additional revenue.[21] And the budget moved into surplus for the first time since 1969 and stayed there from 1998 to 2001. It has not been in the black since.[22]

Kemp said very little in public about the dominant political events of 1998—the Monica Lewinski scandal that exploded in January and led House Republicans to impeach Clinton for perjury and obstruction of justice. On October 24, two weeks after the House voted, 258–176, to authorize an impeachment inquiry and two weeks before the November election, Kemp was asked whether he would vote to impeach Clinton. "The answer is no," he said. . . . "Right now, no. But let the inquiry begin."[23]

Gingrich had expected, on the basis of private polls, to gain from six to thirty House seats in the midterm election owing to Clinton's wrongdoing. But in a political shock, Democrats picked up five seats and reduced the GOP margin in the House to just twenty-one seats. Within days, Gingrich was forced to resign his Speakership and left Congress in January 1999.[24] The day Gingrich announced his departure, Kemp sent him a letter expressing "sadness and great admiration for your willing-ness to put our party and country above personal interests. . . . [We] are fortunate to have had the leadership of a man who not only knew how to seize the reins of power . . . but who also knew how to yield power when the time came." It was signed "Your very good friend, Jack."[25]

As the Judiciary Committee conducted Clinton impeachment hearings during November and voted out four articles of impeachment in December, Kemp was all but silent. The House approved just two articles, splitting along party lines. The Senate overwhelmingly voted to acquit Clinton, ending the matter. During the entire process, Clinton remained popular. Just before he was acquitted, his approval rating in a *Washington Post* poll stood at 68 percent, 8 points higher than when the Lewinsky scandal first broke.[26]

According to Jimmy Kemp, his father "thought it was small of the Republicans" to pursue impeachment. "He never liked those kind of politics. He thought looking at peccadilloes was small" and did not think Clinton's conduct impeachable.[27]

———

On public issues other than impeachment, Kemp weighed in vigorously and often. Through 1999 and election year 2000, Clinton argued that the best use of the federal surplus was to "save Social Security first," depos-iting the funds "in a lockbox" to extend the solvency of the retirement system. Enough Republicans agreed with him that Kemp unleashed a blast in the *Wall Street Journal* headlined, "The Party of Reagan . . . or of Hoover?"[28] A "debt cabal," he charged, comprised large majorities in both parties, "led by President Clinton, and buttressed by Federal Reserve Chairman Alan Greenspan" and included the House's new leadership—Speaker Dennis Hastert of Illinois and Majority Leader Tom DeLay of Texas—which had made even a "timid" proposed 10 percent rate reduction contingent on debt reduction.

Kemp argued that Republicans instead should follow the lead of Ways and Means Committee chairman William Archer of Texas, who advocated further capital gains rate cuts, Social Security reform allowing workers to set up private investment accounts, and income tax rate reductions at least undoing Clinton's increase in the top rate from 31 percent to 39.6 percent—but preferably lowering it to 25 percent. "No balanced budget, and surely no reduction in of an already-shrinking national debt, ever produced prosperity," he wrote.

Kemp took on numerous other controversies during the Clinton years. He teamed up with his Latino successor as HUD Secretary, Henry Cisneros, and a bevy of both liberal and conservative groups to advocate easing immigration restrictions and granting amnesty to thousands of illegal immigrants. The coalition included Americans for Tax Reform and the National Retail Federation as well as the U.S. Catholic Conference and the National Coalition for Human Rights.[29]

When many in the GOP were calling for an end to race-based affirmative action, Kemp joined with Representative J. C. Watts (R-OK), then the only African American Republican in Congress, to advocate creation of the Community Renewal Project to "replace discrimination with opportunity, poverty with jobs and despair with education."[30] The bill contained familiar Kemp ideas: parental choice in schooling, more incentives to work and save in the welfare system, private ownership of public housing, and enterprise zones.

He took on a new issue too, opposing the Kyoto treaty on climate change. "Whether humans are influencing the climate is unknown. Despite the mantra from the Clinton administration that the science is settled, it is not," he wrote in the *New York Times*.[31] Regardless, the treaty did not bind developing countries like China and India to reduce carbon emissions and therefore would be ineffective while damaging the U.S. economy. When the treaty came up for Senate ratification in 1997, Kemp was still a GOP presidential prospect. And since a leading Kyoto advocate was Vice President Al Gore, Novak wrote that a new Kemp-Gore debate on global warming "could affect the succession of both parties."[32]

———

Five days before the 2000 New Hampshire primary, Kemp endorsed Texas governor George W. Bush for the GOP nomination. This was viewed as a setback for Steve Forbes in his second bid for the nomination. Kemp had endorsed Forbes in 1996 and Forbes again was running on a Kempian platform—a flat tax, partial privatization of Social Security, and appointment of federal judges with opposition to abortion as a litmus test. And the Forbes campaign was distributing a book coedited by Kemp, *The IRS vs. the People,* which called for replacement of the income tax code with a flat tax.

At a press conference in Nashua, New Hampshire, Kemp explained: "I am not here against John McCain," Bush's main rival, and "I am certainly not here against Steve Forbes, a dear friend, who I think would make a great Secretary of the Treasury." And "I am not here suggesting that we can pass a flat tax immediately. I really believe that Governor Bush is the one who can inspire the nation and win a mandate for bringing down the Clinton tax rates." Forbes responded coolly at his own press conference: "Jack is a nice fellow, and we worked together. But he is part of the party establishment. So it is no surprise that they are rallying around their own." He called Kemp's endorsement an example of "politics as usual."[33]

Kemp's son Jimmy believes Bush's main attractions for his father were his professed belief in "compassionate conservatism," a concept originated by Kemp, and his liberal attitudes on immigration and inclusiveness in the GOP, which had resulted in Bush's carrying 49 percent of the Hispanic vote and 27 percent of the African American vote in his reelection as Texas governor in 1998.[34] Also, McCain's economic plan was to pay off the national debt by 2013 instead of cutting taxes, anathema to Kemp.[35]

After the endorsement, Kemp received a handwritten note from Bush thanking him and observing "I know you respect Steve so it made the decision difficult. Your statements made good news and helped with our surge."[36]

Actually, McCain won the New Hampshire primary, one of just seven primary and caucus victories to Bush's forty-four. Kemp campaigned for Bush, but also scolded him and McCain for attacking each other. "Ease up, you guys," he said. "We've got a bigger foe to battle with and that's Al Gore." He said the campaign was "getting a bit off the field of friendly strife and into the World Wrestling Federation" as the McCain forces accused Bush's campaign of using phone banks in South Carolina to charge that he'd fathered a black child out of wedlock, which Bush denied. McCain, meanwhile, accused Bush of pandering to the Christian Right.[37]

Kemp cheered Bush's choice of Dick Cheney as his vice presidential running mate, saying it demonstrated that Bush was dedicated to a Reaganite economic policy.[38] Astoundingly, in doing so, he repudiated one of his own signal accomplishments in Congress—Reagan's 1986 tax reform, which he called "badly flawed" and, he said, was partly to blame for the eight-month recession of 1990–91 that led to Clinton's defeat of Bush's father.

During the campaign, Kemp denounced Gore for indulging in "scare tactics" and "demagoguery" for claiming that Bush's support for private savings accounts would "bankrupt Social Security" and that Bush's tax cut proposals would increase the federal debt by $1.6 trillion. And he said Gore's platform was "based on faulty ideas, class warfare and a debating style propelled by high-octane prevarication, exaggeration and condescension"—stronger language than he'd ever employed in any of his own campaigns.[39]

On election eve, he wrote an op-ed, "Memo to the Victor,"[40] in which he suggested policy changes he hoped would be addressed in "a spirit of reconciliation and concern for those most in need"—increasing the growth rate above 4 percent by simplifying the tax code, with a top rate no higher than 25 percent; allowing workers to set up personal savings accounts with their Social Security taxes; pegging the dollar to the value of a basket of commodities; giving parents the opportunity to choose their children's schools; and "America must reevaluate its role in the post–Cold War world," reconsidering "every embargo, sanction or restraint on trade placed on nations with whom we disagree."

Once the U.S. Supreme Court handed Bush his election victory after the contested vote count in Florida and Bush took office, Kemp hailed his cabinet choices as "outstanding."[41]

————

As his "Memo to the Victor" indicated, Kemp had totally changed his outlook on foreign policy once the cold war ended. In 1988, with the Soviet Union weakened but still intact, he'd called himself a "heavily-armed dove" even though he regularly allied himself with anticommunist hawks, such as Defense Secretary Caspar Weinberger and Senator Jesse Helms. In the Clinton and Bush eras, he rarely advocated the use of force anywhere except in Afghanistan after Al Qaeda's 9/11 attacks.

For instance, Kemp was vociferous in denouncing Clinton's three-month bombing of Serbia in 1999 to secure withdrawal of its troops waging a brutal war to hold on to its largely Muslim province of Kosovo. He was equally outspoken in opposing sanctions and bombing of Iraq to punish violations of the peace agreement that followed the first Gulf War, and he opposed the 1998 Iraq Liberation Act. Kemp called for "containment" of Saddam Hussein rather than his ouster, using a term associated with dovish Democrats and Republican "realists" during the cold war, when Kemp favored "rollback."

When NATO bombing ceased in June 1999 and Serbian dictator Slobodan Milošević agreed to pull his troops out of Kosovo, Kemp dissented from such conservative organs as the *Weekly Standard* and *National Review*. "It was an unnecessary, and in my opinion, illegal and unconstitutional war from the beginning," Kemp wrote.[42] He said the Clinton administration had perpetrated a "fog of lies and culture of deceit" and called for the resignation of Secretary of State Madeleine Albright, though not of Republican secretary of defense William Cohen, who joined Kemp at Empower America after leaving office.

Kemp joined an odd coalition in opposing the Iraq Liberation Act, passed 360–38 by the House and by unanimous consent in the Senate in September 1998 and signed by Clinton in October. It committed the United States to a policy of "regime change" in Iraq.

The *Forward*, published in Yiddish and English in New York, identified the "odd coalition" as including "the Christian left, the Rev. Louis Farrakhan's friends, two former Clinton administration National Security Council officials, Martin Luther King III and the Republican vice presidential nominee in the last election, Jack Kemp." The paper noted that "Kemp's emergence in the appeasement, or, as he puts it 'containment' camp is important because it marks a break with many of his longtime political and intellectual friends."[43] Except on civil rights, his new allies formerly had been Kemp's ideological and political adversaries. They hadn't changed their views on foreign policy. Kemp had changed his.

In an interview with the *Forward,* Kemp said, "We are in a never-never land where my conservative brethren, God bless their hearts, don't have a policy to install a Thomas Jefferson in Iraq." He reasoned, "We contain North Korea, we contain Syria, we contain Iran, we can contain Iraq." He denounced United Nations–imposed trade sanctions and seemed to accept Iraq's dubious assertion that "4,500 children under the age of five are dying every month from hunger and disease as a result." He added, "I think this [Clinton] administration has been shameless in bombing first and asking questions later." He recommended lifting the sanctions if Saddam agreed to "unfettered, unencumbered inspections. . . . We've got to give him some light at the end of the tunnel."

The newspaper noted that while Kemp was a staunch supporter of Israel who'd called for the release of convicted American spy Jonathan Pollard, he might be under the influence of Jude Wanniski, who "has been close in recent years to the anti-Semitic Rev. Louis Farrakhan." Wanniski told the *Forward* he intended to meet with Iraq's ambassador to the United States, Nizar Hamdoun, in an effort to have Saddam interviewed by Western journalists to get his views across. The paper also quoted Wanniski as warning American Jews that Israel's failure to compromise with Arab neighbors would lead to disaster. "You lost 6 million in that Holocaust and you will lose 6 million more," he was quoted as saying.

Kemp was deeply influenced by Wanniski, though their relationship was mercurial. Larry Hunter, Kemp's speech and column writer at Empower America from November 1995 until July 2004, said that Wanniski, a close friend, convinced Kemp in the 1990s that President George H. W. Bush had been right in 1991 not to topple Saddam Hussein lest the United States become bogged down in occupying the country. He said Wanniski was in touch with Hamdoun and that Kemp had meetings with him as well.[44]

Hunter said Kemp "never believed the propaganda about there being weapons of mass destruction. And he did a lot of research into it." The conservative magazine the *American Spectator* reported in May 1999 that Wanniski was advising Kemp to accept an invitation to meet with Saddam Hussein himself—which he never did.[45]

In 1999, Kemp broke off direct contact with Wanniski, according to a letter Kemp later wrote to Defense Secretary Don Rumsfeld.[46] Hunter said that Kemp and Wanniski "were always having fallings out and going for long periods of time without speaking. However, even when Jude and Jack weren't speaking to each other, Jack was reading his stuff,"[47] and Hunter remained in close contact with Wanniski and relayed his thoughts to Kemp.

Kemp criticized Clinton also for failing to advance deployment of a missile defense system and charged that Gore had "followed in lockstep with every one of Clinton's and Albright's politically motivated military interventions abroad." He called on Bush to "reassure the American people that as president he would use greater caution and restraint than the Clinton administration has used in deploying our men and women in uniform to remote theaters with no clear mission and no limit on the terms of deployment."

On one other foreign policy issue, Kemp condemned Clinton for "tilting toward the Palestinians" in Mideast diplomacy and for interfering in Israel's internal politics to defeat hard-line Prime Minister Benjamin Netanyahu, Kemp's longtime friend, and install a more pliable Ehud Barak. He also criticized Clinton for failing to exercise a veto when the United Nations deplored Israel's military response to the violent intifada unleashed by Yasir Arafat when he refused to accept more than total control of East Jerusalem as part of a U.S.-brokered peace agreement.[48]

———

Bush did not follow the foreign policy course Kemp hoped for. As Bush took the United States to war in Iraq, Kemp was far less publicly caustic than he was against Clinton's actions. Instead, he argued against going to war in private to his friends Cheney, Powell, and Rumsfeld—to no avail. He did make it clear in columns that he opposed toppling Saddam Hussein, but he never castigated Bush administration war advocates by name. He merely criticized unnamed "neocon friends" who believed "that talking to adversaries while there are outstanding and difficult differences of opinion is tantamount to surrender."[49]

He was fully with the administration, however, in the aftermath of the 9/11 attacks. "Make no mistake. America is at war," Kemp wrote in his first column after the attacks. He compared Osama bin Laden to Hitler[50] but also made it clear that America's war was with jihadists, not with Arabs or Muslims in general.

Kemp wrote a letter to Rumsfeld a month after 9/11 expressing "complete confidence" in the Bush team "in prosecuting this most unconventional of wars."[51] The main purposes of the letter, though, were to dispute Wanniski's call for the ouster of Deputy Secretary of Defense Paul Wolfowitz, a leading neoconservative advocate for ousting Saddam Hussein, and to refute Wanniski's claim that he was responsible for Kemp's not signing an open letter organized by *Weekly Standard* editor William Kristol calling for action against Iraq. "The fact is, I have not spoken to Wanniski for almost two years," he wrote, and "the truth is, Kristol did not ask me to sign," thinking him "too dovish."

Kemp wrote that he agreed with 95 percent of the contents of the Kristol letter, calling for an all-out war against terrorism. "But what I take issue with is the letter's assertion that even if evidence does not link Iraq directly to the attack, a failure by the Bush administration to move against Saddam Hussein and topple him from power would . . . 'constitute an early and perhaps decisive surrender in the war on international terrorism.' I found that statement not only gratuitous and arrogant, but also inflammatory and wrong."

Two months after 9/11, he publicly cautioned that "we must exercise power judiciously in pursuit of well-conceived objectives which precludes lashing out just to settle old scores. . . . "[52]

He wrote that Bush "has the potential to be a great president" because—Kemp thought—he was not yielding to pressure within the administration to "go after Iraq" in the wake of 9/11. Bush had said, Kemp wrote, that the United States was "watching Iraq very carefully" and had offered to reconsider relations if Saddam Hussein allowed UN inspectors back into his country, a course that Kemp urged him to follow.

In a Townhall.com column in December 2001, Kemp wrote: "The obsession of some members of the press and political establishment to attack Iraq right now is disturbing. . . . We have yet to turn up conclusive evidence that Hussein harbors or assists Al Queda terrorists or that he has forged a long-distance alliance with Al Queda to wage war on America."[53]

As President Bush moved toward war through 2002 and into 2003, Kemp asked trenchant questions about his policy, though he never outright questioned his judgment. If he were sitting alone with the president and vice president, he wrote, he would ask them why they "believe Hussein would be irrational or crazy enough to use a weapon of mass destruction against us," especially when he was successfully warned off their use in the 1991 Gulf War. "Does the United States now claim the legal and moral authority to attack any other country preemptively because we fear that country might attack us in the future if it acquired the weapons to do so . . . ? And would other nations, such as India, Pakistan or China be justified in taking similar action on the basis of their fears of other nations?"

Actually, said Hunter, Kemp did talk regularly to Rumsfeld, Cheney, and Powell. "I recall sitting in the Vice President's office. Cheney was being Cheney. Jack was trying to ask questions. . . . [Cheney] gave him a version of, 'if you knew what I know.' He was very condescending. Of course, Jack didn't have the intelligence [data], but he knew a lot of people." Hunter urged Kemp to criticize administration hawks, but "he never came out publicly the way I would have liked him to do, but I don't think he was capable of that. . . . These were his friends."

According to Hunter, Kemp thought "that if only he could maintain good relations with these [administration] people, look them in the eye, grab their flesh, he could ultimately influence them to do the right thing. Jack was convinced of the power of persuasion through rational discourse, and he thought himself the master 'persuader.' Jack always insisted on [seeing] people's good side. . . . Jack never realized, until maybe late in the game, just how much of an outsider he really was."[54]

Kemp called again and again for the administration to demand ever more intrusive inspection rights from Saddam Hussein and kept praising Bush for pushing ultimatums on the Iraqi leader. He lambasted Gore and Senator Edward Kennedy by name among "left-wing critics who have attacked the president's integrity under the guise of raising legitimate differences of opinion as to the proper course of action in Iraq."[55]

Once the war began and, as he had feared, the United States had no coherent plan to control chaos in the country, he wrote, "We now have a moral obligation, which also is in our self-interest, to help rebuild Iraq and to assist the Iraqi people to create the institutions that will generate economic growth and foster democratic self-rule." The idea that U.S. forces had to occupy Iraq militarily, he said, was "dangerous and could lead us into the quagmire of guerilla war"—exactly what happened. He recommended that the Iraqi military, disbanded by the U.S.-run Coalition Provisional Authority, be reconstituted to keep order; that local elections be held promptly, that the Defense Department return management of Iraq's oil fields to Iraqis and that the United States mount a "Marshall Plan" for the region to encourage investment and development.[56]

Kemp said little while Iraq descended into sectarian civil war and jihadists dominated the Sunni province of Anbar, but in 2007, he strongly backed Bush's troop "surge" to reclaim lost ground. He criticized then-Senate Foreign Relations Committee chairman Joe Biden for calling for an end to U.S. involvement in Iraq.

In sum, once the United States had defeated the Soviet empire, Kemp adopted a national security policy at odds with his cold war views, arguing for many of the noninterventionist, pronegotiation positions he'd condemned when State Department "détentists" advocated them. When the United States was attacked on September 11, 2001, he supported an all-out war against terrorist groups. He opposed the second Iraq war, but once U.S. forces were committed, he did not join his antiwar allies in advocating a withdrawal that would have ensured the defeat of the U.S. mission. He was no longer a neoconservative like many of his close friends, but neither could he be called a dove.

———

On economic and domestic social policy, Kemp was utterly consistent. He blamed the eight-month recession of 2001 not on the bursting of a "tech bubble," but on Alan Greenspan's tightening monetary policy after he determined the economy was suffering from "irrational exuberance."[57] Top journalists such as the *Washington Post*'s David Broder and the *New York Times*'s David Leonhardt interpreted Bush's first-year economic policy as a "return to Reaganomics" and a restoration of supply-siders' influence in Washington.[58] But Kemp wrote that projected surpluses—which he calculated would total $8 trillion over the next decade—permitted a tax cut double the size of the $1.6 trillion Bush was proposing.

As enacted, Bush's 2001 bill, officially the Economic Growth and Tax Relief Act of 2001 (EGTRA), phased in a cut in the top individual rate from 39.6 percent to 35 percent and the lowest from 15 percent to 10 percent. It provided taxpayers one-time rebates, reduced the so-called marriage penalty, expanded the child tax credit, eliminated the "death tax" over a nine-year period, and expanded tax benefits for Individual Retirement Accounts. But Congress reduced its overall estimated price tag to $1.35 trillion—still the largest tax cut since 1981—and imposed a ten-year "sunset" on the bill, later extended, which nearly led to fiscal and political crises in 2010 and 2012 over its renewal.[59] Kemp argued that the measure should have included corporate tax cuts and a reduction in the capital gains tax. He and other supply-siders contended that Bush was arguing for tax reductions as a Keynesian "stimulus" rather than as a spur to investment, savings, and production.[60]

He was much more approving of Bush's 2003 tax bill, known as the Jobs and Growth Tax Relief Act of 2003 (JGTRA), which dropped the capital gains rate from 20 percent to 15 percent, lowered the rate on dividends to that level, accelerated the phase in of the 2001 cuts, and allowed for immediate write-offs for small business investments.[61] Even though, at $350 billion, it was only a fourth the size of the 1981 bill, Kemp argued that it was a supply-side bill. "The recovery triggered by the 2003 rate reductions means not only prosperity for all Americans, but more revenue for the government, too."[62]

Kemp stoutly defended the Bush cuts against charges from Democrats and liberal economists that they would balloon deficits, hamper economic growth, threaten inflation, were unfair in benefiting rich people more than the poor and middle class—and that, in wartime, the nation needed to "sacrifice," or at least pay the cost through tax increases. "Sacrifice? What and to what purpose?" Kemp wrote.[63] "[By] keeping tax rates too high and 'sacrificing' economic growth we don't help the war effort. We hinder it." As to benefiting the rich, he argued that the rich were paying a larger share of taxes and would provide more revenue if a lower rate didn't push them into tax shelters.[64]

Kemp was wrong to think that Bush's tax cuts improved the government's fiscal condition. Budget surpluses disappeared in fiscal 2002. Revenues dropped as a percentage of GDP from 18.8 in 2001 to 15.6 percent in 2004, while outlays increased from 17.6 to 19. Cumulative deficits from fiscal 2001 to 2004 totaled $1.5 trillion, though they did drop from a high of $790 billion in 2002 to $442 billion in 2003.[65] Largely on the strength of Bush's response to 9/11, Republicans picked up eight House seats in the 2002 election and two Senate seats, regaining full control of Congress.

———

In the run-up to the 2004 presidential elections, Kemp blamed deficits on spending for defense (necessary) and domestic programs (less so), but said they were tolerable as a percentage of GDP and that "the economy is the strongest it's been in a long time."[66] He said Democratic nominee John Kerry "is pushing protectionism and increased government spending. Bush has called for making his tax cuts permanent, but that alone is not enough. The president needs a big idea to take to the country on a referendum basis much as Ronald Reagan did in 1980." He recommended Social Security reform with large personal retirement accounts.

When New York Republican senator Alfonse D'Amato suggested that Bush drop Dick Cheney as vice president, Kemp leaped to his defense in spite of their differences over Iraq. "Contrary to media stereotypes, Cheney has been controlled, professional, and one of the president's most trusted advisers. Up close, he is not ideologically rigid at all. . . . [He] is affable, thoughtful and almost entirely lacking in pretense. . . . [He] has been one of the most effective vice presidents in our nation's history."[67]

Nearing the election, with opinion polls showing Kerry and Bush in a dead heat, Kemp charged that the "the Democratic Left" was indulging in "their favorite three strategies: class warfare, generational warfare and race-baiting." His race-baiting charge was based on fliers depicting a black civil rights protester being blasted with a fire hose with the accompanying headline "This is what they used to do to keep us from voting." In spite of the attacks, he predicted that Bush's share of the African American vote would rise from 8 percent in 2000 to 20 percent in 2004.

On Election Day, Bush beat Kerry, 51 percent to 48 percent. He carried 11 percent of the African American vote, and increased his percentage among Latinos from 35 percent in 2000 to 44 percent.[68]

———

In midsummer 2004, Empower America concluded a merger with another conservative group, Citizens for a Sound Economy, to form a new entity, FreedomWorks. With Bush in the presidency, there was little need for a "shadow government," as there had been in the Clinton years. Besides, Kemp was tired of raising money for the nonprofit and eager to concentrate on his boards and speeches. Kemp was supposed to remain a principal at FreedomWorks, but disagreements with its chairman, former House majority leader Dick Armey, and its CEO, Matt Kibbe, led to his departure.

Kemp was a strong advocate for Bush's second-term "Ownership Society" agenda and its key component: the opportunity for workers to establish private investment accounts with a portion—Kemp advocated half—of the 6.5 percent of wages they normally paid in Social Security taxes. But he also criticized the way the administration and congressional Republicans were trying to sell the program, especially their calls for reduction in guaranteed benefits or an increase in the retirement age, which he called "politically suicidal and completely unnecessary."[69]

Kemp concurred with the administration that Social Security was doomed to go bankrupt because its funds were being borrowed to pay for other government programs and because younger workers were not numerous enough to support the retirement costs of the baby boom generation. But he wrote that the administration's emphasis on the program's lack of sustainability was helping the "disinformation campaign being waged by the Democrats and their allies, AARP and MoveOn.org." He suggested an alternative means of arguing for and financing reform, but the administration did not adopt them.[70] Though they controlled both chambers, congressional Republicans became skittish under sustained Democratic/AARP/union attack and the Bush plan failed.[71]

Kemp continued trying to make the GOP more attractive to minorities. He backed a twenty-five-year extension of the 1965 Voting Rights Act, which passed, and an effort to enact a comprehensive immigration law, which did not. Kemp favored the bill cosponsored by GOP senator John McCain and Democrat Edward Kennedy to offer "earned citizenship" to illegal immigrants, but it ran afoul of House Republicans and a large bloc of GOP senators. "The House version [with a seven-hundred-mile wall between the United States and Mexico] . . . would be a prescription for electoral and political disaster not unlike what happened to our party in . . . 1964, when Barry Goldwater . . . voted against the Civil Rights Act," Kemp wrote.[72]

When Hurricane Katrina flooded New Orleans in August 2005 and sent Bush's constantly descending approval ratings below 40 percent, Kemp defended Bush and took on both his Democratic and GOP critics. "Imagine what a dispossessed low-income family living in Houston's Astrodome might think of Republican conservatives who talk about not spending the money on necessary emergency relief, restoration and rebuilding the region," he wrote.[73]

In 2006, with Bush's sixth-year approval rating at 33 percent owing to the unpopularity of the Iraq war and his perceived mishandling of the Katrina aftermath, and with House Republicans stained by scandal, the GOP lost control of both chambers of Congress, dropping a net thirty-one House seats and six Senate seats. After the election, moderate Republicans blamed conservatives for pushing the GOP too far to the right, and conservatives asserted that the party had failed to limit the size of government.[74] Kemp did not weigh in at that point, but the fact is that federal outlays increased from 17.6 percent of GDP in fiscal 2001 to 19.4 percent in 2006, and Bush did not veto a single spending bill while his party held its majorities in Congress.[75]

––––––

In a sixteen-month period in 2005 and 2006, three of Kemp's closest long-standing allies died: Jude Wanniski, on August 29, 2005; Kemp's brother, Tom, on April 26, 2006; and Jeane Kirkpatrick, on December 8, 2006. Of the three, Tom's death was the most devastating to Kemp. Tom Kemp was seventy-five and still fit when he died of a heart attack while swimming laps at a pool in Laguna Beach, California. He was Kemp's boyhood hero—a first-class athlete at USC, a successful businessman as CEO of the Coca-Cola Bottling Company of Los Angeles and president of Beatrice/Hunt-Wesson Foods, and Kemp's trusted adviser during the 1988 presidential campaign.

When his oldest brother, Paul, reached him in his car the day of Tom's death, "Jack was just absolutely out of control, he was so upset and crying. . . . Jack was devastated, that's what he expressed to me at the time, that his hero had died."[76]

Kemp was a eulogist at Kirkpatrick's memorial service at the church they both attended, Fourth Presbyterian in Bethesda. He wrote a column honoring her and recalled that when he introduced her at events around the country, he'd first call her "the Margaret Thatcher of the U.S.," then say, "No, Margaret Thatcher is the Jeane Kirkpatrick of the U.S."

According to aides, Kemp and Wanniski were not speaking to each other when Kemp's longtime guru died of a heart attack, though every obituary referred to their connection to the supply-side movement.

––––––

In 2007, Kemp and his successor as HUD secretary, Democrat Henry Cisneros, published a study on state and local success stories in expanding housing opportunities.[77] They were interviewed about the subprime lending crisis then unfolding and the national slide in home sales and housing prices that, a year later, triggered the Great Recession. The two agreed that what was occurring, as Cisneros put it, was "a correction in the abuses of the market" not "a crash." Kemp said that the Federal Reserve was correctly expanding money supply and the Federal Housing Administration and other agencies were correctly tightening up on lending standards to screen out unqualified buyers. "I think this is going to be a soft landing," Kemp said.[78]

He was not alone in failing to foresee the gravest economic crisis since the Great Depression. In January 2008, Kemp recommended that Congress allow "underwater" homeowners to declare bankruptcy like other secured borrowers in order to reset their mortgages under court supervision. The bill he endorsed failed to pass.[79]

Kemp also wrote—several times in the run-up to the 2008 elections, in fact—that however bad the financial news was becoming, it was important to keep in mind that "the past 25 years have been the best stock market for U.S. investors in U.S. history" because of the supply-side policies put into place during the Reagan administration and sustained by Bill Clinton in the 1990s and George W. Bush in the 2000s.[80]

Kemp met with GOP presidential candidate Mitt Romney in December 2007, but decided to endorse Senator John McCain, who assured him a role in his campaign. It was a calculated decision. He didn't think McCain fully understood his economic growth message, but thought he would listen to him. And he respected McCain's heroic military service.[81]

Kemp campaigned vigorously for McCain and, among other down-ticket candidates, for Bob Dole's wife, Elizabeth, running for reelection as senator in North Carolina. (She lost.) At McCain's frequent town-hall-style rallies, Kemp often sat in the front row, and when McCain got a question about economics, he'd call Kemp on stage to answer it. The economic policy differences between McCain and Obama were the main subject of his columns during the campaign—mainly differences on taxes, but also on trade. Obama vowed during the Democratic primaries to renegotiate the North American Free Trade Agreement and opposed a new agreement with Colombia. Kemp disparaged Obama's proposal to give a $500 refundable income tax credit to all but the top 5 percent of workers, which he said would not lower marginal rates and would not benefit the economy. He urged McCain to go beyond his previous proposals by eliminating federal income taxes for the middle 20 percent of wage earners. "Such a tax reform would be an antidote to the class warfare, neo-collectivist policies of Barack Obama. If implemented, it would also jump-start the economy," he wrote.[82]

A week after Obama won the presidency, Kemp wrote "A Letter to My Grandchildren,"[83] saying, "My first thought last week upon learning that a 47-year-old African American Democrat had won the presidency was, 'Is this a great country or not?'" He said he was disappointed that his friend, McCain, had lost, but this was "a monumental event in the life of our nation . . . transformational given the history of race relations in our nation." Just forty years before, he recalled, blacks had trouble voting, let alone thinking about running for president. In his days playing football, "There were no black coaches, no black quarterbacks and certainly no blacks in the front offices of football and other professional sports." He concluded by observing that Obama had spoken in his victory-celebration speech in Chicago of Abraham Lincoln's view of the nation as an "unfinished work." "Well, isn't that true of all of us? Therefore let us all strive to help him be a successful president, so as to help make America an even greater nation."

———

Kemp returned from campaigning saying he was inexplicably exhausted and complaining that his hip hurt. He thought it was the after effects of an old football injury, much like the damaged knee he'd had replaced in 2006. On that occasion, his body was still in such good shape that he walked into a restaurant with Joanne carrying a cane, but walked out without it. And when he could return to skiing without pain, his daughter Jennifer said, he cried.[84]

After the election, Jimmy and his father made a brief business trip to Israel, where he again complained about hip pain. He tried a massage, but the masseur turned out to be a beefy, aggressive Russian émigré who made his pain excruciating. He made a trip to speak to a grandson's political science class at Whitworth University in Spokane, where he talked well beyond his allotted schedule. He felt so tired afterward that he could not fly to Seattle to visit his son Jeff and his family. He went home instead.

At Thanksgiving dinner in Bethesda, Kemp was in so much pain that he could not sit in a chair. Raul Fernandez and J. T. Taylor recommended he see the Wizards' and Capitols' team physician, orthopedic surgeon Benjamin Shaffer. Shaffer scheduled Kemp for an MRI. After looking at the results, Shaffer told him, "I'm not an oncologist, but I think you need to see one right away." Fernandez said Shaffer called him and said, "Look, you have to say whatever you have to say to him as soon as possible because this doesn't look good. It's everywhere."[85] Jimmy Kemp said his father often had seen dermatologists and had lesions removed from his face, doubtless the product of spending years at Southern California beaches in the days before protective sunscreens. The melanoma that metastasized throughout Kemp's body never had been detected.

Instead of Houston's MD Anderson or another nationally renowned cancer center, he chose to receive chemotherapy and radiation close to home.[86] He was able to spend his last months with his family and visitors he selected, including football great Jim Brown. Family friend and political ally Dan Coats went to Kemp's house and played a videotape of a dying Leonard Bernstein conducting Beethoven's Ninth Symphony just after the Berlin Wall fell in 1989, with an orchestra made up of East and West German musicians.

J. T. Taylor made a few visits to Kemp's house, once arriving to see a figure moving quickly across the hallway. Joanne told him Kemp was expecting him in his TV room. Ex-NFL Coach Jim Mora and retired NFL referee Ron Botchan, his college roommates, were with him. Kemp was wearing a visor with a wig that looked like boxing promoter Don King's standup hair—he'd lost his own to chemo. "This was something he'd rarely do. With Jack, it was usually all about Jack. But this time, he did it for me. We both cracked up."[87]

His daughter Jennifer said that Kemp never wanted to talk about death, but changed dramatically after his diagnosis. He pulled her and Jeff aside and told them to look after "this precious woman," Joanne. He had always been strong, but now he softened, accepting care humbly and graciously, no small feat for a man who valued strength as much as Kemp did.

Jeff Kemp talked to his father intensively during his last months, engaging in some of the most deeply intimate conversations of their lives. "I had a four-page bullet point letter of all the things I wanted to thank him for, and I sat Mom and him down in their little family room, maybe in February. He was pretty ill and weak, but not in terrible shape yet. And I read him the list, 15 minutes, and I'm laughing some and then crying. Mom is crying and laughing just a bit. Dad is laughing and then crying, and then we're all hugging."

Jeff is convinced his father ended his life a committed Christian.[88] His last words to Jeff were a prayer: "Dear God, help Jeff to realize his talent. Help him to realize the force for good. . . ." He couldn't finish his sentence, but Jeff knew he meant "the force for good that he can be in this world." Then he said, "And help us both realize the only thing that matters is, Thy will be done."[89]

He could barely speak, but when one of his grandsons had a paper to write on the role of radio in World War II, he called Kemp, who whispered into the phone to him about Winston Churchill's speeches to the British people during the war. "It gave us chills," Jennifer said. "It was really moving, because his brain was still so intact and he cared so much about history."[90]

In February 2009, with doctors giving him no more than four months to live, Kemp wrote his last and longest column for Townhall .com—about his hero Abraham Lincoln. He speculated on what Lincoln might have achieved had he not been assassinated and mourned that America's dream of equality had yet to be realized. "But Lincoln showed us the way. He believed that the American system of upward mobility was the bedrock of our democracy, that no individual is excluded from the American Dream and that poverty is not a permanent condition. And like the story of the 'Good Shepherd' from Hebrew and Christian scripture, he believed we must move forward and not leave anyone behind."[91]

Kemp died on May 2, 2009, a rainy Saturday, with Joanne and his daughters holding his hands, singing songs they all loved—from "How Great Thou Art" and "Amazing Grace" to "Chestnuts Roasting on an Open Fire"—laughing about the incongruity of singing a Christmas song in May. They said prayers, read scripture, and whispered good-byes. Their pastor, the Reverend Dr. Rob Norris, joined them for an hour of the time. Jeff and Jimmy could not make it to his bedside before he passed away. "I remember holding his hand and specifically the quirky finger that had been broken in some game and molded into the shape of a foot-ball," Jennifer recalled.[92] "We told him how much we loved him and that it was good for him to join his Creator and Lord in heaven."

———

For years, Kemp had adamantly ruled out any funeral or memorial service. His wife and children were planning to have one anyway, but he finally relented and said he'd allow one—at Fourth Presbyterian Church, with his children speaking and no politicians. The service was held in a much bigger venue—Washington National Cathedral—and America's second-largest cathedral was filled to its two-thousand-seat capacity. The music was led by the Howard University choir, which mixed a Negro spiritual with traditional hymns.

Many politicians attended, but as he wished, none spoke, though ex–White House aide (and Prison Fellowship leader) Chuck Colson gave the longest tribute, including a section on why Kemp could not be president. "Number one, he was without guile," Colson said.[93] "In all the many, many times we were together over the years, I never heard him say an unkind thing about another human being. Never saw him attack anyone publicly. I don't think he could run an attack ad. . . . How do you get to the White House without attack ads?

"I don't think he could have compromised his convictions. If he believed something was right and just . . . Jack Kemp could not hide that, he would speak out. . . . That great virtue of courage . . . may be what kept him out of the White House."

As Kemp had prescribed, his grandchildren read scripture and his children offered reflections, all loving, some funny. Jimmy revisited his enduring love of football—and his preference for it above all other sports. "He missed every soccer game I ever played, but if I was playing football, he was there." He told of the one time Kemp tried golf. "He took one swing on the driving range with my brand-new three wood. He missed by a foot, broke the club head off, dropped the headless shaft beside me, walked to the car and drove off. I was 13."

He and Jeff named his long list of heroes. Jeff said Kemp called himself "an Abraham Lincoln, William Wilberforce, Teddy Roosevelt, Martin Luther King, Winston Churchill American." Jeff also repeated the list of thanks that he'd previously read to his father privately: for his letters and JFK-grams, "for publicly and privately praising and bragging on us, for his constant words, 'You're a Kemp, be a leader;' for teaching me to throw the football and helping me teach my sons, for giving us freedom to do as we desired but never pushing us in sports, for being at *all* my games (I didn't play soccer), for his love of books and history and dinner table conversation about supply-side economics, about Jackie Robinson, about free trade, about democracy. I thanked him for his identification with and for his championing the cause of black Americans, of aspiring immigrants, of oppressed Jews and Christians across the world; for his optimism and his upward vision. I thanked him for his sunny disposition and offering better ideas instead of attacking, for reveling in our togetherness and our activities as a family. And, finally, I thanked him for my raspy voice."[94]

Kemp's death was greeted with an avalanche of newspaper tributes. Liberal columnist Al Hunt of the *Wall Street Journal* wrote that even if the merits of supply-side economics were "dubious," "in each generation there are a few politicians whose influence is so deep and durable that it rivals, and perhaps exceeds, some of those who get to the White House. Sen. Ted Kennedy is one such figure. Mr. Kemp was another."[95] Liberal Clarence Page of the *Chicago Tribune* wrote that only Kemp had the "desire, the enthusiasm and the steamroller perseverance" to bring Queen Elizabeth to a low-income housing project to be hugged by a tenant.[96] Conservative Michael Gerson wrote that "in his passion for ideas—and in the affection he inspired—Jack was the most influential modern Republican who never became president.[97] The *Wall Street Journal*'s conservative editorial page called him a "Capitalist for the Common Man" and said he was "among the most important Congressmen in U.S. history. . . . He helped to transform the Republican Party . . . [through] the power of his ideas, and from the sincerity and enthusiasm with which he spread them."[98] Any number of writers and editorial pages opined, as the *Dallas Morning News*'s headline put it, "Today's GOP could use a Jack Kemp."[99]

———

On August 12, 2009, Kemp was posthumously awarded the Presidential Medal of Freedom, the nation's highest civilian award, by President Barack Obama. Joanne was at the White House to receive the medal. Obama observed before the presentation, "A conservative thinker, a Republican leader and a defender of civil rights, he was that rare patriot who put country over party, never forgetting what he learned on the gridiron—that it takes each of us doing our part, and all of us working together to achieve a common goal. It's a life from which we can all draw lessons, Democrat and Republican alike." The actual medal citation read: "A statesman and a sports icon, Jack French Kemp advocated for his beliefs with an unwavering integrity and intellectual honesty. On the football field, he earned the respect and admiration of his teammates for his judgment and leadership. As a public servant, he placed country before party, and ideas before ideology. Jack Kemp built bridges where others saw divisions and his legacy serves as a shining example for those who challenge conventional wisdom, stay true to themselves, and better our nation."

Thirteen

LEGACY

Politicians who were never president are usually forgotten once they leave the stage. Jack Kemp hasn't been. Within five years of his death, a Kemp revival was in full flower. With both the Republican Party and the country in desperate need of leadership, conservatives, moderates, and liberals all have joined in the call for one, two, or many more Kemps. And some politicians have begun trying to emulate him.

On the right, Republicans bemoaned the lack of intellectual leadership and willingness to work hard. "The Republican Party can study itself to death and hire the world's best marketers, but without some Jack Kemps it will only be dressing up stasis," wrote Rich Lowry, editor of *National Review.*[1] "Kemp did his most important work as a backbencher in the House. Where is his equivalent today?" GOP leaders in the House should "tell some promising member to spend the next three months coming up with 10 ideas for promoting work in America, or for a new welfare reform agenda, or for replacing Obamacare, or for making college affordable." One of Kemp's signal strengths was policy entrepreneurship: he said again and again that the purpose of a political party was not only to try to win elections, but to also produce better ideas than the opposition, thereby broadening its appeal. Opposing Democrats—foremost, Barack Obama— has been the abiding preoccupation of Republican leaders. "Better ideas" have been slow to emerge, though they are beginning to.

On the left, Sam Tanenhaus of the *New York Times* noted[2] that Kemp has been called a hero by some prominent Democrats, including Senator Cory Booker of New Jersey. Tanenhaus observed, Kemp "preached the gospel of upward mobility, economic opportunity, cultural diversity, and racial justice." Also, he traced Kemp's attitudes on race to his experience as a pro quarterback. In fact, Kemp said that when he fought racism, it was in tribute to the African Americans he'd played with. Liberals legitimately appreciate Kemp's "bleeding heart." They ignore his dedication to low taxes and free markets as the means to foster upward mobility.

The full Kemp model—"bleeding heart" and "conservative"— is what the nation needs. Politicians who are principled, dynamic, positive, cheerful, inclusive, bipartisan, optimistic, unorthodox, disposed to compromise, committed to courting minorities, urban oriented, progrowth, and antibureaucratic—and interested in ideas and action, not political tactics or personal attack. Idealistic. Visionary. "The goal of achieving House majority was too small for Jack," former representative Vin Weber said.[3] "He wanted to transform the country."

———

Yet for all its enduring appeal, the popular Kemp model is neither his most significant achievement nor the heart of his historical legacy. Kemp's style as a politician has many admirers and may yet transform the Republican Party. But it was Kemp's leadership of the supply-side revolution that changed America and the world and altered history. He was the nexus of a movement spawned largely outside the GOP and originally in defiance of senior Republicans. Kemp brought together a renegade band of free market economists in New York and Washington, the influential editorial page of the *Wall Street Journal*, widely read columnist Robert Novak, a group of relatively young Republicans in Congress, and Ronald Reagan, who adopted Kemp's legislation, based on supply-side economics, as the policy of his new administration. All this happened in the decade from the mid-1970s to the mid-1980s before Kemp was fifty.

That the policy of deep tax rate cuts and sweeping tax reform sparked nearly a quarter century of economic growth and prosperity when all else had failed—that is what makes it Kemp's greatest legacy. Not only did the supply-side formula create robust growth, impressive job creation, and a surge in the American stock market, it also had a worldwide effect. After the fall of the Berlin Wall and collapse of the Soviet Union, tax cutting swept through countries liberated from Soviet domination. Bulgaria adopted a flat income tax rate of 10 percent. Estonia settled on a 22 percent rate. Russia cut tax rates. Even Sweden reduced taxes, followed by Finland. To Kemp's dismay, tax rates were later increased in many countries. Nonetheless, income and corporate rates around the world are roughly half what they were a generation ago.

In 2005, Kemp lamented that the concept of supply-side economics had been "all but forgotten in Washington, and many of its principles abandoned by U.S. policymakers."[4] The explanation for supply side's disappearance is simple: government leaders prefer Keynesianism, which relies on government spending often coupled with politically "targeted" tax cuts to revive a bad economy. It gives them control. It is the default position of the governing class. Government decides how much is spent, what it's spent on, and who benefits. With supply-side cuts, government yields control. Thus there is widespread antipathy to supply-side economics among governing elites.

Jack Kemp became famous as a professional football player and important as a congressman. But the success of the supply-side movement has elevated him to a higher status. Without that success, it's unlikely there would be a Kemp revival. With it, he's unavoidable when the Republican Party, the economy, taxes, and political reform are the subject of serious discussion. With the return of Keynesian economics and its subsequent failure in America, Kemp represents a shining alternative. All that's needed now is a leader, a few disciples, and a megaphone.

In 1936, Albert Jay Nock wrote a famous essay in the *Atlantic Monthly* titled "Isaiah's Job." Nock was an intellectual and "individualist." In his essay, he told the story of "Remnant," who, God said, existed and could save civilization. "They are obscure, unorganized, inarticulate, each one rubbing along as best he can. . . . They are the ones who will come back and build up a new society."

Kemp's Remnant of sorts is scattered about the country, but it's not apocalyptic or inarticulate or obscure. They are admirers of the Kemp political model and are committed to turning America away from the policies of liberalism, the left, and Keynes. In their place, the Kemp Remnant believes an updated version of supply side's free market approach should be enacted. And reforms of education and immigration and a new emphasis on reducing poverty and welfare dependence must be pursued as well.

If there's a leader of the Kemp diaspora, it's Paul Ryan. He was Kemp's assistant at Empower America, the now-defunct think tank in Washington. He learned the power and appeal of supply-side economics from Kemp himself. He wrote a paper that hastened Kemp's emergence as a champion of immigration reform. But Ryan is not an exact replica of Kemp. He calls himself a second generation supply-sider. He means the agenda has changed in the twenty-first century.

For Kemp, taxes and growth were everything. "We're focused on growth," Ryan said,[5] "but also on the size of government and deficits and debt. . . . The debt has gotten so big it's growth-retarding." Ryan said, "It never really necessarily sat right with me" that Kemp was agnostic about spending, deficits, and bigger government. Kemp, in turn, felt Ryan should have turned down the chairmanship of the House Budget Committee. He thought it was politically harmful to be identified with cutting programs people like. But Ryan said growth is still the overriding goal, "better than just cut, cut, cut [and] balance the budget." In 2015, Ryan became chairman of the tax-focused House Ways and Means Committee.

Ryan has emulated Kemp in outreach to minorities. Kemp's mentor, Bob Woodson of the Center for Neighborhood Enterprise, has taken Ryan to tour inner-city neighborhoods and talk to residents. "I'm a poor imitator [of Kemp]," Ryan said. "I'm doing the best I can. I'm trying to encourage others to do the same and emulate me." But Republicans have "lost a couple steps from Jack's legacy in speaking to everybody about growth and hope and opportunity and the right to rise," he said. "We have not spread that confident message about how these ideas apply equally to everybody."[6]

Senator Rand Paul of Kentucky, elected in 2010, has made an effort to model himself on Kemp. Over dinner in 2014, he pumped political consultant Scott Reed for hours with questions about Kemp. Reed had worked for Kemp's presidential campaign in 1988, served as his chief of staff at HUD, and engineered the selection of Kemp as Bob Dole's vice presidential running mate in 1996.[7] Like Kemp, Paul has adopted an urban policy that stresses the creation of low-tax enterprise zones to attract business and jobs to depressed cities. He has spoken frequently to African American groups. Paul's supporters see him as a "compassionate conservative," an updated version of Kemp.

But Rand Paul is more Kempian in style than substance. He is a libertarian who favors small government. Kemp was a big government conservative. He believed government had a critical role to play in lifting people out of poverty. This included subsidies, not just incentives. In foreign policy, Paul is not the internationalist that Kemp was. Nor did Kemp think America should restrain its projection of power and influence in the world, as Paul does. During the cold war, Kemp was more hawkish and anti-Soviet than Reagan. Later, he was against George W. Bush's going to war in Iraq, but then in favor of winning it.

Paul's Senate colleague, Marco Rubio of Florida, has a long association with Kemp and said that while he was growing up, Kemp "was an influence on me."[8] Kemp could "distill" his message "down to everyday life and everyday people." In 2006, they talked for hours when Rubio was developing his project to identify "100 innovative ideas for Florida's future." Rubio's priorities, such as immigration reform and a new anti-poverty program, are similar to Kemp's. As speaker of the Florida House, he championed tax reform to reduce property taxes and trim the size of the state government. "We sure could use Kemp right now," he said in a 2012 speech.[9] Kemp is not here, "but his ideas and the principles behind them are."

A handful of Republican governors have strong Kemp leanings. Some speeches of Governor Bobby Jindal of Louisiana have sounded as if Kemp had written them. Governor Sam Brownback of Kansas enacted income tax cuts plucked out of the supply-side playbook. Governor Mike Pence of Indiana, who served in the House from 2001 to 2013, told *Howey Politics Indiana* that he became friends with Kemp in 1988.[10] Kemp encouraged him to run for chairman of the House Republican Conference in 2008. He won. Kemp "was as great an influence and perhaps greater because we were friends," Pence said. "I felt like Jack understood the foundation of Lincoln's party, which is a foundation about quality of opportunity and a boundless confidence in the American people." Running as a "Jack Kemp Republican," Larry Hogan was elected governor of Maryland, the bluest of blue states, in 2014.

Bruce Rauner of Illinois was a special case. He ousted Democratic governor Pat Quinn in a heavily Democratic state with a weak economy and a mounting debt crisis. A businessman, Rauner had spent time in the poor neighborhoods. He visited inner-city schools and is a school reformer. "It was so Kemp-like," Heritage's Steve Moore said.[11] "He picked up on the Kemp message" of tackling poverty. The result: in the election, Rauner did better in poor minority communities than Republicans usually do.

Based on his record as governor of Florida, Jeb Bush is a model Kempian. He was a relentless reformer. He cut taxes. He did more to advance radical changes in his state's school system than any other governor. He was a fervent supporter of charter schools, vouchers, and allowing students to transfer from failing schools. He became a leading advocate for overhauling the immigration system to bring more skilled

people into the country legally. He named his political action committee "Right to Rise," borrowing from Lincoln and Kemp.

There are also many Kemp-minded economists in waiting. Moore
is a major presence in Washington on economic issues. John Mueller of
the Ethics and Public Policy Center worked as Kemp's economist on
Capitol Hill. Cesar Conda is an economic analyst who worked for Kemp
before serving as Rubio's chief of staff for three years. Larry Kudlow,
the chief economist for Reagan's budget office, is a columnist, contributor to CNBC, and a longtime friend of Kemp's. "My relationship with
Jack was, if you call me and ask me, I'm your guy," he said.[12]

A younger group calling themselves Reform Conservatives are
"Kempian in various ways," said Peter Wehner, who was policy director
of Empower America, the Kemp think tank.[13] They reflect a "very real
strain of conservatism that I think Jack and Reagan represented—
forward-looking, reform minded, very Burkean." For them, Wehner
said, "it's not simply about what government can't do, but what the purposes of government are." Like Kemp, they want to use government for
conservative ends. They believe government "can catalyze other institutions in society to make them strong—the large area between the individual and the state. That's something that Jack would be sympathetic
to." Indeed, he would.

In 2014, so-called Reformicons published an online, book-length
policy agenda, "Room to Grow: Conservative Reforms for a Limited
Government and a Thriving Middle Class."[14] It's idea rich, but not
deemed truly conservative by libertarians who claim it "reinvents the
liberal welfare state" instead of supplanting it.[15] On taxes, the book calls
for subsidies to help the middle class. Supply-side veterans such as Dan
Mitchell of the Cato Institute regard this as Keynesian-style tinkering
with the tax code. They propose to follow Kemp's lead with across-the-
board reductions in marginal income tax rates. Ryan, for example,
would cut the top income tax rate to 25 percent. That's impossible,
according to the reformers. A rate that low would generate too little
revenue to fund the government without causing debt to skyrocket.

Senator Mike Lee of Utah, a leading member of the reform camp, would settle for a 35 percent rate.

That there's division inside the camp of Kemp followers is hardly surprising. Yet Kemp disciples of all stripes agree on the new agenda. It would focus on four big issues: taxes, entitlements, immigration, and poverty. Tax reform, passed in 1986, was Kemp's final triumph. A new round of reform would require two things associated with Kemp: a broader tax base with lower rates, and skill at compromise. The first means killing tax preferences and special breaks, as was done in 1986. The second is where compromise comes in. It means tax rate cuts along with tax credits in one package. Kemp would have agreed to that deal.

Kemp's favorite word was *growth*. In his day, spending on Social Security, Medicare, and Medicaid didn't impede growth. That's no longer true. Ryan is the promoter of "premium support," a plan to bring free market incentives and more patient choice to Medicare, the fastest growing entitlement. The Congressional Budget Office projects the return of $1 trillion deficits in 2020. "You can't have public debt rising as a share of GDP," conservative economist Larry Lindsey asserts. "The key to that is entitlement reform."[16]

On immigration, compromise translates as reform in several steps, first with border security and the overhaul of the immigration system that now discriminates in favor of relatives of citizens, later by legalizing illegal immigrants and providing them with a path to citizenship. There's no other way with Republicans in control of Congress. Republicans fear passage of immigration reform in a single massive bill will produce unforeseen—and possibly disruptive—consequences.

On poverty, what's required is more talk and more action. Once fighting poverty becomes a Republican theme, thanks to the Kemp revival, more discussion is assured. Action has gained momentum. Ryan has the most ambitious antipoverty plan. He would expand the earned income tax credit, which has encouraged work and abated poverty. He would turn Head Start into a block grant and allow states to experiment with early education programs. He would consolidate federal jobs programs. He would give judges more discretion in sentencing nonviolent offenders, recognizing that long jail terms reinforce the cycle of poverty in families. Jeb Bush would reform K-12 education and institute German-style apprenticeship programs for those not headed to college. Rubio would promote alternatives to conventional college degrees.

————

In the 1970s, Kemp often gathered his economic and political advisers for dinner at his home in suburban Maryland. The sessions were boisterous and argumentative. Many of the economists didn't like each other. They disagreed strenuously over the strategy for winning approval of tax cuts. Several participants were prima donnas. Irving Kristol was the calming voice. Meanwhile, life in Kemp's congressional office was frenetic because Kemp overscheduled himself. He made snap decisions. His old football pals dropped in for unscheduled visits.

Yet out of this tumult came an intellectual and political revolution and a new era of prosperity in America. It was unexpected by the elites. They were dispirited and had lost the ability to rally the country. The instigator of the economic boom was an ex-football star who had taught himself economics in all its intricacies and lingo. Kemp, with his single-mindedness and boundless energy, turned out to have the most important qualities of a leader. He could bring people together in a cause. He could transform discord into solidarity. And he was always on offense.

The new interest in Kemp is not an accident or a happenstance. It reflects the nation's desire for a different kind of political leader, one with ideas for making the economy work again—for everyone. Kemp filled that role earlier when no one else could. Now the country awaits the arrival of a new leader. Surely that person is on the way.

ACKNOWLEDGMENTS

———

This book originated in 2011, when the Jack Kemp Foundation, encouraged by Kemp's former press secretary, Marci Robinson Shore, retained Kondracke to conduct its Oral History Project. Under direction from foundation president Jimmy Kemp and from Michelle Van Cleave, and invaluably assisted by oral historian Brien Williams, Kondracke interviewed more than hundred of Kemp's lifetime associates—fellow football players, congressional and cabinet colleagues, staff members, friends, and family. Their recollections were a central source for this book and the Kemp Foundation graciously agreed to their use without conditions. Oral History transcripts, recordings, and videos are available on the Kemp Foundation Web site: www.jackkempfoundation.org/kemp-legacy-project.

In 2012 the Kemp Foundation and Librarian of Congress James Billington appointed Kondracke to fill the Kemp Chair in Political Economy at the library's Kluge Center for Scholars. Kemp's papers—more than 400 boxes consisting of 118,500 items—were meticulously organized by the library's manuscript division. Kondracke is indebted for assistance and many kindnesses from the Kluge staff, including its former director, Carolyn Brown; assistant director, Mary Lou Reker; and Travis Hensley, without whom this book often might have been lost in cyberspace. Drs. Billington and Brown allowed Kondracke to occupy Kluge space even after his two-year fellowship expired.

It was former Kemp chief of staff David Smick's idea that Kondracke and Barnes team up in writing this book, and he was an invaluable adviser. Among Kemp's staff and colleagues were John Mueller, Sharon Zelaska, Bruce Bartlett, David Hoppe, Randy Teague, Jeffrey

Bell, Scott Reed, Vin Weber, and Newt Gingrich. We received generous advice on supply-side economics from its foremost historian, Brian Domitrovic, chairman of the history department at Sam Houston State University.

We are indebted for valuable research assistance, especially from Amy Collier and from Michael Randall, Adam Schwarzman, Alescia Hyde, and V. P. Dao. And for help from Kemp Foundation staff members Tim Fisher, Emma Bayer Watkins, and Bona Park. And for generous guidance from Joanne Kemp, sons Jimmy and Jeff, and daughters Jennifer Andrews and Judith Nolan.

We are indebted to our agent, Bob Barnett, for far more than normal "agentry." He was a friend of Kemp's and acted as a good friend and adviser to us. And we are grateful to our editor, Bria Sandford, who conscientiously demonstrated that book editing is not a lost art. And to Adrian Zackheim, our publisher, for believing in this project.

And finally we are boundlessly thankful to our wives, Marguerite Kondracke and Barbara Barnes, for putting up with months upon months of absence while we buried ourselves in our offices—and for giving us wise editorial, psychological, and time-management advice and moral support.

NOTES

———

Symposia and Panels, an Explanation

1. Symposium, "Jack Kemp, the Bills and Buffalo" is the title in the Kemp Foundation's Oral History Project archive transcript for three panels conducted at Ralph Wilson Stadium in Buffalo, New York, on March 3, 2011. Panel 1 is "Quarterback Jack Kemp and the Buffalo Bills." Panels 2 and 3 are both titled "Congressman Kemp, Politics and the Buffalo Office." They're referred to in text as Buffalo Oral History symposium, Panel 1, 2, or 3.

2. Symposium, "Jack Kemp and the Tax Reforms of 1981 and 1986" is the title for two panels at the Miller Center of Public Affairs at the University of Virginia, Charlottesville, Virginia, on April 18, 2011. Panel 1 is titled "Jack Kemp and the Economic Recovery Tax Act of 1981" and Panel 2 is "Jack Kemp and the Tax Reform Act of 1986." In the text and endnotes they are referred to as Miller Center symposium, Panel 1, and Miller, Panel 2, or Miller 1 or Miller 2.

3. Symposium, "Kemp Congressional Staff" is the title for two panels conducted at the Longworth House Office Building, Washington, DC, September 19, 2011. Panel 1 included staff serving Kemp in the 1970s; Panel 2, the 1980s. We've identified them as Congressional Staff symposium, Panel 1 (as with the one above), or Congressional Staff symposium, Panel 2.

4. Symposium, "Jack Kemp and the Reagan Revolutionaries in the House" is the title for two panels conducted March 6, 2012, at the Kluge Center of the Library of Congress. Panel 1 was titled "The Reagan Mandate and Conservative Political Thought." Panel 2 was "The Cold War, Iran Contra, the Politics of the House and the 1988 Campaign." Our endnotes refer either to Reagan Revolutionaries symposium, Panel 1 or Panel 2.

5. Symposium, "On the Road with Jack Kemp" is the title of a panel September 6, 2012, at the Kemp residence in Bethesda, Maryland. It's referred to in the endnotes as Road symposium.

6. Symposium, "Jack Kemp and the 1988 Republican Presidential Primaries" is the title for three panels held on April 14, 2012, at Republican National Committee Headquarters, Washington, DC. Panel 1 was titled "Campaign Strategy, Themes, and Launch." Panel 2, "The Campaign at the State Level: Michigan, New Hampshire, South Carolina, and Georgia." Panel 3, "Campaign Successes and Failures, the Decision to Withdraw and What Came Next." Referred to as 1988 Campaign symposium, Panel 1, 2, or 3.

7. Symposium, "Quarterback in the Cabinet" is the title for a panel conducted on June 29, 2012, at the Bipartisan Policy Center, Washington, DC. It's referred to as the HUD symposium.

8. Symposium, "Jack Kemp and the 1988 Republican Presidential Primary," conducted in April 14, 2012. It is referred to in the notes as the 1988 Campaign symposium.

9. Symposium, "Secretary Kemp Quarterback in the Cabinet," conducted on June 29, 2012, Washington, DC. This is referred in the notes as the HUD symposium.

Introduction

1. The formulation that Kemp was the foremost Republican politician of the twentieth century who was not president is not original with us. It was suggested in various forums by Kemp advisers Jeff Bell, Bruce Bartlett, John Mueller, and Michael Gerson, as well as former *Human Events* editor Allan Ryskind.

2. The "misery index" was invented in the 1960s by Lyndon Johnson's chief economic adviser, Arthur Okun, simply adding the inflation and unemployment rate as a takeoff on the temperature-humidity "discomfort index." United States Misery Index, http://www.miseryindex.us.

3. "Satisfaction with the United States," Gallup; http://www.gallup.com/poll/1669/general-mood-country.aspx.

4. Fredric Smoler, "We Had a Great History, and We Turned Aside," *American Heritage,* October 1993.

5. Ibid.

6. One of Kemp's favorite Lincoln scholars was Gabor Boritt, author of *Lincoln and the Economics of the American Dream* (Urbana and Chicago: University of Illinois Press, 1994), an in-depth study of views on "the right to rise" and its relation to Lincoln's antislavery views.

7. David S. Broder, "A Fervent Kemp Raises Battle Cry," *Washington Post*, October 10, 1987, A3.

8. Michael Lewis, "The Quarterback," *New Republic,* October 14, 1996.

9. This is not an authorized biography. The Jack Kemp Foundation granted use of its Jack Kemp Oral History Project interviews without restriction or right of review.

10. Carmen DeNavas-Walt and Bernadette D. Proctor, "Income and Poverty in the United States: 2013," U.S. Census Bureau, http://www.census.gov/content/dam/Census/library/publications/2014/demo/p60-249.pdf.

11. "Cumulative Increases in Health Insurance Premiums, Workers' Contributions to Premiums, Inflation, and Workers' Earnings, 1999–2013, Kaiser/HRET Survey of Employer Sponsored Health Benefits, 1999–2013, Bureau of Labor Statistics, http://i.huffpost.com/gen/1307260/original.jpg.

12. "Wealth Inequality Has Widened Along Racial, Ethnic Lines Since End of Great Recession," Pew Research Center, http://www.pewresearch.org/fact-tank/2014/12/12/racial-wealth-gaps-great-recession/.

13. Associated Press, "Richest 1% Earn Biggest Shale Since Roaring '20s," CNBC, *Inside Wealth*, http://www.cnbc.com/id/101025377.

14. Table A-15, "Alternative Measures of Labor Underutilization," Bureau of Labor Statistics, U.S. Department of Labor, http://www.bls.gov/news.release/empsit .t15.htm.
15. CNN/ORC Poll, May 29–June 1, 2014, http://www.pollingreport.com/life.htm.
16. Robert Rector, "Marriage: America's Greatest Weapon Against Child Poverty," Heritage Foundation, Special Report 117, http://www.heritage.org/research/ reports/2012/09/marriage-americas-greatest-weapon-against-child-poverty.
17. "How NOT to Fight Inflation," remarks at the 44th Annual Convention of the International Longshoremen's Association, AFL-CIO, Miami, Florida, July 16, 1979, reprinted in Jack Kemp, *The American Idea: Ending Limits to Growth* (Washington, DC: American Studies Center, 1984), 23.
18. "Annual Secondary Education per Student," U.S. Department of Education, https:// www2.ed.gov/about/overview/fed/10facts/edlite-chart.html.
19. "The Condition of College & Career Readiness 2014," ACT, http://www.act .org/research/policymakers/cccr14/index.html.
20. Andrew Flowers, "Why We Still Can't Afford to Fix America's Broken Infrastructure," FiveThirtyEight Economics, http://fivethirtyeight.com/features/why-we -still-cant-afford-to-fix-americas-broken-infrastructure.
21. "Health Expenditure per Capita," World Bank, http://data.worldbank.org/indicator/ SH.XPD.PCAP.
22. http://www.whitehouse.gov/omb/budget/historicals, Table 7.1.
23. "Our Debt Problems Are Still Far from Solved," Committee for a Responsible Federal Budget, May 15, 2013, http://crfb.org/document/report-our-debt-problems -are-still-far-solved.
24. "Honest money is a populist, blue-collar, middle-class, bread-and-butter concern," Kemp told a Federal Reserve Bank/Emory University audience, March 17, 1982, in a speech titled "How to Fight Inflation: The Supply-Side Strategy for Lower Interest Rates." Reprinted in Kemp, *The American Idea*, 69.
25. In February 2015, with the U.S. rate at 5.5 percent, the European Union rate was 9.8. Norway (3.9), Switzerland (3.5), and Germany (5.1) had lower rates, but France (10.6), the Netherlands (7.1), Denmark (6.2), Sweden (7.8), Finland (9.1), Italy (12.7), and Spain (23.7) had higher. The United Kingdom rate was 5.7. http://epp.eurostat .ec.europa.eu/cache/ITY_PUBLIC/3-01042014-AP/EN/3-01042014-AP-EN.PDF and http://en.wikipedia.org/wiki/List_of_countries_by_unemployment_rate.
26. Smoler, "We Had a Great History."
27. Fred Barnes, "Corporations Get 'Welfare,' 2 in GOP Say," *Baltimore Sun*, January 18, 1982, A1.

Chapter 1: Quarterback

1. Ed Abramoski, Buffalo Oral History symposium, Panel 1, 8.
2. Jeff Kemp, Kemp Oral History Project interview, Washington, DC, December 5, 2012, 27.
3. Paul Kemp, Kemp Oral History interview, San Francisco, August 2, 2011, 14.
4. Dick Kemp, Kemp Oral History interview, Irvine, CA, August 3, 2011, 6.
5. Paul Kemp, Kemp Oral History interview, 20.

6. Ibid., 27.

7. Dick Kemp, Kemp Oral History interview, 17.

8. Juan Williams, "The Disappearing Candidate: Maybe If Jack Kemp Weren't So Worried About Winning, He Wouldn't Be Losing," *Washington Post*, October 11, 1987, W19.

9. Jeff Kemp, Kemp Oral History interview, 26.

10. Paul Kemp, Kemp Oral History interview, 6.

11. Dick Kemp, Kemp Oral History interview, 10.

12. Richard Kemp, *Little Brother* (Irvine, CA: self-published, 2010), 33.

13. Tom Kemp, quoted in Marie Brenner, "Jack the Jock," *Vanity Fair*, January 1986, 102.

14. Jordan was also Occidental's track coach (Kemp threw javelin) and went on to coach at Stanford and for the 1968 U.S. Olympic track team. In college at USC, he was the roommate of 1936 Olympian Louis Zamperini, central figure in Laura Hillenbrand's *Unbroken*.

15. Jim Mora, Kemp Oral History Interview, August 5, 2011, 48.

16. Charles E. Ferguson, Buffalo Oral History symposium, Panel 1, 9.

17. Joanne Kemp, Kemp Oral History interview, December 10, 2012, Bethesda, MD, 7.

18. Ibid., 27.

19. Abramoski, Buffalo Oral History symposium, Panel 1, 9.

20. Joanne Kemp, Kemp Oral History interview, 22.

21. Dick Kemp, Kemp Oral History interview, 13. Dick himself pursued a career as a Christian Science chaplain in the U.S. Navy.

22. Paul Kemp, Kemp Oral History interview, 49.

23. Al McGuire, Buffalo Oral History symposium, Panel 1, 24.

24. Ed Gruver, *The American Football League: A Year-by-Year History, 1960–1969* (Jefferson, NC: McFarland & Company, 1997), 82–83.

25. Ed Rutkowski, Buffalo Oral History interview, July 7, 2011, 2.

26. Larry Felser, Buffalo Oral History symposium, Panel 1, 7.

27. Rutkowski, Buffalo Oral History symposium, Panel 1, 13.

28. Ibid., 32.

29. Rutkowski, e-mail, March 25, 2015.

30. Rick Azar, Buffalo Oral History symposium, 23.

31. http://www.pro-football-reference.co./players/K/Kempja00.htm.

32. Azar, Buffalo Oral History symposium, 18.

33. Felser, Buffalo Oral History symposium, Panel 1, 55.

34. Rutkowski, Buffalo Oral History symposium, 51.

35. Rutkowski, Kemp Oral History interview, 9.

36. Ibid., 4.

37. Felser, Buffalo Oral History symposium, Panel 1, 54.

38. Rowland Evans and Robert Novak, "Ugly Political Rumors," *Washington Post*, December 29, 1978, A15.

39. Robert D. Novak, *The Prince of Darkness: 50 Years of Reporting in Washington* (New York: Crown Forum, 2007), 354.

40. Rutkowski, Buffalo Oral History symposium, Panel 1, 32.

41. Rutkowski, Kemp Oral History interview, 17.

42. Guy Gugliotta, "The Ardor of a Conservative," *Washington Post,* August 11, 1996, A1.

43. Lloyd Grove, "Jack Kemp and the Whole Nine Yards," *Washington Post,* August 21, 1992, B1.

44. Adam Clymer, "Jack Kemp, Star on Field and in Politics, Dies at 73," *New York Times,* May 3, 2009, A1.

Chapter 2: Supply-Sider

1. Bureau of Labor Statistics, *Handbook of Labor Statistics,* Table 51. Civilian Labor Force and Unemployment (Washington, DC: Government Printing Office, 1973), 119; http://books.google.com/books?id=4uKTf_cU42gC&pg=PA119&lpg=PA119&dq =buffalo+unemployment+rate+1971&source=bl&ots=NWINNH4CRV&sig=XZY3 _P6wfeQWh0f1SKCdafbC0xA&hl=en&sa=X&ei=Jj-HVPSBHIr1oATPjYCoBg&ved =0CCAQ6AEwATgK#v=onepage&q=buffalo%20unemployment%20rate%201971& f=false.

2. The term "stagflation" was coined in 1965 by the British chancellor of the exchequer in 1970, Iain Macleod. Online Etymology Dictionary: http://dictionary .reference.com/browse/stagflation. It was brought to the United States by economist Paul Samuelson in a *Newsweek* column, "What's Wrong," March 19, 1973. Edward Nelson and Kalin Nikolov, introduction to Bank of England Working Paper, 2002, 9. http://www.bankofengland.co.uk.publications/workingpapers/wp155.pdf.

3. John Mueller, Kemp Oral History interview, Washington, DC, January 18, 2012, 2.

4. Bruce Bartlett, Miller Center symposium, Panel 1, 16.

5. Arthur Laffer, Kemp Oral History interview, June 13, 2011, Nashville, TN.

6. Bruce Bartlett, "Revolution of 1978," *National Review,* October 27, 1978, 1333.

7. Kemp's very first House floor speech on economics, May 3, 1971 (Congressional Record, 130860), was a call for reinstatement of the investment tax credit to revive the machine tool industry. He argued for it in similar terms: "It should be obvious to all that the better the tools for production which American workers use in their jobs, the more productive they are and, consequently, the higher will be their wages."

8. Robert Livingston, Reagan Revolutionaries symposium, Panel 1, 17.

9. Bill Brock, Miller Center symposium, Panel 1, 20.

10. Al Bemiller, quoted in Ray Didinger, "Kemp Making a Pass at the White House," *Philadelphia Daily News,* June 11, 1986.

11. David S. Broder, "The Right Signals: Kemp's Game in Policy Arena Recalls Style of 'Happy Warrior,'" *Washington Post,* September 2, 1986, A1.

12. Randal Teague, interview with Fred Barnes, February 12, 2015.

13. Allan Ryskind, Reagan Revolutionaries symposium, Panel 1, 19.

14. Brian Domitrovic, *Econoclasts: The Rebels Who Sparked the Supply-Side Revolution and Restored American Prosperity* (Wilmington, DE: ISI Books, 2009), 62 ff. This book is the definitive history of the supply-side movement and an indispensable guide to the authors.

15. Ibid., 159.

16. Ryskind, Reagan Revolutionaries symposium, Panel 1, 29.

17. "It's Time to Cut Taxes," *Wall Street Journal,* December 1, 1978, 46.

18. Bartlett, "Revolution of 1978."

19. Irwin Ross, "Jack Kemp Wants to Cut Your Taxes—a Lot, *Fortune,* April 10, 1978, 38.

20. Rowland Evans and Robert Novak, *The Reagan Revolution: An Inside Look at the Transformation of the U.S. Government* (New York: E. P. Dutton, 1981), 64.

21. Marie Brenner, "Jack the Jock," *Vanity Fair,* January 1986, 102.

22. Arthur Laffer, Kemp Oral History interview, 9.

23. Bartlett, "Revolution of 1978," 31.

24. Martin Tolchin, "Jack Kemp's Bootleg Run to the Right," *Esquire,* October 24, 1978, 68.

25. Domitrovic estimates there were as many as two hundred adherents at the time, *Econoclasts,* 127.

26. Ibid., 125–26.

27. Joanne Kemp, Kemp Oral History interview, December 10, 2012, 58.

28. Congressional Record, December 18, 1975, 41702.

29. Jude Wanniski, "Taxes and a Two-Santa Theory," *National Observer,* March 6, 1976, 14.

30. Ross, "Jack Kemp Wants to Cut Your Taxes—a Lot," 38.

31. Bartlett, *Reaganomics: Supply Side Economics in Action* (Westport, CT: Arlington House Publishers, 1981), 126.

32. Jude Wanniski, "Looking for the Right Broom," *Wall Street Journal,* August 17, 1976, 18.

33. Bartlett, *Reaganomics,* 218–20.

34. Laffer, Kemp Oral History interview, 24.

35. David Smick, interview with Fred Barnes, April 18, 2014.

36. Mueller, Kemp Oral History interview, 23.

37. Paul Craig Roberts, *The Supply-Side Revolution: An Insider's Account of Policymaking in Washington* (Cambridge, MA: Harvard University Press, 1984), 28.

38. Congressional Record, 5049, February 23, 1977.

39. Bartlett, Kemp Oral History interview, June 3, 2011, Great Falls, VA, 4.

40. Roberts, *The Supply-Side Revolution,* 15–16.

41. Ibid., 7.

42. Bartlett, *Reaganomics,* 169.

43. Ibid., 130.

44. Bartlett, Kemp Oral History interview, 6.

45. Ibid., 22.

46. Brock, Kemp Oral History interview, Washington, DC, June 23, 2011, 20, 24.

47. Ibid., 23.

48. Ronald Reagan, "Why Not Cut the Income Tax?" *Washington Post,* October 12, 1976, A19.

49. Congressional Record, March 15, 1978, 7038–47.

50. Domitrovic, *Econoclasts,* 162.

51. Jack Kemp Oral History Archive, Library of Congress, Box 78, folder 4.

52. Bartlett, Miller Center symposium, Panel 1, 34; and Bartlett, "Revolution of 1978," 1335–36.

53. Bartlett, "Revolution of 1978."

54. Ross, "Jack Kemp Wants to Cut Your Taxes—a Lot," 41.

55. Bartlett, "Revolution of 1978."

56. *CQ Almanac,* 1978, 233.

57. Domitrovic, *Econoclasts,* 171.

58. David Gergen, "Wanted: A GOP Program," *Washington Post,* November 19, 1978, C8.

59. Editorial, *Wall Street Journal,* December 4, 1978, 26.

60. William F. Buckley, *Firing Line* transcript, Program S0351, January 2, 1979, 8–9, 30, http://hoohila.stanford.edu/firingline/programView2.php?programID =787.

Chapter 3: Turning Point

1. David A. Stockman, *The Triumph of Politics: How the Reagan Revolution Failed* (New York: Harper & Row, 1986), 47.

2. Martin Tolchin, "Kemp's Bootleg to the Right," *Esquire,* October 1978, 59ff.

3. Jeff Bell, Kemp Oral History interview, Washington, DC, July 15, 2011, 26.

4. Tolchin, "Kemp's Bootleg to the Right," 59ff.

5. Irwin Ross, "Jack Kemp Wants to Cut Your Taxes—a Lot," *Fortune,* April 10, 1978, 37ff.

6. John Sears, interview with Morton Kondracke, February 27, 2014.

7. Robert D. Novak, *The Prince of Darkness: 50 Years of Reporting in Washington* (New York: Crown Forum, 2007), 334, 336.

8. David Smick, Kemp Oral History interview, Vero Beach, FL, January 19, 2012, 24.

9. Bell, Kemp Oral History interview, 27.

10. Novak, *The Prince of Darkness,* 334.

11. Rowland Evans and Robert Novak, *The Reagan Revolution: An Inside Look at the Transformation of the U.S. Government* (New York: E. P. Dutton, 1981), 70.

12. Novak, *The Prince of Darkness,* 336.

13. The italics were Kemp's, 13.

14. Jack Kemp, *An American Renaissance: A Strategy for the 1980s* (New York: Harper & Row, 1979), 197.

15. Domitrovic, *Econoclasts: The Rebels Who Sparked the Supply-Side Revolution and Restored American Prosperity* (Wilmington, DE: ISI Books, 2009), 190–91.

16. On March 18, 1981, Kemp received a letter from Donald E. Johnson, president of the Hoover Presidential Library Association, asking "that you acquaint yourself more intimately with the Hoover record and desist from further defamation of a distinguished Republican statesman and humanitarian." Kemp replied politely, but did not cease disparaging Hoover's economic policy. Jack Kemp Archive, Library of Congress, Box 26, folder 1.

17. "How NOT to Fight Inflation," remarks at the 44th Annual Convention of the International Longshoremen's Association, AFL-CIO, July 16, 1979 Miami, FL, reprinted in Jack Kemp, *The American Idea: Ending Limits to Growth* (Washington, DC: American Studies Center, 1984), 23.

18. John Mueller, Kemp Oral History interview, 12.

19. In Johnson's time the misery index was 6 or 7. In Carter's it rose to 21.9 in June 1980. Domitrovic, *Econoclasts,* 105.

20. Reagan was accused of fabricating the "welfare queen" story and indulging in "racial malarkey," but his target, Diana Taylor, was first exposed by the *Chicago Tribune* and

convicted of theft and perjury in 1977. A *Slate* magazine investigation in 2013 developed strong evidence that she was involved in kidnappings, child trafficking, and murder. Josh Levin, "The Welfare Queen," *Slate*, December 19, 2013, http://www.slate.com/articles/news_and_politics/history/2013/12/linda_taylor_welfare_queen_ronald_reagan _made_her_a_notorious_american_villain.html.

21. Ronald Reagan, *An American Life: The Autobiography* (New York: Threshold, 1990), 231.

22. Evans and Novak, *The Reagan Revolution*, 28.

23. Bell, Kemp Oral History interview, 54.

24. Allan Ryskind, Reagan Revolutionaries symposium, Panel 1, 10.

25. Arthur Laffer, Kemp Oral History interview, Nashville, TN, June 14, 2011, 37.

26. Kemp appointment books at the Library of Congress (Box 5, folder 7) show no Reagan lunch or Laffer dinner, but Kemp's only visit of the year to Los Angeles occurred during the week of August 19–26. Wednesday, August 22, is the lone day for which no speeches or other appointments were scheduled.

27. Cannon, *President Reagan: The Role of a Lifetime* (New York: Simon & Schuster, 1991), 236.

28. Jude Wanniski, *The Way the World Works,* introduction to the second edition, reprinted in the third edition (Morristown, NJ: Polynomics Inc., 1989), 336.

29. Evans and Novak, "Reagan-Kemp Team Possible," Glens Falls, NY, *Post-Star,* October 23, 1979.

30. Cannon, "Reagan Refuses to Debate His GOP Opponents," *Washington Post*, November 15, 1981, A3.

31. Cannon, *Governor Reagan: His Rise to Power* (New York: Public Affairs, 2003), 453.

32. John Sears interview with Morton Kondracke, February 27, 2014.

33. Smick, Kemp Oral History interview, 33.

34. Lew Lehrman, Kemp Oral History interview, Greenwich, CT, December 11, 2011, 25.

35. Edwin Meese III, *With Reagan: The Inside Story* (Washington, DC: Regnery Publishing, 1992), 121–24.

36. Martin Anderson, *Revolution: The Reagan Legacy* (Stanford, CA: Hoover Institution Press, 1990), 161.

37. Wanniski, who got fired by the *Wall Street Journal* for one act of indiscretion—handing out fliers for Jeff Bell's Senate campaign in 1978—also asserted he was the principal father of supply-side economics, offending fellow members of the movement, and referred to himself and those in it as "wild men." He had to apologize for his assertions in a letter to the *Village Voice.* Alexander Cockburn and James Ridgeway, "Worlds in Collision: The Battle for Reagan's Mind," *Village Voice*, April 10, 1980; Letter to the Editor, *Village Voice*, April 28, 1980.

38. Meese, *With Reagan,* 123, 124.

39. http://www.c-span.org/video/?5221-1/president-reagan-jack-kemp-tribute.

40. Stockman, *The Triumph of Politics*, 50.

41. Cannon, *President Reagan*, 67.

42. Ibid.

43. Domitrovic, *Econoclasts*, 206.

44. Evans and Novak, "Reagan, JFK and Taxes," *Washington Post,* April 7, 1980, A25.

45. Smick, Kemp Oral History interview, 42. Sears continues to dismiss Reagan as a "performer" who "rarely made a decision himself." His advisers were "in the position of a movie director" telling him what to do. "Actually, the person you had to convince was not Reagan. It was Mrs. Reagan. Not the substance of it. If it looked good to her, you could do it. And being for tax cuts looked good to her." Sears, despite his long association with Reagan, still isn't sure whether Reagan is "the most complicated guy I ever knew or the simplest." Sears interview with Morton Kondracke, February 27, 2014, Miami, FL.

46. Domitrovic, *Econoclasts,* 206.

47. Congressional Staff symposium, Panel 2, 19.

48. Jack Kemp Archive, Library of Congress, Box 79, folder 12.

49. Congressional Staff symposium, Panel 1, 44.

50. Ibid., 19.

51. "Platform Quarterback," *Washington Post,* July 14, 1980, A19.

52. After Kemp's death, James C. Roberts, once director of Kemp's political action committee, wrote an article, "Don't Forget the 1980 Draft Kemp for Vice President," on *Human Events.com,* http://www.humanevents.com/article.php?print=yes&id, posted May 20, 2009, describing a six-month unauthorized campaign touting Kemp for the number two spot. It attracted support from representatives Trent Lott of Mississippi and Connie Mack of Florida as well as Iowa governor Terry Branstad. Roberts said Kemp pleaded with him to cease the effort because Laxalt thought Kemp was behind it and was furious. Roberts claims credit for sneaking five thousand "Kemp for Vice President" signs onto the convention floor.

53. Smick, Kemp Oral History interview, 27–30.

54. Speech, "A Republican Tidal Wave," July 15, 1980, reprinted in Kemp, *The American Idea,* 3.

55. Meese, Kemp Oral History interview, October 13, 2011, Washington, DC, 6.

56. "How the Ford Deal Collapsed," *Newsweek,* July 28, 1980, 20.

57. Meese, Kemp Oral History interview, 11.

58. Ibid., 9.

59. Evans and Novak, *The Reagan Revolution,* 80.

60. "Republican National Convention Acceptance Speech," http://www.reagan.utexas.edu/archives/reference/7.17.80.html, 5.

61. Stockman, *The Triumph of Politics,* 64.

62. John Brooks, "Annals of Finance," *New Yorker,* April 19, 1982, 108.

63. Evans and Novak, *The Reagan Revolution,* 82.

64. William Niskanen, *Reaganomics: An Insider's Account of the Policies and the People* (New York: Oxford University Press, 1988), 12.

65. Cannon, *Reagan* (New York: G. P. Putnam's Sons, 1982), 297n.

66. The American Presidency Project, Presidential Debates, Presidential Debate in Baltimore (Reagan-Anderson), September 21, 1980, http://www.presidency.ucsb.edu/ws/?pid=29407.

67. Smick, Kemp Oral History interview, 50.

68. Commission on Presidential Debates, the Carter-Reagan Presidential debate, October 28, 1980, http://www.debates.org/index.php?page=october-28-1980-debate-transcript.

Chapter 4: Reagan Revolutionary

1. David Lynch, "'Modesty,' Called Debts Bring Kemp House Post," *Buffalo Courier Express*, December 9, 1980, 1.
2. Vin Weber, Kemp Oral History interview, December 3, 2012, 2.
3. Jean-Baptiste Say (1767–1832) was a French free market economist best known for "Say's Law," holding that increasing the supply of goods creates demand for them, not the reverse. He was a patron saint of supply-siders.
4. Weber, Kemp Oral History interview, 5.
5. Ibid., 12.
6. Dan Lungren, Reagan Revolutionaries symposium, Panel 1, 9.
7. Dan Coats, Kemp Oral History interview, June 14, 2012, 2.
8. Newt Gingrich, Kemp Oral History interview, December 13, 2012, 5.
9. Ibid., 24.
10. Connie Mack, Reagan Revolutionaries symposium, Panel 1, 22.
11. Sharon Zelaska telephone interview, September 19, 2014. The Dow Jones Industrial Average stood at 758 when Reagan was elected in 1980 and stood at 1,287 in 1983. It rose to 2,722 in mid-1987 before dropping to 1,738 later that year. It stood at 2,000 at the end of Reagan's term, rose to 3,000 by the end of George H. W. Bush's, then surged to 10,000 in mid-1998 and 11,500 at the end of 1999, before the tech bubble burst sent it crashing back to 7,286 in 2001; http://stockcharts.com/freecharts/historical/djia19802000.html.
12. Karen Tumulty, "Trent Lott's Segregationist College Days," *Time*, December 12, 2002, http://content.time.com/time/nation/article/0,8599,399310,00.html.
13. Trent Lott, Kemp Oral History interview, June 13 2012, Washington, DC, 6.
14. Ibid., 5.
15. Ibid., 45, 11.
16. Paul Craig Roberts, *The Supply-Side Revolution: An Insider's Account of Policymaking in Washington* (Cambridge, MA: Harvard University Press, 1984), 89–90.
17. Alexander Cockburn and James Ridgeway, "Worlds in Collision: The Battle for Reagan's Mind," *Village Voice*, April 7, 1980.
18. Lehrman did not get the job. Donald Regan, CEO of Merrill Lynch, did. But in addition to Roberts, Kemp ally Norman Ture was named undersecretary for taxation, and Steve Entin, Roberts's deputy.
19. Steven F. Hayward, *The Age of Reagan: The Conservative Counterrevolution, 1980–1989*, vol. 2 (New York: Three Rivers Press, 2009), 58.
20. "Prime Interest Rate History," http://www.fedprimerate.com/wall_street_journal_prime_rate_history.htm.
21. "Economics: Memo to Reagan: 'Avoiding an Economic Dunkirk,'" *New York Times*, December 14, 1980, A19.
22. Brian Domitrovic, *Econoclasts: The Rebels Who Sparked the Supply-Side Revolution and Restored American Prosperity* (Wilmington, DE: ISI Books, 2009), 213.
23. Ibid., 65.
24. Indexing ensures that the value of taxpayers' incomes do not rise from year to year solely due to inflation, thereby protecting them from being taxed at a higher rate because they are judged to have higher real incomes than they do. See Institute on

Taxation and Economic Policy, "Indexing Income Taxes for Inflation: Why It Matters," http://itepnet.org/pdf/pb8infl.pdf.

25. Rowland Evans and Robert Novak, *The Reagan Revolution: An Inside Look at the Transformation of the U.S. Government* (New York: E. P. Dutton, 1981), 112.

26. Ibid., 124.

27. Robert D. Novak, *The Prince of Darkness: Fifty Years of Reporting in Washington* (New York: Crown Forum, 2007), 375.

28. Roberts, *The Supply-Side Revolution*, 112.

29. Ibid., 92.

30. Evans and Novak, *The Reagan Revolution,* 126.

31. Ibid., 124, 126.

32. Meg Greenfield, "Today (Let Us Suppose) Is January 20, 1985—How Will the Winner Have Got There," *Washington Post,* January 20, 1981, A21.

33. Arthur Laffer, Kemp Oral History interview, June 14, 2011, 33.

34. Steven Rattner, *New York Times,* February 17, 1981, 1.

35. Evans and Novak, *The Reagan Revolution* 84.

36. Roberts, *The Supply-Side Revolution,* 104.

37. Hayward, *The Age of Reagan,* 652n.

38. James Baker, Kemp Oral History interview, March 13, 2013, Houston, TX, 26.

39. Evans and Novak, *The Reagan Revolution,* 85.

40. Ibid., 102.

41. Fred Barnes, "Tax Break for Rich Gaining; Democrats Issue Plan," *Baltimore Sun,* April 7, 1981, A1.

42. Roberts, *The Supply-Side Revolution,* 129.

43. David K. Lynch, "Kemp Quote Aids Dems in Battle of Budget," *Buffalo Courier Express,* April 12, 1981, C1.

44. Roberts, *The Supply-Side Revolution,* 120.

45. Ibid., 121.

46. Roland Powell, "Kemp Opposes Compromise on Tax Cuts," *Buffalo News,* April 12, 1981, 1.

47. Roberts, *The Supply-Side Revolution,* 130.

48. "Address on the Program for Economic Recovery," April 28, 1981, millercenter .org/president/speeches/speech-5446.

49. Roberts, *The Supply-Side Revolution,* 130.

50. Hayward, *The Age of Reagan,* 150.

51. Roberts, *The Supply-Side Revolution,* 137.

52. Ibid., 143.

53. Ibid., 144.

54. Ibid., 145.

55. Hayward, *The Age of Reagan,* 152.

56. Ibid., 160.

57. Roberts, *The Supply-Side Revolution,* 162.

58. *CQ Almanac,* 1981, 92.

59. Karen W. Anderson, "Graffitti Cluttering Up the Tax Bill," *New York Times,* July 5, 1981, A1.

60. Steven R. Weisman, "Reagan, in Speech, Asks Tax Cut Help and Attacks Foes," *New York Times*, July 28, 1981, A1.
61. Hayward, *The Age of Reagan*, 165.
62. Congressional Record, June 29, 1981, 18244–5.
63. Ibid., 18260.
64. "Kemp's Lonely Road Makes Victory Sweet," *Buffalo Courier Express*, July 30, 1981, A1.
65. Gingrich, Kemp Oral History interview, 17.
66. *CQ Almanac*, 1981, 93.
67. Hayward, *The Age of Reagan*, 166.
68. Roberts, *The Supply-Side Revolution*, 167.
69. The National Bureau of Economic Research, "US Business Cycle Expansions and Contractions," www.nber.org/cycles.html.
70. Roberts, *The Supply-Side Revolution*, 168.
71. Ibid., 171.
72. Domitrovic, *Econoclasts*, 233.
73. Jack Kemp Archive, Library of Congress, Box 82, folder 13.
74. Roberts, *The Supply-Side Revolution*, 195.
75. Ibid., 191.
76. Ibid., 190–91.
77. Congressional Record, November 10, 1981, S13224ff.
78. William Greider, "The Education of David Stockman," *Atlantic*, December 1981.
79. Stockman now says (Kemp Oral History interview, Greenwich, Connecticut, December 8, 2011, 34) that instead of "Trojan Horse," he should have said that reducing the top rate would be a "silver lining" or "associated benefit" of across-the-board cuts. He said he favored deep budget cuts and tax increases because he was "terrified by the (deficit) numbers" he saw emerging from the 1981 bill's add-ons, plus Reagan's defense proposals and Congress's refusal to cut domestic spending.
80. "Trickle down" is the classic label liberals use to attack GOP economics, sometimes justifiably. Republicans allegedly lard benefits on the rich—"job creators"—believing they will eventually "trickle down" to the masses. Democrats constantly argue for benefiting the middle class or the poor, though the results tend to be temporary for the economy as whole.
81. Novak, *The Prince of Darkness*, 376.
82. John Mueller, Kemp Oral History interview, 44; David Smick, Kemp Oral History interview, 39.
83. Robert D. Hershey Jr., "The Supply-Siders Respond," *New York Times*, November 16, 1981, D1.
84. James Baker, Kemp Oral History interview, 59.
85. Lou Cannon, *President Reagan*, 261.
86. Roberts, *The Supply-Side Revolution*, 210.

Chapter 5: Front Line

1. Congressional Record, May 3, 1983, H2546.
2. Congressional Staff symposium, Panel 2, 98.

3. Jerry Brewer, "Thanks, Dad: Jeff Kemp's Ode to His Famous Father," *Seattle Times*, June 21, 2009, http://www.seattletimes.com/html/brewer/2009364035_brewer21.html.

4. In Old English, "Kemp" did mean "strong, brave warrior" or "athletic champion," http://dictionary.reference.com/browse/kemp.

5. James Kemp, Kemp Oral History interview, November 9, 2010, 11.

6. Jeff Kemp, Kemp Oral History interview, Washington, DC, December 5, 2012, 30.

7. Jennifer Kemp Andrews and Judith Kemp Nolan, Kemp Oral History interview, November 7, 2012, 1.

8. Ibid., 3.

9. Ibid., 39.

10. Ibid., 28.

11. Ibid.

12. Jeff Kemp, Kemp Oral History interview, 37.

13. Ibid., 38.

14. Brewer, "Thanks, Dad."

15. Jennifer Kemp Andrews and Judith Kemp Nolan, Kemp Oral History interview, 46.

16. Ibid., 45.

17. Ibid., 44.

18. Jeff Kemp, Kemp Oral History interview, 10.

19. Dan Coats, Oral History interview, Washington, DC, June 14, 2012, 5.

20. James Kemp, Kemp Oral History interview, 3.

21. Jennifer Kemp Andrews and Judith Kemp Nolan, Kemp Oral History interview, 36.

22. James Kemp, Kemp Oral History interview, 6.

23. Jennifer Kemp Andrews and Judith Kemp Nolan, Kemp Oral History interview, 37.

24. James Kemp, Kemp Oral History interview, 4.

25. Joanne Kemp, Kemp Oral History interview, December 10, 2012, Bethesda, MD, 72.

26. Coats, Kemp Oral History interview, 7.

27. James Kemp, Kemp Oral History interview, 10.

28. Jeff Kemp, Kemp Oral History interview, 23.

29. Ibid., 2.

30. Jennifer Kemp Andrews and Judith Kemp Nolan, Kemp Oral History interview, 15.

31. Jeff Kemp, Kemp Oral History interview, 42.

32. Ibid., 41.

33. Ibid., 42.

34. Jennifer Kemp Andrews and Judith Kemp Nolan, Kemp Oral History interview, 33.

35. "Longest JFK-Gram in History," undated, written to Jeff Kemp, undated but late 1994, copy provided to authors by Jeff Kemp.

36. David Smick, Kemp Oral History interview, Vero Beach, FL, January 19, 2012, 3.

37. Ibid., 38.

38. Ibid.

39. Ibid., 40.

40. Congressional Staff symposium, Panel 1, 5.

41. Sharon Zelaska, Kemp Oral History interview, January 23, 2012, Manassas, VA, 1.

42. Ibid., 9.

43. Jennifer Kemp Andrews and Judith Kemp Nolan, Kemp Oral History interview, 27.

44. Zelaska, Kemp Oral History interview, 21.

45. Ibid., 20.

46. Ibid., 11.

47. Ibid., 12.

48. Zelaska, Kemp Oral History interview, 9. House staffers were paid on the last day of every month, but in the last month of the year, payday was on December 15, so they wouldn't be paid again until January 31.

49. Randall Teague, Congressional Staff symposium, Panel 1, 60.

50. Congressional Staff symposium, Panel 1, 16.

51. Richard Billmire, Congressional Staff symposium, Panel 2, 30.

52. David Hoppe, ibid., 85.

53. Congressional Staff symposium, Panel 1, 78.

54. *Human Events,* September 1, 1979, 742; Jack Kemp Archive, Library of Congress, Box 197, folder 20.

55. John Buckley, Congressional Staff symposium, Panel 2, 40.

56. David Hoppe, Congressional Staff symposium, Panel 2, 83.

57. Ibid., 83.

58. Ibid., 84.

59. Ibid., 101.

60. Billmire, ibid., 31.

61. Zelaska, Kemp Oral History interview, 10.

62. Road symposium, 3.

63. Rick Ahearn, ibid., 37.

64. Ed Brady, ibid., 14.

65. J. T. Taylor, ibid., 24.

66. Zelaska, Kemp Oral History interview, 33.

67. Michael O'Connell, Road symposium, 39.

68. Ahearn, ibid., 40.

69. Ibid., 70.

70. Ibid., 19.

71. Ed Rutkowski, Buffalo Oral History symposium, Panel 2, 22.

72. Marie Shattuck, ibid., 21.

73. E-mail, Russ Gugino, September 6, 2014.

74. Brady, Road symposium, 26.

75. Ahearn, ibid., 9.

76. Bill Dal Col, ibid., 45.

77. Taylor, ibid., 44.

78. Ibid., 45.

79. John Mueller, Congressional Staff symposium, Panel 1, 30.

80. Ahearn, Road symposium, 74.

81. Van Cleave, Congressional Staff symposium, Panel 2, 103.

82. Teague, ibid., Panel 1, 45.

Chapter 6: Courage

1. John Buckley, Congressional Staff symposium, Panel 2, 14, confirmed by Trent Lott, interview with Morton Kondracke, Washington, DC, June 10, 2012.

2. Mary Cannon, ibid., 15.

3. Office of Management and Budget, Budget of the United States Government, Fiscal Year 1990, 4-4, listed in Bruce Bartlett, *The New American Economy: The Failure of Reaganomics and a New Way Forward* (New York: Macmillan, 2009), 153. The list of "Legislated Tax Changes by Ronald Reagan as of 1998" listed four tax cuts totaling $275 billion, including ERTA of 1981, $264.4 billion; Interest and Dividends Compliance Act of 1983, $1.8 billion; Federal Employees' Retirement System Act of 1986, $0.2 billion; and the Tax Reform Act of 1986, $8.9 billion. Tax increases totaled $132.7 billion, including TEFRA of 1982, $57.3 billion; Highway Revenue Act of 1982, $4.9 billion; Social Security Amendments of 1983, $24.6 billion; Railroad Retirement Revenue Act of 1983, $1.2 billion; Deficit Reduction Act of 1984, $25.4 billion; Consolidated Omnibus Budget Reconciliation Act of 1985, $2.9 billion; Omnibus Budget Reconciliation Act of 1985, $2.4 billion; Superfund Amendments and Reauthorization Act of 1986, $0.6 billion; Continuing Resolution for 1987, $2.8 billion; Omnibus Budget Reconciliation Act of 1987, $8.6 billion; Continuing Resolution for 1988, $2.0 billion. Reagan defenders point out that, regardless of the tax increases he agreed to, Reagan reduced the top individual income tax rate during his presidency from 70 percent to 28 percent.

4. Ronald Reagan, *The Reagan Diaries*, December 22, 1981, Douglas Brinkley, ed. (New York: HarperPerennial, 2007), 57.

5. At the December 1, 1988, dinner marking Kemp's retirement from Congress, Baker praised Kemp as "the idea man behind the Reagan revolution" and said "a lot of us have eaten our share of crow because what some of us thought best termed as 'voodoo economics' turned out to be can-do economics"; http://www.c-span.org/video/?5221-1/president-reagan-jack-kemp-tribute.

6. James A. Baker III with Steve Fiffer, *"Work Hard, Study . . . and Keep Out of Politics!": Adventures and Lessons from an Unexpected Public Life* (New York: G. P. Putnam Sons, 2007), 187.

7. James Baker, Kemp Oral History interview, March 13, 2013, Houston, TX, 33, 8, 59, 47.

8. Steven R. Weisman, "On Taxes, the President's Men Versus the President," *New York Times*, January 10, 1982, E3.

9. Lee Lescaze and John M. Berry, "President 'Facing Reality' on Tax Increases," *Washington Post*, January 12, 1982, A2.

10. Jack Kemp Archive, Library of Congress, Box 82, folder 14.

11. Reagan, *Diaries*, 64.

12. "Aides Say Reagan Will Ask Congress for Excise Tax Rise," *New York Times*, January 21, 1982, 1.

13. Ronald Reagan, *The Reagan Diaries*, January 21, 1982, Douglas Brinkley, ed. (New York: HarperPerennial, 2007), 64.

14. William J. Eaton and Robert Shogan, "Dilemma on Taxes Confronts President," *Los Angeles Times*, January 23, 1982, 1.

15. Reagan, *Reagan Diaries*, January 22, 1982, 64–65.

16. The American Presidency Project, State of the Union address, January 26, 1982, http://www.presidency.ucsb.edu/ws/index.php?pid=42687ly.

17. Paul Craig Roberts, *The Supply-Side Revolution: An Insider's Account of Policymaking in Washington* (Cambridge, MA: Harvard University Press, 1984), 216.

18. Rowland Evans and Robert Novak, "Making Peace with Paul Volcker," *Washington Post*, February 22, 1982, A11.

19. Roberts, *The Supply-Side Revolution*, 224–25.

20. "Tax Plan Seeks to Lift Revenue and Trim Deficit," *Wall Street Journal*, February 8, 1992, 3.

21. Roberts, *The Supply-Side Revolution*, 229.

22. Steven F. Hayward, *The Age of Reagan: The Conservative Counterrevolution 1980–1989*, vol. 2 (New York: Three Rivers Press, 2009), 209–10.

23. Roberts, *The Supply-Side Revolution*, 234.

24. Philip Lentz, "Kemp Defends Reaganomics," *Chicago Tribune*, March 6, 1982, 3.

25. Evans and Novak, "Aides Increase Reagan's Isolation," *Washington Post*, April 9, 1982, A19.

26. Baker, *Work Hard, Study,* 187.

27. The actual deficits came in at $207.8 billion for 1983, $185.4 billion for 1984, and $221.3 billion for 1985; http://www.whitehouse.gov/omb/budget/Historicals, Table 1.3.

28. David S. Broder, "Kennedy and Kemp vs. the Fed," *Washington Post,* June 16, 1982, C7.

29. Roberts, *The Supply-Side Revolution*, 237.

30. Thomas B. Edsall, "House Votes to Accept Senate's $98.5 Billion Tax Bill," *Washington Post*, July 29, 1982, A14.

31. Evans and Novak, "Revolt Against Tax Bill," *Washington Post*, August 4, 1982, A19.

32. Reagan, *Diaries*, August 4, 1982, 96; Reagan, *An American Life*, 321.

33. David Hoffman and Thomas B. Edsall, "Reaganauts Scramble on Tax Rise," *Washington Post*, August 5, 1982, A1.

34. "Reagan Reportedly Takes Kemp to Woodshed," *Los Angeles Times*, August 5, 1982, A2.

35. George Skelton and Robert A. Rosenblatt, "President Fights Growing GOP Revolt on Tax Hike," *Los Angeles Times,* August 6, 1982, B1.

36. Rich Jaroslovsky, "Reagan Seeks to Reassure Conservatives Upset by His Support for Tax Increase," *Wall Street Journal,* August 6, 1982, 6.

37. Robert Dole, "Taxes: The Republican Identity Crisis," *Washington Post*, August 9 1982, C8.

38. Howell Raines, "Reagan Recruits Dissident Adviser to Aid on Tax Bill," *New York Times*, August 10, 1982, A1.

39. Hoffman, "Nofziger Changes Mind, Backs Reagan's Tax Boost Package," *Washington Post*, August 10, 1982, A1.

40. Hoffman, "Reagan Presses for Tax Bill," *Hartford Courant*, August 11, 1982, A1.

41. Jack Kemp, "What This Fight Is All About," *Washington Post*, August 12, 1982, A23.

42. Raines, "For Kemp, Tax Policy and Politics Seem to Merge," August 13, 1982, A12.

43. Evans and Novak, "White House vs. Jack Kemp," *Washington Post*, August 13, 1982, A19.

44. Edwin Meese III, Kemp Oral History interview, Washington, DC, October 13, 2011, 17.

45. James Baker, Kemp Oral History interview, 34.

46. The American Presidency Project, Ronald Reagan, Interview with Jeremiah O'Leary of the *Washington Times*, August 13, 1982, http://www.presidency.ucsb .edu/ws/index.php?pid=42859.

47. There was widespread speculation that Reagan, then seventy-one, might not seek a second term.

48. Hoffman, "White House Admits Supply-Side Slump," *Washington Post,* August 16, 1982, A1.

49. "Address to the Nation on Federal Tax and Budget Reconciliation Legislation," August 16, 1982, http://www.reagan.utexas.edu/archives/speeches/1982 /82aug.htm.

50. Albert Hunt, "Tax Fight Enhanced Kemp's Standing Even Though He Lost and Made Enemies," *Wall Street Journal,* August 20, 23.

51. Ibid.

52. Broder, "What the Voters Said: Sway the Course," *Washington Post,* November 7, 1982, B3.

53. "The Needed Correction," *Wall Street Journal*, November 4, 1982, 30.

54. Vin Weber, Reagan Revolutionaries symposium, Panel 1, 34.

55. Ibid., 37.

56. Ibid., 14.

57. Ibid., 12.

58. Bob Walker, Reagan Revolutionaries symposium, Panel 1, 12.

59. Weber, ibid., 37.

60. Gingrich, Kemp Oral History interview, December 13, 2012, Arlington, VA, 27.

61. John LaFalce, Buffalo Oral History symposium, Panel 3, 12.

62. Chris Matthews telephone interview with Morton Kondracke, September 24, 2014.

63. Norman Ornstein telephone interview with Morton Kondracke, March 23, 2014.

64. Broder, "The Right Signals," *Washington Post,* September 2, 1986, A1.

65. Roberts, *The Supply-Side Revolution,* 304.

66. David A. Stockman, *The Triumph of Politics: How the Reagan Revolution Failed* (New York: Harper & Row, 1986), 356.

67. Ibid., 364.

68. Fiscal Year 2012 Historical Tables, Budget of the United States Government (Washington, DC: U.S. Government Printing Office), Table 21, 139; https://www .gpo.gov/fdsys/pkg/BUDGET-2012-TAB/content-detail.html.

69. Brian Domitrovic, *Econoclasts: The Rebels Who Sparked the Supply-Side Revolution and Restored American Prosperity* (Wilmington, DE: ISI Books, 2009), 263.

70. Evans and Novak, "The Republican Letters," *Washington Post,* July 4, 1093, A15.

71. Jack Kemp, "A Floating Dollar Costs Us Jobs," *Washington Post,* May 15, 1983, B5.

72. Evans and Novak, "The Gloom Brothers," *Washington Post,* March 18, 1983, A19.

73. "Kemp Opposes Nomination of Volcker if Fed Moves to Tighten Money Supply," *Los Angeles Times,* July 14, 1983, B4.

74. William Greider, *Secrets of the Temple: How the Federal Reserve Runs the Country* (New York: Simon & Schuster, 1988), 608.

75. Jack Kemp, "Six Questions for Chairman Volcker," *Wall Street Journal,* February 7, 1984, 31.

76. Paul Blustein, "Reagan Says Money Supply Is Increasing at Pace Consistent with 'Sound Recovery,'" *Wall Street Journal*, February 23, 1984, 4.

77. Bureau of Labor Statistics, "Labor Force Statistics from the Current Population Survey, 1984," http://data.bls.gov/pdq/SurveyOutputServlet.

78. Dan Rostenkowski interview with Morton Kondracke, July 19, 1984.

79. David S. Broder and Lou Cannon, "Both Wings of GOP Hope to Spice Up a Bland Party Platform," *Washington Post*, July 25, 1984, A3.

80. "Dole Opposes No-Tax-Rise Plank," *Washington Post*, July 27, 1984, A6.

81. Cannon and Broder, "Reagan Says Tax Boost Is 'Last Resort,'" *Washington Post*, August 13, 1984, A1.

82. Dave Hoppe, Kemp Oral History interview, 13.

83. Bill Peterson, "Platform Bears Kemp's Mark," *Washington Post*, August 19, 1984, A10.

84. Fred Barnes, "Right Wing Prevails in GOP Platform," *Baltimore Sun*, August 17, 1984, 1A.

85. Speech, "This American Revolution," August 21, 1984, Dallas, TX, reprinted in Jack Kemp, *The American Idea: Ending Limits to Growth*, (Washington, DC: American Studies Center, Goodrich Printers, 1985), 6.

86. David Stockman, *The Triumph of Politics*, 39.

87. Elizabeth Kolbert, "Dole, in Choosing Kemp, Buried a Bitter Past Rooted in Doctrine," *New York Times*, September 29, 1996, 1.

88. http://www.jimmycarterlibrary.gov/documents/speeches/acceptance_speech.pdf.

Chapter 7: Tax Reformer

1. Robert Hall and Alvin Rabushka, "A Proposal to Simplify Our Tax System," *Wall Street Journal*, December 10, 1981, 30.

2. David A. Stockman, *The Triumph of Politics: How the Reagan Revolution Failed* (New York: Harper & Row, 1986), 361.

3. John Mueller, Miller Center symposium, Panel 2, 6; Alan Murray and Jeffrey Birnbaum, *Showdown at Gucci Gulch* (New York: Random House, 1988), 39.

4. Murray and Birnbaum, *Showdown at Gucci*, 23–24.

5. Ibid., 26.

6. Ibid., Appendix A.

7. Ibid., 34.

8. Ibid., 38.

9. Mueller, Miller Center symposium, Panel 2, 3.

10. Congressional Record, April 26, 1984, 10227.

11. Paul Blustein, "Bill Imposing Flat 25% Tax Rate, Cutting Many Deductions, Is Proposed in Congress," *Wall Street Journal*, April 27, 1984.

12. Blustein, "The Outlook: Tax Reform in '85? Don't Bet on It," *Wall Street Journal*, April 30, 1984, 1.

13. "Bradley-Kemp-Reagan?," *Wall Street Journal*, March 5, 1984, 30.

14. Murray and Birnbaum, *Showdown at Gucci*, 38.

15. Ibid., 39.

16. Ibid., 41.

17. "A Dialogue: Kemp and Bradley on Tax Reform," *New York Times*, September 30, 1984, A5.

18. Jeffrey Birnbaum, "Bradley, Kemp Aren't Yet a Team," *Wall Street Journal*, December 21, 1984, 44.

19. Bill Bradley, Kemp Oral History interview, March 11, 2011, New York, 13.

20. Ibid., 18.

21. Murray and Birnbaum, *Showdown at Gucci*, 72.

22. Ibid., 63.

23. James A. Baker III, *"Work Hard, Study . . . and Keep Out of Politics!": Adventures and Lessons from an Unexpected Public Life* (New York: G. P. Putnam Sons, 2006), 219.

24. Murray and Birnbaum, *Showdown at Gucci*, 64.

25. Ibid., 72; Fred Barnes, "Cynics Could Be in for Shock as Tax Reform Pressure Builds," *Baltimore Sun*, December 30, 1984, 1.

26. Murray and Birnbaum, *Showdown at Gucci*, 66.

27. Paul Blustein and Jeffrey Birnbaum, "Reagan Seen Backing a Plan to Revise Taxes When It Gets Bipartisan Support," *Wall Street Journal*, January 30, 1985, 1; Ernest B. Ferguson, "Merger of All Tax-Reform Bills Likely, Kemp Says," *Baltimore Sun*, January 30, 1985, 10A.

28. Jonathan Fuerbringer, "1985 Tax Overhaul Unlikely, Says Dole," *New York Times*, January 25, 1985, D16.

29. Murray and Birnbaum, *Showdown at Gucci*, 77.

30. David E. Rosenbaum, "A Decidedly Different Tax Debate," *New York Times*, March 24, 1985, F1.

31. Jane Seaberry and Anne Swardson, "Tax Plan More Enticing To Business, Baker Says," *Washington Post*, May 24, 1985, A7.

32. Blustein and Birnbaum, "Reagan's Tax-Overhaul Plan Will Keep Top Capital-Gains Rate Close to 20%," *Wall Street Journal*, May 8, 1985, 3.

33. David Shribman, "Bipartisan Hill Support Enhances Tax Proposal's Chances This Year," *Wall Street Journal*, May 30, 1985, 3.

34. Robert Timberg, "GOP Strategists Pin Great Hopes to Reagan's Tax Reform Plan," *Baltimore Sun*, May 26, 1985, 18A.

35. Rowland Evans and Robert Novak, "Kemp Comes Home," *Washington Post*, June 17, 1985, A11.

36. "37 in House Assail Rostenkowski Plan," *Los Angeles Times*, September 29, 1985, 6.

37. Mueller, Miller Center symposium, Panel 2, 26.

38. Ibid., 4.

39. Ibid., 24.

40. Ibid., 28.

41. Anne Swardson, "Ways and Means Approves Higher Standard Deduction," *Washington Post*, October 9, 1985, 1.

42. Mueller, Miller Center symposium, Panel 2, 32.

43. Murray and Birnbaum, *Showdown at Gucci*, 157.

44. Ibid., 159.

45. Ibid., 160.

46. Ibid., 161.

47. Congressional Record, December 11, 1985, 35951.

48. Murray and Birnbaum, *Showdown at Gucci*, 165.

49. Ronald Reagan, *An American Life: The Autobiography* (New York: Threshold, 1990), 376.
50. Murray and Birnbaum, *Showdown at Gucci*, 166.
51. Text supplied by John Mueller from personal files.
52. Murray and Birnbaum, *Showdown at Gucci*, 170.
53. Ibid., 170–71.
54. Text supplied by John Mueller from personal files.
55. David Hoppe, Miller Center symposium, Panel 2, 35.
56. Evans and Novak, "After the Fiasco," *Washington Post*, December 16, 1985, A15.
57. Evans and Novak, "Kemp's Transition," *Washington Post*, December 20, 1985, A23.
58. Edward Walsh, "GOP Points Fingers on Tax-Bill Blunders," *Washington Post*, December 19, 1985, A6.
59. Evans and Novak, "Kemp's Transition," A23.
60. Murray and Birnbaum, *Showdown at Gucci*, 203.
61. Ibid., 207.
62. Ibid., 210.
63. Michael Wines, "Massive Tax Reform Bill Passed by House," *Los Angeles Times*, September 26, 1986, 12.
64. Bradley, Kemp Oral History interview, 26.
65. http://www.taxfoundation.org/article/brief-history-tax-expenditures.
66. Gerald M. Boyd, "Claiming the Credit in 1988," *New York Times*, October 23, 1986, D18.

Chapter 8: Freedom Fighter

1. Douglas Turner, "Kemp Gets Soviet Line on Rights," *Buffalo News*, July 18, 1983.
2. Mary Cannon telephone interview with Morton Kondracke, April 30, 2014.
3. Speech, "The Roots of American Foreign Policy," delivered before the Council on Foreign Relations, New York, March 29, 1983, reprinted in Jack Kemp, *The American Idea: Ending Limits to Growth* (Washington, DC: American Studies Center, 1984), 170.
4. Ronald Reagan, *The Reagan Diaries,* Douglas Brinkley, ed. (New York: Harper Perennial, 2007), Wednesday, July 27, 1983, 170.
5. Ibid., Thursday, July 28, 1983, 170.
6. Ibid., Tuesday, August 1, 171.
7. Eric Gelman, "Reagan Holds Kemp in Contempt," *Newsweek*, August 15, 1983, 15.
8. Richard Billmire, Kemp Oral History interview, February 7, 2012, 37; Hobart Rowen, "Kemp Now Backs Funds for Global Aid Banks," *Washington Post*, May 21, 1985, E3; David R. Francis," "US Stepping Up Push for Free Enterprise via Third-World Aid," *Christian Science Monitor*, May 30, 1985. Joe Rogers, who left as Kemp's foreign operations subcommittee staff assistant in 1984 to become ambassador to the Asian Development Bank, said (Kemp Oral History interview, April 10, 2012, 21) that the Baker Plan reforms were "very short-lived" and that the banks swiftly returned to their previous policies.
9. David Obey, Kemp Oral History interview, December 13, 2011, 2.
10. Billmire, Kemp Oral History interview, 42.
11. Fenyvesi, Charles, "After Moscow, 'Yes, Yes, Yes,'" *Washington Post*, December 13, 1982, C1; Jack Kemp, "Lozansky Family Overcomes Soviet Monolith," *Evans Journal*

(Angola, New York), December 30, 1982, 3; "Under This Chupah: It's Best Man Dole and Witness Kemp," *Forward*, September 6, 1996, 1.

12. Billmire, Kemp Oral History interview, 53.

13. Kemp attended Fairfax High School in Los Angeles, where the student body was 95 percent Jewish, and dated the daughter of one of Los Angeles's leading rabbis.

14. Congressional Record, October 14, 1981, H23828.

15. Rudy Abramson, "Reagan Plans Quick Report to Congress," *Boston Globe*, June 10, 1981, 1.

16. Ronald Reagan, *An American Life: The Autobiography* (New York: Threshold, 1990), 410.

17. Ibid., 416.

18. Reagan described Sharon as "a bellicose man who seemed to be champing at the bit to start a war," ibid., 491.

19. Ibid., 422.

20. Ibid., 425.

21. Ibid., 423.

22. Steven F. Hayward, *The Age of Reagan: The Conservative Counterrevolution*, 1980–1989, vol. 2 (New York: Three Rivers Press, 2009), 314.

23. Wolf Blitzer, "A Supporter in Congress," *Jerusalem Post*, October 15, 1982, 1.

24. Reagan, *An American Life*, 437.

25. Blitzer, "A Supporter in Congress," *Jerusalem Post*, October 15, 1982, 4.

26. Ibid.

27. Address before The American Israel Public Affairs Committee, March 20, 1983, Jack Kemp Archive, Library of Congress, Box 131, folder 9.

28. Reagan, *An American Life*, 434.

29. Blitzer, "A Supporter in Congress," *Jerusalem Post*, October 15, 1982, 4.

30. Jack Kemp Archive, Library of Congress, Box 371, folder 9.

31. Benjamin Netanyahu, Kemp Oral History interview, March 26, 2014.

32. Ibid., 10.

33. Ibid., 9.

34. Robert S. Greenberg, "Bill Requiring Closure of PLO's Washington, UN Office May Be Propaganda Blow to US," *Wall Street Journal*, December 24, 1987, 28.

35. Interview with Marci Robinson, May 22, 2013; Robert Pear, "US Will Allow PLO to Maintain Its Office at UN," *New York Times*, August 30, 1988, A1.

36. "Reagan Doctrine" was coined by Charles Krauthammer in a *Time* essay, April 1, 1985. It was counter to the "Brezhnev Doctrine" laid down by Soviet leader Leonid Brezhnev on November 13, 1968, who justified the August 1968 Soviet invasion of Czechoslovakia by saying "forces hostile to socialism" had tried to turn the country toward capitalism.

37. "US Halts Economic Aid to Nicaragua," *New York Times*, April 2, 1981.

38. Hayward, *The Age of Reagan*, 301.

39. Eleanor Randolph, "Conservative Kemp Denounces El Salvador Right Wing Squads," *Hartford Courant*, October 29, 1983, A6. Kemp did so on a trip to the region with a bipartisan commission he'd helped to create to study Central America policy, headed by former secretary of state Henry Kissinger.

40. Hayward, *The Age of Reagan*, 319.

41. Jack Kemp, "Nicaragua's Stolen Democratic Revolution Must Be Restored," *Washington Times*, April 22, 1985.

42. Congressional Record, March 19, 1986, 5538.

43. Kemp letter to Reagan, May 22, 1986, Jack Kemp Archive, Library of Congress, Box 127, folder 3.

44. Hayward, *The Age of Reagan*, 552.

45. Ibid., 555; http://articles.latimes.com/1987-11-13/news/mn-13755_1_house-speaker-jim-wright.

46. Reagan, *Diaries*, August 6, 1987, 523.

47. From 67 percent to 46 percent in November 1986, according to a New York Times/CBS News poll. Jane Mayer and Doyle McManus, *Landslide: The Unmaking of the President, 1984–1988* (New York: Houghton Mifflin, 1988), 292. Reagan recovered and by the close of his presidency was approved by 64 percent of the public, according to the Gallup poll. Dalia Sussman, "Improving with Age: Reagan's Approval Grows Better in Retrospect," ABC News, August 6, 2001.

48. Michelle Van Cleave, Kemp Oral History interview, Washington, DC, February 3, 2012, 22, 38.

49. Hayward, *The Age of Reagan*, 516.

50. "Members of Congress Vow to Wash It All Out," *Los Angeles Times*, November 25, 1986.

51. Thomas Palmer, "Kemp Backs Reagan's Reluctance to Disclose Arms Sales," *Boston Globe*, July 27, 1987, 4.

52. "Kemp Backpedals on Subject of Pardoning North, Poindexter," *Washington Post*, December 4, 1987, 3.

53. Kemp, "Trust the President's Foreign Policy," *New York Times*, December 23, 1986, A21.

54. On October 25, 1983, Reagan sent 7,600 U.S. troops to the Caribbean nation after a military coup ousted its leftist government. The United States asserted that U.S. medical students were endangered. The invasion occurred two days after the Beirut bombing killed 241 U.S. Marines.

55. Reagan, *An American Life*, 294.

56. Fiscal Year 2012 Historical Tables, Budget of the United States Government (Washington, DC: U.S. Government Printing Office), Table 3.1, 51.

57. Congressional Record, April 13, 1983, 8419.

58. Hayward, *The Age of Reagan*, 305.

59. Eleanor Randolph and Karen Tumulty, "Senate Rejects Demand for Immediate Nuclear Freeze," *Los Angeles Times*, November 1, 1983, 1.

60. David Shribman, "House Votes to Buy More Pershing 2 Missiles," *New York Times*, October 27, 1983, A10.

61. Harold Jackson, "President Prepared to Stop Start Talks in MX Budget Storm," *Guardian*, January 8, 1983, 4.

62. James McCartney, "Reagan Gets MX Victory in the House," *Philadelphia Inquirer*, May 25, 1983, A1.

63. David S. Broder, "Gephardt, Kemp Hit Hard, but Keep Smiling in Bout Over SDI and Contra Aid," *Washington Post*, August 28, 1987, A6.

64. Lou Cannon, *President Reagan: The Role of a Lifetime* (New York: Simon & Schuster, 1991), 666.

65. Hayward, *The Age of Reagan,* 294–95.

66. Reagan, *An American Life,* 666.

67. Letter to Reagan, July 28, 1986, Jack Kemp Archive, Library of Congress, Box 122, folder 5.

68. Reagan, *An American Life,* 608.

69. Ibid., 676. President George W. Bush formally withdrew from the ABM treaty in 2002.

70. Reagan, *An American Life,* 268.

71. Ibid., 660.

72. Ibid., 677.

73. "Remarks Prepared for Delivery by Congressman Jack Kemp, Concord, New Hampshire, December 4, 1987," reprinted in Jack Kemp, *Advancing the American Idea into the '90s* (Washington, DC: Campaign for a New Majority State 1988), 61.

74. Speech to the Heritage Foundation, May 22, 1987, Jack Kemp Archive, Library of Congress, Box 365, folder 2.

75. Former Kemp aide William Schneider, undersecretary of state for science under Shultz and a nuclear expert, still claims that INF was a "bad deal" because it permitted the Soviets—and, now, Russia—to alter their ICBM range to pose as great a threat to Europe as the dismantled SS20s. William Schneider telephone interview, May 28, 2014. The Obama administration has charged Russia with violating the treaty, http://www.politico.com/story/2015/02/ash-carter-russia-vladimir-putin-defense-115421.html.

76. Douglas Turner, "He'd Clean House at State Dept. by Ousting Shultz, Kemp Says," *Buffalo News,* January 13, 1986, Jack Kemp Archive, Library of Congress, Box 178, folder 8.

77. Hayward, *The Age of Reagan,* 432; Cannon, *President Reagan: The Role of a Lifetime,* 321.

78. Hayward, *The Age of Reagan,* 321.

79. Bernard Gwertzman, "Aid to Angola Rebels Is Debated in Administration and Congress," *New York Times,* October 29, 1985, A4.

80. Reagan, *Diaries,* November 8, 1985, 367.

81. George Shultz, *Turmoil and Triumph: My Years as Secretary of State* (New York: Charles Scribner's Sons, 1993), 1118.

82. Fred Barnes, "Angola Options," *New Republic,* December 23, 1985, 7.

83. Cannon, *President Reagan: The Role of a Lifetime,* 321.

84. Reagan letter, November 8, 1988, Jack Kemp Archive, Library of Congress, Box 385, folder 11.

85. CIA Library, The World Factbook, Angola, https://www.cia.gov/library/publications/the-world-factbook/geos/ao.html.

86. Lou Cannon, *President Reagan: The Role of a Lifetime,* 324.

87. Ibid., 323.

88. Ibid., 332.

89. Sidney Blumenthal, "South African Sanctions Issue Divides U.S. Conservatives," *Washington Post,* August 22, 1985, A1.

90. Letter to Mrs. Libba Barnes, October 1, 1985, Jack Kemp Archive, Library of Congress, Box 119, folder 7.

91. David Hoppe telephone interview, May 7, 2014.

92. Congressional Record, September 12, 1986, 23152.

93. Letter to Mrs. Libba Barnes, October 1, 1985.

94. Broder, "Conservatives Cheer Kemp's Call for Shultz to Quit," *Washington Post,* February 21, 1987, A4.

95. CPAC speech text, Jack Kemp Archive, Box 364, folder 18.

96. *Buffalo Evening News,* January 12, 1986.

97. David Hoppe, telephone interview, May 7, 2014.

98. John Buckley, Oral History interview, April 24, 2012, 38.

99. The American Presidency Project, Ronald Reagan, News Conference, January 29, 1981, http://www.presidency.ucsb.edu/ws/?pid=44101.

100. Robert M. Gates, *From the Shadows* (New York: Simon & Schuster, 2011), 197.

101. "Address at Commencement Exercises at the University of Notre Dame," May 17, 1981, http://www.reagan.utexas.edu/archives/speeches/1981/51781a.htm.

102. Van Cleave, Kemp Oral History interview, 33.

103. Reagan, *An American Life,* 548.

104. Ibid., 273.

105. George Shultz interview with Morton Kondracke, February 6, 2013, Stanford, CA.

106. Reagan, *An American Life,* 641.

107. "Shultz Has the Last Laugh," *San Francisco Chronicle,* March 11, 1988, A20.

Chapter 9: Also Ran

1. Vin Weber, Kemp Oral History interview, 42.

2. David Hoffman and Paul Taylor, "Republicans Clash Over Trade Policy," *Washington Post,* February 29, 1988, A10.

3. Ronald Reagan, *An American Life: The Autobiography* (New York: Threshold, 1990), 719. As Reagan recounted its history, the "Eleventh Commandment" was first enunciated by California state GOP chairman Gaylord Parkinson in 1966 after Reagan was attacked by a gubernatorial primary rival: "Thou Shalt Not Speak Ill of Any Fellow Republican," *American Life,* 150. Technically, he could have endorsed Bush without violating the commandment by not criticizing Bush's rivals.

4. Steven V. Roberts, "Is the President in Favor of a Bush Nomination?" *New York Times,* December 1, 1987, B24.

5. Dale Russakoff, "Bush: The Loyal Subordinate," *Washington Post,* January 21, 1985, G4.

6. Jack Germond and Jules Witcover, "Bush Gets the Blessing and Curse of Being Vice President," *Baltimore Sun,* February 16, 1986, 21.

7. Edwin Meese III, *With Reagan: The Inside Story* (Washington, DC: Regnery Publishing, 1992), 44.

8. Fred Barnes, "Jack and George," *New Republic,* April 28, 1982, 20.

9. Peter Goldman and Tom Mathews, *The Quest for the Presidency: The 1988 Campaign* (New York: Touchstone, 1989), 188.

10. John Dillin, "Speculation About '88 Upstages '84," *Christian Science Monitor,* August 21, 1984, 22.

11. Goldman and Mathews, *"The Quest for the Presidency,"* 210.

12. Elizabeth Kolbert, "Dole, in Choosing Kemp, Buried a Bitter Past Rooted in Doctrine," *New York Times,* September 29, 1996, 1.

13. Barry Sussman, "Bush Leads Likely '88 GOP Candidates in Public Favor, Poll Finds," *Washington Post,* August 12, 1985, A4.

14. Maureen Dowd, "Kemp to Seek Presidential Nomination," *New York Times,* April 7, 1987, A1.

15. David S. Broder, "Buzzwords from Kemp," *Washington Post,* April 12, 1987, D7.

16. Jude Wanniski letter to Kemp, December 14, 1987, Wanniski Archive, Hoover Institution, Stanford University, Box 4, folder 6.

17. Weber, Kemp Oral History interview, 43.

18. Henry Clay in 1824, James A. Garfield in 1880.

19. Charles Black, Symposium, "Jack Kemp and the 1988 Republican Presidential Primary," Panel 1, 8.

20. John Buckley, Kemp Oral History interview, 12.

21. Black, 1988, Campaign symposium, Panel 1, 16.

22. Clark Durant, 1988 Campaign symposium, Panel 3, 12.

23. James Baker, Kemp Oral History interview, 35.

24. Robert Shogan, "Robertson Holds Limelight in Michigan," *Los Angeles Times,* June 23, 1986, A4.

25. Rowland Evans and Robert Novak, "Kemp's Quagmire," *Washington Post,* July 23, 1986, A21; Phil Gailey, "Aide Stresses Reagan's Neutrality in GOP Race," *New York Times,* July 22, 1986, A18.

26. David Shribman, "Michigan Results Expose Weakness of Robertson and Other Republican Presidential Contenders," *Wall Street Journal,* August 7, 1986.

27. Buckley, Congressional Staff symposium, Panel 2, 57.

28. Ibid., 59.

29. Scott Reed, Kemp Oral History interview, Washington, DC, November 26, 2012, 5.

30. Mary Cannon, Congressional Staff symposium, Panel 2, 61.

31. Frank Gifford, "Kemp Defends Campaign After Bias Incident," *Los Angeles Times,* December 9, 1987, 5.

32. Weber, Kemp Oral History interview, 44.

33. Laurence I. Barnett, "Tacking Further to the Right," *Time,* March 2, 1987.

34. E. J. Dionne, "Bush Draws Fire in First Debate," *New York Times,* October 29, 1987, A25.

35. Paul West, "Poll, Observers Report Bush Won TV Debate by Maintaining Status Quo," *Baltimore Sun,* October 30, 1987, 14A.

36. Steve Neal, "Secret Chicago Talks Launch Kemp Race," *Chicago Tribune,* August 28, 1986, 1.

37. James Dickenson, "Buchanan Says He Won't Run for President," *Washington Post,* January 21, 1987, A4.

38. Barnes, "Jack and George," *New Republic,* April 28, 1982, 20; Fred Barnes, "Kemp's Seeming Drift," *Baltimore Sun,* March 3, 1986; Barnes, "Kemp and the Cons," *New Republic,* December 28, 1987, 10.

39. Buckley, Kemp Oral History interview, 56.

40. Robin Toner, "Bush Backers Rally at Capitol in Attempt to Show Strength," *New York Times,* July 1, 1987, B8.

41. Buckley, Kemp Oral History interview, 22.

42. John Balzar, "Bush Tears Up Kemp Flyer Criticizing Him on Abortion," *Los Angeles Times,* January 19, 1988, C16.

43. Cathleen Decker, "An Exultant Kemp Draws Blood in NH," *Los Angeles Times,* 17.

44. Broder, "Kemp Announces GOP Presidential Bid," *Washington Post,* April 7, 1987, A1.

45. Clifford D. May, "Gallup Poll Sees Rise in Support for Kemp in New Hampshire," *New York Times,* January 13, 1988, D26.

46. George Skelton, "The Times Poll: Bush, Dukakis Take Big Leads in NH Races," *Los Angeles Times,* January 24, 1988, 1.

47. "Dole and Gephardt Lead Poll," *New York Times,* February 7, 1988, 30.

48. Paul Young, 1988 Campaign symposium, Panel 2, 17.

49. Fred Barnes, "Kemp and the Cons," *New Republic,* December 28, 1987, 10.

50. Black, 1988 Campaign symposium, Panel 3, 12.

51. Buckley, Congressional Staff symposium, Panel 2, 69.

52. Thomas Edsall, "Critical Vote Today in South Carolina," *Washington Post,* March 5, 1988, 1.

53. Broder, "Dole, Robertson, Kemp Swamped at the Polls in 16 of 17 States," *Washington Post,* March 9, 1988, A1.

54. Maureen Dowd, "Kemp Bows Out, but Drops Hint on No. 2 Spot," *New York Times,* March 11, 1988, A1.

55. Gerald Boyd, "Kemp, in Call for Unity, Endorses Vice President," *New York Times,* March 29, 1988, D26.

56. Jack Kemp, "1988's Lessons for Conservatives," reprinted in *Advancing the American Idea into the 90s* (Washington, DC: Campaign for a New Majority State, 1988), 103.

57. Congressional Staff symposium, Panel 2, 65.

58. Buckley, Kemp Oral History interview, 18.

59. Buckley, Congressional Staff symposium, Panel 2, 94.

60. Ed Rollins with Tom DeFrank, *Bare Knuckles and Back Rooms: My Life in American Politics* (New York: Broadway Books, 1996), 183.

61. Mosheh Maimonides, 1138–1204, was a Sephardic Jewish scholar who adapted Aristotelian philosophy to biblical teaching. Cecil Roth, *A History of the Jews,* rev. ed. (New York: Schocken Books, 1970), 175–79.

62. Mary Cannon, Congressional Staff symposium, Panel 2, 94.

63. Paul Young, ibid., 4.

64. Black, 1988 Campaign symposium, Panel 1, 24.

65. Reed, Kemp Oral History interview, 12.

66. Buckley, Congressional Staff symposium, Panel 2, 78.

67. David Smick, Kemp Oral History interview, 3.

68. Letter, January 28, 1988, Wanniski Archive, Hoover Institution, Box 4, folder 6.

69. Smick, Kemp Oral History interview, 6.

70. Reed, Kemp Oral History interview, 14.

71. Sharon Zelaska, Congressional Staff symposium, Panel 2, 52.

72. David Hoppe, ibid., 35.

73. Buckley, ibid., 51.

74. Goldman and Mathews, *The Quest for the Presidency,* 207.

75. Brooks Jackson, "Bush, Dole and Dukakis Lead the Race to Build the Biggest Campaign Funds," *Wall Street Journal,* January 4, 1988, 40.

76. Frank Cannon, 1988 Campaign symposium, Panel 1, 10.

77. http://www.fec.gov/audits/1988/Title26/JackKemp1988.pdf#search=JackKemp1988.

78. Jack Kemp Archive, Library of Congress, Box 214, folder 8.

79. Evans and Novak, "10 Pros Favor Jack Kemp as Bush's Running Mate," *Chicago Sun-Times,* July 27, 1988, 23.

80. Goldman and Mathews, *The Quest for the Presidency,* 317.

81. Bob Woodward and David S. Broder, "Dan Quayle: The Premeditated Surprise," *Washington Post,* January 5, 1992, A1.

82. Dan Quayle, *Standing Firm: A Vice-Presidential Memoir* (New York: HarperCollins, 1995), 4.

83. Hoppe, Congressional Staff symposium, Panel 2, 70.

84. Hoppe, 1988 Campaign symposium, Panel 3, 22.

85. John Mueller, Congressional Staff symposium, Panel 2, 72.

86. "Official Proceedings of the 34th Republican National Convention," 104ff.

87. Hoppe, Congressional Staff symposium, Panel 2, 24.

88. Ibid., 71.

89. Ibid., 72.

90. Congressional Staff symposium, Panel 2, 74.

91. Buckley, Kemp Oral History interview, 56.

92. Reed, Kemp Oral History interview, 23.

93. Dave Ernst, "Good Sport Kemp Pledges Support for the GOP Team," *Buffalo News,* August 17, 1988, 1.

94. Polls taken after the Democratic convention showed Bush trailing Dukakis by 17 points. After the GOP convention, Bush moved into the lead by 6 points. Michael Oreskes, "Bush Overtakes Dukakis in a Poll," *New York Times,* August 23, 1986. Ultimately, Bush won the election with 53.4 percent of the popular vote and carried all but ten states and the District of Columbia.

95. Hoppe e-mail to Morton Kondracke, March 27, 2015.

96. Hoppe, 1988 Campaign symposium, Panel 3, 7.

97. Hoppe, Congressional Staff symposium, Panel 2, 72.

98. Quayle, *Standing Firm,* 37, 52.

99. "The Day the Ticket Came Together," *Washington Post,* August 17, 1988, D1.

100. Robert D. Novak, *The Prince of Darkness: 50 Years of Reporting in Washington* (New York: Crown Forum, 2007), 451.

101. Jennifer Kemp Andrews and Judith Kemp Nolan, Kemp Oral History interview, 69.

102. Despite Bush's strong victory over Democrat Michael Dukakis, 53.3 percent to 45.6 in the popular vote and 426–111 in the Electoral College, Republicans lost a net two House seats and one Senate seat, leaving Democrats in charge of both chambers.

Chapter 10: Poverty Warrior

1. Ernie Warlick, Buffalo Oral History symposium, Panel 1, 24.

2. Pro Football Hall of Fame, JonKendle, "Players Boycott AFL All-Star Game," February 18, 2010, http://www.profootballhof.com/history/2010/2/18/players -boycott-afl-all-star-game/.

3. Richard Kemp, *Little Brother* (Irvine, CA: self-published, 2010), 19.

4. One of Kemp's favorite Lincoln scholars was Gabor S. Boritt, author of *Lincoln and the Economics of the American Dream,* who quoted Lincoln (page 173) saying that "a

black man is entitled to it . . . to be a hired laborer this year and the next work for himself and afterward, hire men to work for him!" Slavery, in Lincoln's view, threatened free labor everywhere in America and winning the Civil War was necessary, as he told Ohio soldiers in 1864, to preserve a nation that offered "an open field and a fair chance for your industry, enterprise and intelligence; that you may all have equal privileges in the race of life."

5. Craig Fuller telephone interview with Morton Kondracke, January 8, 2014.
6. Charlie Black telephone interview with Morton Kondracke, December 12, 2013.
7. Fred Barnes, "The Poverty Thing," *New Republic*, January 16, 1989, 14.
8. http://www.c-span.org/video/?5222-1/tribute-rep-jack-kemp.
9. Barnes, "The Poverty Thing," 14.
10. John Sununu telephone interview with Morton Kondracke, February 7, 2014.
11. Joanne Kemp, Kemp Oral History interview, 110.
12. Jason DeParle, "How Jack Kemp Lost the War on Poverty," *New York Times Magazine*, February 28, 1993, 47.
13. Ibid.
14. The references were in appearances before the National Urban League, August 8, 1989, National Association of Realtors, November 10, 1989, and American Legislative Exchange Council, April 27, 1990, http://www.Bush41library.tamu .edu/archives. Public Papers—Searchable/Search by Content/War on Poverty.
15. http://www.presidency.ucsb.edu/george_bush.php. American Presidency Project, University of California Santa Barbara. Papers of George Bush, December 19, 1988. Excerpts of the President-elect's News Conference Announcing the Nomination of Jack Kemp as Secretary of Housing and Urban Development.
16. "Remarks at the Swearing-in Ceremony for Jack F. Kemp as Secretary of Housing and Urban Development," http://www.Bush41library.tamu.edu/archives. Public Papers/1989.
17. DeParle, "How Jack Kemp Lost," 56.
18. David Treadwell, "'Activist' Kemp Tours Atlanta to Examine Housing Problems Faced by Inner Cities," *Los Angeles Times*, February 15, 1989, 17.
19. James Traub, "Jack Kemp Faces Reality," *New York Times*, May 7, 1989, A38.
20. Jack Kemp Archive, Library of Congress, Box 287, folder 14.
21. Robert Woodson, Symposium, "Secretary Kemp Quarterback in the Cabinet," Washington, DC, June 29, 2012, 35.
22. Rick Ahearn, Road symposium, 67.
23. HUD symposium, 31.
24. Al DelliBovi, HUD symposium, 11.
25. Philip Shenon, "Samuel R. Pierce Jr., Ex-Housing Secretary, Dies at 78," *New York Times*, November 3, 2000, B13.
26. Jason DeParle, "'Robin HUD' Given a Stiff Sentence," *New York Times*, June 23, 1990, 6.
27. Jack Kemp Archive, Library of Congress, Box 245, folder 11.
28. Bill McAllister and Chris Spolar, "The Transformation of HUD: 'Brat Pack' Filled Vacuum at Agency," *Washington Post*, August 6, 1989, A1.
29. Edward T. Pound and Jill Abramson, "Pierce May Have Kept Hands Off, but Projects of Pals Sailed Through," *Wall Street Journal*, July 12, 1989, A1.

30. Fiscal Year 2012 Historical Tables, Budget of the United States Government, Table 5.2, 106–7 (Washington, DC: U.S. Government Printing Office), https://www .whitehouse.gov/sites/default/files/omb/budget/fy2012/assets/hist.pdf.

31. Clifford D. May, "Housing Troubles Raise Kemp's Political Stature," *New York Times,* July 10, 1989, B6.

32. "Final Report and Recommendations," Subcommittee on HUD/MOD Rehab Investigation, Committee on Banking, Housing and Urban Affairs, November 1990, 243.

33. Larry D. Thompson, in Gerald S. Greenberg, ed., *Historical Encyclopedia of U.S. Independent Counsel Investigations* (Westport, CT: Greenwood Press, 2000).

34. "Still Rising: the HUD Bill, and Smell," *New York Times* editorial, July 13, 1999, A22.

35. Kenneth J. Cooper, "Pierce Misled Hill, Panel Concludes," *Washington Post,* November 2, 1990, A23.

36. Pierre Thomas and Toni Locy, "U.S. Won't Prosecute Ex-Secretary in HUD Probe," *Washington Post,* January 12, 1995, A1.

37. Sharon Zelaska, Kemp Oral History interview, January 23, 2012, 38.

38. Mary Cannon, Kemp Oral History interview, June 18, 2012, 24.

39. Sherrie Rollins telephone interview with Morton Kondracke, February 17, 2014.

40. A description of the team's reform efforts is covered in an op-ed by Francis Keating, "Jack Kemp and His Trowel," *Washington Post,* April 8, 1993, A21.

41. John Weicher, HUD symposium, 19.

42. Gaylord Shaw, "Up to $2 Billion Lost in HUD Scandal, Kemp Testifies," *Newsday,* July 12, 1989, 15.

43. Scott Reed, Kemp Oral History interview, 34.

44. Jack Kemp Archive, Library of Congress, Box 368, folder 6.

45. Ibid.

46. David S. Broder, "Urban Recipe: From Back Burner to Hot Spot: Initiatives Brought Forth as Bush's Response to LA Violence Had Languished Since 1989," *Washington Post,* May 24, 1992, A4.

47. Reed, Kemp Oral History interview, 30.

48. Mary Cannon telephone interview with Morton Kondracke, February 10, 2014.

49. http://www.Bushlibrary.tamu.edu/archive. Textual Archives/Public Papers —Searchable/Search by Content/.

50. DeParle, "How Jack Kemp Lost the War on Poverty," 57.

51. Richard Darman, *Who's in Control? Polar Politics and the Sensible Center* (New York: Simon & Schuster, 1996), 202.

52. Mary Cannon telephone interview.

53. Steven A. Holmes, "Kemp's Legacy as Housing Secretary: One of Ideas, Not Accomplishments," *New York Times,* August 20, 1996, A15.

54. DeParle, "How Jack Kemp Lost the War on Poverty," 56.

55. Ibid.

56. http://www.whitehouse.gov/omb/budget/historicals, Table 1.2, and U.S. Census Bureau, Statistical Abstract of the United States, 2012, 310.

57. Darman, *Who's in Control?,* 191.

58. Peggy Noonan, *What I Saw at the Revolution: A Political Life in the Reagan Era* (New York: Random House, 1990), 307.

59. Andrew Rosenthal, "Bush Now Concedes a Need for 'Tax Revenue Increases' to Reduce Deficits in Budget," *New York Times,* June 27, 1990, 1.

60. DeParle, "How Jack Kemp Lost," 47.

61. HUD symposium, 61.

62. Fred Barnes, "The Urban Cowboy," *USA Today Weekend,* August 14–16, 1992, 8.

63. DeParle, "How Jack Kemp Lost," 47.

64. Rowland Evans and Robert Novak, "Darman's Disdain," *Washington Post,* November 23, 1990, A17.

65. DeParle, "How Jack Kemp Lost," 56.

66. Evans and Novak, "Darman's Disdain."

67. DeParle, "How Jack Kemp Lost," 56.

68. Ibid., 57.

69. University of Virginia Miller Center Presidential Speech Archive.

70. DeParle, "How Jack Kemp Lost," 57.

71. Michael McQueen and Gerald Seib, "Bush Seen as Uncaring on Domestic Issues," Asia Edition, *Wall Street Journal,* July 31, 1991, 24. (Same as "While Bush Stars on Yet Another Foreign Stage, Critics Say He Should Play Bigger Role at Home," in the U.S. *Wall Street Journal,* July 30, 1991), 18.

72. Holmes, "Kemp's Legacy as Housing Secretary," A15.

73. U.S. Census Bureau, Statistical Abstract of the United States, 2011, Table 711, 464.

74. Bill Dal Col telephone interview, January 31, 2014.

75. DeParle, "How Jack Kemp Lost," 47.

76. Lawrence M. O'Rourke, *GENO: The Life and Mission of Geno Baroni* (n.p.: Paulist Press, 1991), 87.

77. Gwen Ifill, "Kemp Wants $93 Million Rescinded," *Washington Post,* November 28, 1989, A15.

78. DeParle, "How Jack Kemp Lost," 47.

79. Gwen Ifill, "Kemp Assails Senate Funding Curbs," *Washington Post,* September 29, 1990, A6.

80. Ann Mariano, "Kemp's Initiatives for Public Housing Are the Big Loser," *Washington Post,* November 8, 1991, A23.

81. Jason DeParle, "Amid Housing Crisis, a Bitter Feud Over Policy," *New York Times,* October 23, 1991, A15.

82. Ifill, "Kemp Assails Senate Funding Curbs," A6.

83. Gwen Ifill, "Housing Sale to Tenants Threatened by Conflict," *Washington Post,* September 28, 1990, A25.

84. Woodson, HUD symposium, 47.

85. Ann Mariano, "Kemp's Initiatives for Public Housing Are the Big Loser," *Washington Post,* November 8, 1991, A23.

86. DeParle, "Amid Housing Crisis."

87. Ifill, "Kemp Assails Senate Funding Curbs," A6.

88. James Baker, Kemp Oral History interview, Houston, TX, March 13, 2013, 10.

89. Marvin Fitzwater, *Call the Briefing! A Memoir: Ten Years in the White House with Presidents Reagan and Bush* (New York: Crown, 1995), 43.

90. Baker, Kemp Oral History interview, 12.

91. Ibid., 44.

92. Evans and Novak, "Fixing Budget Blame," *Washington Post,* August 10, 1990, A15.

93. Barnes, "War Dividend," *New Republic,* March 25, 1991, 12.

94. Barnes, "The Slump Thing," *New Republic,* November 4, 1991, 22.

95. Vin Weber, Kemp Oral History interview, 53.

96. Alan Murray and David Wessel, "Darman Says Taxes Won't Be Trimmed in '91, but May Be Cut Next Year if Economy Stays Limp," *Wall Street Journal,* November 4, 1991, A20.

97. Jack Kemp Archive, Library of Congress, Box 387, folder 4.

98. John Sununu telephone interview with Morton Kondracke, February 6, 2014.

99. John Judis, "Jack Kemp Scrambles for Daylight," *GQ,* July 1992, 154.

100. Ann Devroy, "Kemp Apologizes to Bush for Remark; HUD Chief Regrets Context, Not Content of 'Gimmicks' Statement," *Washington Post,* February 6, 1992, A1.

101. Mary Cannon, Kemp Oral History interview, Washington, DC, June 18, 2012, 34.

102. Devroy, "Kemp Apologizes to Bush for Remark," A1.

103. Dan Quayle, *Standing Firm: A Vice-Presidential Memoir* (New York: HarperCollins, 1994), 100.

104. Ibid., 105.

105. "The L.A. Riots: 20 Years Later, 1992 Riots Timeline," *Los Angeles Times* staff, http://www.nbclosangeles.com/news/local/Los-Angeles-1992-Riots-By-the-Mumbers-148340405.html; http://timelines.latimes.com/los-angeles-riots/.

106. Judis, "Jack Kemp Scrambles for Daylight," 154.

107. Barnes, "Unkempt," *New Republic,* June 1, 1992, 11.

108. Ibid.

109. DeParle, "How Jack Kemp Lost," 57.

110. Lamar Alexander interview with Morton Kondracke, February 12, 2014, Washington, D.C.

111. The American Presidency Project, George Bush, "Address to the Nation on the Civil Disturbances in Los Angeles, California," May 1, 1992, http://www.presidency.ucsb.edu/ws/?pid=20910.

112. John E. Yang, "Address City Issues, Kemp Urges Bush," *Washington Post,* May 3, 1992, A26.

113. Jack Kemp, "A New Agenda for Ending Poverty: Give People a Stake in Their Own Communities," *Washington Post,* May 3, 1992, C7.

114. Robert Pear, "Riots in Los Angeles: Clinton Tours City's Damaged Areas and Chides Bush," *New York Times,* May 5, 1992, A26.

115. Jason DeParle, "After the Riots: As Los Angeles Smoke Lifts, Bush Can See Kemp Clearly," *New York Times,* May 7, 1992, A1.

116. DeParle, "How Kemp Lost."

117. DeParle, "After the Riots."

118. Fred Barnes, "Unkempt," 11.

119. Ibid.

120. "Remarks on Urban Aid Initiatives and an Exchange with Reporters," http://www.bush41library.tamu.edu/archives/public papers. Public Papers—Searchable. Search by Date. 1992-05-12.

121. www.upi.com/archives/1992/11/04/Bush-vetoes-urban-aid-tax-bill1/265720853200.

122. Ahearn, telephone interview with Morton Kondracke, January 31, 2014.

123. George Will, "Five Things Bush Must Do in Order to Win in November," *Baltimore Sun,* July 24, 1992, 11A.

124. Tom Morganthau, "The Quayle Question," *Newsweek,* August 3, 1992, 25.

125. Fitzwater, *Call The Briefing!*, 432–34.
126. Dal Col telephone interview with Morton Kondracke, January 31, 2014.
127. Dal Col, Ahearn, HUD symposium, 47.
128. Tom Raum, "Bush: No Shakeup in the Works," *New Orleans Times Picayune*, August 20, 1992, A16.
129. Dal Col, Road symposium, 48.
130. Timothy Noah, "Kemp Seems to Be Diverging from Bush Even While Stumping for the GOP Ticket," *Wall Street Journal*, September 28, 1992, A14.
131. Black telephone interview, December 13, 2013; and Evans and Novak, "Dud Baker Bomb," *Washington Post*, October 14, 1992, A21.
132. Broder, "Late, but Not a Bad Start," *Washington Post*, August 23, 1992, C7.
133. Broder, "What Future for the GOP?" *Washington Post*, November 8, 1992, C7.
134. Robert J. McCarthy, "Kemp Looks Presidential to State Delegation," *Buffalo News* August 19, 1992, A16.
135. Evans and Novak, "GOP Heir Apparent," *Washington Post*, November 4, 1992, C19.

Chapter 11: Veep

1. Gerald F. Seib, "Conservatives Form Group in Attempt to Consolidate Power, Sharpen Message," *Wall Street Journal*, January 13, 1993, A16.
2. Vin Weber, Kemp Oral History interview, December 3, 2012, 56.
3. Douglas Frantz, "Influential Group Brought into Campaign by Kemp," *New York Times*, September 1, 1996, 32.
4. David Rogers, "At Empower America, Refuge for Conservatives; First Year Has Been a Tale of Money and Ego," *Wall Street Journal*, January 6, 1994, A14.
5. Richard Estrada, "Kemp Metamorphoses from Quarterback to Cheerleader," *Dallas Morning News*, September 17, 1996, 1A; Marc Lacey, "Kemp Releases Tax Records: He's Worth at Least $5 million," *Los Angeles Times*, September 6, 1996, 15.
6. Douglas Turner, "Kemp Assails Clinton's Call for Sacrifice," *Buffalo News*, January 24, 1993, A8.
7. Jack Kemp, "The Next 100 Days," *Wall Street Journal*, April 27, 1993, A20.
8. John Dillin, "Empower America Says Clinton Will Help GOP," *Christian Science Monitor*, June 21, 1993, 4.
9. Lally Weymouth, "Kemp, Kemp: Is He Their Man?," *Washington Post*, September 27, 1993, A19.
10. Empower America News Release, December 21, 1994, Jack Kemp Archive, Library of Congress, Box 355, folder 5.
11. Richard L. Berke, "GOP Challenges Clinton's Agenda," *New York Times*, January 23, 1994, 14.
12. Editorial, "Heresy from Jack Kemp," *Washington Post*, March 15, 1993, A19.
13. Steve Forbes, Kemp Oral History interview, February 2, 2012, 16.
14. Bill Bennett, Kemp Oral History interview, December 11, 2012, 37.
15. Editorial, "The Fortress Party?," *Wall Street Journal*, October 21, 1994, A14.
16. Robert Novak, "Jack Kemp: Flawed GOP Jewel," *Washington Post*, October 27, 1994, A23. Rowland Evans retired from writing the Evans-Novak column on May 15, 1993. Novak was the sole author thereafter, *Prince of Darkness*, 505.

17. Gebe Martinez, "California Elections/Prop. 187. Kemp Draws Criticism for Voicing Opposition," *Los Angeles Times,* October 20, 1994, 1.

18. On November 8, 1994, Proposition 187 was approved by voters, 59 percent to 41 percent. It never went into effect, first enjoined and then struck down by a federal judge who declared it infringed on the federal government's exclusive jurisdiction over immigration matters. Wilson, reelected with 55 percent of the vote, appealed the ruling to the 9th Circuit Court of Appeals, but his successor, Democrat Gray Davis, dropped the appeal in 1999, effectively killing the law.

19. Dan Balz, "Bull Market Takes Off in 1996 GOP Futures," *Washington Post,* August 22, 1992.

20. Fred Barnes, "The Obsessions of Jack Kemp," *New Republic,* May 9, 1994, 18.

21. Ibid.

22. Ibid.

23. "Kemp Agrees to Pay Campaign Penalties," *New York Times,* June 22, 1994, A16.

24. Barnes, "The Obsessions."

25. Jack Nelson, "Kemp Says GOP Must Reach Out to Minorities," *Los Angeles Times,* June 10, 1994, 11.

26. "Longest JFK-Gram in History," undated, written to Jeff Kemp, undated but late 1994, copy provided to authors by Jeff Kemp.

27. Weber, Kemp Oral History interview, 60.

28. Kemp, "GOP Contract—My Amendments," *Wall Street Journal,* September 23, 1994, A14.

29. Kemp, "Contract Hitters . . . and Contract Hopes," *Washington Times,* October 21, 1994.

30. Neil A. Lewis, "Kemp Rejects Presidential Bid, Citing Dislike of Fund Raising," *New York Times,* January 31, 1995, A12.

31. Institute of Politics, Harvard University, *Campaign for President: The Managers Look at '96* (Hollis, NH: Hollis Publishing Co., 1997), 38.

32. "Longest JFK-Gram in History."

33. Dole press release, April 3, 1995, Jack Kemp Archive, Library of Congress, Box 280, folder 8.

34. John Mueller, Congressional Staff symposium, Panel 2, 91.

35. Report of the National Commission on Economic Growth and Tax Reform, "Unleashing America's Potential," January 1996, 8.

36. "Tax Notes," August 14, 1995. Kemp Archive, Box 281, folder 1.

37. Dan Balz, "Gramm Sets Outline of 16% Flat Tax," *Washington Post,* January 17, 1996, A6.

38. Alan Murray, "The Outlook: GOP Adherents Study Merits of a Flat Tax," *Wall Street Journal,* January 29, 1996, A1.

39. Eric Pianin, "Dole's Turnabout on Tax Issue Demonstrates Rightward Lean," *Washington Post,* August 6, 1995, 8.

40. Gerald Seib and Christina Duff, "Kemp Commission to Avoid Endorsing Flat Tax, Likely Fueling Debate Within Republican Party, *Wall Street Journal,* January 1, 1996, A16.

41. Ibid.

42. Jack Kemp, "Lower Taxes, Higher Revenues," *New York Times,* February 11, 1996, E15.

43. Clay Chandler, "On the Road to a Flat Tax, a Curve or Two," *Washington Post,* January 21, 1996, A1.

44. John Mueller, Kemp Oral History interview, 68.

45. John Mueller telephone interview with Morton Kondracke, July 28, 2014.

46. Forbes, Kemp Oral History interview, 3, 13.

47. Ibid., 24.

48. Ibid., 25.

49. Bob Woodward, *The Choice: How Bill Clinton Won* (New York: Simon & Schuster, 1996), 274.

50. Ibid., 281.

51. Wanniski letter to Kemp, February 19, 1996, Wanniski Archive, Hoover Institution, Box 15, folder 12.

52. Forbes, Kemp Oral History interview, 27.

53. Ruth Marcus and Walter Pincus, "Forbes Spent $18 million on Race Last Year," *Washington Post,* February 6, 1996, A1.

54. Woodward, *The Choice,* 373–75.

55. Richard L. Berke, "Politics: The Overview; Dole Endorsed by Alexander and Lugar," *New York Times,* March 7, 1996, B9.

56. Actually, Churchill joined the Liberal Party on May 31, 1904, opposing the Conservatives' policy of protectionism and high tariffs. The last straw, however, was the Aliens Bill, which drastically curbed Jewish immigration from Russia. Martin Gilbert, *Churchill: A Life* (New York: Henry Holt & Co., 1991), 165.

57. Novak, "Kemp's Last Straw," *Washington Post,* March 11, 1996, A9.

58. Ernest Tollerson, "Politics; Endorsement; Kemp Supports Forbes in Bid to Salvage Flat-Tax Plan as an Issue in the Campaign," *New York Times,* March 7, 1996, B10.

59. Ron Scherer, "Forbes Leaves '96 Race and a Flat-Tax Legacy: What $25 Million Bought," *Christian Science Monitor,* March 15, 1996, 3.

60. "The Flat Tax Is Losing Its Appeal Among US Voters, Poll Finds," *Wall Street Journal,* March 8, 1996, R2.

61. Kevin Merida, "A Party Stalwart Who Continues to Puzzle," *Washington Post,* March 17, 1996, A10.

62. Edwin Chen, "News Analysis: Can Gingrich Hold His Tongue for Good of Party?," *Los Angeles Times,* December 24, 1995, 1.

63. Institute of Politics, ed. *Campaign for President,* 44.

64. Woodward, *The Choice,* 418.

65. Scott Reed, Dole Oral History Project interview, November 8, 2007, 16. Robert J. Dole Archive and Special Collections, Robert J. Dole Institute of Politics, University of Kansas, The Dole Institute Oral History Project. Dolearchives.ku.edu/oralhistory -legacy#orallegacy_nz.

66. Ibid., 17.

67. Ronald Brownstein, "Dole Camp Weighs Plan to Cut Income Tax Rates," *Los Angeles Times,* May 9, 1996, 1.

68. Blaine Harden, "Dole Invests His Hopes in Middle Class Anxiety; Tax-Cut Speech Takes a Populist Approach," *Washington Post,* August 6, 1996, 1.

69. Richard Morin, "Poll Shows Dole Still Narrowing Gap as More Voters Say They're Undecided," *Washington Post,* August 11, 1996, A15.

70. Bob Woodward, "A Onetime Running Mate Starts Early for His Own Series," *Washington Post*, June 26, 1996, 1.

71. Dan Balz, "For Dole, the Hunt for a No. 2 Was Always About Winning," *Washington Post*, August 11, 1996, A19.

72. Ibid.

73. Reed, Kemp Oral History interview, November 26, 2012, Washington, DC, 52.

74. Reed, Kemp Oral History interview, 52; John Buckley, Kemp Oral History interview, 57; Balz, "For Dole, the Hunt"; Ronald Brownstein and Edwin Chen, "Kemp Has Inside Track in Dole VP Race," *Los Angeles Times*, August 9, 1996, 1.

75. Bennett, Kemp Oral History interview, 22.

76. Buckley, Kemp Oral History interview, 57.

77. Reed telephone interview with Morton Kondracke, June 27, 2014.

78. Bennett, Kemp Oral History interview, 21.

79. Reed telephone interview.

80. Ibid.

81. Joanne Kemp, Kemp Oral History interview, December 10, 2012, 114.

82. By all reports, it would have been Connie Mack.

83. Dole Oral History Project, May 23, 2007, 10.

84. Reed telephone interview.

85. Buckley, Kemp Oral History interview, 58.

86. Reed Oral History interview, 58.

87. Ibid.

88. Robert Novak, "Amazing Choice," *Washington Post*, August 12, 1996, A13.

89. Buckley, Congressional Staff symposium, Panel 2, 95.

90. Maria LaGanga, "Dole Makes It Clear He's the Boss," *Los Angeles Times*, August 11, 1996, 1.

91. Reed, Kemp Oral History interview, 60.

92. Buckley, Kemp Oral History interview, 60.

93. Kemp, Dole Oral History Project, May 23, 2007, 12.

94. Blaine Harden, "Dole Brings Kemp, a '15,' to His Team," *Washington Post*, August 11, 1996, A1.

95. *Time* cover story, August 12, 1996; David Broder, "GOP Odd Couple Is an Odd Choice for Party," *Washington Post*, August 12, 1996, A1.

96. Maureen Dowd, "Dole and Kemp: The Party's Odd Couple," *Milwaukee Journal Sentinel*, August 13, 1996, 10.

97. Novak, *The Prince of Darkness: Fifty Years of Reporting in Washington* (New York: Crown Forum, 2007), 534.

98. Reed telephone Interview.

99. *Time* cover story, August 12, 1996.

100. Institute of Politics, ed. *Campaign for President '96*, 200–1.

101. http://www.cnn.com/ALLPOLITICS/1996/conventions/san.diego/transcripts/0815/kemp.fdch.shtml.

102. On the day Dole was nominated, Kemp wrote him a handwritten letter marked "personal and confidential" beginning "Dear Bob, Tonight, for you, this is your destiny, your career in the service of your country." He wrote his old adversary that "you are the shadow President right now" and that both God and history were on

his side. (Letter from J. T. Taylor personal files, e-mail to Morton Kondracke, October 4, 2012.)

103. Wayne Berman, Kemp Oral History interview, March 21, 2013, 3, 10, 13.

104. R. Drummond Ayers, "In New Role, Kemp Fights with His Past Over Ideology," *New York Times*, August 15, 1996, A19.

105. Ronald Brownstein, "Kemp Now Backs Immigration Curbs, End to Preferences," *Los Angeles Times*, August 14, 1996, 1.

106. Marc Lacy, "Kemp Keeps Prop. 209 at Arm's Length," *Los Angeles Times*, October 30, 1996, 6.

107. Berke, "Poll Shows Dole Slicing Away Lead Clinton Had Held," *New York Times*, August 20, 1996, A1.

108. Dan Coats, Kemp Oral History interview, Washington, DC, June 14, 2012, 13.

109. Berman, Kemp Oral History interview, 7.

110. Ibid., 8.

111. Frank Bruni, "Kemp Stumps for the Votes of Minorities," *New York Times*, August 29, 1996, B8.

112. Jerry Gray, "In Inner-City Chicago, Kemp Makes Pitch for Black Votes," *New York Times*, September 4, 1996, 8.

113. Gray, "Kemp Courts Harlem Voters with Open Arms, Little Hope," *New York Times*, September 7, 1996, 8; Marc Lacy, "Kemp Makes Appeal to Black Voters," *Los Angeles Times*, September 7, 1996, 14.

114. Michael Rezendes, "Muslim's Self-help Praised by Kemp," *Boston Globe*, September 8, 1996, A1.

115. Wanniski letter to Kemp, April 24, 1996. Wanniski Archive, Hoover Institution, Box 15, folder 12.

116. "Kemp Stirs Storm by Complimenting Nation of Islam Big," *Forward*, September 13, 1996, 1.

117. Ed Feulner, Kemp Oral History interview, Washington, DC, April 12, 2012, 7.

118. Berman, Kemp Oral History interview, 5.

119. "Kemp Stirs Storm," *Forward*.

120. Berman, Kemp Oral History interview, 7.

121. Paul Duggan, "Kemp, After Praising Farrakhan's Message, Seeks Condemnation of Anti-Semitism," *Washington Post*, September 11, 1996, A9.

122. Novak, "Trouble for Newt if Democrats Win," *Buffalo News*, September 16, 1996, B3.

123. A. M. Rosenthal, "Kemp and Farrakhan," *New York Times*, October 15, 1996, A17.

124. Novak, "The Man Who Didn't Dare," *Washington Post*, November 4, 1996, A19.

125. John F. Harris and Dan Balz, "Democratic Nominees Revive Campaign Bushing," *Washington Post*, August 31, 1996, A20.

126. Richard Morin and Dan Balz, "Economy, Growing Optimism Help Clinton Keep Lead in Poll," *Washington Post*, September 6, 1996, 1.

127. Alan Miller, "Democrats Return Illegal Contribution," *Los Angeles Times*, September 21, 1996, 16.

128. Institute for Politics, ed. *Campaign for President*, 250; "DNC Says It Erred by Holding Fund-Raiser at Buddhist Temple," by Rich Connell and Alan C. Miller, October 17, 1996, 15; Edith B. Richburg, "For Clinton Donor, Just Business As Usual," *Washington Post*,

October 20, 1996, 1; Kevin Merida and Serge F. Kovaleski, "Mysteries Arise All Along the Asian Money Trail," *Washington Post*, November 1, 1996, 1.

129. Edwin Chen and Maria LaGanga, "Dole Hammers Clinton's Credibility," *Los Angeles Times*, October 2, 1996, 4.

130. Marc Lacy and Jonathan Peterson, "Politics: For Gore and Kemp, Different Stump Roles," *Los Angeles Times*, September 10, 1996, 5.

131. "A Transcript of First Televised Debate Between Clinton and Dole," *New York Times*, October 7, 1996, B8.

132. Balz, "Silence on Character Issue Puzzles Some Republicans," *Washington Post*, October 11, 1996, A1.

133. Institute of Politics, ed. *Campaign for President*, 215.

134. Reed telephone interview.

135. Katherine Q. Seelye, "Changing Tactics, Dole Challenges Clinton's Ethics," *New York Times*, October 9, 1996, A1.

136. Reed telephone interview.

137. Feulner Kemp Oral History interview, 35.

138. Berman, Kemp Oral History interview, 16.

139. Judd Gregg telephone interview with Morton Kondracke, June 30, 2014.

140. Berman, Kemp Oral History interview, 17.

141. Feulner, Kemp Oral History interview, 36.

142. Bill Dal Col, Road symposium, 45.

143. Jeff Bell, Kemp Oral History Project, 92.

144. Ed Brady, Road symposium, 45.

145. Commission on Presidential Debates, "October 9, 1996 Debate Transcript," http://www.debates.org/index.php?page=october-9-1996-debate-transcript.

146. Reed, Kemp Oral History interview, 68.

147. Reed telephone interview with Morton Kondracke, June 27, 2014.

148. Gloria Borger, David Fischer, Linda Kulman, Kenneth Walsh, and Jason Vest, "Should Dole Swing Away?," *U.S. News & World Report*, October 13, 1996.

149. Bennett, Kemp Oral History interview, 4.

150. Berman, Kemp Oral History interview, 18.

151. Buckley, Kemp Oral History interview, 63.

152. Mary McGrory, "Kemp Gets Gored," *Washington Post*, October 13, 1996, C1.

153. Novak, "Better Luck Next Time," *Washington Post*, October 14, 1996, A27.

154. "Quarterback Drops the Ball," *Buffalo News*, October 14, 1996, B2.

155. James Gerstenzang and Marc Lacy, "Gore, Kemp Clash on Tax Cuts and Economic Growth," *Los Angeles Times*, October 10, 1996, 1.

156. Reed, Oral History interview, 72.

157. Ibid., 71.

158. Buckley Oral History interview 63.

159. Berman, Kemp Oral History interview, 20.

160. Commission on Presidential Debates, "October 16, 1996 Debate Transcript," http://www.debates.org/index.php?page=october-16-1996-debate-transcript.

161. Borger, Fisher, Kulman, Walsh, and Vest, "Should Dole Swing Away?," 14.

162. Adam Nagourney, "Dole Campaign in Discord Over Attacking President," *New York Times*, October 11, 1996, A1.

163. Marc Lacy and Maria LaGanga, "Kemp Goes on Offensive with Blast at Clinton," *Los Angeles Times,* October 13, 1996, 1.

164. Michael Weisskopf, "Gore Scores Kemp for 'Low Road Attack' as GOP Pounds Away on Ethics Issues," *Washington Post,* October 14, 1996, A13.

165. Gray, "Kemp Backers Still Seeking Pit Bull, but He's Not Biting," *New York Times,* October 17, 1996, 8.

166. Buckley, Kemp Oral History interview, 61.

167. Reed interview with Morton Kondracke, June 24, 2015.

168. Berke, "GOP Leaders Doubtful That Dole Can Close Gap," *New York Times,* October 20, 1996, 1.

169. Adam Nagourney, "Dole Warns Against Influence of 'Foreign Aid' on Democrats," *New York Times,* October 20, 1996, 20.

170. Berke, "Aggressive Turn by Dole Appears to Be Backfiring," *New York Times,* October 22, 1996, A1.

171. Seelye, "Dole Is Imploring Voters to 'Rise Up' Against the Press," *New York Times,* October 26, 1996, 1.

172. Institute of Politics, ed. *Campaign for President,* 250.

173. Gray, "Kemp Ruffled by Reports of Republican Pessimists and His Being Defeatist," *New York Times,* October 30, 1996, A16.

174. Reed, Kemp Oral History interview, 74.

175. Rick Ahearn, Road symposium, 50.

176. "Stay Involved and Keep Fighting," *Washington Post,* November 6, 1996, B6.

177. Albert Hunt, "Can Kemp Be Ready for Prime Time?" *Wall Street Journal,* December 12, 1996, A13.

178. Berman Oral History interview, 12.

Chapter 12: Fourth Quarter

1. Dan Coats, Kemp Oral History interview, June 14, 2012, Washington, DC, 9; Associated Press, "Bomb Carrier in US House Prompts Tightened Security," November 2, 1983, http://www.nytimes.com/1983/11/02/us/bomb-carrier-in-us-home-prompts-tightened-security.html.

2. Joanne Kemp, Kemp Oral History interview, 100.

3. Shannon Henry, "A High-Flying Friendship," *Washington Post,* January 21, 1999, E1.

4. "Supporting Cast," *New York Times,* August 2, 2000, A20.

5. Raul Fernandez, Kemp Oral History Project interview, February 22, 2012, 25.

6. Michael Weisskopf, "In 'Wilderness,' Kemp Mined Lode Via Speeches, Directorships," *Washington Post,* August 23, 1996, A14; Richard Estrada, "Kemp Metamorphoses from Quarterback to Cheerleader," *Dallas Morning News,* September 17, 1996, 1A; Marc Lacy, "Kemp Releases Tax Records: He's Worth at Least $5 Million," *Los Angeles Times,* September 6, 1996, 15; Phil Kuntz, "Board Seats Have Boosted Kemp's Wealth," *Wall Street Journal,* August 16, 1996, A2.

7. "Kemp Comes Up with Way to Retain Stock Options," *Wall Street Journal,* September 6, 1996, B12.

8. Chris Woodyard, "Kemp Says First Class Is a Must," April 11, 2000, 2E.

9. Bill Ritter, "Financier Indicted in Mineral Scheme," *Los Angeles Times,* September 10, 1986.

10. Marc Lifsher, "Venezuela Wants Trading Company to Sell Oil in US," *Wall Street Journal,* June 2, 2003, A13; Mary Anastasia O'Grady, "Americas: In Chavez's Crosshairs," *Wall Street Journal,* September 22, 2006, A11.

11. J. T. Taylor interview, September 29, 2014.

12. Robert Novak, "Is Kemp Alive?," *Washington Post,* February 10, 1997, A7.

13. Ralph Z. Hallow, "Kemp Won't Run in 2000, Ends Formal Political Career," *Washington Times,* April 2, 1999, A4.

14. Robert Shogan, "A Liberated Kemp Now Free to Shape Public Policy," *Los Angeles Times,* May 12, 1999, 5.

15. Ibid.

16. Curt Anderson, Associated Press, "Ethics Committee Drops Last of 84 Charges Against Gingrich," *Washington Post,* October 11, 1998, A13; Leslie Lenkowski, "Gingrich's Vindication Should Spur Tax Code Changes," *Wall Street Journal,* February 9, 1999, A22.

17. Alan Elsner, Reuters, "Kemp Assails GOP Leaders for Pulling Back on Tax Cuts," *Buffalo News,* March 12, 1997, A12.

18. Patrice Hill, "Gingrich's Priority on Budget Sparks Feud with Tax Cutters," *Washington Times,* March 12, 1997, A12.

19. Hallow, "Hopefuls Tell GOP to Focus on Issues," *Washington Times,* September 10, 1997.

20. Ceci Connolly, "Disappointment on the Right Over Budget Deal," *Washington Post,* August 13, 1997, A4.

21. Paul Gigot, "Gingrich Gets Tax Windfall from Kemp," *Wall Street Journal,* A14.

22. http://www.whitehouse.gov/omb/budget/historicals, Table 1.3.

23. Joyce Howard Price, "Kemp Would Let Pollard Go, Vote Not to Impeach Clinton," *Washington Times,* October 25, 1998, A4.

24. Nancy Giffs and Michael Duffy, "Fall of the House of Newt," *Time,* November 16, 1998.

25. Jack Kemp Archive, Library of Congress, Box 239, folder 4.

26. Richard Morin, "Public Blames Clinton, Gives Record Support," *Washington Post,* February 15, 1999, A1.

27. James Kemp interview, September 22, 2014.

28. Jack Kemp, "The Party of Reagan . . . or of Hoover?," *Wall Street Journal,* July 30, 1999, A18.

29. Steven Greenhouse, "Coalition Urges Easing of Immigration Laws," *New York Times,* May 16, 2000, A16.

30. Jack Kemp and J. C. Watts Jr., "Better than Affirmative Action," *Washington Post,* July 8, 1997, A15.

31. Kemp, "An Indefensible Treaty," *New York Times,* October 27, 1997, 23.

32. Novak, "Kemp's Environmental Edge," *Washington Post,* September 1, 1997, A21.

33. Leslie Wayne with Frank Bruni, "Kemp Endorses Bush in Move Embarrassing to Forbes, Whom He Backed in '96 Race," *New York Times,* January 28, 2000, A19.

34. Sam Fulwood III, "Decision '98/the Final Count," *Los Angeles Times,* November 5, 1998, 2.

35. Walter Mears, "Kemp Endorsement Boosts Bush in New Hampshire," Bergen County, NJ, *Record*, January 28, 2000, A8.
36. Jack Kemp Archive, Library of Congress, Box 398, folder 1.
37. Jack Kemp, "Kemp Says McCain, Bush Too Negative," Bloomington, IL, *Pantagraph* February 29, 2000, A1.
38. "Cheney Opens the Door to Supply Side of Bush Administration," Townhall.com, August 2, 2000.
39. Kemp, "Al Gore's Economics of Fear," Townhall.com, October 11, 2000; "Scare Tactics Won't Work," Townhall.com, November 1, 2000.
40. Kemp, "Memo to the Victor," *Washington Times*, November 9, 2000, A20.
41. Joseph Kahn, "Bush Selections Signal a Widening of Cabinet's Role," *New York Times*, December 31, 2000, 1.
42. Kemp, "Artfully Woven Web of Deceit," *Washington Times*, June 17, 1999, B1.
43. Seth Gitell, "Drive to Rollback Saddam Is Generating Opposition of Odd Political Coalition," *Forward*, January 1, 1999, 1.
44. Larry Hunter interview, October 2, 2014.
45. "Wandering Jude," *American Spectator*, May 1999, 13.
46. Letter to Donald Rumsfeld, October 12, 2001.
47. Hunter e-mail, November 3, 2014.
48. Kemp, "Arafat's Diplomacy in Extremis," Townhall.com, October 18, 2000.
49. Kemp, "'Soft Diplomacy' Is the Best Plan," Townhall.com, March 13, 2007.
50. Kemp, "United States at War," Townhall.com, September 19, 2001.
51. Letter to Rumsfeld, October 12, 2001.
52. Kemp, "Consider Mideast Reality in the War on Terrorism," Townhall.com, November 7, 2001.
53. Kemp, "Straight Talk on Iraq," Townhall.com, December 5, 2001.
54. Hunter e-mail, November 3, 2014.
55. Kemp, "Shotgun Behind the Door—Loaded and Cocked," Townhall.com, October 1, 2002.
56. Kemp, "Iraq for the Iraqis," Townhall.com, August 26, 2003.
57. Kemp, "The Greenspan Recession," Townhall.com, August 15, 2001.
58. David S. Broder, "Return to Reaganomics," *Washington Post*, February 6, 2001; David Leonhardt, "Supply-Side Economists Regain Influence Under Bush," *New York Times*, April 10, 2001, C1.
59. "The Bush Tax Cuts of 2001 and 2003: A Brief Legislative History, Harvard Law School, Federal Budget Policy Seminar, Briefing Paper No. 37," http://www.law.harvard.edu/faculty/hjackson/2001-2003TaxCuts_37.pdf.
60. Kemp, "We Can Afford a Much Bigger Tax Cut," *New York Times*, February 21, 2001, A19; "Ignore the Double Talk and Double the Tax Cuts," Townhall.com, March 21, 2001; Leonhardt, "Supply-Side Economists."
61. Harvard Law School, "The Bush Tax Cuts."
62. Kemp, "A Tale of Two Tax Cuts," Townhall.com, June 13, 2005.
63. Kemp, "Senate Should Learn from History About Tax Cuts," Townhall.com, April 1, 2003.
64. Kemp, "Guns, Butter and Tax Code Reform," Townhall.com, December 19, 2006.
65. http://www.whitehouse.gov/omb/budget/historicals, Table 1.3.

66. Kemp, "Rising Tide, Sinking Ship," Townhall.com, July 5, 2004.
67. Kemp, "The Vision Thing," Townhall.com, July 16, 2004.
68. Roper Center, University of Connecticut, "How Groups Voted in 2004," http://www.ropercenter.uconn.edu/elections/how_groups_voted/voted_04.html.
69. "Mandate on Social Security Doesn't Include Benefit Cuts," *Investor's Business Daily,* November 10, 2004, A16.
70. Richard W. Stevenson, "With Bush Safely Re-elected, Rove Turns Intensity to Policy," *New York Times,* March 28, 2005, A1.
71. Jackie Calmes, "Lost Appeal: How a Victorious Bush Fumbled Plan to Revamp Social Security," *Wall Street Journal,* October 20, 2005, A1.
72. Kemp, "America Can Be a Nation of Immigrants and a Nation of Laws," Townhall.com, April 3, 2006.
73. Kemp, "New Start for Katrina's Victims," Townhall.com, September 20, 2005.
74. Michael Grunwald, "Republicans' Angry Factions Point Fingers at Each Other," *Washington Post,* November 9, 2006, A31.
75. http://www.uspolitics.about.com/od/electionissues/tp/Bush-Vetos.htm.
76. Kemp Oral History Project, 28.
77. "Our Communities, Our Homes: Pathways to Housing and Homeownership in America's Cities and States," Joint Center for Housing Studies, Harvard University.
78. CEO Wire, September 27, 2007.
79. Jack Kemp, "Bringing Bankruptcy Home," *Los Angeles Times,* January 18, 2008, A23.
80. Kemp, "The 25-Year Bull Market," Townhall.com, August 14, 2007.
81. James Kemp interview, September 22, 2014.
82. Jack Kemp and Peter Ferrara, "It's Time to Think Big on Tax Cuts," *Wall Street Journal,* October 8, 2008, A17.
83. Kemp, "A Letter to My Grandchildren," Townhall.com, November 12, 2008.
84. Jennifer Kemp Andrews and Judith Kemp Nolan, Kemp Oral History interview, 80.
85. Raul Fernandez, ibid. 33.
86. Joanne Kemp, Kemp Oral History interview, December 10, 2012, 125.
87. J. T. Taylor telephone interview with Morton Kondracke, September 29, 2014.
88. Kemp Oral History Project, 48ff.
89. Jerry Brewer, "Thanks, Dad: Jeff Kemp's Ode to His Famous Father," *Seattle Times,* June 21, 2009.
90. Nolan and Andrews, Kemp Oral History interview, 14.
91. Kemp, "Honoring Lincoln," Townhall.com, February 3, 2009.
92. E-mail from Jennifer Kemp Andrews, October 22, 2014.
93. "Chuck Colson Eulogy for Jack Kemp," https://www.youtube.com/watch?v=aMkFj4oehCs.
94. Washington National Cathedral, Memorial Service for Jack Kemp, http://www.nationalcathedral.org/events/kemp090508.shtml#.VFcicvTF9ts.
95. Albert R. Hunt, "U.S. Conservatives Lose an Optimist," *New York Times,* May 10, 2009.
96. Clarence Page, "The GOP Should Have Listened," *Chicago Tribune,* May 6, 2009.
97. Michael Gerson, "Head and Heart," *Washington Post,* May 4, 2009.

98. "Capitalist for the Common Man," *Wall Street Journal*, May 4, 2009.
99. Editorial, "Today's GOP Could Use a Jack Kemp," *Dallas Morning News*, May 6, 2009.

Chapter 13: Legacy

1. Rich Lowry, "Where Is Today's Jack Kemp?," *Jewish World Review*, March 22, 2013.
2. Sam Tanenhaus, "Note to Republicans: Channel Jack Kemp," *New York Times,* April 5, 2004, http://www.nytimes.com/2014/04/06/sunday-review/note-to-republicans-channel-jack-kemp.html?_r=o.
3. Vin Weber interview, December 3, 2012.
4. Kemp, "Time for a Supply-Side Revival," Townhall.com, December 19, 2005.
5. Paul Ryan, interview with authors, February 6, 2014.
6. Ibid.
7. Scott Reed interview, September 18, 2014.
8. Marco Rubio interview, October 7, 2014.
9. Rubio speech, December 4, 2012.
10. *Howey Politics Indiana,* November 13, 2014, 7.
11. Steve Moore interview, December 2, 2014.
12. Larry Kudlow interview, December 8, 2011.
13. Peter Wehner interview, August 14, 2014.
14. "Room to Grow: Conservative Reform for a Limited Government and a Thriving Middle Class," YGNetwork.org.
15. Shikha Dalmia, "Reform Conservatism Won't End the Liberal Welfare State, It'll Reinvent It," Reason.com, http://reason.com/archives/2015/02/18/reform-conservatism-wont-end-the-liberal.
16. Larry Lindsey interview with Fred Barnes, October 14, 2014.

Index

AARP, 310
ABC, 24, 106, 198, 248, 284
ABC polls, 198, 267, 274, 277
abolitionism, 202
abortion, 252, 298
Adams, Paul, 225
affirmative action, 272, 273–74, 275, 282, 297
Afghanistan, 300
  Soviet occupation of, 1, 178
AFL-CIO, 27, 51, 61, 158, 199
Africa, 1, 178
African Americans, 4, 61, 82–83, 197, 222–25,
    229, 257, 277, 323
  as athletes, 217, 222, 320
  Republican Party and, 3, 9, 128, 207–8, 297
  support for JK among, 56
  voting of, 142, 221, 275, 299, 309, 313
  see also civil rights movement; racial
    integration; racism
African National Congress (ANC), 191
Ahearn, Rick, 122, 124–27, 223, 275, 286
Aid to Families with Dependent Children
  (AFDC), 9–10
Airborne Warning and Control System
  (AWACS), 175–76
Air Force One, 266
Albright, Madeleine, 301, 303
Alexander, Lamar, 213, 260–61, 265
Al Qaeda, 178, 300, 304
Amer-I-Can, 249
American Dream, 7, 88, 222, 224, 290,
  315–16
American Enterprise Institute (AEI), 37, 39,
  113, 142
American Football League (AFL), 20–24,
  123, 290
  All-Star game of, 217

NFL merger with, 23, 248–49
  racial discrimination in, 4, 21, 23, 217
American Football League Players
  Association, 4, 23, 24, 27
American Israel Public Affairs Committee
  (AIPAC), 241
*American Renaissance, An: A Strategy for the
  1980s* (Kemp), 59
American Revolution, 202
Americans for Tax Reform, 297
American University (Moscow), 175
Ames, Iowa, 201–2, 203–4
Anderson, John, 74–75
Anderson, Martin, 41, 57, 64–66, 74, 84, 86–87,
  101, 135–36
Andrews, Jennifer Kemp (daughter), 111, 330
  childhood and adolescence of, 28, 97, 105
  JK and, 105, 206, 216, 315–16
Andropov, Yuri, 194
Angola, 178, 188–90
Anti-Ballistic Missile Treaty, 186
anticommunism, 188–89
Anti-Defamation League, 276
anti-Semitism, 202, 276–77, 302
Arab-Israeli conflict, 175–78, 302, 303
Arafat, Yasir, 303
Archer, William, 297
Arias, Oscar, 180–81
Arizona, 31, 265
Arkansas, 45, 277
Arledge, Roone, 24
Armey, Dick, 261, 309
arms control, 76, 171, 172, 183–88, 190, 193
arms race, 183–85
Armstrong, William, 53, 95, 213
Army, U.S., 120
  JK's service in, 19

Arnett, Grace-Marie, 262
Arnett, Jon, 19
Ash-Shiraa, 181
Asian Americans, 222
Atlantic Coast Conference, 109
Atlantic Monthly, 100, 322
Atwater, Lee, 169
Azar, Rick, 23

Baker, Howard, 57, 197–98, 213, 215
Baker, James, 90, 111, 130, 136–37, 219,
    250–51, 268
  as chief of staff, 84, 92, 101–2, 132–34, 190
  as secretary of state, 111, 240–42
  as treasury secretary, 158–60, 162–63, 166,
    173, 200
Baker, Susan, 111, 242
Baltimore, Md., 74, 222–23
Baltimore Colts, 20, 23, 248
Baltimore Sun, 6
Barak, Ehud, 303
Barbour, Haley, 281
Bare Knuckles and Back Rooms (Rollins), 208
Barnes, Barbara, 6
Barnes, Fred, 6
Barnes, Karen, 6
Barnett, Bob, 330
Bartlett, Bruce, 39, 43, 45, 52, 267, 329
Baseball Hall of Fame, 81
Beatrice/Hunt-Wesson Foods, 311
Begin, Menachem, 176, 177
Beirut, 176, 185
Bell, Jeffrey, 49, 55–56, 57–58, 62, 73, 152, 206,
    262, 280, 329–30
Bellanca, Al, 26
Bennett, Bill, 10, 215, 252, 255–56, 268–69,
    278, 283
Bennett, Elayne, 215
Bentsen, Lloyd, 212–13
Berlin Wall, fall of, 314, 321
Berman, Wayne, 273–75, 276–77, 280, 283, 287
Bernstein, Leonard, 314
Bethesda, Md., 38, 105, 150, 293, 311, 314
Bethlehem Steel, 27
Bible, 6, 216
Biden, Joe, 306
Billington, James, 329

Billmire, Richard, 69, 117–18, 120–21, 175
bin Laden, Osama, 303
Black, Charlie, 199, 201, 205–6, 210–12,
    218–19, 250
Blixseth, Tim, 292
Bob Jones University, 128
Boeing, 10, 131
Boland, Edward, 180
Bond, Rich, 249
Booker, Cory, 320
Book of Virtues, The (Bennett), 256
Bork, Robert, 202
Boston Globe, 204–5, 275–76
Boston Patriots, 290
Botchan, Ron, 314
Bradley, Bill, 95
  basketball career of, 151, 156
  as "father" of tax code reform, 151–60, 164,
    168–69
  JK and, 154–57, 164
Bradley-Gephardt tax bill, 151–55
Brady, Ed, 122–23, 125–26, 242–43, 245,
    249–50, 281
Breen, Jon, 67–68
Bretton Woods Conference of 1944, 144
Brezhnev, Leonid, 183, 193–94, 197
Brock, Bill, 32, 46–47, 49, 56, 69, 72, 80
Broder, David, 142, 214, 251, 272, 306–7
Brodhead, William, 91
Brodie, John, 20
Brookings Institution, 160
Brooks, John, 74
Brown, Carolyn, 329
Brown, Jim, 248–49, 314
Brownback, Sam, 324
Bryan, William Jennings, 145
Buchanan, Patrick, 189, 192, 203, 234–35, 245,
    260–61, 264–65, 267
Buckley, John, 203–4, 209–11, 214, 270,
    278–79
  on JK, 119, 128, 192, 199, 201, 207,
    209–10, 216
Buckley, Reid, 279–81, 283–85
Buckley, William F., 249, 279
budgets, 92
  balancing of, 39–40, 50, 60, 64, 80, 87,
    92–93, 99–100, 295

Buffalo, N.Y., 6, 22–23, 25–27, 31, 57, 59, 60, 63, 97, 105, 125, 139, 141, 170, 214, 265, 273, 274
  blue-collar suburbs of, 29
  War Memorial Stadium in, 26
Buffalo, University of, 274
Buffalo Bills, 20–24
  AFL championships of, 22, 23, 24
  JK as quarterback with, 4, 21–24, 25, 26, 47, 88, 105, 109, 217
Buffalo Courier Express, 92, 119
Buffalo Evening News, 119
Buffalo News, 22, 24, 283
Buoniconti, Nick, 290
Bush, Barbara, 203, 215, 218, 223
Bush, George H. W., 53, 57, 67–68, 139, 169, 191, 192
  as CIA director, 72, 197
  JK's political relationship with, 218–21, 230–32, 234, 241–45
  military service of, 197
  Points of Light program of, 220
  presidency of, 5, 111, 181, 216, 218–21, 224, 227, 230–37, 239, 241–51, 259, 302
  presidential campaigns and election of, 196–204, 206–7, 211–16, 218, 219, 221, 233–35, 249–51, 265, 299
  "Read My Lips" promise of, 221, 233–34
  speeches of, 221, 231, 233–35, 244, 246, 250
  as vice president, 88, 90, 196–98, 203
Bush, George W., 253
  JK's endorsement of, 298–99, 300
  "Ownership Society" agenda of, 309
  presidency of, 289, 291, 303–5, 307–12, 323
  presidential campaigns of, 280, 298–300, 308–9
  as Texas governor, 286, 298
Bush, Jeb, 324–25, 327
Butler, Stuart, 76

Calgary Stampeders, 20
California, 3, 4, 14–18, 20, 25–26, 33, 76, 112, 118, 136, 239, 245, 272–74
  Proposition 13 of, 49
  Proposition 187 of, 5, 256–57, 264, 273
  Proposition 209 of, 273–74
California, University of, at Los Angeles (UCLA), 17

Call the Briefing (Fitzwater), 241, 249
Campbell, Carroll, 268
Camp David, 52, 131, 138, 192
Canada, 20, 36, 291
Canadian Football League (CFL), 20, 108
Cannon, Frank, 212
Cannon, Lou, 101, 190
Cannon, Mary Brunette, 128, 225–27, 230–32, 244
capitalism, 4
  democratic, 1, 2, 103, 194, 228
Capitalism and Freedom (Friedman), 25, 119
Carter, Jimmy, 42, 84
  "malaise" speech of, 71
  1980 campaign of, 68, 71, 73–77
  presidency of, 1, 30, 51–53, 60, 68, 71, 75–77, 99, 132, 142–43, 149, 175, 179, 183–84
Case, Clifford, 49, 58
Casey, William, 179, 190
Castine, Michael, 123
Catholic Conference, U.S., 297
Cato Institute, 325
CBS, 55, 139, 182, 214
CBS/*New York Times* poll, 274
Center for Neighborhood Enterprise, 323
Central America, 1, 106, 178–79, 181, 188, 289–90
Central Intelligence Agency (CIA), 72, 179, 180, 189, 193, 197
Chamber of Commerce, U.S., 31, 51, 131–32, 152, 163
Charles, Prince of Wales, 97, 124
Chavez, Hugo, 292
Cheney, Richard, 37, 166, 268
  vice presidency of, 299, 303, 305, 308
Chernenko, Konstantin, 194
Chertoff, Michael, 279
Chicago, Ill., 36, 61, 133, 157, 277, 313
  Cabrini-Green project in, 223
  South Side, 275
Chicago, University of, 34, 35, 36
Chicago Tribune, 318
China, 72, 197, 298, 305
  one child policy of, 171, 174
Choice, The (Woodward), 268
Chowder and Marching (C&M) Club, 32, 82
Christianity, 315, 316
  born-again, 106

Christian Right, 299

Christian Science, 4, 15–16, 18, 20, 216

Churchill, Winston, 111, 206, 252, 265, 273, 274, 315, 317

Churchill High School, 105, 107, 109

Cisneros, Henry, 297, 311–12

Citizens for a Sound Economy, 309

Civil Rights Act of 1964, 310

civil rights movement, 46, 309

    JK's commitment to, 3, 4, 21, 23, 82, 157, 190–91, 202, 217–18, 222, 257, 313, 317–18, 320

"Clair de Lune" (Debussy), 106

Claremont McKenna College, 293

Clark, Dick, 188

Clark, William, 176, 179, 190

Clark Amendment, 188

class warfare, 309

Cleveland Browns, 248–49

climate change, 297–98

Clinton, Bill:

    ethical problems and scandals of, 5, 277–79, 284–85, 295–96

    foreign policy of, 300–303

    impeachment of, 295–96

    presidency of, 5, 252, 254–55, 257–59, 261, 263, 266–67, 277–79, 281–82, 294–98, 300–303, 309, 312

    presidential campaigns of, 231–32, 247, 250–51, 253, 267, 270, 273, 277–79, 281–82, 284–86, 299

Clinton, Hillary:

    health-care plan of, 254

    law practice of, 277

CNBC, 325

CNN, 244

CNN/ORC (Opinion Research Corporation), 7

Coats, Dan, 2, 80–81, 83, 107, 140, 191, 274, 288, 314

Coats, Marsha, 81

Coca-Cola Bottling Company, 311

Cohen, William, 301

Cold War, 10, 300, 323

College National Republican Committee, 214–15

Collier, Amy, 330

Colorado, 53, 95, 100, 213

Colson, Chuck, 106, 316–17

Columbus Realty Trust, 290

Commentary, 119

Commerce Department, U.S., 240

communism, 173, 178, 183, 186, 187, 193

Community Renewal Project, 297

Conable, Barber, 95, 99

Conable-Hance bill, 95, 96–97

Conda, Cesar, 325

Conference of Presidents, 277

Congress, U.S., 10, 26–34

    see also House of Representatives, U.S.: Senate, U.S.

Congressional Black Caucus, 142, 174

Congressional Budget Office, 295, 326

Congressional Club, 203

Congressional Record, 100, 103

Congressional Research Service, 48–49

Conservative Caucus, 191

Conservative Opportunity Society (COS), 139–41

Conservative Political Action Conference (CPAC) of 1987, 192, 202–3

conservativism, 5, 6, 25, 30, 31, 198, 218, 235

    "compassionate," 142, 172, 228, 298, 323

    populist, 228

    progressive, 252

    reform, 325

Constitution, U.S., 160, 202

    First Amendment of, 281

Constitution of Liberty, The (Hayek), 25, 119

Contras, 106, 178–81, 190

    JK's support for, 178, 180

    U.S. aid to, 178–81

    see also Iran-Contra scandal

Coopers and Lybrand, 262

Cranston-Gonzales Act of 1990, 239

Crocker, Chester, 189–90

Cuba, 1, 178, 179

Cuomo, Mario, 228

Dal Col, Bill, 237, 249, 250, 253, 263, 280

Dallas, Tex., 21, 147–48, 271, 285

Dallas Cowboys, 109, 290

Dallas Morning News, 197, 318

Dallas Texans, 22

D'Amato, Alfonse, 69, 308

Danforth, John, 213
Daniels, Mitch, 201
Dao, V. P., 330
Darman, Richard, 84, 97, 148, 151, 158–63, 166, 230–35, 242–43, 248
  JK and, 220, 230–32, 235–37, 245, 247, 250–51
Dartmouth College, 107, 109
d'Aubuisson, Roberto, 179
Deaver, Mike, 70, 89, 101, 134
Declaration of Independence, 4, 71
DeLay, Tom, 297
DelliBovi, Al, 225–27, 246
democracy, 9, 33, 175, 281, 306
  capitalism and, 1, 2, 193, 194, 228
Democratic Congressional Campaign Committee, 170
Democratic Leadership Council, 253
Democratic National Committee (DNC), 278, 285
Democratic National Convention:
  of 1980, 73–74
  of 1984, 147, 152, 228
  of 1988, 213
  of 1996, 277
Democratic Party, 1, 3, 8, 25, 26–27, 43, 71, 99, 152
  African Americans in, 277
  conservative wing of, 54, 94–95
  liberal wing of, 9, 91
Denny, Reginald, 245
DeParle, Jason, 232
Depression, Great, 14, 34, 129, 138, 312
Detroit, Mich., 58–59, 69, 72
Detroit Lions, JK as quarterback of, 5–6, 18
Deukmejian, George, 213
Devine, Sam, 79
Devroy, Ann, 244–45
Diefenderfer, William, 168
Dixon, Julian, 142
Dole, Bob, 5, 6, 57, 84, 94, 148, 153, 159, 168, 174–75, 257–58, 260–61
  animosity between JK and, 13, 60, 111, 132–33, 135, 137, 149, 174, 198, 251, 272, 284
  JK as running mate of, 271–87
  1988 presidential and vice presidential campaign of, 196–206, 211–13, 265
  1996 presidential campaign of, 263–87, 323
  as Senate majority leader, 259, 267
  war injury of, 198
Dole, Elizabeth, 111, 198, 213, 270–71, 312
Dole, Kenny, 278
dollars, 2, 209
  gold standard and, 8, 144–46, 192
  printing of, 34, 35–36
  see also money supply
Domenici, Pete, 84, 92, 132, 213, 261
Domitrovic, Brian, 330
Doonesbury, 197
Dorgan, Byron, 142
dos Santos, José Eduardo, 190
dot-com bust, 291
Dowd, Maureen, 272
Downey, Tom, 141–42
drugs, 257
  dealing in, 224
Duarte, José Napoleón, 179, 181
Dubenion, Elbert "Duby," 23
Dukakis, Michael, 212
DuPont, Pierre, 203, 205, 211

Eagle Forum, 203
Economic Club of New York, 262
Economic Empowerment Task Force, 235, 237
Economic Growth and Tax Relief Act of 2001 (EGTRA), 307
Economic Recovery and Tax Act of 1981 (ERTA), 98
  see also Kemp-Roth tax bill
economics:
  austerity, 61, 87, 99
  JK's intellectual revolution in, 29
  "trickle-down," 44, 101, 283
  "voodoo," 68, 72, 197
  see also Keynes, John Maynard; supply-side economics
Eddy, Mary Baker, 216
education:
  apprenticeship programs in, 327
  poor results of, 8
  school selection in, 9
Education Department, U.S., 246, 282
Edwards, Mickey, 194
Eisenhower, Dwight D., 34

elections, U.S.:
of 1932, 15, 59
of 1960, 272
of 1964, 25, 27
of 1968, 57
of 1970, 26–28
of 1974, 46, 195
of 1976, 40–42, 46, 47, 57, 60, 62, 66, 69, 198, 271
of 1978, 49–50, 53, 54, 80, 81
of 1980, 2, 5, 26, 53, 55–59, 62–78, 83, 90, 184, 196, 198
of 1982, 58, 85, 139
of 1984, 147–50, 152, 154, 157, 184
of 1986, 170
of 1988, 2, 5, 6, 26, 53, 69, 117, 128, 129, 149, 167, 169, 182, 192, 194–216, 219, 265, 311, 323
of 1992, 5, 215, 231–32, 235, 244, 245, 248, 249–51
of 1994, 254, 260, 263
of 1996, 5, 111, 175, 237, 251, 252–55, 257–60, 262–87, 293–95, 301, 323
of 2000, 280, 286, 293, 294, 298–300
of 2004, 280, 308–9
of 2008, 312–13
of 2010, 323
of 2012, 142
Electronic Industries Association, 93
Elizabeth II, Queen of England, 223, 318
Ellison, Larry, 290
Ellsworth, Robert, 267–68
El Salvador, 179, 181
Emancipation Proclamation, 5
Empower America, 252–56, 263, 281, 289, 291, 301, 302, 309, 322
Engler, John, 268
Ethics and Public Policy Center, 325
Evans, Michael, 51
Evans, Rowland, 56, 62
Evans, Tommy, 70
Evans and Novak, 56, 62, 84, 86, 87, 136–37, 161, 167, 200–201, 212, 242, 244, 251
Exxon, 10, 131

Face the Nation, 139, 182
Fahrenkopf, Frank, 259
Fair and Simple Tax (FAST) bill, 153–55

Fairfax High School, 17
Falwell, Jerry, 135, 202
Family and Medical Leave Act of 1993, 282
Farrakhan, Louis, 275–77, 301, 302
Fauntroy, Walter, 142
Federal Bureau of Investigation (FBI), 225, 278, 283, 284
Federal Election Commission, 211–12, 258
Federal Housing Administration, 312
Federal Reserve, 34, 35, 48, 84, 98–99, 129, 136, 142, 146–47, 240, 259, 297, 312
Open Market Committee of (FOMC), 147
Felser, Larry, 24, 25
Fenwick, Millicent, 52
Fernandez, Raul, 289–90, 314
Feulner, Ed, 274–75, 276, 279–80
"Filegate" scandal, 278, 284
Findley, Paul, 52
Fiscal Integrity Act (proposed), 39
Fisher, Tim, 330
Fitzwater, Marlin, 241, 244, 247, 249, 250
Flaherty, Tom, 27
Florida, 290, 300, 323–24
food stamps, 9–10, 131
Forbes, 290
Forbes, Malcolm, 262
Forbes, Steve, 253, 255, 260–61, 262–66, 272, 298–99
Ford, Gerald R., 40–43, 55, 60, 62, 72, 197, 198, 249, 271
presidency of, 30–32, 37, 53, 74, 77, 188
Forstmann, Ted, 253
Fortune, 40, 51–52, 56–57
Forward, 301–2
Foss, Joe, 22
Foster, Vince, 277
Foundation for Economic Education (FEE), 25
Fourth Presbyterian Church, 105, 316
Fox, Richard, 210
Foxman, Abe, 276
Frazier, Alice, 223
FreedomWorks, 309
Free Market Petroleum LLC, 292
Friedman, Milton, 25, 29, 119, 145, 151
Full Employment and Balanced Growth Act, 47–49
Fund for American Studies, 117

Gallup polls, 169, 204, 286
Garcia, Robert, 76, 142
Gates, Robert, 193
gay rights, 252
Georgia, 51, 53, 81, 96, 141
Gephardt, Dick, 151–53, 158–60
Gergen, David, 53–54, 84
Germany, Federal Republic of, 183, 184
Gerson, Michael, 253, 318
Gifford, Frank, 20
Gilchrist, Cookie, 23, 106, 217
Gilder, George, 90
Gillman, Sid, 20–22
Gingrich, Newt, 7, 53, 256, 257, 260–61,
    266–67, 278, 330
  Contract with America proposed by, 258–59
  JK and, 2, 34, 81, 106, 139–41, 147, 166, 191,
    198, 234, 265, 294–96
  as Speaker of the House, 140, 294–96
Glen, Alixe, 286
global warming, 298
gold standard, 8, 9, 10, 144–46, 148, 192,
    208–9, 276
Goldwater, Barry, 25, 27, 70, 255, 310
Gonzales, Henry, 239
Gorbachev, Mikhail, 169, 186–88, 192, 194, 241
Gore, Al, 302–3, 305
  JK's debate with, 5, 111, 142, 279–84, 286
  presidential campaign of, 299
  vice presidency of, 5, 142, 254, 270,
    276–81, 298
Graham, Clifford, 292
Gramm, Phil, 93, 99, 257, 260–61, 266
Gramm-Latta bills, 93–94, 95
Gray, Kimi, 219, 239
Great Society, 35, 144, 220, 238, 247
Greenfield, Meg, 88
Greenspan, Alan, 51, 74, 146, 297, 306
Gregg, Judd, 279–80
Greider, William, 100–101
Grenada, 183, 185
Gulf War, 231, 251, 300, 305

Habitat for Humanity, 292, 293
Haig, Al, 203
Haiti, 174
Hall, Robert, 150, 260–61, 262

Hamdoun, Nizar, 302
Hance, Kent, 95
Hannaford, Peter, 58
Hart, Gary, 100
Harvard University, 86, 151, 231
Hastert, Dennis, 297
Hatch, Orrin, 202
Hawkins, Augustus "Gus," 47–48
Hayek, Friedrich, 25, 29, 119
Head Start, 203, 255, 282, 326
Health and Human Services Department,
    U.S., 246
health-care insurance, 7, 319
health-care system, 8, 254, 258
Heisman Trophy, 24
Heller, Walter, 35, 43
Helms, Jesse, 188, 203, 300
Hensley, Travis, 329
Heritage Foundation, 76, 187, 207, 228, 253, 274
Heritage Review, 207
Hezbollah, 176, 181, 182
Hilton, Barron, 21
Hinckley, John, Jr., 91
Hispanics, 9, 197, 208, 223, 229, 256, 275, 290–91
  voting of, 142, 299
Hitler, Adolf, 180, 185, 303
Hogan, Larry, 324
Hollywood, Calif., 14–15, 61
Holocaust, 176, 180, 302
Holt, Marjorie, 49, 51
Home Ownership for People Everywhere
    (HOPE), 233, 235, 236, 239–40, 248
Honduras, 174, 180
Hooks, Benjamin, 221
Hoover, Herbert, 3, 60, 62, 196, 297
Hoover Institution, 260–61
Hoppe, David, 116, 117, 118–20, 166, 192, 210–11,
    213–15, 329
House of Representatives, U.S., 10, 39–42, 226
  Appropriations Committee of, 51, 78, 172,
    175, 238
  bills introduced by JK in, 31–32, 39, 40,
    43–54
  Budget Committee of, 42–43, 78, 92, 172,
    253, 322
  Defense and International Affairs
    subcommittee of, 78

House of Representatives, U.S. (*cont.*)
　Democratic members of, 47, 49–50, 53, 80,
　　92–93, 96, 99, 134, 138, 179, 184
　Ethics Committee of, 294
　Government Operations investigative
　　subcommittee of, 227
　JK's career in, 1–2, 5–6, 10, 28–34, 38–54,
　　59–60, 78–83, 88–105, 113–19, 128–49,
　　172–74, 289–91, 319
　JK's retirement from, 66, 219
　Judiciary Committee of, 296
　Republican members of, 43–46, 49, 73,
　　77–78, 80, 96, 129, 132, 133–34, 137–38,
　　149, 159, 170, 173, 243, 286, 320, 326
　Rules Committee of, 52, 164, 166–67
　Ways and Means Committee of, 32, 45, 49,
　　88, 91, 95, 96, 133, 159, 162, 167, 253,
　　297, 322
House Republican Conference, 75, 86, 114,
　163, 172, 324
Housing & Urban Development Department
　(HUD), 218–28, 311
　funding of, 225, 232, 237–40
　headquarters of, 221, 226–27
　JK as secretary of, 5, 6, 8, 111, 116, 117,
　　120–24, 216, 219–49, 255, 263, 275, 323
　JK's reform of, 227–28, 238
　JK's retirement from, 252–53, 292
　morale at, 226–27
　Office of Public Affairs in, 238
　scandal, mismanagement, and corruption
　　in, 224–26, 238
Houston, Tex., 21, 249
Houston, University of, 21
Houston Oilers, 21
Howey Politics Indiana, 324
Hubbell, Webb, 277
HUD Reform Act of 1989, 227, 239
Human Action (Mises), 25, 119
Human Events, 119
human rights, 174, 180, 202
Humbert, Thomas, 233
Hume, Brit, 106, 248
Hume, Kim, 106
Humphrey, Hubert, 3, 47–48, 142
Humphrey-Hawkins bill, 47–48
Hunt, Albert, 106, 138, 317–18

Hunter, Larry, 302, 305
Hurricane Katrina, 310
Hussein, Saddam, 289, 300–305
Hyde, Henry, 166

Illinois, 44, 52, 74, 140, 166, 324
immigration, 8, 274, 298
　illegal, 297, 310
　reform of, 9, 289, 310, 322, 324–25, 326
Index of Leading Cultural Indicators, 256
India, 298, 305
Individual Retirement Accounts (IRAs), 155,
　243–44, 307, 308
inflation, 1, 29–30, 31–32, 35, 39, 51–52, 143–47
　curbing of, 34, 37, 47–48, 60, 62, 89, 132,
　145–46
Inter-American Development Bank, 174
interest rates, 34, 93, 99, 146
Intermediate-Range Nuclear Forces (INF)
　Treaty, 187–88, 203
Internal Revenue Service (IRS), 113, 153, 294
International Football Association, 103
International Longshoremen's Association, 8,
　60–61
International Monetary Fund (IMF), 172–73
Iowa, 174, 200–202, 205, 208
　caucuses of, 67, 200, 204–5, 265
Iran, 170, 301
　American hostages held in, 1
　terrorism sponsored by, 176, 181
　U.S. arms sale to, 170, 180, 181–82
Iran-Contra scandal, 180, 181–82, 196
Iraq, 302–6, 308
　nuclear facility destroyed in, 175
　regime change in, 301
　sectarian civil war in, 306
Iraq Liberation Act of 1998, 300–301
Iraq War, 242, 310
　JK's opposition to, 289, 303–6, 323
　U.S. victory in, 234
IRS vs. the People, The (Kemp and Forbes,
　eds.), 298
"Isaiah's Job" (Nock), 322
Israel, 120, 276, 302, 313
　Palestinian rocket attacks on, 176, 303
　U.S. relations with, 175–78, 241, 303
　see also Arab-Israeli conflict

Israeli Air Force, 175
Israeli Army, 176
Italian Americans, 23

Jack Kemp Foundation, 6
Jaruzelski, Wojciech, 175
Javits, Jacob, 55, 58, 69
Jefferson, Thomas, 301
Jeffords, Jim, 97
Jerusalem, East, 303
Jerusalem Post, 177
Jesus Christ, 39
Jews, 175, 241, 276–77, 302, 317
   Soviet, 171, 174
Jindal, Bobby, 324
jobs, 145, 326–27
   creation of, 30, 31, 34, 169, 219, 224
Jobs and Growth Tax Relief Act of 2003
   (JGTRA), 307
Jobs Creation Act of 2004, 40, 43–44, 73
Job Training Partnership Act of 1982, 214–15
John Paul II, Pope, 128
Johnson, Lyndon B., 27, 35–36, 220, 272
Joint Congressional Committee on Taxation,
   98, 154
Jones, Jim, 92, 96
Jones, Paula, 277, 284
Jordan, Vernon, 223
Justice Department, U.S., 182, 225

Kansas, 198, 251, 271–72, 324
   Russell County Courthouse in, 272
Kansas City Chiefs, 22
Kasten, Bob, 148, 153–55, 158–60
Keane, James, 170
Kearns, David, 246
Keating, Frank, 225, 227, 268
Kemp, Dick (brother), 16, 20
Kemp, Elva (grandmother), 15–16, 217–18
Kemp, Frances (mother), 4, 14–16, 20, 104, 216
Kemp, Jack:
   "American Idea" of, 71–72
   bipartisanship of, 141–42
   "bleeding heart" predilections of, 6, 172,
      218, 288–89, 298, 320
   cancer diagnosis of, 314–15
   celebrity of, 27, 28, 32, 53, 54, 105, 121, 231–32

childhood and adolescence of, 4, 13, 14–18,
   28, 111, 217
corporate board memberships of, 289, 290–92
courage of, 139, 147–49, 317
debating of, 5, 11, 25, 27, 142, 157, 218,
   279–84, 286
education of, 4, 17–19, 24, 156
fatherhood and family life of, 15, 16, 28, 97,
   103–12, 114, 120, 289
final illness and death of, 110, 123, 156,
   315–16, 319
football career of, 3, 4, 5–6, 7, 10, 13–14,
   16–28, 32–33, 70, 72, 83, 88, 102, 105, 109,
   111, 123, 156, 195, 210, 217, 219, 222, 238,
   248–49, 272, 273, 289, 291, 318, 321
football injuries of, 13, 21–22, 24, 313, 316
foreign and defense policies of, 5, 10, 141,
   171–94, 240–41, 300–303
grandchildren of, 110, 293, 313–15, 317
homosexual rumors about, 25–26
income and wealth of, 24, 82, 253, 258,
   288–90, 292–93
inner circle and political team of, 33–34,
   79–83, 92, 102, 104, 112–27, 150, 280–81
"JFK-grams" of, 104, 109–10, 111, 317
leadership and influence of, 4, 8, 13–14, 17,
   22, 23, 28–29, 33, 77, 79–80, 82, 83, 94,
   104, 170, 173, 199, 263, 293, 317–18, 320,
   324, 327
Medal of Freedom awarded to, 318
memorial service of, 316–17
military service of, 19
1988 presidential campaign of, 5, 6, 26, 128,
   129, 149, 167, 169, 182, 192, 194–212, 216,
   260, 311, 323
1996 vice presidential campaign of, 5, 175,
   237, 271–88, 290–91, 293, 294, 301, 323
pro-life record of, 199, 202
property of, 20, 26, 105, 107, 292–93
religious background and belief of, 4,
   15–16, 18, 20, 216, 315
speeches of, 8, 10, 25, 26, 31, 33, 41, 50, 59,
   60, 62, 68, 69–72, 80, 93, 97, 119–20, 122,
   128, 148, 161, 164, 185, 187, 208, 213–14,
   228–30, 243, 249–50, 253, 258, 273, 274,
   286, 291, 314
transformative legacy of, 1, 3, 319–27

Kemp, Jack (*cont.*)
    voter appeal of, 56–57, 60–61
    "wilderness years" of, 252–53, 257, 266, 289
Kemp, Jack (uncle), 14
Kemp, Jeff (son), 314, 330
    childhood and adolescence of, 28, 104–6, 109
    football career of, 104, 105, 109, 120
    on JK, 14, 16, 104, 106, 107, 109, 317
    JK's relationship with, 258, 259–60, 273, 315
Kemp, Jennifer (daughter), *see* Andrews,
    Jennifer Kemp
Kemp, Jimmy (son), 292, 313–14, 330
    childhood and adolescence of, 28, 97, 104,
        105, 107–9
    football career of, 108–9, 120, 211, 214,
        291, 317
    on JK, 104, 107–8, 289, 291, 296, 298, 314, 317
Kemp, Joanne Main (wife), 38, 39, 63, 81, 83,
        87–88, 90, 171, 215, 218, 242, 243, 292, 330
    courtship and marriage of, 19
    JK's relationship with, 16, 18–19, 28, 97,
        104–5, 107, 111, 126, 219, 259, 269–70, 272,
        280, 286, 289, 313–16
    political activism of, 27, 104, 174
    prayer and study groups of, 6, 104
Kemp, Judith (daughter), *see* Nolan, Judith
    Kemp
Kemp, Paul (father), 4, 14–16
Kemp, Paul, Jr. (brother), 14–16
    on JK, 16, 21, 311
Kemp, Tom (brother), 16–17, 210–11, 311
Kemp, Willard (uncle), 14
Kemp-Kasten tax bill, *see* Fair and Simple Tax
    (FAST) bill
Kemp Partners, 292
Kemp-Roth tax bill, 2, 44–56, 58–63, 65–68,
    70, 73–78, 80, 85–86, 91, 96, 98, 101,
    170, 263
    opposition to, 76–77, 92, 142
    watering down of, 89, 94
Kennedy, Edward M., 3, 68, 214–15, 305,
    310, 318
Kennedy, John F., 2, 8, 208, 272
    assassination of, 35
    economic policy of, 35, 40, 43–46, 49, 61, 67,
    97, 262
Keogh accounts, 155

Kerry, John, presidential campaign of, 308–9
Keynes, John Maynard, 2, 6, 9, 34–35, 39,
    48–49, 61, 117, 307, 321, 325
Kilpatrick, James J., 57–58
King, Coretta Scott, 222
King, Don, 314
King, Martin Luther, III, 301
King, Martin Luther, Jr., 222, 224, 272, 273, 317
    birthday celebration of, 142, 203
King, Rodney, 231, 245
Kirkland, Lane, 27
Kirkpatrick, Jeane, 106, 179, 188, 190, 252,
    256, 311
Kissinger, Henry, 70
Kissinger Commission, 289
Klein, Herb, 25
Koch, Ed, 241, 257
Kohl, Helmut, 183, 184
Kondracke, Morton, 6–7
Korean War, Inchon landing in, 85
Kristol, Gertrude Himmelfarb "Bea," 106
Kristol, Irving, 2, 30, 37, 55, 56, 119, 152,
    158, 327
    JK's relationship with, 106, 112, 135, 304
Kudlow, Lawrence, 98–99, 325
Kyoto treaty, 297–98

labor force, 7–8, 262
    blue-collar, 29, 46, 67
    JK's support of, 27, 30, 31, 83
labor unions, 31, 46, 60–61, 158, 175, 218
    collective bargaining of, 27, 56, 60
Ladd, Ernie, 28
LaFalce, John, 141–42
Laffer, Arthur, 2, 31, 34, 36–38, 41–42, 44–45,
    49, 63, 74, 87, 101–2, 149
Laffer curve, 37, 38, 67, 106
LaHaye, Tim, 202
Lamonica, Daryle, 23, 27
Lantos, Tom, 227
Latta, Delbert, 93
Laxalt, Paul, 64–65, 67, 135
Layne, Bobby, 18
League of Women Voters, 76
Leahy, Frank, 20, 27
Lebanon, 176–77
    U.S. hostages in, 170, 181, 182

Lee, Mike, 325–26
Lehrer, Jim, 280–81
Lehrman, Lew, 42, 65, 84–85, 87, 152
Leonhardt, David, 306–7
Leonsis, Ted, 290
Levitas, Elliott, 96–97
Lewinsky, Monica, 295–96
Lewis, Ann, 273
Lewis, C. S., 111
Lewis, John, 222
Liberal Party, *53*
liberals, 3, 6, 9, 30, 54, 193, 221, 237–38
"Liberal Welfare State," 140
libertarianism, 43, 323
Library of Congress, 6, 43, 118–19
Likud Party, 178
Lincoln, Abraham, 214, 273, 281, 313, 315–17
    Emancipation Proclamation of, *5*, 128
    Republican Party and, 3–5, 9, 216, 221–22, 264
    "right to rise" principle of, 4, 71, 218, 325
Lindsey, Larry, 326
Livingston, Bob, 32
Lodge, Henry Cabot, 3
Long, Russell, 159
Los Angeles, Calif., 14–18, 68, 84–86, 89, 124,
    245–49, 275, 278
    Crips and Bloods gangs in, 249
    1992 riots in, 231, 237, 245–48
    Pacific Palisades neighborhood of, 62
Los Angeles Chargers, *see* San Diego Chargers
Los Angeles International Airport (LAX),
    65–66, 67
Los Angeles Rams, 18, 19, 109
Los Angeles Times, 135, 205, 278
Lott, Trent, 2, 82–83, 106, 117, 128, 140, 148,
    161, 164–67, 258
Lott, Tricia, 83
Louisiana, 32, 324
Lowry, Rich, 319
Lozansky, Edward, 174–75
Lozansky, Tatiana, 174–75
Lugar, Richard, 268
Lungren, Dan, 33, 80, 140

MacArthur, Douglas, 85
McCain, John, 268, 298–99, 310
    2008 presidential campaign of, 312–13

McCarthy, Max, 26–27
McFarlane, Robert, 180
McGrory, Mary, 283
Mack, Connie, 81
Mack, Connie, III, 2, 81–82, 106, 140, 268
Mackey, John, 23, 248–49
McLaughlin, Ann, 268
McLaughlin Group, 6
Madison, James, 162
Maguire, Paul, 21
Maimonides, 208, 209
Manchester Union Leader, 205
Mandela, Nelson, 191
Mao Tse-tung, 141
Marines, U.S., 176–77, 184–85
Martin, Preston, 146
Martin Luther King Jr. Center, 222
Martin Luther King Jr. Memorial
    Foundation, 292
Marxism, 178–79, 187–90, 255
Maryland, 95, 238, 324, 327
Matthews, Chris, 106, 142
Matthews, Kathleen, 106
Medicaid, 9–10, 131, 266, 326
Medicare, 76, 203, 282, 326
Meet the Press, 238, 255, 258
Mexico, 310
Michel, Bob, 131, 140, 165–66, 259
Michigan, 75, 86, 200–201
Michigan State University, 86
Middle East, 106, 303
Middle East peace process, 3, 231
Mikulski, Barbara, 237–40
Miller, Warren, 292
Milošević, Slobodan, 300
Minnesota, 79, 149, 195
Mises, Ludwig von, 25, 29, 119
Mississippi, University of (Ole Miss), 82, 83
Missouri, 213, 250
Mondale, Walter, 147–49, 152, 155, 158
Monday Night Football, 122, 279
money supply, 98–99, 144
    JK's policy on, 142–46, 148, 150–70
    loosening of, 84, 146
    tightening of, 34–35, 85, 132, 306, 312
    see also dollars

Montana, Joe, 104, 109
Moore, Henson, 162
Moore, Steve, 324, 325
Mora, Jim, 17, 314
Moral Majority, 135, 161, 202
Moran, John, 269
Morris, Dick, 266–67
Moscow, 175, 186, 193
Moynihan, Daniel Patrick, 86–87
Mueller, John, 30, 42, 65, 116–19, 127, 152–53,
    161–63, 166, 168, 213, 266, 329
  on JK, 260
  JK and, 262, 289, 325
mujahideen, 178
Mundell, Robert, 2, 34–38, 42, 74, 80
"Mundell-Laffer Hypothesis, The: A New
    View of the World Economy"
    (Wanniski), 37–38
Muslims, 300, 303
  Shiite, 176
  Sunni, 306

Namath, Joe, 24
Namibia, 189–90
National Aeronautics and Space
    Administration (NASA), 239
National Affordable Housing Act of 1990, 239
National Association for the Advancement of
    Colored People (NAACP), 199, 221
National Association of Manufacturers, 158, 163
National Collegiate Athletic Association
    (NCAA), 156
National Conference on Soviet Jewry, 104
National Football League (NFL), 17, 18–21,
    115, 118
  AFL merger with, 23, 248–49
National Liberation Front, *see* Sandinistas
National Observer, 36, 39
National Review, 25, 119, 254, 257, 301, 319
National Rifle Association, 255
National Security Council (NSC), 189, 197, 301
National Union for Total Independence of
    Angola (UNITA), 178, 188–90
Nation of Islam, 275
Naval Academy, U.S., 120
Navy, U.S., 14, 197
Navy football team, 109

NBC, 106, 238, 250, 255
NBC/*Wall Street Journal* polls, 285, 286
Netanyahu, Benjamin, 106, 177–78, 303
Netanyahu, Jonathan, 177
New Deal, 59, 238
New Hampshire, 62, 209
  primary elections in, 67–68, 200–205, 245,
    264–65, 298–99
New Jersey, 37, 49, 52, 58, 268, 320
"New Left," 235
New Mexico, 92, 213
New Orleans, La., 23, 200, 215, 310
New Republic, 6, 119, 262
"New Right," 134
Newsweek, 173, 197
New York, N.Y., 2, 36, 37, 69, 228, 275
New Yorker, 74
New York Giants, 20
New York Jets, 21, 24
New York Knicks, 151
New York Post, 241
New York State, 25, 26, 56, 69, 76
New York Times, 84, 94, 96, 100, 101, 119, 122,
    232, 285, 298, 306–7
  on JK, 56, 89–90, 136, 154–55, 160, 237, 272,
    274, 320
  JK's op-ed in, 182–83
New York Times vs. Sullivan, 224
New York Titans, *see* New York Jets
Nicaragua, 178, 180
  Somoza rule in, 179
  see also Contras
Nickles, Don, 268
9/11 terrorist attacks, 300, 306
  aftermath of, 303–4
Nixon, Richard M., 34, 36, 39, 106, 137
  presidency of, 57, 74, 144, 183, 186, 192, 224
  wage and price controls of, 30
  Watergate scandal and, 31, 46
Nobel Prize, 36, 118, 174, 180
Nock, Albert Jay, 322
Nofziger, Lyn, 58–59, 135–36
Nolan, Judith Kemp (daughter), 330:
  childhood and adolescence of, 97, 105–10, 120
  on JK, 105, 106–7, 108, 109–11, 216
Noonan, Peggy, 233–34
North, Oliver, 180, 181–82

North American Free Trade Agreement (NAFTA), 254, 312
North Atlantic Treaty Organization (NATO), 183, 184, 187, 300
North Carolina, 188, 203, 312
North Dakota, 142, 265
North Korea, 301
Notre Dame University, 193
  football team of, 23, 27
Novak, Robert, 26, 65, 86, 231, 271
  on JK, 63, 70, 216, 265, 272, 277, 298
  JK and, 6, 56–59, 101, 255, 258, 263
nuclear weapons, 76, 183–88
  mutually assured destruction (MAD) with, 185
Nunn, Sam, 51–52, 141, 261

Obama, Barack, 157, 312–13, 319
Obamacare, 319
Obey, David, 173–75
Occidental College:
  JK's education at, 4, 17–19, 156
Office of Management and Budget (OMB), 36, 78–79, 100, 225, 227
Ohio, 52, 79, 93
Oklahoma, 96, 194
O'Leary, Jeremiah, 137
O'Neill, Thomas P. "Tip," 52, 92, 94–97, 140–42, 164–66, 168, 179–80
Oracle, 290–91, 292
Oregon, 168–69
Ornstein, Norman, 142

Packwood, Robert, 159, 163–65, 167–68
Page, Clarence, 318
Pakistan, 305
Palestinian Liberation Organization (PLO), 176–78
Palestinians, 176–78
  intifada of, 303
Park, Bona, 330
Parker, Buddy, 18, 19–20
Parks, Rosa, 22
Paul, Rand, 323
Paul, Ron, 43
Pearl Harbor, Japanese attack on, 282
Pearson, Drew, 26

Pechman, Joseph, 160
Pence, Mike, 324
Penn, Mark, 273
Pennsylvania, 142, 213
Pepper, Claude, 189
Perot, Ross, 253, 257, 277, 285
Phillips, Howard, 191
Pierce, Samuel, 224–26, 238
Pinkerton, James, 235–36
Pittsburgh Steelers, JK with, 18, 19–20
Planned Parenthood, 202
Poindexter, John, 182
Poland, 173, 175
politics, 141, 293
  JK's view of, 3, 7, 8, 11, 25, 50, 319
  polarization in, 8, 139
Pollard, Jonathan, 302
Popular Movement for the Liberation of Angola (MPLA), 190
populism, 148, 198, 228
Portugal, 188
poverty, 30, 75, 247, 316
  illegitimacy and, 7, 257
  JK's agenda against, 216, 219–24, 228–33, 236–37, 245, 289
  "war" on, 220–24, 232, 242, 245, 326
Powell, Colin, 257, 268, 283, 286, 303, 305
prices, 84
  rising of, 29–30, 84
  stability of, 48, 144
Prince of Darkness, The (Novak), 26
Princeton University, 151, 156
Prison Fellowship, 104, 106, 316
Pro Basketball Hall of Fame, 156
Pro Football Hall of Fame, 18, 24, 104, 118, 248, 290
Proxicom, 290–91
Public Interest, 37–38, 119
public works projects, 30, 31
Puerto Rico, 141

Quayle, Dan, 213–16, 219, 245, 249, 250, 251, 257
Quayle, Marilyn, 213
Quinn, Pat, 324

Rabin, Yitzhak, 266
Rabushka, Alvin, 150, 261, 262

racial integration, 4, 21, 23, 82, 217
racism, 61, 222, 229, 320
Rahn, Richard, 152
Rangel, Charlie, 275
Rauner, Bruce, 324
Reagan, Nancy, 65, 67, 90, 130
Reagan, Ronald, 9, 10, 32, 33, 81, 219, 251, 255, 295, 308, 325
  autobiography of, 61, 175, 184
  California governorship of, 25–26, 136
  conservatism of, 98
  diary of, 130, 131, 135, 164, 173, 189
  economic successes of, 6, 93–98, 147–49, 196, 197
  foreign and defense policies of, 171, 173–81, 196, 323
  JK's political relationship with, 5, 25–26, 40–41, 47, 49, 57–59, 61–67, 72–74, 77, 83, 86, 89–91, 97–99, 102, 128–31, 133–37, 144, 146, 148, 165, 167, 170, 171, 173–75, 178, 181–83, 192–93, 289
  legislative victories of, 78, 93–95, 97–99
  Mideast peace plan of, 177
  movie career of, 151
  1980 presidential campaign and election of, 2, 5, 26, 53, 55–59, 62–78, 82, 88, 90, 117, 196
  1984 presidential campaign and reelection of, 147–49, 195–96, 208
  presidency of, 42, 47, 78–79, 83–102, 112, 117, 128–39, 142–51, 154, 157–71, 173, 175–99, 201, 221, 225, 232, 233, 243, 256, 289, 312
  shooting and recuperation of, 91, 92–93
  speeches of, 73, 89–91, 93, 96, 100, 130–33, 138, 154, 158, 159, 163, 185–86, 193
  supply-side economics adopted by, 1, 2–3, 6, 63–67, 74, 79, 88, 100–101, 129, 196, 312, 320
  tax cuts of, 2–3, 6, 88–98, 157, 169, 196
  tax increases of, 100, 129, 131–39, 143, 150–51, 243
  tax reform plans of, 157–61, 163–70
  White House staff of, 84, 88, 90, 129–30, 133, 136, 196
Reagan Doctrine, 178, 192
Reaganomics, 2–3, 68, 89, 139, 142, 196, 299, 306
Reagan revolution, b, 78, 82, 169, 196

Rebuilding Our Communities, 293
recession, 242, 251, 299
  Great, 7, 312
  1982, 138, 142
  2001, 306
Reed, Scott, 117, 201–2, 209–11, 214, 224, 225, 227–28, 230–31, 234, 263–65, 267–72, 275, 279, 281–86, 323, 330
Regan, Donald, 88, 98, 154, 157, 158, 168
Reker, Mary Lou, 329
RENAMO, 188
Republican National Committee (RNC), 46–47, 58–59, 62, 198, 249, 259
Republican National Convention:
  of 1976, 41, 69
  of 1980, 63, 69–74, 172
  of 1984, 147–50, 172, 197, 199
  of 1988, 6, 200, 215, 221, 233–34
  of 1992, 235, 249–51, 253
  of 1996, 267, 268, 272–74
Republican Party, 8, 13, 61, 319
  African Americans and, 3, 9, 128, 217–18, 297
  "big tent" advocacy in, 9, 46, 298, 310
  conservative wing of, 5, 25, 31, 46, 205, 310
  JK's affiliation with, 1–6, 9–10, 15, 25–27, 31, 41–42, 55–59, 78, 195, 282, 294
  JK's criticism of, 3, 9–10
  liberal wing of, 49, 58
  Old Guard, 79, 82, 129
  as party of Lincoln, 3–5, 9, 216, 221–22, 264
  primogeniture "law" of, 208, 265
  Reagan wing of, 206
Revenue Act of 1978, 52–53
Reykjavik summit, 169, 186–87
Rhodes, John, 41
Rhodes Scholars, 151, 156
Ridge, Tom, 268
right-to-work laws, 27
Road to Serfdom, The (Hayek), 25, 119
Roberts, Paul Craig, 42–44, 83–84, 90, 94, 98–99, 135
Robertson, Pat, 200–203, 205–6, 211
"Robin HUD" scandal, 225
Rockefeller, Nelson, 3
Roe v. Wade, 199
Rogers, Joe, 117
Rohrabacher, Dana, 257

Roll Call, 6

Rollins, Ed, 208, 210–11, 272

Rollins, Sherrie, 227

Roman Catholic Church, 23, 27, 114, 116, 180, 202, 256

Romney, Mitt, 142, 312

Roosevelt, Franklin D., 3, 15, 25, 85, 87, 112

Roosevelt, Theodore, 81, 317

Rostenkowski, Dan, 91, 95–96, 133, 147

   tax reform and, 159–61, 163–65, 167–68

Roth, William, 45–47

   see also Kemp-Roth tax bill

Rousselot, John, 43–44, 79

Rowen, Hobart, 100

Rozelle, Pete, 118

Rubio, Marco, 323–24, 325, 327

Rumsfeld, Donald, 188, 268, 302–5

Russert, Tim, 250

Russia, 225, 321

Rutkowski, Ed, 22–23, 25, 27, 125

Ryan, Paul, 253, 322–23, 325, 326

Saban, Lou, 23, 27

St. Louis, Mo., 228, 236, 250

Sakharov, Andrei, 174

Samuelson, Paul, 35, 36

San Diego, Calif., 267, 271–74, 284

San Diego Chargers, JK as quarterback with, 4, 13, 20–21, 25, 28, 70

Sandinistas, 179–81

San Francisco, Calif., 147, 256

San Francisco 49ers, 20, 104, 109

Sarbanes-Oxley Act of 2002, 291

Saudi Arabia, 175, 180, 197, 204

Save Our State initiative, 257

Savimbi, Jonas, 188–90

Savings and Investment Act of 1974, 31–32, 40

Say, Jean-Baptiste, 80

Schlafly, Phyllis, 203

Schwarzenegger, Arnold, 118

Scowcroft, Brent, 241

Sears, John, 57–58, 62–65, 67–68, 112, 276–77

Seattle Seahawks, 109

Senate, U.S., 2, 26, 42, 45–46, 51–53, 55, 58, 64, 69, 80, 153, 226, 238

   Appropriations subcommittee of, 237

   Budget Committee of, 84, 93, 134

   Democratic members of, 53, 95

   Finance Committee of, 45, 51, 52, 73–74, 84, 94, 95, 132, 134, 159, 163, 167–68, 198, 212–13

   Foreign Relations Committee of, 306

   Intelligence Committee of, 187–88

   Republican members of, 44, 77, 95, 133, 139, 149, 170, 184, 259, 286

Shakespeare, Frank, 55

Sharon, Ariel, 176, 241

Shcharansky, Anatoly, 174

Shevardnadze, Eduard, 241

Shore, Marci Robinson, 329

Shultz, George, 74, 86, 121, 151, 174, 176, 179, 181–82, 185–86, 187–92

   JK's attacks on, 182, 188–89, 192, 194, 203

Sigma Nu fraternity, 82

Simon, Paul, 44, 49

Simpson, Alan, 213

Simpson, O. J., 24, 27

Smick, David, 57–58, 64–65, 68, 116, 117, 156, 262, 329

   on JK, 65, 70, 76, 112–13, 210

Smith, Adam, 228

Smith, Richard Norton, 270

socialism, 193, 194, 229

Social Security, 76, 134, 203, 204, 209, 264, 295–300, 326

   reform of, 308, 309–10

South Africa, 188–89, 190–91

South Carolina, 68, 128, 206, 265, 299

South Dakota, 15–16, 217, 265

Southern California, University of (USC), 17, 36, 311

Soviet Union, 10, 179, 289, 300, 323

   Afghanistan invaded by, 1, 178

   collapse of, 1, 175, 193, 241, 321

   as "evil empire," 185–86

   nuclear arsenal of, 183–88, 193

   political dissidents in, 174–75

   U.S. relations with, 75, 76, 169, 171, 174–75, 183–88, 190, 192–94, 203, 241

Speakes, Larry, 94, 132

stagflation, 1, 29–30, 34, 36

Stalin, Joseph, 187

Standing Firm: A Vice-Presidential Memoir (Quayle), 245

Stanford University, 36, 150
Starr, Kenneth, 277
State Department, U.S., 172, 179, 180, 188,
    189, 190, 192, 240–41, 306
Staubach, Roger, 109, 290
Steiger, Bill, 46, 49, 52–53
Stein, Herbert, 39, 51, 56
Stephanopoulos, George, 273
Stockman, David, 9–10, 67, 75, 78–79, 84–88,
    97–101, 132, 151, 233
    criticism of, 101, 131
    Dunkirk memo of, 9, 85, 87
    JK and, 106, 131, 149
    Reagan and, 92, 94, 97–98, 143, 149
stock market, 30, 84–85, 312, 321
    JK's investments in, 82
    1987 crash of, 207
Strategic Arms Limitation Treaty, 172, 183
Strategic Arms Reduction Talks, 183
Strategic Defense Initiative (SDI) "Star Wars,"
    185–87, 192, 199, 207
Strategic Petroleum Reserve, U.S., 292
sub-prime lending crisis, 311–12
Sununu, John, 116, 219, 233–34, 236, 242–43
Super Bowl, 103, 293
supply-side economics, 29–54, 57–58, 83–85,
    87, 90, 128, 150, 267, 306–7
    JK's advocacy of, 1, 2–3, 6, 8, 31, 38–55, 57,
        61–62, 66, 77–79, 81, 83, 86–87, 102,
        130, 136–37, 156, 172–73, 195, 256, 312,
        320, 321
    national movement of, 2, 40, 53, 65, 77, 320
    opposition to, 68, 73, 78, 79, 198
    Reagan's adoption of, 1, 2–3, 6, 63–67, 74,
        79, 88, 100–101, 129, 196, 312, 320
    skepticism about, 6, 317
    as a term, 39
Supply Side Revolution, The (Roberts), 83–84
Supreme Court, U.S., 202, 224, 300
Syria, 176–77, 301

Taft, Robert, 3
Taliban, 178
Tambo, Oliver, 191–92
Tanenhaus, Sam, 320
Tax and Fiscal Responsibility Act of 1982
    (TEFRA), 134–38, 150–51

tax code reform, 8–9, 149–70, 313, 324, 326
    Bradley as "father" of, 151–59, 164, 169
    flat tax concept and, 155, 260–62, 264,
        265–66, 298
    JK's policy on, 150, 152–57, 160–70, 194,
        230, 243–44, 246, 260–62
    legislation stemming from, 151–55, 157–70,
        207, 242
    Reagan's plans for, 157–61, 163–70, 299
Tax Cut News, 50–51
taxes, 4, 13, 325
    capital gains, 31, 46, 49, 53, 89, 91, 152, 158,
        169, 242–43, 250, 262, 295, 297, 307
    corporate, 31, 35, 46, 95, 152, 157, 254
    credits and write-offs of, 31, 151–53, 230,
        244, 307, 313
    creeping brackets of, 30, 48, 51–53, 60, 86, 95
    cutting of, 2–3, 6, 8, 31, 34, 35, 37, 39–56, 62,
        67, 70, 85–86, 88–98, 134, 150, 156, 169,
        242, 282–83, 295, 308
    "death," 307
    excise, 100, 131, 234
    gasoline, 75, 234
    income, 9, 62, 73, 94, 95, 243, 260, 313
    indexation of, 153, 158, 295
    JK's policy on, 2, 13, 29–54, 56, 102, 307–8
    payroll, 9, 234
    property, 49
    raising of, 9, 34, 35, 40, 51–52, 98, 100, 129,
        131–39, 143, 150–51, 221, 234, 243, 259, 321
    revenues from, 60, 143, 152, 234, 307, 308
    standard deduction on, 151, 260
    state and local, 151–52
Tax Reform Act of 1986, 168–70, 299
Taylor, J. T., 123, 126, 280–81, 291, 314
Teague, Randal, 31, 32–33, 116–17, 119, 127, 329
Teeter, Bob, 218, 244
Tennessee, 32, 46, 213
terrorism, 184–85, 288, 304
    Iranian sponsorhip of, 176, 181
    see also Al Qaeda; Hezbollah; 9/11 terrorist
        attacks
Texas, 43, 44, 93, 95, 239, 286
Thatcher, Margaret, 183, 199, 230, 240,
    295, 311
Thornburgh, Dick, 213
Thurmond, Strom, 135

Tittle, Y. A., 20

Tolchin, Martin, 55–56

Tower, John, 120, 182

trade, 171
  enterprise zones for, 9, 76, 203, 220, 221, 224, 231, 232, 236, 248, 250, 254, 297
  free market, 9, 14, 25, 29, 36, 172, 252, 320, 322, 326

"Travelgate" scandal, 278, 284

Treasury Department, U.S., 40, 42–43, 49, 51, 56, 79, 84, 90, 144, 152, 154, 157, 158, 212, 224, 225, 240, 243, 261

Treasury 1 tax reform bill, 157–58

Treasury 2 tax reform bill, 160–61

Triumph of Politics, The: Why the Reagan Revolution Failed (Stockman), 149

Ture, Norman, 40, 45, 51, 135, 152

unemployment, 1, 7, 9, 29–30, 35, 48, 60, 84, 129, 196, 230, 258
  decline of, 48, 196, 258

United Nations (UN), 106, 172, 176, 178, 179, 188, 197, 252, 301, 303, 304

United States, 7
  economic booms in, 3, 35, 40
  economic downturns in, 1, 7, 14, 29–30, 34, 36, 89, 98–99, 102, 129–30, 138, 147, 242, 251, 299, 306, 312
  federal debt of, 8, 34, 233, 295
  federal deficits of, 31, 35, 60, 85, 89, 92–93, 95, 99, 143, 233, 307–8
  government shut-downs in, 266, 295
  gross domestic product (GDP) of, 8, 39, 40, 59, 102, 143–44, 169, 184, 233, 242, 262, 308, 311, 326
  gross national product (GNP) of, 36, 147
  income gains of top one percent in, 7, 8
  infrastructure of, 8, 218
  nuclear arsenal of, 183–88
  Soviet relations with, 75–76, 169, 171, 174–75, 183–88, 190, 192–94, 203, 241

Urban Mass Transit Administration, 225

USA Today, 257, 291

Vail, Colo., 107, 292–93

Van Cleave, Michelle, 120, 127, 329

Venezuela, 292

Vermont, 75, 97

Vietnam War, 1, 35, 46, 144, 182
  opposition to, 86

Viguerie, Richard, 203

Volcker, Paul, 84, 89, 142, 144, 157
  JK's criticism of, 129, 132, 146–47

Voting Rights Act of 1965, 203, 310

Walker, Bob, 140–41, 191

Wall Street Journal, 25, 36–38, 40, 54, 84, 92, 99–100, 106, 119, 122, 139, 150, 237, 243, 250, 285, 292, 320
  Bennett and JK's op-ed in, 256–57
  on JK, 32, 138, 153, 201, 265, 297, 317–18

Wanniski, Jude, 2, 36–42, 49, 62, 74, 80, 101, 113, 117, 118, 152, 272
  JK's relationship with, 36, 38–44, 55, 56, 58–59, 63–66, 87, 106–7, 135, 149, 199, 210, 258, 263, 275–77, 280, 302, 304, 311

Warren, Earl, as chief justice, 3

Washington, D.C., 2, 28, 29, 32, 36, 37, 64, 105, 219, 223, 276
  Capitol in, 33, 166, 175, 236
  Israeli embassy in, 106, 178
  Kenilworth-Parkside project in, 239, 240
  public housing in, 233, 239, 240
  Rayburn Building in, 114, 123
  voting in, 142, 149, 203
  Watergate apartments in, 269, 270–71

Washington National Cathedral, 316–17

Washington Post, 47, 53, 84, 94, 100, 116, 119, 122, 139, 142, 198, 262, 267–68, 296, 306–7
  on JK, 56, 88, 230–31, 244, 251, 283
  JK's op-ed in, 247

Washington Post/ABC poll, 198, 267, 274, 277

Washington Speakers Bureau, 253

Washington Star, 119

Washington Times, 137

Waterfield, Bob, 18

Watergate scandal, 31, 42, 46, 53, 195

Waters, Maxine, 248–49

Watkins, Emma Bayer, 330

Watts, J. C., 297

Way the World Works, The (Wanniski), 49, 80, 87, 117

Wealth of Nations (Smith), 228

weapons of mass destruction, 289, 305
Weber, Vin, 106, 140–41, 191, 249, 252–53, 256,
    281, 330
  on JK, 202, 230–31, 258, 320
  JK and, 2, 79–80, 83, 195, 199, 243
Weekly Standard, 301, 304
Wehner, Peter, 325
Weicher, John, 227
Weinberger, Caspar, 176, 186, 190, 300
welfare, 50, 198, 219, 230, 236–37, 297
  reform of, 61, 220, 319
White House Council of Economic Advisers,
  51, 90
Whitewater Development Corporation, 277,
  279, 284
Whitman, Christine "Christie" Todd,
  268, 271
Whitworth university, 314
Will, George, 197, 249
Williams, Brien, 330
Wilson, Pete, 256
Wirthlin, Richard, 72, 89, 154, 197, 251

Wisconsin, 46, 148
  primary elections in, 206–7
Wolfowitz, Paul, 304
Women, Infants and Children (WIC)
  nutrition program, 255
Woodruff, Judy, 106
Woodson, Bob, 223, 240, 323
Woodward, Bob, 268
World Bank, 172
World Cup of 1986, 103
World War I, 14, 252
World War II, 8, 60, 85, 160, 197, 252, 315
Wright, Jeremiah, 157
Wright, Jim, 44, 48–49, 93, 140, 181, 294

Yellowstone Club, 292
Yiddish language, 273, 301
Young, Andrew, 222
Young, Paul, 205, 209

Zelaska, Sharon, 113–17, 119, 121–23, 125–26,
  211–12, 225, 329